TOM WOLFE

The Purple Decades

A READER

By Tom Wolfe

THE KANDY-KOLORED TANGERINE-FLAKE STREAMLINE BABY (1965)

THE PUMP HOUSE GANG (1968)

THE ELECTRIC KOOL-AID ACID TEST (1968)

RADICAL CHIC & MAU-MAUING THE FLAK CATCHERS (1970)

THE NEW JOURNALISM (1973)

THE PAINTED WORD (1975)

MAUVE GLOVES & MADMEN, CLUTTER & VINE (1976)

THE RIGHT STUFF (1979)

IN OUR TIME (1980)

FROM BAUHAUS TO OUR HOUSE (1981)

THE PURPLE DECADES (1982)

Those Whom God Hath Joined Together

"You've been living together for four years. Why get married now?"
"I'm tired of being snubbed by the doormen."

TOM WOLFE

The Purple Decades

A READER

BERKLEY BOOKS, NEW YORK

This Berkley book contains the complete text of the original hardcover edition.

THE PURPLE DECADES

A Berkley Book / published by arrangement with
Farrar, Straus and Giroux

PRINTING HISTORY
Farrar, Straus edition published 1982
Berkley trade paperback edition / November 1983
Second printing / March 1984

ISBN: 0-425-06266-X

A BERKLEY BOOK ® TM 757,375
Berkley Books are published by The Berkley Publishing Group, 200 Madison Avenue, New York, New York 10016.
The name "BERKLEY" and the stylized "B" with design are trademarks belonging to Berkley Publishing Corporation.
PRINTED IN THE UNITED STATES OF AMERICA

CONTENTS

INTRODUCTION

The Purple Decades—if we hadn't lived through them, we wouldn't have believed them possible. Already they begin to seem very far away. Luckily, we have Tom Wolfe to remember them by. Luckily, future historians, curiosity-seekers, and literate citizens will be able to turn to Tom Wolfe for the definitive, comprehensive, tuned-in portrait of our age.

In the Introduction to his first book, *The Kandy-Kolored Tangerine-Flake Streamline Baby*, Tom Wolfe explains how "the whole thing started" accidentally one afternoon in the early sixties when he was sent to do a newspaper story on the Hot Rod & Custom Car Show at the Coliseum in New York and how this led to his eventual interest in stock car racing and free-form Las Vegas neon-sign sculpture and "all these . . . *weird* . . . nutty-looking, crazy baroque custom cars, sitting in little nests of pink angora angel's hair for the purpose of 'glamorous' display." While he was trying to understand why the conventional newspaper story he wrote failed to capture some essential truth of the experience, Wolfe was struck by the animating insight that "the proles, peasants, and petty burghers" of America were "creating new styles . . . and changing the life of the whole country in ways that nobody even seems to bother to record, much less analyze." He was on to something.

Wolfe goes on to relate how *Esquire* became interested in the custom-car phenomenon, how they sent him to California, and how he ended up staying up all night, "typing along like a madman," in order to meet the *Esquire* deadline, elaborating the perception that suddenly "classes of people whose styles of life had been practically invisible had the money to build monuments to their own styles." Among teenagers, this meant custom cars, rock 'n' roll, stretch pants, and decal eyes. In the South, he was to discover, it took the form of stock car racing, which in fifteen years had replaced baseball as the number-one spectator sport. All over the country, at every suburb, supermarket, and hamburger stand, Las Vegas-style neon sculpture was transforming the American skyline. "The incredible postwar American electro-pastel surge into the suburbs," Wolfe would later call it. It was "sweeping the Valley, with superhighways, dreamboat cars, shopping centers, soaring thirty-foot Federal Sign & Signal Company electric supersculptures—Eight New Plexiglas Display Features!—a surge of freedom and mobility . . ."[1] The *Esquire* story Wolfe finished that morning long ago was eventually called "The Kandy-Kolored Tangerine-Flake Streamline Baby," and thus the New Journalism was born.

Tom Wolfe's ascendancy as spokesperson for this era in American life developed through the medium that came to be called the New Journalism, but by reason of his own special gifts. The novelists, those erstwhile cultural chroniclers, failed to fulfill this role, according to Wolfe, because they were "all crowded into one phone booth . . . doing these poor, frantic little exercises in form."[2] Therefore, the New Journalists "had the whole crazed obscene uproarious Mammon-faced drug-soaked mau-mau lust-oozing Sixties in America all to themselves,"[3] and the seventies too, for that matter—"the Me Decade," as Wolfe described it.

But Wolfe's success is based on realities that go beyond the theory that the novelists weren't paying attention and the fact that Wolfe himself came to be the most accomplished and notorious practitioner of the New Journalism, and its chief architect and advocate. Wolfe's banner of the New Journalism was flown, in large part, to gain acceptance for a whole new set of literary conventions—conventions that, not accidentally, allowed full expression of his particular virtuosity. Encompassing the aesthetics and methodology of the nineteenth-century realist novel and the *modus operandi* of the big-city streetwise police-beat reporter, it was a form, Wolfe noted, that consumed "devices that happen to have originated with the novel and mixed them with every other device known to prose. And all the while, quite beyond matters of technique, it enjoyed an advantage so obvious, so built-in, one almost forgets what a power it has: the simple fact that the reader knows *all this actually happened.*"[4]

Probably, the New Journalism was also part of the same evolution in consciousness that led, in different ways, to the new fiction, the new poetry, and the old psychology: an idea about the importance of focusing attention on subjective emotional experience, dramatized point-of-view, unique sensibility, and of delving beneath appearances for deeper meanings. In formulating new conventions and then serving as a propagandist for his own kind of art, Tom Wolfe, like Fielding, like Zola or Joyce, was following in a time-honored tradition, the formal innovator modifying received forms and methods to suit his own, historically exceptional, circumstances. "Every great and original writer," wrote William Wordsworth, "in proportion as he is great and original, must create the taste by which he is to be relished."

Among the trickiest of the conventions Wolfe entertained was his inventive application of the principles of point-of-view. Wolfe describes in *The New Journalism* how and why he aspired to treat point-of-view in non-fiction writing "in the Jamesian sense in which fiction writers understand it, entering directly into the mind of a character, experiencing the world through his central nervous system throughout a given scene."[5] The idea, he says, "was to give the full objective description, plus something that readers had always had to go to novels and short stories for: namely, the subjective or emotional life of the characters."[6]

How can a non-fiction writer pretend to know exactly what a person is thinking or feeling at any given moment? He asks them. If a reporter bases his reconstruction of the subjective life of the character on the most scrupulous reporting, Wolfe would contend, he can get close to the truth of the inner life. Wolfe's ideal of saturation reporting is far more ambitious than anything the old journalists had thought to try. His approach is to cultivate the habit of staying with potential subjects for days, weeks, or months at a time, taking notes, interviewing, watching, and waiting for something dramatic and revealing to happen. Only through the most persistent and searching methods of reporting, Wolfe would emphasize, can the journalist's entrée into point-of-view, the subjective life, inner voices, the creation of scenes and dialogue, and so on, be justified.

Another aspect of Wolfe's treatment of point-of-view is his playful use of the downstage voice, the devil's-advocate voice, and other voices in his work. Here is a writer with a marvelous ear for dialogue, an easily galvanized, chameleonlike faculty for empathy, and a ventriloquist's delight in speaking other people's lines. From the start of his career, he was bored silly by the "pale beige tone" of conventional non-fiction writing, which seemed to him "like the standard announcer's voice . . . a drag, a droning," a signal to the reader "that a well-known bore was here again, 'the journalist,' a pedestrian mind, a phlegmatic spirit, a faded personality. . . ."[7] So, early on, he began experimenting with outlandish voices and with the principle of skipping rapidly from one voice or viewpoint to the next, sometimes unexpectedly in the middle of a sentence, and often enough without identifying the voice or viewpoint except through context. Anything to avoid the stupefying monotony of the pale beige tone.

Even in expository sections, he often adopts the tone or characteristic lingo, point-of-view, or pretense of a character he is writing about: the "good old boy" voice he assumes, for example, in the narration of "The Last American Hero"; the slangy L.A. vernacular of the Mac Meda Destruction Company in *The Pump House Gang*; the freaked-out lingo of the Merry Pranksters in *The Electric Kool-Aid Acid Test*; the ghetto jive of *Mau-Mauing the Flak Catchers*; or the sugary, gossipy persona of *Radical Chic.* Any voice he wishes to take on, he assumes with unerring smoothness and fidelity. Frequently, however, the voice produced turns out to be a put-on voice that reveals and dramatizes personality as it revels in the flaws, prejudices, and affectations of the character. The voice, that is, is both part of the character and, at the same time, above or outside it, interpreting and passing judgment.

Literal-minded critics have sometimes leapt to the assumption that Wolfe's put-on voice was expressing his actual opinions on a subject. Thomas R. Edwards does this, for instance, in discussing a passage about the Watts riots from *The Pump House Gang*:

> Watts was a blast . . . Artie and John had a tape-recorder and decided they were going to make a record called "Random Sounds from the Watts Riots." They drove right into Watts . . . and there was blood on the streets and roofs blowing off the stores and all these apricot flames and drunk Negroes falling through the busted plate glass of the liquor stores. Artie got a nice recording of a lot of Negroes chanting "Burn, baby, burn."

Edwards claims that Wolfe's "general view of 'serious' social concern makes the passage a virtual endorsement of the attitudes it mimics,"[8] when, obviously, the passage is expressing the lack of social concern of the Pump House Gang. The mercilessness of their attitude toward the Negroes serves to document the insularity of their tribal bond. The put-on voice here is Wolfe's way of dramatizing the group's attitude toward other groups, a trait he also illustrates in showing the kids' outrageous prejudices against anyone over the "horror age" of twenty-five.

Now, in any case, the New Journalism is a *fait accompli.* Whatever quibbling one might still occasionally hear about the dubiousness of its procedures, it is practiced every day across the land, from *Rolling Stone* to *The New Yorker*, from *The Atlantic Monthly* and *Esquire* to the sports pages of *The New York Times,* the *Fresno Bee,* and the *Bangor Daily News*—in some cases by writers who don't even know what to call it, who might be surprised to learn they are committing it. Though Wolfe has always remained loyal to the journalistic calling and has expropriated its methods in all earnestness for his own purposes and has thus permanently changed the definition and the shape of journalism, he clearly is, and always has been, more than a journalist.

Temperamentally, Tom Wolfe is, from first to last, with every word and deed, a *comic* writer with an exuberant sense of humor, a baroque sensibility, and an irresistible inclination toward hyperbole. His antecedents are primarily literary—not journalistic, and not political, except in the largest sense. All these years, Tom Wolfe has been writing Comedy with a capital C, Comedy like that of Henry Fielding and Jane Austen and Joseph Addison, like that of Thackeray and Shaw and Mark Twain. Like these writers, Tom Wolfe might be described as a brooding humanistic presence. There is a decided moral edge to his humor. Wolfe never tells us what to believe exactly; rather, he shows us examples of good and (most often) bad form. He has always proffered these humanistic and moral perspectives on his subjects.

Which is not to say that beneath the cool surface of the hyped-up prose we should expect to find either a fire-and-brimstone preacher or a Juvenalian sort of satirist seething with indignation about the corruption of his fellow men. Neither will we discover, in Wolfe's work, any sign at all of a political or social activist who might argue on behalf of a particular party, issue, system, creed, or cause.

The satirical element in Wolfe's sort of comedic writing is most often sunny, urbane, and smiling. Like all Horatian comedy, it aims to reform through laughter that is never vindictive or merely personal, but broadly sympathetic:

> Comedy may be considered to deal with man in his human state, restrained and often made ridiculous by his limitations, his faults, his bodily functions, and his animal nature . . . Comedy has always viewed man more realistically than tragedy, and drawn its laughter or its satire from the spectacle of human weakness or failure. Hence its tendency to juxtapose appearance and reality, to deflate pretense, and to mock excess.[9]

Classical comedy outlives causes and headlines because of its freedom from parochial ideology. It is a human response based on the conviction that human nature is so prone to folly and vanity that it cannot be helped or changed, except possibly through self-awareness, through admission of its innate silliness. Whatever side of whatever issue we are on, the comedian believes, we are likely to end up making fools of ourselves. Yet there is always a forgiving or good-natured quality to Horatian (and Wolfean) comedy, since it assumes that this peculiar flawed human condition is universal and any one of us (including the writer poking fun) may be guilty of demonstrating it at any moment.

A close connection between laughter and reproof is evident throughout Wolfe's oeuvre. In works such as *The Electric Kool-Aid Acid Test* and "The Me Decade," for example, Wolfe mocks the idea that "letting it all hang out" is likely to offer a road to salvation or improvement. In *The Electric Kool-Aid Acid Test*, Wolfe shows again and again how destructive the sixties phony wisdom about the "joys" of abandonment to chemical cornucopias, in particular, could be. Similarly, by parodying facile aspects of the human potential movement in "The Me Decade" ("Esalen's specialty was lube jobs for the personality"[10]), Wolfe demonstrates his concern about the exploitation and misdirection of human energies in what he sees as a foolish, limited, and petty cause. In "The Intelligent Coed's Guide to America," Wolfe exposes the preposterous ironies of a certain brand of fashionable intellectual bellyaching in the seventies and shows how the pronouncements of certain American intellectuals may have had more to do with their own status and identity needs than with any authentic repression or doom worth taking seriously. In *From Bauhaus to Our House*, Wolfe shows how a status-related infatuation with things European in the 1930s and 1940s led to a redirection of American music, art, psychology, and especially architecture, that was ultimately reductive, excessive, and nonsensical.

Or in *Radical Chic*, as Wolfe observes the socially elite of Manhattan indulging the fad of inviting members of the Black Panthers to their opulent parties, he poses the theory that the ostensible desire for social justice and the display of generosity involved had somewhat less to do with the proceedings than had the secret motive, which was the longing of the aristocrats to feel in its fullest degree the heady sensation of "How chic we are." Switching his angle of vision diametrically in *Mau-Mauing the Flak Catchers*, Wolfe shows, hilariously, how enterprising blacks gleefully intimidated, outwitted, and hoodwinked social-agency do-gooders during the heydays of the poverty program.

All these perspectives arise out of a sense of the moral insufficiency of the participants and reveal Tom Wolfe pointing a finger and laughing wholeheartedly at what people do when they fly in the face of the hard facts about their own natures or their unconscious or concealed motives or aspirations. The merriment is intense; the laughter is real. But there is little cause for feeling vastly superior to the miserable fools, tarnished folk heroes, rebels, fanatics, and hustlers from Wolfe's rogue's gallery of humanity. For lurking just beneath the swirling surface of his prose is the sobering realization that the potential for vanity of similar proportion is common to us all.

One indirect moral service that great comedic writers perform is to promote self-awareness, and Wolfe's major contribution here has been his emphasis on the hidden and sometimes peculiar manifestations of status-seeking in American life. In the manner of a conscientious Martian anthropologist, he has tried rigorously to apply the principle that all primates, including humans, organize their societies according to status hierarchies and struggles for dominance. The importance of status behavior as the source of society's most mysterious subtleties has, of course, been recognized and studied by the social sciences for years. The proof of the existence of such behavior is not original to Tom Wolfe, but the wholesale exploration of its features in American culture and its exploitation for comical purposes are certainly important aspects of Wolfe's novelty and uniqueness. The tool of status-analysis, and other gleanings from the social sciences, has led Wolfe, over the last two decades, to these basic assumptions about American life: (1) That the fragmentation and diversity of American culture resulted in the emergence of subcultures or enclaves that have evolved their own bizarre art forms, life styles, and status rituals independent from the "elite" culture of the past, the "high" culture of the American Northeast via Europe ("the big amoeba-God of Anglo-European sophistication"[11]), or other common references. (2) That these enclaves, generally ignored by serious social observers, deserve the closest scrutiny, both because they are the truest, most authentic, examples of "the way we live now" and because they illustrate comically that human nature follows the same quaint, barbaric patterns regardless of class, region, or circumstance. (3) That fragmentation of American society has sometimes caused rampant status confusion (as in *Radical Chic*); emphasis upon enunciating weird new tribal identities (as in *The Pump House Gang*, *The Electric Kool-Aid Acid Test*, or *The Right Stuff*); the evolution of status dropouts who discover they can compete more favorably with some new set of rules in life style (as in "The Mid-Atlantic Man"); and a remarkable array of bewildering or ridiculous behavior (as in "The Voices of Village Square" or "The Girl of the Year")—all ripe for Wolfean analysis—including the widespread frantic search for spurious forms of salvation (as in "The Me Decade" or *The Electric Kool-Aid Acid Test*).

Thus, Junior Johnson's stock cars of "The Last American Hero," as seen through Wolfe's eyes, are like the totems of the Easter Islanders or the formal architecture of the Regency period, critically important cultural artifacts that are the focus of both veneration and status competition for their creators. Or, as in *The Right Stuff*, among the test pilots, the fraternity of "the right stuff" is the basis for the display of almost incredible forms of heroism, which Wolfe clearly admires. But, even here, it is the fierce status competition within the group that serves to motivate the men, a desire for the "sinfully inconfessable . . . feeling of superiority, appropriate to him and his kind, lone bearers of the right stuff."

Grounding his insights about human nature firmly on his belief in the potent force of status in human affairs, and its expression through fashion, Wolfe claims—in *The Painted Word* and in *From Bauhaus to Our House*, for instance—that styles in contemporary painting and architecture can be understood more plainly by examining the ambitions and status games of influential artists, architects, critics, and patrons than by trying to comprehend their creations as personal miracles, a position that has been somewhat less than stupendously popular in the art world.

As his career has matured, Wolfe's aspirations as a cultural chronicler have been greatly enhanced by his ability to grasp, to digest, and to stimulate human interest in large, sometimes esoteric, subject areas usually thought to be the domain of art historians, sociobiologists, or other specialists. Few would have dared, as Wolfe does in *The Painted Word*, for example, to take on the whole bloody history of Modern Art and to offer a waggish, but devilishly shrewd, critique of how Modern Art came to serve fashion and theory instead of humankind; or, as in the scorching sequel, *From Bauhaus to Our House*, to deal with "what went wrong" during the past fifty years of American architecture.

Wolfe's unfailing wit and his faculty for selecting the truly memorable example are undoubtedly a part of this ability to assimilate, transform, and humanize his subject matter. "Yale had completed a building program of vast proportions," he explains in *From Bauhaus to Our House*, "that had turned the campus into as close an approximation of Oxford and Cambridge as the mind of man could devise on short notice in southern Connecticut . . . For better or worse, Yale became the business barons' vision of a luxurious collegium for the sons of the upper classes who would run the new American empire." But when an addition was built for the Yale art gallery after the Second World War, "the building could scarcely have been distinguished from a Woolco discount store in a shopping center" and the interior "had the look of an underground parking garage." And all this in the name of "unconcealed structure"—another instance for Wolfe of how mindless fashion and buzz-word aesthetic theory were allowed to undermine good sense and consistency of design—but also an instance of how Wolfe is able to concretize and persuade by skillful elaboration of the perfect example.

Typically, as Wolfe unspools yard after yard of theory, he forces us to test it against our own understanding of the nature of things. And he compels us to ask questions: Why in the name of God should painting and architecture in our time have become so trivialized, so specialized, so uniform? Why would an accomplished, clever man want to give up his work and French-fry his brains and invest his earthly time tooling around the countryside in a psychedelic schoolbus? Why in the world would a normal, sane, healthy person want to risk his life on a day-to-day basis as a test pilot or an astronaut? Why do people *behave* as they do? How do we live? How should we live?

Clearly, as Wolfe has grown in stature, he has become more interested in reform and more concerned about what he sees as "the wrong stuff" and "the right stuff." At the heart of *Bauhaus* and *The Painted Word* is a straightforward wish to humanize art and architecture by showing how "the freight train of history"[12] got off on the wrong track by the most ludicrous sort of historical coincidence. All of Wolfe's recent books, and many of his earlier essays, are also parables offered as intellectual history. They show how political power and orthodoxy and fashion-mongering have often run roughshod over originality, virtue, fair play, exuberance, and panache. The moral would seem to be that those who succumb to the temptation to aspire to the merely fashionable, who thus sacrifice the noble impulse toward individual vision, may end up "succeeding" and thereby mucking up whole centuries. This failing, he seems to warn us, is so common that all of us should be on guard against it, lest we, too, be tempted to repeat it. Substance over surface, he proclaims, should be our guide—be alert to the frailties of human nature and pay attention to values that truly matter. Yet there is nothing self-righteous in Tom Wolfe's moral stance, and it is so well disguised that the average reader often may be unaware that an implicit moral position is being assumed.

After roughly twenty years of development—by combining the methodology of the journalist with his own special sense and sensibility—the young writer whose life was forever changed by one amazed afternoon at the Coliseum at the Hot Rod & Custom Car Show has gone on to become the most astute and popular social observer and cultural chronicler on his generation. If Tom Wolfe sometimes interprets the American scene with the apparent detachment and freedom from constraints of a visiting Martian, he remains a Martian with an enviable sense of humor, energy, and playfulness. If he is often the maverick skeptic among us, the ultimate "King-Has-No-Clothes-On" man of principle, he is a skeptic with the power of empathy. If, at times, he seems to be viewing his own culture like an anthropologist studying the strange habits of the Trobriand Islanders, he is an anthropologist with an ear for every kind of idiomatic speech, loaded language and the multiple meanings it contains, and a conviction about the value of skewering pretentiousness wherever it may be found. No other writer of our time has aspired to capture the fabled Spirit of the Age so fully and has succeeded so well.

JOE DAVID BELLAMY

Notes

[1] Tom Wolfe, *The Electric Kool-Aid Acid Test* (New York: Farrar, Straus and Giroux, 1968), p. 39.

[2] Joe David Bellamy, *The New Fiction: Interviews with Innovative American Writers* (Urbana, Chicago, London: University of Illinois Press, 1974), p. 80.

[3] Tom Wolfe, *The New Journalism* (New York: Harper and Row, 1973), p. 31.

[4] Wolfe, *Journalism*, p. 34.

[5] Wolfe, *Journalism*, p. 19.

[6] Wolfe, *Journalism*, p. 21.

[7] Wolfe, *Journalism*, p. 17.

[8] Thomas R. Edwards, "The Electric Indian," *Partisan Review*, 3, 1969, p. 540.

[9] C. Hugh Holman, William Flint Thrall, and Addison Hibbard, *A Handbook to Literature* (Indianapolis: Bobbs-Merrill, 1972), p. 108.

[10] Tom Wolfe, *Mauve Gloves & Madmen, Clutter & Vine* (New York: Farrar, Straus and Giroux, 1976), p. 145.

[11] Tom Wolfe, *The Kandy-Kolored Tangerine-Flake Streamline Baby* (New York: Farrar, Straus and Giroux, 1966), p. 82.

[12] Tom Wolfe, *Radical Chic & Mau-Mauing the Flak Catchers* (New York: Farrar, Straus and Giroux, 1970), p. 17.

The Purple Decades

BOB & SPIKE

Look! She beckons! With those deep high-class black eyes! Here at a dinner party in Alfred Barr's apartment, in a room full of men who get their shirts hand-laundered at 90 cents a shirt by Forziati on East 74th Street and women who start getting ready for dinner with, first off, a little hair action at 4 p.m. by Kenneth on East 54th Street—here in this room she beckons. Liza, Liza Parkinson, Mrs. Bliss Parkinson, president of the Museum of Modern Art, daughter of Cornelius Bliss, niece of Lillie P. Bliss, who was one of the founders of the museum, sister of Anthony Bliss, the president of the Metropolitan Opera Association—Liza, the very embodiment of all that is most social, high class, Protestant tree-of-life and embossed-watermark-writing-paper in this whole art world social thing—Liza beckons to Spike. And Spike catches Bob's eye across the room. And Bob gives Spike the high sign. Go, girl, go. This is the moment—beckoning black eyes!—

Bob and Spike—*Spike*—when Bob, Robert Scull, America's most famous collector of pop and other avant-garde art, first met his wife, Ethel, Ethel Redner of West 86th Street, on a blind date back in 1943, he said to himself, "Ethel, what a terrible name." So he called her Spike. Spike's family had some dough, but Bob and Spike were so broke that they were living in one room on West 56th Street with a Murphy bed. They got a $12 membership in the Museum of Modern Art, three blocks away, on West 53rd Street, and used the museum, the garden, the restaurant and everything, as their living room, to entertain guests in. Is that irony or isn't it? Bob got very interested in

From *The Pump House Gang* (New York: Farrar, Straus and Giroux, 1968). First published as "Upward with the Arts—The Success Story of Robert & Ethel Scull" in *New York*, the *World Journal Tribune*'s Sunday magazine, October 30, 1966.

the art there and started a phantom art collection, writing down the names of pictures he wished he had, on a piece of shirt cardboard in his wallet. In 1947 or 1948 Bob started in the New York taxicab business, which was a very rough business at that time, full of—well, don't ask. Half the guys were rejects from the Mafia shape-up for hotel house dicks. But Bob started making money, and the rest is history. He started actually buying pictures himself. He had to put up with a lot of ridicule and everything, like the time in 1959 when he bought Jasper Johns's beer cans, two cans of Ballantine Ale, as a matter of fact, but everybody called them the beer cans, and the magazines and newspapers came around to take pictures, and he was very proud about buying Jap's beer cans. Would you believe they were only making fun of him? Yeah! Kids used to come to his kids in school and say, "Hey, is your old man the nut who bought the beer cans?" But he kept on collecting, and pretty soon Robert Scull became synonymous with pop art, and Bob and Spike are just getting in tight with the very social Museum of Modern Art crowd and finally here is the big dinner in Alfred's apartment—Alfred Barr is the curator of the Museum of Modern Art—

Here amid the crystal and the silver asparagus holders and the Forziati ironing jobs are people the magnitude of Liza and Philip—that's Philip Johnson, the architect, socialite and art savant—and Bob and Spike are looking great. Bob, who is 49, is just emerging, sartorially, from the 57th Street Biggie phase. The 57th Street Biggie look is the look of the men in New York who are in their 40s or 50s and the money is starting to come in and their hair is thinning in the crown but they comb it straight back like the real studs of the American business world do, like Lyndon Johnson does, as a matter of fact. They are getting an opulent plumpness about them, not fat exactly, and they don't have double chins, just sort of a great smooth tan fullness in the jowls set off by some good Sulka shirt work and a little Countess Mara in the necktie and a suit from Frank Brothers and a wife with apricot-colored hair—they all have wives with apricot-colored hair for some reason—and they take the Christmas cruise on the S.S. *France*. Only Spike didn't go the apricot-hair route. She has already graduated to the big time in fashion. She is slender and quite pretty. Her hair, which is mostly kind of pineapple blond, is great, and Kenneth does it. Her dresses come from St. Laurent, Dior, Chanel, Courrèges, Mainbocher, Cardin, Ken Scott, you name it. And she didn't like the Christmas cruise on the S.S. *France*. All the women came to the breakfast table wearing furs and enough diamonds to sink the boat. Spike took to her stateroom and wouldn't come out.

Finally—the moment arrives. Bob and Spike are both eating with the Continental style they now use, holding the fork in the left hand and the knife in the right. Liza Parkinson beckons, motions to Spike to come aside so she can talk to her. Those deep dark aristocratic eyes—she is the *whole thing* in the whole social thing of the art world—and Bob gives Spike the high sign, and right away, without having to say a word to each other, Bob and Spike both figure the same thing. This is the moment. Liza is going to say to Spike something like, Could you serve on this board or whatever, or could we get yours and Bob's advice on this or that vital project, or, at the very least, would you come to such-and-such a dinner—you know, something that will symbolize the fact that Robert and Ethel Scull are now in the inner circle of the whole thing—and Liza draws Ethel aside and then Liza—regal eyes!—pops the question—

Afterwards, when Spike comes back, Bob can hardly wait.

"What did she say?"

"Are you all set?" says Spike.

"Yeah—"

"You sure your heart's O.K.?"

"Yeah—"

"She said, 'Ethel, would you mind telling me who does your hair?' "

Who does your hair?

"Well—what did you say to that?"

"I told her."

"Then what did she say?"

"She said would I ask him if he could do hers."

"That's all she said?"

"No. She wanted to know how much it was."

Well, there it is. It is just an incident, but it gives an idea of what Bob and Spike are up against in this whole art world thing. Bob does everything right, better than right, in fact. He rises out of the Lower East Side and its psychological affiliates, the Bronx and Long Island, to an eight-room apartment on Fifth Avenue overlooking the park and a summer place in East Hampton. He amasses a collection of pop art and op art and primary art, in fact, everything since abstract expressionism, that is actually better than the Museum of Modern Art's in that area. Like a lot of ambitious guys who had to take the night-school route, he studies his field very thoroughly, talks to the artists themselves for hours on end, until he probably knows more about pop art and post-pop art than anybody in the country except for Leo Castelli, Ivan Karp, Henry Geldzahler and a couple of others. He probably knows a lot more about it than Alfred Barr. Yet what do they want from Bob and Ethel Scull at the Museum of Modern Art? They want $1,000 a year so they can be on the International

Council and they want Ethel to help organize a party—and where does she get her hair done?

Who needs that? This season Robert and Ethel Scull are transferring their backing from the Museum of Modern Art to the Whitney. All right, the whole art world is not going to flip over backward like Charlie Brown in the comic strip over this, but it's a sign of this whole social thing in the art world that nobody knows anything about. They can talk about *modern art and contemporary art* all they want. But it's the same old social thing that's been going on in art for a hundred years, the flutey bitones of the Protestant cultural establishment, and—

But then Spike looks at Bob, and Bob looks at Spike and he shrugs and wraps his clavicles up around his head and breaks into a smile, in a primordial gesture of the New York streets, the What Are You Gonna Do Shrug, and he says:

"Spike, you know what my philosophy is? My philosophy is, *Enjoy.*"

Enjoy! So a few things aren't panning out here at the top of the ladder. The main thing is that you're up here. Right? That is one thing nobody ever seems to understand about people who go through something like the Lower East Side–West Bronx route and make it in New York. A few slights, a few disappointments, a little sniggering along the way—you're going to cut your throat over that? The main thing is that Robert and Ethel Scull are one of *the* great social success stories of New York since World War II.

In eighteen years they have *made it* all the way, or practically all the way, from point zero—up from the Lower East Side, the West Bronx, up from that point just eighteen years ago when Bob Scull was a nobody, a 31-year-old businessman whose business had gone down the chute and he and Spike woke up every morning in that Murphy bed, to . . . Today. Today they have made it to the greatest address in New York, Fifth Avenue across from Central Park, and not just in terms of money, but right into that whole world of opening nights and the parties they write about in the papers, chauffeurs who are practically one of the family, apartments where the lobby and the doorman look so great you feel like you have to dress up to step on the sidewalk or you're letting down the building, esoteric New York day schools for the younger children and boarding schools for the older ones, lunches at La Grenouille where expensive matrons in Chanel suits have two bloody marys and smile—teeth!—at tailored young men with names like Freddy, Ferdi and Tug, petite plaques on the exhibition wall that say "from the collection of Mr. and Mrs.

Robert C. Scull," photographs in the women's magazines in court-photographer Shah and Farah Diba poses, fashion stories in which they say that this new madras wool gabardine coat is on the backs of Mrs. William Paley, Mrs. Palmer Dixon, Mrs. Samuel Pryor Reed and Mrs. Robert C. Scull, and a social set in which Chester is Chester Beatty who owns the diamond mines, and Nicole is Nicole Alphand the wife of the former French ambassador, and Bob is Robert Kintner the former chairman of NBC, Susan is Susan Stein the heiress, Alex is Alex Liberman the editorial director of *Vogue*, Marina is Marina Consort the wife of Prince Michael of Greece, Jap is Jasper Johns the painter, Dean is Dean Acheson, Sammy is Sammy Davis, Ave is Averell Harriman, Andy is Andy Warhol, Lady Bird is Lady Bird—All right! People are getting shot and blown up in Vietnam. China is a restless giant. The black ghettos are brandishing the fist of liberation. God has gone and died. And yet what Bob and Spike have done, made it, is still the only name of the game in New York. What is more, they have made it the way people dream of making it in New York; namely, right now. The hell with just making the money and setting things up for your children and waiting for the reflected glory of it when your daughter at Wellesley, the bird-song genius, gets invited up for a weekend in the country at the Detergent King's in North Egremont.

Make it—now!

That cry, that cry, burning like valvulitis in so many hearts in New York tonight . . .

Bob and Spike are the folk heroes of every social climber who ever hit New York. What Juarez was to the Mexican mestizo—what John L. Sullivan was to the Boston Irish—what Garibaldi was to the Sardinian farmers—what the Beatles are to the O-level-dropout £8-a-week office boys of England—what Antonino Rocca is to the Garment Center aviator Puerto Ricans of New York—what Moishe Dayan is to the kibbutzim shock workers of the Shephelah—all these things are Bob and Spike to the social climbers of New York.

In a blaze of publicity they illuminated the secret route: *collecting wacked-out art.* It was a tricky business. Art has been a point of entry into New York Society for seventy-five years or more. Duveen, of course, made millions selling *cultural immortality* to John D. Rockefeller and Henry Clay Frick in the form of Old Masters. After World War I the Protestant elite turned to Recent Masters as well. The Museum of Modern Art, after all, was not founded by intellectual revolutionaries. It was founded in John D. Rockefeller, Jr.'s living room, with Goodyears, Blisses, and Crowinshields in attendance. They founded the museum in order to import to New York the cultural cachet of the European upper classes, who were suddenly excited over the Impressionists and post-Impressionist masters such as Cézanne, Picasso, and Braque. In either case, Old Masters or New, the route was through art that had been certified in Europe.

Bob Scull had started out collecting Renaissance bronzes, but he quickly found out two things: (1) after World War II the prices of certified art, even in an esoteric field like Renaissance bronzes, were rising at a rate that made serious collecting out of the question; (2) the social world of certified art, even modern art, was a closed shop controlled—despite a dazzling aura of cultural liberalism—by the same old Protestant elite.

Then, in the late 1950's, a great thing happened: Pop Art; and pop publicity for Pop Art. In the financial world they speak of the tens of millions a man would be worth today had he invested $10,000 in IBM in 1926. But who ever has the daring or the foresight to do these things at the time? Bob Scull. Socially, Scull achieved a stock coup of IBM magnitude by plunging on the work of a painter, Jasper Johns, in 1959 and 1960. Rather amateurish stuff it was, too, renderings of flags, targets, numbers—and two bronzed ale cans. *How they sniggered over that!* But Johns became the "axe man for abstract expressionism," as Scull likes to put it. The ten-year-rule of abstract expressionism, which had seemed like *the final style*, was over, and in came a new movement, with Johns and Robert Rauschenberg as the key figures. Two years later, in 1962, it picked up a name: Pop Art.

Abstract expressionism was so esoteric it had all but defied exploitation by the press. But all the media embraced Pop Art with an outraged, scandalized, priapic delight. Art generally became the focus of social excitement in New York. Art openings began to take over from theater openings as the place where the chic, the ambitious, and the beautiful congregated. Art museum committees replaced charity committees as the place where ambitious newcomers could start scoring socially.

By 1961 the Sculls were being invited everywhere. "It was a whole thing going on," Scull told me, "where we got invitations from important people we didn't even know. You feel a little strange—you know, you go to some famous person's to a party or a dinner and you don't even know them, but you figure some friend of yours asked them to invite you, and then you get there and you find out there's nobody you know there. They just invited you. And everybody is very friendly. It's great. They come up and embrace you like you're the oldest friends in the world.

"I'll never forget once in Washington, at a gallery, Dean Acheson was there and I heard that he wanted to meet me. He came all the way over and shook hands with me very warmly and congratulated me on my collection—the whole thing was just as if we had gone to school together or something. Acheson—he was always practically a *god* to me, you know? One of the great leaders. And I walked in and here he walks all the way across the room and says *he* had looked forward to meeting *me*. And all the time I had always thought there were two worlds, this world full of all these people who did these great things, all these great, faultless people, and then this other world the rest of us were in."

From *hoi polloi* to *haute monde*—just so!

The success of Bob's original plunge, investing in twenty of Johns's works at one clip like he did, might be called luck. But the way Bob and Spike traversed that difficult interval from *hoi* to *haute* proved they had something else: *Fifth Avenue guts*, east side of the Park.

Throughout the period of transition—*how they sniggered!*—Bob and Spike were blessed with that gyroscope a few lucky people get built into them growing up in New York. It is an attitude, a Sat'dy aftuh-noon *Weltanschauung*, that always keeps them steady somehow. It is the cynicism of the cab driver with his cap over one eye. It is the fatalism of those old guys who sit out in front of the stores in the Lower East Side on Saturday afternoon in old bentwood chairs of the 1930's drugstore variety and just survey the scene with half a smile on, as if to say, look around you, this town is a nuthouse to start with, right? So don't get your bowels in an uproar. Relax. Enjoy.

There was, for example, the ticklish business—*how they sniggered*—of Bob learning how to dress. As I said, Scull is emerging from the 57th Street Biggie phase. Somebody turned him on to the big time in men's fashion, the English tailor shops on Savile Row, which is in the sort of 57th Street and Fifth Avenue area of London. The Savile Row shops still like to maintain the impression that they are some kind of private clubs and that you have to be recommended by an old customer. O.K., said Bob Scull, enjoy, enjoy, and he had two wealthy English friends, Harry Lawton and Murray Leonard, recommend him. All the same he can't resist it; he has to swing from the heels. So he walks into this place, amid all the linenfold paneling and engraved glass with all the "by appointment" crests, HRH King George, The Prince of Wales, etc., and a man about 55 in a nailhead worsted suit with a step-collared vest comes up and Scull announces that Harry Lawton and Murray Leonard recommended him and he wants . . . a sport jacket made of the material they make riding pinks out of.

"I beg your pardon, sir?" says the man, turning his mouth down and putting a cataractic dimness into his eyes as if he hopes to God he didn't hear correctly.

"You know that material they make the riding pinks out of, those coats when they go hunting, riding to the hounds and everything, that material, they call it riding pink."

"I am familiar with that, yes, sir."

"Well, I want a sport jacket made out of that."

"I'm afraid that's impossible, sir."

"You don't have the material?"

"It's not that—"

"I know where I can get you the material," says Scull. "There's this place, Hunt & Winterbotham."

Now the man looks at Scull with his lips tight and tilts his head back and opens his nostrils wide as if his eyes are located somewhere up his nose. Telling a Savile Row tailor that there is this place, Hunt & Winterbotham, is like telling a Seventh Avenue coffee shop that there is this thing called a cheese Danish.

"We are aware of the availability of the material, sir," he says. "It's just that we don't do that sort of thing."

"You can make a sport jacket, can't you?"

"Oh, yes, sir."

"And you can get the riding pink."

"Yes, sir."

"Then why can't you get the riding pink and make a sport jacket out of it?"

"As I said, sir, I'm afraid we don't . . ."

". . . do that sort of thing," says Scull, finishing the sentence.

"Yes, sir."

"Well, all I know is, Harry Lawton and Murray Leonard said you could take care of me."

"Oh, you come very highly recommended, sir, it's just that we . . ."

". . . I know . . ."

It is at this point, if not before, that Savile Row tailors are used to seeing Americans, 1960's style, at any rate, bow out, shuffling backwards like they are leaving the throne room, thoroughly beaten, cowed, humiliated, hangdog over the terrible gaffe they have committed—*a sport jacket out of traditional riding pink*—but Bob Scull just starts in again, still exuberant, smiling, happy to be on Savile Row in Harry Lawton and Murray Leonard country, and he says, "All right, let's go over this thing again. You can make a sport jacket and you can get the material . . ." They are so amazed to see an American still standing there and talking that they go ahead and agree to do it, and they take his measurements.

A week or so later Scull comes back in for the first fitting, and they bring out the riding pink, with the body of the coat cut and basted up and one arm basted on, the usual first fitting, and they put it on him—and Scull notices a funny thing. Everything has stopped in the shop. There, in the dimness of the woodwork and the bolt racks, the other men are looking up toward him, and in the back, from behind curtains, around door edges, from behind tiers of cloth, are all these eyes, staring.

Scull motions back toward all the eyes and asks his man, Nostrils, "Hey, what are they doing?"

Nostrils leans forward and says, very softly and very sincerely, "They're rooting for you, sir."

Enjoy! Enjoy!

Scull is so pleased with this, he goes back and starts shaking hands with everybody in the place, right down to the Cypriot seamstresses who made buttonholes and can't speak any English.

"I got news for you," says Scull, by way of congratulating those who are happy and consoling those who are desolate over the riding pink sports jacket, "you're going to be very proud of this jacket when we get through."

Later on, as Scull tells it, he saw one of his friends and said, "Well, I went to your tailor, and I want to thank you, because they made me a very nice jacket."

"Oh, that's very nice. I'm very glad."

"You know, it was funny. They didn't want to make it at first. I walked in and I said, 'I want a sport jacket made out of riding pink' and . . ."

"You *what!* Bob—you didn't use my name, did you . . ."

Afterwards Bob Scull tells me, "It's funny. The English treat their tailors like they were clergymen. Yeah. And their clergymen like they were tailors."

Spike's parents had money, and, if the truth were known, helped set Bob up in the taxi business in 1948. But as for social cachet—well, Spike had to learn all the subtleties of *chic* the same way Bob did, namely, the hard way—*how they sniggered*—but she always showed *class*, in the New York street sense of that term; *moxie*. When the going got tough, Spike just bulled it through and made it work. In the midst of the social galas attendant upon the opening of the Venice Biennale in 1966, I saw Ethel Scull stroll at twilight through Venice, heading for Countess Anna Camerana's in a dress of silver gossamer see-through by St. Laurent and silver shoes. The citizens of Venice and the tourists of all nations, including a man whose monocle fell out of his skull, stared bug-eyed at this vision of Scientific Cinderella chic with her head held high and one perfect rose in her hair. She topped this off by standing on one foot and hoisting the other one up and rubbing it and delivering the last word on strolls through Venice at twilight: "I got news for you, this girl's got sore feet."

Bob hasn't lost the common touch, either. Today he has 130 cabs in his fleet, the Super Operating Corporation, which is $2,625,000 worth of medallions alone, and a big taxi insurance business involving a lot of fleets. He goes up there every day to his garage in the Bronx, at 144th Street and Gerard Avenue, in the Mott Haven section, about ten blocks south of Yankee Stadium, and he deals directly with the drivers right there in the garage, guys like Jakey, The Owl, Cream Cheese, Moon and this guy who used to be there, Do-Nut or whatever they called him.

You know what would be funny? It would be funny to pick up Liza or Philip or Nicole or Peggy—that's Mrs. Peggy Guggenheim of New York and Venice, who has one of the world's greatest private art collections—or Chester or Alex or Bob or Dean or any of the other wonderful people who make up the art world set Robert Scull now moves in—it would be funny to pick up some of these people and suddenly sit them down in the grease moss at the Scull garage in the Bronx and let them try to handle a New York taxi operation for about one hulking hour. Never mind the heavy problems. Just imagine Philip or Alex or Ave dealing with a minor problem, like Do-Nut.

Philip! Ave! Do-Nut was a driver, a huge guy, and every morning he started out from the garage with a big brown paper bag full of donuts and pastries on the seat beside him. He kept on eating the day away and getting bigger and bigger and Scull tried everything. He had them push the seat in Do-Nut's cab back so far, to make room for his belly, it got so the only fares he could pick up were infants and midgets. Then they took the padding off the seats so he was back up against the metal plates. And then one day it was all over. He managed to get into the seat, but he couldn't turn the wheel. It would turn about 15 degrees and then just lodge in his belly.

"Bob, I got news for you," says Do-Nut, there behind the wheel. "This don't make it."

"You want to know something?" says Scull. "This is the day I dreaded."

"Wait a minute," says Do-Nut, "look at this. If I hold my breath, I can turn it."

"Yeah," says Scull, "but what about when you let it out."

Do-Nut exhales and the wheel disappears like a strawberry under a gush of whipped cream. Do-Nut looks up at Scull. Scull shrugs, pulling his shoulders up over his ears like a turtle, in a primordial gesture of the New York streets, the Hopeless Shrug, which says, What can I do after I've said I'm sorry. The guy had eaten himself out of the profession.

Scull still has to shake his head over that. Those guys. But the great thing is, the men, Scull says, the men . . . "generally speaking they're very proud of my art kick. They're proud that their boss is something special. They want a boss they can look up to. That's class."

Bob's art kick, as I say, was tricky business. The economics of collecting *the latest thing* in art, as Bob has been doing, are irrational. A collector can count on *the latest work* by almost any of the current avant-garde artists to depreciate more drastically than a new car; it will lose one third to one half its value the moment it is bought. The explanation gets at the heart of the whole business of collecting the latest, the most avant-garde, the most wacked-out in painting. The price of, say, a new Lichtenstein or a new Johns or a new Stella is not determined by market demand in the usual sense (i.e., a mass of undifferentiated consumers). Aside from museums, the market is, in effect, some ten or twenty collectors, most of whom are striving to become Bobs and Spikes, although they would bridle if it were ever put to them just that way. The game, when one is collecting the *latest thing*—as opposed to certified Old or Recent Masters—is to get one's hands on just that: *the latest thing* by a promising avant-garde artist and, preferably, to be publicized for purchasing it. One has . . . *the new Lichtenstein! the new Poons! the new Rauschenberg! the new Dine! the new Oldenburg!* The competition to buy it hot from the studio is what drives the price up in the galleries. Once that little game is played out, the re-sale value may be but a fraction. The galleries dealing in the hottest avant-garde artists are driven to frantic juggling to make sure each of the handful of players wins a bout every now and then and remains interested. Collector X got the first shot at the last hot one—so Y gets first shot at the next one; and so on.

So Bob Scull got an idea. Why not get to the artists before their work reaches the gallery even? Why not do even better than that—why not *discover* them?

One evening a friend of Bob's, a psychiatrist, said to him: "Bob, did it ever occur to you that when you commission young artists to create works of art, you may be influencing the course of art history?"

Patron. Shaper of history. If the truth be known, it had already crossed Bob's mind that he had influenced art history by buying twenty works by Johns in 1959 and 1960. Before that, Johns was just some kind of odd man out in the art world, some guy from South Carolina trying to bug the establishment with his fey, representational rendition of banal objects. The fact that he was actually being *collected*—well, that's what started Pop Art. Yes, that thought had crossed Bob's mind. But why not go even one step further—*discover* the greats of tomorrow yourself and *commission* the future of art history. Stalk their very studios. That was how Bob ran into Walter De Maria.

It was a Saturday. Another Culture Sabbath. Bob Scull was walking down Madison Avenue, and you know, it's funny on Saturday in New York, especially on one of those Indian summer days—God, somehow Culture just seems to be in the air, like part of the weather, all of the antique shops on Madison Avenue, with a little blaze of golden ormolu here and a little oxblood-red leathery marquetry there, and the rugs hung up in the second-floor display windows—rich!—a Bakhtiari with a little pale yellow setting off the red—and the galleries, God, gallery after gallery, with the pristine white walls of Culture, the black wooden floors, and the Culture buds, a little Renoirish softness in the autumn faces.

Through the window of this particular gallery, Scull can see two girls who are tending the place, and one is sitting with her legs crossed, a short skirt on, great pre-Raphaelite hair, the perfect Culture bud, and it is not that he wants to make a pass or anything, it is just part of this beautiful atmosphere of Culture in New York, Indian summer, Culture Sabbath, all the rest—so he goes in. It is just a pleasure to go on in there and let the whole thing just sort of seep through you like hot coffee.

But what a freaking show. Here is some wooden sculpture of some sort, two very tall pillars of wood—and then there is a bunch of drawings. Except that there doesn't seem to be anything on the paper, just a lot of framed blank paper on the wall. What the hell is this? Scull goes up very close to a drawing and then he can see there is a hard little design on the paper done with a hard pencil, a No. 8 or something, so you can hardly see it. Then down at the bottom, also in this hard pencil, are these poverty-stricken little words: "Water, water, water."

So Scull turns to the girl and he says, "I've seen a lot of things, but how does this guy think he's going to sell these?"

"Well . . ."

"I mean, I don't know what this whole art thing is coming to. You can't even *see* what's on the paper."

He looks back at it again and it still says "Water, water, water." That's all that's up there. Well, the girl says, it's by a young artist, they never handled him before. She shrugs. Scull is really bugged by this whole thing.

"All right," he says, finally, "how much is this drawing?"

She gives him a look—what the hell, this girl never even thought about the price before. Nobody ever asked. Finally she says, "It's $110."

"All right," says Scull, "I tell you what. This whole thing bugs me. I'll buy this drawing for $110 if you'll give me the artist's name, address and telephone number. I want to see what he has to say about this."

So she says all right, and it's Walter De Maria. So the following week Scull calls up the number. The thing is, the whole thing *disturbs* him, and so this guy may have something he ought to know about. The telephone conversation disturbs him some more. This Walter De Maria comes to the phone and Scull says, "This is Robert Scull."

"Yes." That's all he says.

"Do you know who I am?"

There's this long pause. Then this hesitant voice: "Yes. You're the man who bought my drawing."

"That's right," Scull says. "I'd like to come to your studio and see some more of your work."

There's a big silence. Scull starts saying, Hello, hello. He thinks the guy must have hung up.

"I don't know," the guy says. "I won't be available."

"Look," says Scull, "I bought your drawing and I want to see some more of your work. Can't I even come and look at it?"

"I don't know. I'm glad you bought the drawing, but you bought the drawing from the gallery, not from me, and I'm not available."

Scull is really rocked by this, but he keeps arguing and finally De Maria gives in and says O.K., come on down to his studio. The studio is downtown up in a loft building, about five flights up, and Scull climbs up there. His heart is banging away from the freaking stairs. There's a small room and then a bigger room beyond, and in the small room here are these two pale, slender figures, Walter De Maria and his wife. Mrs. De Maria is kind of backed off into a corner. She doesn't say anything.

"Well," says Scull to De Maria, "I'd like to see some more of your drawings."

So he shows him one and this time Scull has to put on his *glasses* to see if there's anything on paper. He looks up, and by this time De Maria is pacing around the room and running his hands through his hair in a terrible state of agitation.

What the hell is this? Scull says to himself. You could get a heart attack walking up these freaking stairs, and after you get up here, what's going on? He's sorry he even came up. But as a last gesture, he asks De Maria to show him what he had been doing before he did the drawings. Here, says De Maria, that's what I've done. What's that? says Scull. That's a sculpture, says De Maria. Here is this Skee-Ball, like in the amusement arcades, on a wooden board, and it says on there, "Place ball in upper hole," and so Scull dutifully places it in the upper hole and pow! it falls down into a hole at the bottom. Scull stares at the ball. And De Maria, like, he's watching Scull this whole time, waiting for a reaction, but Scull can't come up with any, except that he's still bugged.

"How long have you been a sculptor?" he says.

"Six years."

"Well, can I see some of your earlier work?"

"It's in the other room."

The other room is bigger, a studio room, with all white walls and a white floor—and nothing else. It's empty. Yeah, well, where is it? Scull says. Over here, says De Maria. Over here? De Maria is pointing to a little filing cabinet. He's done a lot of successful sculptures, he says. The only thing is, he never made them. He never made them? No. He couldn't afford the materials. Well, yeah, says Scull, then he says, What's in the file? De Maria riffles through and here are more of these sheets of paper with something on there you can't even see, a few lines and more "Water, water, water" and so forth.

The whole thing now has Scull so bugged he says, "Look—if I commission you to do one for me and I get you the materials, will you make one?"

De Maria says O.K. A couple of months go by and finally De Maria says he has completed a design and he'll need a large plate of silver. Silver? says Scull. Why can't he use stainless steel. It's got to be silver, says De Maria. So Scull gets him the silver. Through all this Bob and Spike get to know De Maria a little better, but it's an unusual relationship. Sometimes one of them says something and there is no response, nothing at all. Other times, they're all out on the street and De Maria walks way ahead, as if he didn't know them. Who are these people following him? Bob says to himself: Ah, he's been through a lot of excitement because of all this. That's all it is.

Then three and a half or four more months go by, and—nothing. Bob is on the verge of going back there and getting his silver back. But then one day De Maria calls up and says the sculpture is ready. He brings it up in a truck, and they bring it up into the apartment; it's the big moment and everything, and here is this big object with a velvet drapery over it. Bob pulls a string and opens up the drapes—and there it is, the piece of silver, the original plate of silver, with nothing on it. Bob stares at the piece of silver. De Maria is watching him just like he did the first day with the Skee-Ball.

"What is it?" says Scull.

"Look on the back."

On the back is a little piece of chrome inscribed "Nov. 5, 1965, made for Mr. and Mrs. Robert C. Scull." There are also instructions to photograph the plate of silver every three months and keep the pictures in a photograph album. The sculpture is entitled *The Portrait of Dorian Gray*. The thing is, says De Maria, the silver will tarnish, and the plate will get blacker and more and more corroded and the film will record the whole process. Every three months until 1975, presumably, Bob or Spike will pull the velvet drapes and take a picture of this piece of corroded metal and then paste it in the scrapbook. *The Portrait of Dorian Gray!* But of course!

"I was overwhelmed by it," Scull told me later. "It's impossible to describe what happens to a collector when he commissions something and it turns out right."

Bob and Spike went out to New Jersey to the studio of George Segal. Segal is famous for his plaster-cast sculptures. Bob and Spike commissioned him to make one of them. So Segal started encasing them in the plaster. It was kind of a wild time. Sometimes the plaster starts sticking to the skin when it dries. Spike lost one of her Courrèges boots in the struggle to get out, and Bob—they had to pull his Levi's off him to keep him from being a permanent living cast. The shape of history, all right. Bob and Spike decided to unveil the sculpture at a party for a couple of hundred celebrities, artists, columnists, and editors. They didn't even know half of them—but they would come, they would come.

The afternoon before the party, Jasper Johns's latest show opened at the Leo Castelli gallery, 4 East 77th Street. There were four huge paintings in the show and Bob wasn't going to get any of them. For a variety of reasons. For one thing, three of them had been spoken for, by museums. Nevertheless, Bob was in a good mood. Spike didn't even show up, but Bob was in a good mood. Castelli's, especially at an opening like this, was where it was at. You could tell that at a glance. Not by the paintings, but by the Culture buds. They were all there, all these gorgeous little Culture buds, 20, 21, 22, 23, 24 years old, along in there, their little *montes Veneris* in the sweet honey grip of Jax slax that finger into every fissure, their serious little Culture pouts hooded in Sassoon thrusts and black Egypt eyes—their lubricous presence, like that of the whalebird, indicating where the biggest fish in the sea is.

Out in the middle of the bud coveys Bob is talking to Leo Castelli. Castelli, New York's number-one dealer in avant-garde art, is a small, trim man in his late fifties. Bob is Leo's number-one customer. Leo is the eternal Continental diplomat, with a Louis-salon accent that is no longer Italian; rather, Continental. Every word he utters slips through a small velvet Mediterranean smile. His voice is soft, suave, and slightly humid, like a cross between Peter Lorre and the first secretary of a French embassy.

"Leo," says Bob, "you remember what you told me at Jap's last show?"

"Noooooooo——"

"You told me—I was *vulgar!*"—only Bob says it with his eyes turned up bright, as if Leo should agree and they can have a marvelous laugh over it.

"Noooooo, Bob——"

"Listen, Leo! I got news——"

"Nooooooo, Bob, I didn't——"

"I got news for you, Leo——"

"Noooooooooooo, Bob, I merely said——" Nobody says No like Leo Castelli. He utters it as if no word in the entire language could be more pleasing to the listener. His lips purse into a small lubricated O, and the Nooooooo comes out like a strand of tiny, perfect satiny-white pearls . . .

"Leo, I got news for you——"

"Nooooooooo, Bob, I merely said that at that stage of Johns's career, it would be wrong—"

"*Vulgar* you said, Leo—"

"—would be wrong for one collector to buy up the whole show—"

"You said it was *vulgar*, Leo, and you know what?"

"What, Bob?"

"I got news for you—*you were right!* It *was* vulgar!" Bob's eyes now shine like two megawatt beacons of truth; triumphant, for the truth now shines in the land. For one of the few times in his life, Castelli stares back blank; in velvet stupefaction.

That night, the big party—it was freezing. For a start, Spike was very icy on the subject of Jasper Johns; another of their personal tiffs, and Johns wasn't coming to the party. But enjoy! Who else is even in a position to *have* tiffs with the great of the avant garde? It was also cold as hell outside, about 17 degrees, and all these people in tuxedos and mini-evening dresses came up into the Sculls' apartment at 1010 Fifth Avenue with frozen heads and—*kheeew!*—right inside the door is a dark velvet settee with a slightly larger than life plaster cast of Ethel Scull sitting on it, legs crossed, and Bob standing behind it. Standing next to it, here in the foyer, are the real Bob and Spike, beaming, laughing, greeting everybody—*Gong*—the apartment has been turned into a gallery of Bob's most spectacular acquisitions.

Everywhere, on these great smooth white walls, are de Koonings, Newmans, Jasper Johns's targets and flags, John Chamberlain's sculpture of crushed automobile parts, Andy Warhol's portrait of Spike made of thirty-five blown-up photos from the Photo-Matic machine in the pinball arcade at 52nd Street and Broadway, op art by Larry Poons with color spots that vibrate so hard you can turn your head and still, literally, see spots in front of your eyes. That is on the dining room walls. There used to be a Rosenquist billboard-style painting in there with huge automobile tire treads showing. Tonight there is a painting by James Rosenquist on the ceiling, a painting of a floor plan, the original idea being that the Sculls could wake up in the morning and look over their bed and see the floor plan and orient themselves for the day. Over the headboard of their king-size bed is an "American nude" by Tom Wesselmann with two erect nipples sitting up like hot cherries.

Many prominent people are moving about in the hubbub, talking, drinking, staring: George Segal the movie actor, George Segal the sculptor, Leonard Lyons the columnist, Aileen Mehle, who is Suzy Knickerbocker the columnist; Alex Liberman; Mrs. Jacob Javits; Robert Kintner. Larry Poons comes in with his great curly head hung solemnly, wearing a terry cloth Hawaiian shirt with a picture of a shark on it. *Poonsy!* Spike calls him Poonsy. Her voice penetrates. It goes right through this boilup of heads, throats, tuxedoes. She says this is a big concession for Poonsy. She is talking about the Hawaiian shirt. This is *formal* for Poonsy. To some parties he wears a T-shirt and a pair of clodhoppers with Kelly green paint sloshed on them. *Awash.* People are pouring through all the rooms. *Gong*—the World's Fair. Everybody leaves the apartment and goes downstairs to where they have three Campus Coach Line buses out on Fifth Avenue to take everybody out to the World's Fair, out in Flushing.

The World's Fair is over, but the Top o' the Fair restaurant is still going, up in the top of a big mushroom tower. The wreckage of the fair, the half-demolished buildings, are all hulking around it in silhouette, like some gigantic magnified city dump. The restaurant itself, up there at the top, turns out to be a great piece of 1930's *Mo-dren* elegance, great slabs of glass, curved wood, wall-to-wall, and, everywhere, huge plate-glass views of the borough of Queens at night.

Scull has taken over half the big complex at the top of the tower, including a whole bandstand and dance floor with tables around it, sort of like the old Tropicana night club in Havana, Cuba.

After dinner a rock 'n' roll band starts playing and people start dancing. Mrs. Claes Oldenburg, a pretty, petite girl in a silver minidress, does a dance, the newest boogaloo, with Robert Rauschenberg, the artist. The band plays "Hang on, Sloopy." Rauschenberg has had an outrageous smile on all evening and he ululates to himself from time to time—Oooooooooo—Gong—the dancing stops and everybody is shepherded into a convention hall.

There is a movie screen in here and rows of seats. The lights go out. The first movie is called *Camp*, by Andy Warhol. A group of men and women in evening clothes are sitting in a very formal pose in a loft. One of them is Jane Holzer. A fat boy in some kind of Wagnerian opera costume comes out in front of them and does some ballet leaps, sagging and flopping about. The men and women in the evening clothes watch very stiffly and respectfully. Another fat boy comes out with a yo-yo act. A man in drag, looking like a faded Argentinian torch singer, comes out and does a crazy dance. The basic idea is pretty funny, all these people in evening clothes watching stiffly and respectfully while the performers come out and go into insane acts. It is also exquisitely boring. People start drifting out of the convention hall in the darkness at the Top o' the Fair. So they stop that film, and the lights go on and a young man named Robert Whitman comes up and puts on his film, which has no title.

This one is more elaborate. It involves three screens and three projectors. The lights go out. On the left screen, in color, a slender, good-looking girl, kind of a nude Culture bud, with long pre-Raphaelite hair and good beach skin, is taking a shower, turning this way and that. At first water comes out of the nozzle, and then something black, like oil, and then something red, like wine. She keeps waffling around. On the righthand screen, also in color, some nice-looking buds are lying on the floor with their mouths open. You're looking down at their faces. Food and liquid start falling, cascading down, into their mouths, onto their faces, onto their noses, their eyes, all this stuff, something soft and mushy like pancake mix, then a thin liquid like pineapple juice, then chopped meat, chopped liver or something, raw liver, red and runny, all hitting the old bud face there or going straight down the gullet. Only they keep smiling. Then the whole thing goes in reverse and all the stuff comes back up out of their mouths, like they're vomiting, only they're smiling out of these pretty faces the whole time.

On the center screen, all this time, in black and white—nobody can tell what the hell is going on at first. There are these sort of, well, *abstract* shapes, some fissures, folds, creases, apertures, some kind of rim, and some liquid that comes from somewhere. But it doesn't add up to anything. Of course, it could be some of the abstract forms that Stan Brakhage uses in his films, or—but then, after about fifteen minutes, while Black-haired Beauty on the left waffles in the shower and the Open-jawed Beauties on the right grin into eternal ingestion, it adds up—the girl who was sitting on the rim gets up, and then some large testicles lower into view, and then the organism begins to defecate. The film has somehow been made by slicing off the bottom of a toilet bowl and putting a glass shield in place and photographing straight up from inside the bowl. Black-haired Beauty pivots in the shower, luxuriating in oil, Strawberry Beauty smiles and luxuriates in chopped liver.

And here, descending head-on into the faces of the 200 celebrities, artists, columnists, editors . . . is an enormous human turd.

Marvelous! The lights go on. All these illuminati are sitting here in their tuxedos and mini-evening dresses at the Top o' the Fair above grand old Nighttime City Lights New York City, above the frozen city-dump silhouette of the New York World's Fair, like an assembly of poleaxed lambs.

Walter De Maria! Walter De Maria is on the drums, high up on the Tropicana bandstand, snares, brushes, blond wood, those sturdy five-story loft walkup arms going like hell—Walter De Maria is on the rise. Bob Scull patronized him, helped him out, and De Maria is now among the rising young sculptors. Blam! He beats the hell out of the drums. On the dance floor they've seized all the equipment at the Top o' the Fair, the artists. The band looks on from the side. Walter De Maria has the drums, Claes Oldenburg has a tambourine, his wife Pat, in the silver dress, has a microphone, and Rauschenberg has a microphone. Rauschenberg's friend Steve Paxton, the dancer, is dancing, waffling, by himself. Rauschenberg and Pat Oldenburg are both ululating into the microphones, wild loon wails—*Sloopy!*—filling up this whole mushroom-head glass building overlooking frozen Queens. Where are the poleaxed lambs? They have been drifting off. The Campus Coach Line buses have been leaving every half hour, like a bus route. The pop artists, the op artists, the primary artists, have the place: De Maria, Rauschenberg, Rosenquist, Segal, Poons, Oldenburg, they have the Top o' the Fair. Larry Poons pulls off his shark terry cloth Hawaiian shirt and strips down to his Ford Motor Company Cobra T-shirt, with the word COBRA stacked up the front about eight times. Poons waffles about on the edge of the dance floor, with his head down but grinning.

Bob Scull beams. Spike is delighted. Her voice penetrates—yes!

"Look at Poonsy! When I see that boy smile, I really enjoy it, I'm telling you!"

Bob Scull sits at a table on the edge of the dance floor, beaming. Rauschenberg and Pat Oldenburg go into ululation, mimicking rock 'n' roll singers, and then somebody there says, "Sing the dirty song!" Just as if she knows what he means, Pat Oldenburg starts singing the Dirty Song. She has the microphone in that Show Biz grip and her legs roil around in her silver mini-gown and she sings.

"You got a dirty ceiling, you got a dirty floor, you got a dirty window, you got a dirty door, oh dirty dirty, dirty dirty dirty, oh dirty dirty, dirty dirty dirty—"

Scull just beams and gets up from the table and takes his chair practically out onto the dance floor in front of her and sits down—

"—oh dirty dirty, dirty dirty dirty, dirty dirty, oh, you got dirty hair, you got dirty shoes, you got dirty ears, you got dirty booze, dirty dirty, dirty dirty dirty, oh you got a dirty face you got a dirty shirt, you got dirty hands—"

Rauschenberg ululates in the background, De Maria explodes all over the drums in some secret my-own-bag fury, Oldenburg beats the tambourine, Poons waffles and grins, everybody looks at Scull to see what he's going to do. Scull seems to sense this as some sort of test. Enjoy!

"I like it!" he says to Pat Oldenburg.

"—oh dirty dirty, dirty dirty dirty, dirty dirty—"

"That's very good! I like it!"

He beams, Rauschenberg ululates, blam bong—*Gong—2:30 a.m.*, out, out of here, Poons, De Maria, Segal, Rauschenberg, Rosenquist, they're off, down the elevator, they disappear. Bob and Spike take the last elevator down, with Jonathan and Stephen. They get to the bottom, and it is cold as hell, 2:30 a.m., 17 degrees, in the middle of Flushing, Queens, frozen Flushing with the troglodyte ruins of the World's Fair, frozen-dump garbage, sticking up in the black—and suddenly the artists are gone—and so is the last bus. It's unbelievable —Bob and Spike—deserted—abandoned—in the middle of Queens. There must have been some stupid mistake! Either that or somebody told the last bus, and the last bus driver, "This is it, we're all here, take off," and he took off, all those Campus Coach Line buses. A station wagon pulls out. It has a few remaining magazine editors in it, the *Time* and *Life* crowd. It disappears. Suddenly it is all quiet as hell here, and cold. Bob Scull stares out into the galactal Tastee-Freeze darkness of Queens and watches his breath turn white in front of him.

Mens Sana in Corpore Sano

"We'll give you a full scholarship, and you won't have to take but one class a week during basketball season, and you'll have your own apartment, rent-free, and eighteen hundred dollars a month for books, and a Corvette for yourself and a Caprice Classic for your folks and when you graduate you'll be able to read the newspaper and the stereo ads and add and subtract on a portable calculator and direct-dial anywhere in the world."

THE LAST AMERICAN HERO

Ten o'clock Sunday morning in the hills of North Carolina. Cars, miles of cars, in every direction, millions of cars, pastel cars, aqua green, aqua blue, aqua beige, aqua buff, aqua dawn, aqua dusk, aqua Malacca, Malacca lacquer, Cloud lavender, Assassin pink, Rake-a-cheek raspberry, Nude Strand coral, Honest Thrill orange, and Baby Fawn Lust cream-colored cars are all going to the stock car races, and that old mothering North Carolina sun keeps exploding off the windshields.

Seventeen thousand people, me included, all of us driving out Route 421, out to the stock car races at the North Wilkesboro Speedway, 17,000 going out to a five-eighths-mile stock car track with a Coca-Cola sign out front. This is not to say there is no preaching and shouting in the South this morning. There is preaching and shouting. Any of us can turn on the old automobile transistor radio and get all we want:

"They are greedy dogs. Yeah! They ride around in big cars. Unnh-hunh! And chase women. Yeah! And drink liquor. Unnh-hunh! And smoke cigars. Oh yes! And they are greedy dogs. Yeah! Unh-hunh! Oh yes! Amen!"

There are also some commercials on the radio for Aunt Jemima grits, which cost ten cents a pound. There are also the Gospel Harmonettes, singing: "If you dig a ditch, you better dig two. . . ."

There are also three fools in a panel discussion on the New South, which they seem to conceive of as General Lee running the new Dulcidreme Labial Cream factory down at Griffin, Georgia.

And suddenly my car is stopped still on Sunday morning in the middle of the biggest traffic jam in the history of the world. It goes

From *The Kandy-Kolored Tangerine-Flake Streamline Baby* (New York: Farrar, Straus and Giroux, 1965). First published as "The Last American Hero Is Junior Johnson. Yes!" in *Esquire*, March 1965.

for ten miles in every direction from the North Wilkesboro Speedway. And right there it dawns on me that as far as this situation is concerned, anyway, all the conventional notions about the South are confined to . . . the Sunday radio. The South has preaching and shouting, the South has grits, the South has country songs, old mimosa traditions, clay dust, Old Bigots, New Liberals—and all of it, all of that old mental cholesterol, is confined to the Sunday radio. What I was in the middle of—well, it wasn't anything one hears about in panels about the South today. Miles and miles of eye-busting pastel cars on the expressway, which roar right up into the hills, going to the stock car races. Fifteen years of stock car racing, and baseball—and the state of North Carolina alone used to have forty-four professional baseball teams—baseball is all over with in the South. We were all in the middle of a wild new thing, the Southern car world, and heading down the road on my way to see a breed such as sports never saw before, Southern stock car drivers, all lined up in these two-ton mothers that go over 175 m.p.h., Fireball Roberts, Freddie Lorenzen, Ned Jarrett, Richard Petty, and—the hardest of all the hard chargers, one of the fastest automobile racing drivers in history—yes! Junior Johnson.

The legend of Junior Johnson! In this legend, here is a country boy, Junior Johnson, who learns to drive by running whiskey for his father, Johnson, Senior, one of the biggest copper-still operators of all time, up in Ingle Hollow, near North Wilkesboro, in northwestern North Carolina, and grows up to be a famous stock car racing driver, rich, grossing $100,000 in 1963, for example, respected, solid, idolized in his hometown and throughout the rural South. There is all this about how good old boys would wake up in the middle of the night in the apple shacks and hear a supercharged Oldsmobile engine roaring over Brushy Mountain and say, "Listen at him—there he goes!" although that part is doubtful, since some nights there were so many good old boys taking off down the road in supercharged automobiles out of Wilkes County, and running loads to Charlotte, Salisbury, Greensboro, Winston-Salem, High Point, or wherever, it would be pretty hard to pick out one. It was Junior Johnson specifically, however, who was famous for the "bootleg turn" or "about-face," in which, if the Alcohol Tax agents had a roadblock up for you or were too close behind, you threw the car up into second gear, cocked the wheel, stepped on the accelerator and made the car's rear end skid around in a complete 180-degree arc, a complete about-face, and tore on back up the road exactly the way you came from. God! The Alcohol Tax agents used to burn over Junior Johnson. Practically every good old boy in town in Wilkesboro, the county seat, got to know the agents by sight in a very short time. They would rag them practically to their faces on the subject of Junior Johnson, so that it got to be an obsession. Finally, one night they had Junior trapped on the road up toward the bridge around Millersville, there's no way out of there, they had the barricades up and they could hear this souped-up car roaring around the bend, and here it comes—but suddenly they can hear a siren and see a red light flashing in the grille, so they think it's another agent, and boy, they run out like ants and pull those barrels and boards and sawhorses out of the way, and then—Ggghhzzzzzzzhhhhhhgggggzzzzzzzeeeeeong! —gawdam! there he goes again, it was him, Junior Johnson! with a gawdam agent's si-reen and a red light in his grille!

I wasn't in the South five minutes before people started making oaths, having visions, telling these hulking great stories, all on the subject of Junior Johnson. At the Greensboro, North Carolina, Airport there was one good old boy who vowed he would have eaten "a bucket of it" if that would have kept Junior Johnson from switching from a Dodge racer to a Ford. Hell yes, and after that—God-almighty, remember that 1963 Chevrolet of Junior's? Whatever happened to that car? A couple of more good old boys join in. A good old boy, I ought to explain, is a generic term in the rural South referring to a man, of any age, but more often young than not, who fits in with the status system of the region. It usually means he has a good sense of humor and enjoys ironic jokes, is tolerant and easygoing enough to get along in long conversations at places like on the corner, and has a reasonable amount of physical courage. The term is usually heard in some such form as: "Lud? He's a good old boy from over at Crozet." These good old boys in the airport, by the way, were in their twenties, except for one fellow who was a cabdriver and was about forty-five, I would say. Except for the cabdriver, they all wore neo-Brummellian clothes such as Lacoste tennis shirts, Slim Jim pants, windbreakers with the collars turned up, "fast" shoes of the winkle-picker genre, and so on. I mention these details just by way of pointing out that very few grits, Iron Boy overalls, clodhoppers or hats with ventilation holes up near the crown enter into this story. Anyway, these good old boys are talking about Junior Johnson and how he has switched to Ford. This they unanimously regard as some kind of betrayal on Johnson's part. Ford, it seems, they regard as the car symbolizing the established power structure. Dodge is kind of a middle ground. Dodge is at least a challenger, not a ruler. But the Junior Johnson they like to remember is the Junior Johnson of 1963, who took on the whole field of NASCAR (National Association for Stock Car Auto Racing) Grand National racing with a Chevrolet. All the other drivers, the drivers driving Fords, Mercurys, Plymouths, Dodges, had millions, literally millions when it is all added up, millions of dollars in backing from the Ford and Chrysler Corporations. Junior Johnson took them all on in a Chevrolet without one cent of backing from Detroit. Chevrolet had pulled out of stock car racing. Yet every race it was the same. It was never a question of whether anybody was going to *outrun* Junior Johnson. It was just a question of whether he was going to win or his car was going to break down, since, for one thing, half the time he had to make his own racing parts. God! Junior Johnson was like Robin Hood or Jesse James or Little David or something. Every time that Chevrolet, No. 3, appeared on the track, wild curdled yells, "Rebel" yells, they still have those, would rise up. At Daytona, at Atlanta, at Charlotte, at Darlington, South Carolina; Bristol, Tennessee; Martinsville, Virginia—Junior Johnson!

And then the good old boys get to talking about whatever happened to that Chevrolet of Junior's, and the cabdriver says he knows. He says Junior Johnson is using that car to run liquor out of Wilkes County. What does he mean? For Junior Johnson ever to go near another load of bootleg whiskey again—he would have to be insane. He has this huge racing income. He has two other businesses, a whole automated chicken farm with 42,000 chickens, a road-grading business—but the cabdriver says he has this dream Junior is still roaring down from Wilkes County, down through the clay cuts, with the Atlas Arc Lip jars full in the back of that Chevrolet. It is in Junior's blood—and then at this point he puts his right hand up in front of him as if he is groping through fog, and his eyeballs glaze over and he looks out in the distance and he describes Junior Johnson roaring over the ridges of Wilkes County as if it is the ghost of Zapata he is describing, bounding over the Sierras on a white horse to rouse the peasants.

A stubborn notion! A crazy notion! Yet Junior Johnson has followers who need to keep him, symbolically, riding through nighttime like a demon. Madness! But Junior Johnson is one of the last of those sports stars who is not just an ace at the game itself, but a hero a whole people or class of people can identify with. Other, older examples are the way Jack Dempsey stirred up the Irish or the way Joe Louis stirred up the Negroes. Junior Johnson is a modern figure. He is only thirty-three years old and still racing. He should be compared to two other sports heroes whose cultural impact is not too well known. One is Antonino Rocca, the professional wrestler, whose triumphs mean so much to New York City's Puerto Ricans that he can fill Madison Square Garden, despite the fact that everybody, the Puerto Ricans included, knows that wrestling is nothing but a crude form of folk theatre. The other is Ingemar Johanssen, who had a tremendous meaning to the Swedish masses—they were tired of that old king who played tennis all the time and all his friends who keep on drinking Cointreau behind the screen of socialism. Junior Johnson is a modern hero, all involved with car culture and car symbolism in the South. A wild new thing—

Wild—gone wild, Fireball Roberts' Ford spins out on the first turn at the North Wilkesboro Speedway, spinning, spinning, the spin seems almost like slow motion—and then it smashes into the wooden guardrail. It lies up there with the frame bent. Roberts is all right. There is a new layer of asphalt on the track, it is like glass, the cars keep spinning off the first turn. Ned Jarrett spins, smashes through the wood. "Now, boys, this ice ain't gonna get one goddamn bit better, so you can either line up and qualify or pack up and go home—"

I had driven from the Greensboro Airport up to Wilkes County to see Junior Johnson on the occasion of one of the two yearly NASCAR Grand National stock car races at the North Wilkesboro Speedway.

It is a long, very gradual climb from Greensboro to Wilkes County. Wilkes County is all hills, ridges, woods and underbrush, full of pin oaks, sweet-gum maples, ash, birch, apple trees, rhododendron, rocks, vines, tin roofs, little clapboard places like the Mount Olive Baptist Church, signs for things like Double Cola, Sherrill's Ice Cream, Eckard's Grocery, Dr. Pepper, Diel's Apples, Google's Place, Suddith's Place and—yes!—cars. Up onto the highway, out of a side road from a hollow, here comes a 1947 Hudson. To almost anybody it would look like just some old piece of junk left over from God knows when, rolling down a country road . . . the 1947 Hudson was one of the first real "hot" cars made after the war. Some of the others were the 1946 Chrysler, which had a "kick-down" gear for sudden bursts of speed, the 1955 Pontiac and a lot of the Fords. To a great many good old boys a hot car was a symbol of heating up life itself. The war! Money even for country boys! And the money bought cars. In California they suddenly found kids of all sorts involved in vast drag racing orgies and couldn't figure out what was going on. But in the South the mania for cars was even more intense, although much less publicized. To millions of good old boys, and girls, the automobile represented not only liberation from what was still pretty much a land-bound form of social organization but also a great leap forward into twentieth-century glamor, an idea that was being dinned in on the South like everywhere else. It got so that one of the typical rural sights, in addition to the red rooster, the gray split-rail fence, the Edgeworth Tobacco sign and the rusted-out harrow, one of the typical rural sights would be . . . you would be driving along the dirt roads and there beside the house would be an automobile up on blocks or something, with a rope over the tree for hoisting up the motor or some other heavy part, and a couple of good old boys would be practically disappearing into its innards, from below and from above, draped over the side under the hood. It got so that on Sundays there wouldn't be a safe straight stretch of road in the county, because so many wild country boys would be out racing or just raising hell on the roads. A lot of other kids, who weren't basically wild, would be driving like hell every morning and every night, driving to jobs perhaps thirty or forty miles away, jobs that were available only because of automobiles. In the morning they would be driving through the dapple shadows like madmen. In the hollows, sometimes one would come upon the most incredible tar-paper hovels, down near the stream, and out front would be an incredible automobile creation, a late-model car with aerials, Continental kit overhangs in the back, mudguards studded with reflectors, fender skirts, spotlights, God knows what all, with a girl and perhaps a couple of good old boys communing over it and giving you rotten looks as you drive by. On Saturday night everybody would drive into town and park under the lights on the main street and neck. Yes! There was something about being right in there in town underneath the lights and having them reflecting off the baked enamel on the hood. Then if a good old boy insinuated his hands here and there on the front seat with a girl and began . . . necking . . . somehow it was all more *complete*. After the war there was a great deal of stout-burgher talk about people who lived in hovels and bought big-yacht cars to park out front. This was one of the symbols of a new, spendthrift age. But there was a great deal of unconscious resentment buried in the talk. It was resentment against (a) the fact that the good old boy had his money at all and (b) the fact that the car symbolized freedom, a slightly wild, careening emancipation from the old social order. Stock car racing got started about this time, right after the war, and it was immediately regarded as some kind of manifestation of the animal irresponsibility of the lower orders. It had a truly terrible reputation. It was—well, it looked *rowdy* or something. The cars were likely to be used cars, the tracks were dirt, the stands were rickety wood, the drivers were country boys, and they had regular feuds out there, putting each other "up against the wall" and "cutting tires" and everything else. Those country boys would drive into the curves full tilt, then slide maniacally, sometimes coming around the curve sideways, with red dirt showering up. Sometimes they would race at night, under those weak-eyed yellow-ochre lights they have at small tracks and baseball fields, and the clay dust would start showering up in the air, where the evening dew would catch it, and all evening long you would be sitting in the stands or standing out in the infield with a fine clay-mud drizzle coming down on you, not that anybody gave a damn—except for the Southern upper and middle classes, who never attended in those days, but spoke of the "rowdiness."

But mainly it was the fact that stock car racing was something that was welling up out of the lower orders. From somewhere these country boys and urban proles were getting the money and starting this hellish sport.

Stock car racing was beginning all over the country, at places like Allentown, Langhorne and Lancaster, Pennsylvania, and out in California and even out on Long Island, but wherever it cropped up, the Establishment tried to wish it away, largely, and stock car racing went on in a kind of underground world of tracks built on cheap stretches of land well out from the town or the city, a world of diners, drive-ins, motels, gasoline stations, and the good burghers might drive by from time to time, happen by on a Sunday or something, and see the crowd gathered from out of nowhere, the cars coming in, crowding up the highway a little, but Monday morning they would be all gone, and all would be as it was.

Stock car racing was building up a terrific following in the South during the early fifties. Here was a sport not using any abstract devices, any *bat* and *ball*, but the same automobile that was changing a man's own life, his own symbol of liberation, and it didn't require size, strength and all that, all it required was a taste for speed, and the guts. The newspapers in the South didn't seem to catch onto what was happening until late in the game. Of course, newspapers all over the country have looked backward over the tremendous rise in automobile sports, now the second-biggest type of sport in the country in terms of attendance. The sports pages generally have an inexorable lower-middle-class outlook. The sportswriter's "zest for life" usually amounts, in the end, to some sort of gruff Mom's Pie sentimentality at a hideously cozy bar somewhere. The sportswriters caught onto Grand Prix racing first because it had "tone," a touch of defrocked European nobility about it, what with a few counts racing here and there, although, in fact, it is the least popular form of racing in the United States. What finally put stock car racing onto the sports pages in the South was the intervention of the Detroit automobile firms. Detroit began putting so much money into the sport that it took on a kind of massive economic respectability and thereby, in the lower-middle-class brain, status.

What Detroit discovered was that thousands of good old boys in the South were starting to form allegiances to brands of automobiles, according to which were hottest on the stock car circuits, the way they used to have them for the hometown baseball team. The South was one of the hottest car-buying areas in the country. Cars like Hudsons, Oldsmobiles and Lincolns, not the cheapest automobiles by any means, were selling in disproportionate numbers in the South, and a lot of young good old boys were buying them. In 1955, Pontiac started easing into stock car racing, and suddenly the big surge was on. Everybody jumped into the sport to grab for themselves The Speed Image. Suddenly, where a good old boy used to have to bring his gasoline to the track in old filling-station pails and pour it into the tank through a funnel when he made a pit stop, and change his tires with a hand wrench, suddenly, now, he had these "gravity" tanks of gasoline that you just jam into the gas pipe, and air wrenches to take the wheels off, and whole crews of men in white coveralls to leap all over a car when it came rolling into the pit, just like they do at Indianapolis, as if they are mechanical apparati *merging* with the machine as it rolls in, forcing water into the radiator, jacking up the car, taking off wheels, wiping off the windshield, handing the driver a cup of orange juice, all in one synchronized operation. And now, today, the *big money* starts descending on this little place, the North Wilkesboro, North Carolina, Speedway, a little five-eighths-of-a-mile stock car track with a Coca-Cola sign out by the highway where the road in starts.

The private planes start landing out at the Wilkesboro Airport. Freddie Lorenzen, the driver, the biggest money winner last year in stock car racing, comes sailing in out of the sky in a twin-engine Aero Commander, and there are a few good old boys out there in the tall grass by the runway already with their heads sticking up watching this hero of the modern age come in and taxi up and get out of that twin-engine airplane with his blonde hair swept back as if by the mother internal combustion engine of them all. And then Paul Goldsmith, the driver, comes in in a 310 Cessna, and *he* gets out, all these tall, lanky hard-boned Americans in their thirties with these great profiles like a comic-strip hero or something, and then Glenn (Fireball) Roberts—Fireball Roberts!—Fireball is *hard*—he comes in a Comanche 250, like a flying yacht, and then Ray Nichels and Ray Fox, the chief mechanics, who run big racing crews for the Chrysler Corporation, this being Fox's last race for Junior as his mechanic, before Junior switches over to Ford, they come in in two-engine planes. And even old Buck Baker—hell, Buck Baker is a middling driver for Dodge, but even he comes rolling in down the landing strip at two hundred miles an hour with his Southern-hero face at the window of the cockpit of a twin-engine Apache, traveling first class in the big status boat that has replaced the yacht in America, the private plane.

And then the Firestone and Goodyear vans pull in, huge mothers, bringing in huge stacks of racing tires for the race, big wide ones, 8.20's, with special treads, which are like a lot of bumps on the tire instead of grooves. They even have special tires for qualifying, soft tires, called "gumballs," they wouldn't last more than ten times around the track in a race, but for qualifying, which is generally three laps, one to pick up speed and two to race against the clock, they are great, because they hold tight on the corners. And on a hot day, when somebody like Junior Johnson, one of the fastest qualifying runners in the history of the sport, 170.777 m.p.h. in a one-hundred-mile qualifying race at Daytona in 1964, when somebody like Junior Johnson really pushes it on a qualifying run, there will be a ring of blue smoke up over the whole goddamned track, a ring like an oval halo over the whole thing from the gumballs burning, and some good old boy will say, "Great smokin' blue gumballs god almighty dog! There goes Junior Johnson!"

The thing is, each one of these tires costs fifty-five to sixty dollars, and on a track that is fast and hard on tires, like Atlanta, one car might go through ten complete tire changes, easily, forty tires, or almost $2500 worth of tires just for one race. And he may even be out of the money. And then the Ford van and the Dodge van and the Mercury van and the Plymouth van roll in with new motors, a whole new motor every few races, a 427-cubic-inch stock car racing motor, 600 horsepower, the largest and most powerful allowed on the track, that probably costs the company $1000 or more, when you consider that they are not mass produced. And still the advertising appeal. You can buy the very same car that these fabulous wild men drive every week at these fabulous wild speeds, and some of their power and charisma is yours. After every NASCAR Grand National stock car race, whichever company has the car that wins, this company will put big ads in the Southern papers, and papers all over the country if it is a very big race, like the Daytona 500, the Daytona Firecracker 400 or the Atlanta and Charlotte races. They sell a certain number of these 427-cubic-inch cars to the general public, a couple of hundred a year, perhaps, at eight or nine thousand dollars apiece, but it is no secret that these motors are specially reworked just for stock car racing. Down at Charlotte there is a company called Holman & Moody that is supposed to be the "garage" or "automotive-engineering" concern that prepares automobiles for Freddy Lorenzen and some of the other Ford drivers. But if you go by Holman & Moody out by the airport and Charlotte, suddenly you come upon a huge place that is a *factory*, for godsake, a big long thing, devoted mainly to the business of turning out stock car racers. A whole lot of other parts in stock car racers are heavier than the same parts on a street automobile, although they are made to the same scale. The shock absorbers are bigger, the wheels are wider and bulkier, the swaybars and steering mechanisms are heavier, the axles are much heavier, they have double sets of wheel bearings, and so forth and so on. The bodies of the cars are pretty much the same, except that they use lighter sheet metal, practically tinfoil. Inside, there is only the driver's seat and a heavy set of roll bars and diagonal struts that turn the inside of the car into a rigid cage, actually.

That is why the drivers can walk away unhurt—most of the time—from the most spectacular crackups. The gearshift is the floor kind, although it doesn't make much difference, as there is almost no shifting gears in stock car racing. You just get into high gear and go. The dashboard has no speedometer, the main thing being the dial for engine revolutions per minute. So, anyway, it costs about $15,000 to prepare a stock car racer in the first place and another three or four thousand for each new race and this does not even count the costs of mechanics' work and transportation. All in all, Detroit will throw around a quarter of a million dollars into it every week while the season is on, and the season runs, roughly, from February to October, with a few big races after that. And all this turns up even out at the North Wilkesboro Speedway in the up-country of Wilkes County, North Carolina.

Sunday! Racing day! There is the Coca-Cola sign out where the road leads in from the highway, and hills and trees, but here are long concrete grandstands for about 17,000 and a paved five-eighths-mile oval. Practically all the drivers are out there with their cars and their crews, a lot of guys in white coveralls. The cars look huge . . . and curiously nude and blind. All the chrome is stripped off, except for the grilles. The headlights are blanked out. Most of the cars are in the pits. The so-called "pit" is a paved cutoff on the edge of the infield. It cuts off from the track itself like a service road off an expressway at the shopping center. Every now and then a car splutters, hacks, coughs, hocks a lunga, rumbles out onto the track itself for a practice run. There is a lot of esoteric conversation going on, speculation, worries, memoirs:

"What happened?"

"Mother—condensed on me. Al brought it up here with him. Water in the line."

"Better keep Al away from a stable, he'll fill you up with horse manure."

". . . they told me to give him one, a creampuff, so I give him one, a creampuff. One goddamn race and the son of a bitch, he *melted* it. . . ."

". . . he's down there right now pettin' and rubbin' and huggin' that car just like those guys do a horse at the Kentucky Derby. . . ."

". . . They'll blow you right out of the tub. . . ."

". . . No, the quarter inch, and go on over and see if you can get Ned's blowtorch. . . ."

". . . Rear end's loose. . . ."

". . . I don't reckon this right here's got nothing to do with it, do you? . . ."

". . . Aw, I don't know, about yea big. . . ."

". . . Who the hell stacked them gumballs on the bottom? . . ."

". . . th'owing rocks. . . ."

". . . won't turn seven thousand. . . ."

". . . strokin' it. . . ."

". . . blistered. . . ."

". . . spun out. . . ."

". . . muvva. . . ."

Then, finally, here comes Junior Johnson. How he does come on. He comes tooling across the infield in a big white dreamboat, a brand-new white Pontiac Catalina four-door hard-top sedan. He pulls up and as he gets out he seems to get more and more huge. First his crew-cut head and then a big jaw and then a bigger neck and then a huge torso, like a wrestler's, all done up rather modish and California modern, with a red-and-white candy-striped sport shirt, white ducks and loafers.

"How you doing?" says Junior Johnson, shaking hands, and then he says, "Hot enough for ye'uns?"

Junior is in an amiable mood. Like most up-hollow people, it turns out, Junior is reserved. His face seldom shows an emotion. He has three basic looks: amiable, amiable and a little shy, and dead serious. To a lot of people, apparently, Junior's dead-serious look seems menacing. There are no cowards left in stock car racing, but a couple of drivers tell me that one of the things that can shake you up is to look into your rear-view mirror going around a curve and see Junior Johnson's car on your tail to "root you out of the groove," and then get a glimpse of Junior's dead-serious look. I think some of the sportswriters are afraid of him. One of them tells me Junior is strong, silent—and explosive. Junior will only give you three answers, "Uh-huh," "Uh-unh," and "I don't know," and so forth and so on. Actually, I found he handles questions easily. He has a great technical knowledge of automobiles and the physics of speed, including things he never fools with, such as Offenhauser engines. What he never does offer, however, is small talk. This gives him a built-in poise, since it deprives him of the chance to say anything asinine. "Ye'uns," "we'uns," "H'it" for "it," "growed" for "grew" and a lot of other unusual past participles—Junior uses certain older forms of English, not exactly "Elizabethan," as they are sometimes called, but older forms of English preserved up-country in his territory, Ingle Hollow.

Kids keep coming up for Junior's autograph and others are just hanging around and one little boy comes up, he is about thirteen, and Junior says: "This boy here goes coon hunting with me."

One of the sportswriters is standing around, saying: "What do you shoot a coon with?"

"Don't shoot 'em. The dogs tree 'em and then you flush 'em out and the dogs fight 'em."

"Flush 'em out?"

"Yeah. This boy right here can flush 'em out better than anybody you ever did see. You go out at night with the dogs, and soon as they get the scent, they start barking. They go on out ahead of you and when they tree a coon, you can tell it, by the way they sound. They all start baying up at that coon—h'it sounds like, I don't know, you hear it once and you not likely to forget it. Then you send a little boy up to flush him out and he jumps down and the dogs fight him."

"How does a boy flush him out?"

"Aw, he just climbs up there to the limb he's on and starts shaking h'it and the coon'll jump."

"What happens if the coon decides he'd rather come back after the boy instead of jumping down to a bunch of dogs?"

"He won't do that. A coon's afraid of a person, but he can kill a dog. A coon can take any dog you set against him if they's just the two of them fighting. The coon jumps down on the ground and he rolls right over on his back with his feet up, and he's *got* claws about like this. All he has to do is get a dog once in the throat or in the belly, and he can kill him, cut him wide open just like you took a knife and did it. Won't any dog even fight a coon except a coon dog."

"What kind of dogs are they?"

"*Coon* dogs, I guess. Black and tans they call 'em sometimes. They's bred for it. If his mammy and pappy wasn't coon dogs, he ain't likely to be one either. After you got one, you got to train him. You trap a coon, live, and then you put him in a pen and tie him to a post with a rope on him and then you put your dog in there and he has to fight him. Sometimes you get a dog just don't have any fight in him and he ain't no good to you."

Junior is in the pit area, standing around with his brother Fred, who is part of his crew, and Ray Fox and some other good old boys, in a general atmosphere of big stock car money, a big ramp truck for his car, a white Dodge, number 3, a big crew in white coveralls, huge stacks of racing tires, a Dodge P.R. man, big portable cans of gasoline, compressed air hoses, compressed water hoses, the whole business. Herb Nab, Freddie Lorenzen's chief mechanic, comes over and sits down on his haunches and Junior sits down on his haunches and Nab says:

"So Junior Johnson's going to drive a Ford."

Junior is switching from Dodge to Ford mainly because he hasn't been winning with the Dodge. Lorenzen drives a Ford, too, and the last year, when Junior was driving the Chevrolet, their duels were the biggest excitement in stock car racing.

"Well," says Nab, "I'll tell you, Junior. My ambition is going to be to outrun your ass every goddamned time we go out."

"That was your ambition last year," says Junior.

"I know it was," says Nab, "and you took all the money, didn't you? You know what my strategy was. I was going to outrun everybody else and outlast Junior, that was my strategy."

Setting off his California modern sport shirt and white ducks Junior has on a pair of twenty-dollar rimless sunglasses and a big gold Timex watch, and Flossie, his fiancée, is out there in the infield somewhere with the white Pontiac, and the white Dodge that Dodge gave Junior is parked up near the pit area—and then a little thing happens that brings the whole thing right back there to Wilkes County, North Carolina, to Ingle Hollow and to hard muscle in the clay gulches. A couple of good old boys come down to the front of the stands with the screen and the width of the track between them and Junior, and one of the good old boys comes down and yells out in the age-old baritone raw curdle yell of the Southern hills:

"Hey! Hog jaw!"

Everybody gets quiet. They know he's yelling at Junior, but nobody says a thing. Junior doesn't even turn around.

"Hey, hog jaw! . . ."

Junior, he does nothing.

"Hey, hog jaw, I'm gonna get me one of them fastback roosters, too, and come down there and get you!"

Fastback rooster refers to the Ford—it has a "fastback" design—Junior is switching to.

"Hey, hog jaw, I'm gonna get me one of them fastback roosters and run you right out of here, you hear me, hog jaw!"

One of the good old boys alongside Junior says, "Junior, go on up there and clear out those stands."

Then everybody stares at Junior to see what he's gonna do. Junior, he don't even look around. He just looks a bit dead serious.

"Hey, hog jaw, you got six cases of whiskey in the back of that car you want to let me have?"

"What you hauling in that car, hog jaw!"

"Tell him you're out of that business, Junior," one of the good old boys says.

"Go on up there and clean house, Junior," says another good old boy.

Then Junior looks up, without looking at the stands and smiles a little and says, "You flush him down here out of that tree—and I'll take keer of him."

Such a howl goes up from the good old boys! It is almost a blood curdle—

"Goddamn, he *will*, too!"

"Lord, he better know how to do an *about-face* hisself if he comes down here!"

"Goddamn, get him, Junior!"

"Whooeeee!"

"Mother dog!"

—a kind of orgy of reminiscence of the old Junior before the Detroit money started flowing, wild *combats d'honneur* up-hollow—and, suddenly, when he heard that unearthly baying coming up from the good old boys in the pits, the good old boy retreated from the edge of the stands and never came back.

Later on Junior told me, sort of apologetically, "H'it used to be, if a fellow crowded me just a little bit, I was ready to crawl him. I reckon that was one good thing about Chillicothe.

"I don't want to pull any more time," Junior tells me, "but I wouldn't take anything in the world for the experience I had in prison. If a man needed to change, that was the place to change. H'it's not a waste of time there, h'it's good experience.

"H'it's that they's so many people in the world that feel that nobody is going to tell them what to do. I had quite a temper, I reckon. I always had the idea that I had as much sense as the other person and I didn't want them to tell me what to do. In the penitentiary there I found out that I could listen to another fellow and be told what to do and h'it wouldn't kill me."

Starting time! Linda Vaughn, with the big blonde hair and blossomy breasts, puts down her Coca-Cola and the potato chips and slips off her red stretch pants and her white blouse and walks out of the officials' booth in her Rake-a-cheek red showgirl's costume with her long honeydew legs in net stockings and climbs up on the red Firebird float. The Life Symbol of stock car racing! Yes! Linda, every luscious morsel of Linda, is a good old girl from Atlanta who was made Miss Atlanta International Raceway one year and was paraded around the track on a float and she liked it so much and all the good old boys liked it so much, Linda's flowing hair and blossomy breasts and honeydew legs, that she became the permanent glamor symbol of stock car racing, and never mind this other modeling she was doing . . . this, she liked it. Right before practically every race on the Grand National circuit Linda Vaughn puts down her Coca-Cola and potato chips. Her momma is there, she generally comes around to see Linda go around the track on the float, it's such a nice spectacle seeing Linda looking so lovely, and the applause and all. "Linda, I'm thirstin', would you bring me a Coca-Cola?" "A lot of them think I'm Freddie Lorenzen's girl friend, but I'm not any of 'em's girl friend, I'm real good friends with 'em all, even Wendell," he being Wendell Scott, the only Negro in big-league stock car racing. Linda gets up on the Firebird float. This is an extraordinary object, made of wood, about twenty feet tall, in the shape of a huge bird, an eagle or something, blazing red, and Linda, with her red showgirl's suit on, gets up on the seat, which is up between the wings, like a saddle, high enough so her long honeydew legs stretch down, and a new car pulls her—Miss Firebird! —slowly once around the track just before the race. It is more of a ceremony by now than the national anthem. Miss Firebird sails slowly in front of the stands and the good old boys let out some real curdle Rebel yells, "Yaaaaaaaaaaaaghhhhoooooo! Let me at that car!" "Honey, you sure do start my motor, I swear to God!" "Great God and Poonadingdong, I mean!"

And suddenly there's a big roar from behind, down in the infield, and then I see one of the great sights in stock car racing. That infield! The cars have been piling into the infield by the hundreds, parking in there on the clay and the grass, every which way, angled down and angled up, this way and that, where the ground is uneven, these beautiful blazing brand-new cars with the sun exploding off the windshields and the baked enamel and the glassy lacquer, hundreds, thousands of cars stacked this way and that in the infield with the sun bolting down and no shade, none at all, just a couple of Coca-Cola stands out there. And already the good old boys and girls are out beside the cars, with all these beautiful little buds in short shorts already spread-eagled out on top of the car roofs, pressing down on good hard slick automobile sheet metal, their little cupcake bottoms aimed up at the sun. The good old boys are lollygagging around with their shirts off and straw hats on that have miniature beer cans on the brims and buttons that read, "Girls Wanted—No Experience Required." And everybody, good old boys and girls of all ages, are out there with portable charcoal barbecue ovens set up, and folding tubular steel terrace furniture, deck chairs and things, and Thermos jugs and coolers full of beer—and suddenly it is not the up-country South at all but a concentration of the modern suburbs, all jammed into that one space, from all over America, with blazing cars and instant goodies, all cooking under the bare blaze—inside a strange bowl. The infield is like the bottom of a bowl. The track around it is banked so steeply at the corners and even on the straightaways, it is like the steep sides of a bowl. The wall around the track, and the stands and the bleachers are like the rim of a bowl. And from the infield, in this great incredible press of blazing new cars, there is no horizon but the bowl, up above only that cobalt-blue North Carolina sky. And then suddenly, on a signal, thirty stock car engines start up where they are lined up in front of the stands. The roar of these engines is impossible to describe. They have a simultaneous rasp, thunder and rumble that goes right through a body and fills the whole bowl with a noise of internal combustion. Then they start around on two build-up runs, just to build up speed, and then they come around the fourth turn and onto the straightaway in front of the stands at—here, 130 miles an hour, in Atlanta, 160 miles an hour, at Daytona, 180 miles an hour—and the flag goes down and everybody in the infield and in the stands is up on their feet going mad, and suddenly here is a bowl that is one great orgy of everything in the way of excitement and liberation the automobile has meant to Americans. An orgy!

The first lap of a stock car race is horrendous, a wildly horrendous spectacle such as no other sport approaches. Twenty, thirty, forty automobiles, each of them weighing almost two tons, 3700 pounds, with 427-cubic-inch engines, 600 horsepower, are practically locked together, side to side and tail to nose, on a narrow band of asphalt at 130, 160, 180 miles an hour, hitting the curves so hard the rubber burns off the tires in front of your eyes. To the driver, it is like being inside a car going down the West Side Highway in New York City at rush hour, only with everybody going literally three to four times as fast, at speeds a man who has gone eighty-five miles an hour down a highway cannot conceive of, and with every other driver an enemy who is willing to cut inside of you, around you or in front of you, or ricochet off your side in the battle to get into a curve first.

The speeds are faster than those in the Indianapolis 500 race, the cars are more powerful and much heavier. The prize money in Southern stock car racing is far greater than that in Indianapolis-style or European Grand Prix racing, but few Indianapolis or Grand Prix drivers have the raw nerve required to succeed at it.

Although they will deny it, it is still true that stock car drivers will put each other "up against the wall"—cut inside on the left of another car and ram it into a spin—if they get mad enough. Crashes are not the only danger, however. The cars are now literally too fast for their own parts, especially the tires. Firestone and Goodyear have poured millions into stock car racing, but neither they nor anybody so far have been able to come up with a tire for this kind of racing at the current speeds. Three well-known stock car drivers were killed last year, two of them champion drivers, Joe Weatherly and Fireball Roberts, and another, one of the best new drivers, Jimmy Pardue, from Junior Johnson's own home territory, Wilkes County, North Carolina. Roberts was the only one killed in a crash. Junior Johnson was in the crash but was not injured. Weatherly and Pardue both lost control on curves. Pardue's death came during a tire test. In a tire test, engineers from Firestone or Goodyear try out various tires on a car, and the driver, always one of the top competitors, tests them at top speed, usually on the Atlanta track. The drivers are paid three dollars a mile and may drive as much as five or six hundred miles in a single day. At 145 miles an hour average that does not take very long. Anyway, these drivers are going at speeds that, on curves, can tear tires off their casings or break axles. They practically run off from over their own wheels.

Junior Johnson was over in the garden by the house some years ago, plowing the garden barefooted, behind a mule, just wearing an old pair of overalls, when a couple of good old boys drove up and told him to come on up to the speedway and get in a stock car race. They wanted some local boys to race, as a preliminary to the main race, "as a kind of side show," as Junior remembers it.

"So I just put the reins down," Junior is telling me, "and rode on over 'ere with them. They didn't give us seat belts or nothing, they just roped us in. H'it was a dirt track then. I come in second."

Junior was a sensation in dirt-track racing right from the start. Instead of going into the curves and just sliding and holding on for dear life like the other drivers, Junior developed the technique of throwing himself into a slide about seventy-five feet before the curve by cocking the wheel to the left slightly and gunning it, using the slide, not the brake, to slow down, so that he could pick up speed again halfway through the curve and come out of it like a shot. This was known as his "power slide," and—yes! of course!—every good old boy in North Carolina started saying Junior Johnson had learned that stunt doing those goddamned *about-faces* running away from the Alcohol Tax agents. Junior put on such a show one night on a dirt track in Charlotte that he broke two axles, and he thought he was out of the race because he didn't have any more axles, when a good old boy came running up out of the infield and said, "Goddamn it, Junior Johnson, you take the axle off my car here, I got a Pontiac just like yours," and Junior took it off and put it on his and went out and broke *it* too. Mother dog! To this day Junior Johnson loves dirt-track racing like nothing else in this world, even though there is not much money in it. Every year he sets new dirt track speed records, such as at Hickory, North Carolina, one of the most popular dirt tracks, last spring. As far as Junior is concerned, dirt track racing is not so much of a mechanical test for the car as those long five- and six-hundred-mile races on asphalt are. Gasoline, tire and engine wear aren't so much of a problem. It is all the driver, his skill, his courage—his willingness to mix it up with the other cars, smash and carom off of them at a hundred miles an hour or so to get into the curves first. Junior has a lot of fond recollections of mixing it up at places like Bowman Gray Stadium in Winston-Salem, one of the minor league tracks, a very narrow track, hardly wide enough for two cars. "You could always figure Bowman Gray was gonna cost you two fenders, two doors and two quarter panels," Junior tells me with nostalgia.

Anyway, at Hickory, which was a Saturday night race, all the good old boys started pouring into the stands before sundown, so they wouldn't miss anything, the practice runs or the qualifying or anything. And pretty soon, the dew hasn't even started falling before Junior Johnson and David Pearson, one of Dodge's best drivers, are out there on practice runs, just warming up, and they happen to come up alongside each other on the second curve, and—the thing is, here are two men, each of them driving $15,000 automobiles, each of them standing to make $50,000 to $100,000 for the season if they don't get themselves killed, and they meet on a curve on a goddamned practice run on a dirt track, and neither of them can resist it. Coming out of the turn they go into a wildass race down the backstretch, both of them trying to get into the third turn first, and all the way across the infield you can hear them ricocheting off each other and bouncing at a hundred miles an hour on loose dirt, and then they go into ferocious power slides, red dust all over the goddamned place, and then out of this goddamned red-dust cloud, out of the fourth turn, here comes Junior Johnson first, like a shot, with Pearson right on his tail, and the good old boys in the stands going wild, and the *qualifying* runs haven't started yet, let alone the race.

Junior worked his way up through the minor leagues, the Sportsman and Modified classifications, as they are called, winning championships in both, and won his first Grand National race, the big leagues, in 1955 at Hickory, on dirt. He was becoming known as "the hardest of the hard-chargers," power sliding, rooting them out of the groove, raising hell, and already the Junior Johnson legend was beginning.

He kept hard-charging, power sliding, going after other drivers as though there wasn't room on the track but for one, and became the most popular driver in stock car racing by 1959. The presence of Detroit and Detroit's big money had begun to calm the drivers down a little. Detroit was concerned about Image. The last great duel of the dying dog-eat-dog era of stock car racing came in 1959, when Junior and Lee Petty, who was then leading the league in points, had it out on the Charlotte raceway. Junior was in the lead, and Petty was right on his tail, but couldn't get by Junior. Junior kept coming out of the curves faster. So every chance he got, Petty would get up right on Junior's rear bumper and start banging it, gradually forcing the fender in to where the metal would cut Junior's rear tire. With only a few laps to go, Junior had a blowout and spun out up against the guardrail. That is Junior's version. Petty claimed Junior hit a pop bottle and spun out. The fans in Charlotte were always throwing pop bottles and other stuff onto the track late in the race, looking for blood. In any case, Junior eased back into the pits, had the tire changed, and charged out after Petty. He caught him on a curve and—well, whatever really happened, Petty was suddenly "up against the wall" and out of the race, and Junior won.

What a howl went up. The Charlotte chief of police charged out onto the track after the race, according to Petty, and offered to have Junior arrested for "assault with a dangerous weapon," the hassling went on for weeks—

"Back then," Junior tells me, "when you got into a guy and racked him up, you might as well get ready, because he's coming back for you. H'it was dog eat dog. That straightened Lee Petty out right smart. They don't do stuff like that anymore, though, because the guys don't stand for it."

Anyway, the Junior Johnson legend kept building up and building up, and in 1960 it got better than ever when Junior won the biggest race of the year, the Daytona 500, by discovering a new technique called "drafting." That year stock car racing was full of big powerful Pontiacs manned by top drivers, and they would go like nothing else anybody ever saw. Junior went down to Daytona with a Chevrolet.

"My car was about ten miles an hour slower than the rest of the cars, the Pontiacs," Junior tells me. "In the preliminary races, the warmups and stuff like that, they was smoking me off the track. Then I remember once I went out for a practice run, and Fireball Roberts was out there in a Pontiac and I got in right behind him on a curve, right on his bumper. I knew I couldn't stay with him on the straight-away, but I came out of the curve fast, right in behind him, running flat out, and then I noticed a funny thing. As long as I stayed right in behind him, I noticed I picked up speed and stayed right with him and my car was going faster than it had ever gone before. I could tell on the tachometer. My car wasn't running no more than 6000 before, but when I got into this drafting position, I was turning 6800 to 7000. H'it felt like the car was plumb off the ground, floating along."

"Drafting," it was discovered at Daytona, created a vacuum behind the lead car and both cars would go faster than they normally would. Junior "hitched rides" on the Pontiacs most of the afternoon, but was still second to Bobby Johns, the lead Pontiac. Then, late in the race, Johns got into a drafting position with a fellow Pontiac that was actually one lap behind him and the vacuum got so intense that the rear window blew out of Johns' car and he spun out and crashed and Junior won.

This made Junior the Lion Killer, the Little David of stock car racing, and his performance in the 1963 season made him even more so.

Junior raced for Chevrolet at Daytona in February, 1963, and set the all-time stock car speed record in a hundred-mile qualifying race, 164.083 miles an hour, twenty-one miles an hour faster than Parnelli Jones's winning time at Indianapolis that year. Junior topped that at

Daytona in July of 1963, qualifying at 166.005 miles per hour in a five-mile run, the fastest that anyone had ever averaged that distance in a racing car of any type. Junior's Chevrolet lasted only twenty-six laps in the Daytona 500 in 1963, however. He went out with a broken push rod. Although Chevrolet announced they were pulling out of racing at this time, Junior took his car and started out on the wildest performance in the history of stock car racing. Chevrolet wouldn't give him a cent of backing. They wouldn't even speak to him on the telephone. Half the time he had to have his own parts made. Plymouth, Mercury, Dodge and Ford, meantime, were pouring more money than ever into stock car racing. Yet Junior won seven Grand National races out of the thirty-three he entered and led most others before mechanical trouble forced him out.

All the while, Junior was making record qualifying runs, year after year. In the usual type of qualifying run, a driver has the track to himself and makes two circuits, with the driver with the fastest average time getting the "pole" position for the start of the race. In a way this presents stock car danger in its purest form. Driving a stock car does not require much handling ability, at least not as compared to Grand Prix racing, because the tracks are simple banked ovals and there is almost no shifting of gears. So qualifying becomes a test of raw nerve—of how fast a man is willing to take a curve. Many of the top drivers in competition are poor at qualifying. In effect, they are willing to calculate their risks only against the risks the other drivers are taking. Junior takes the pure risk as no other driver has ever taken it.

"Pure" risk or total risk, whichever, Indianapolis and Grand Prix drivers have seldom been willing to face the challenge of Southern stock car drivers. A. J. Foyt, last year's winner at Indianapolis, is one exception. He has raced against the Southerners and beaten them. Parnelli Jones has tried and fared badly. Driving "Southern style" has a quality that shakes a man up. The Southerners went on a tour of northern tracks last fall. They raced at Bridgehampton, New York, and went into the corners so hard the marshals stationed at each corner kept radioing frantically to the control booth: "They're going off the track. They're all going off the track!"

But this, Junior Johnson's last race in a Dodge, was not his day, neither for qualifying nor racing. Lorenzen took the lead early and won the 250-mile race a lap ahead of the field. Junior finished third, but was never in contention for the lead.

"Come on, Junior, do my hand—"

Two or three hundred people come out of the stands and up out of the infield and onto the track to be around Junior Johnson. Junior is signing autographs in a neat left-handed script he has. It looks like it came right out of the Locker book. The girls! Levi's, stretch pants, sneaky shorts, stretch jeans, they press into the crowd with lively narbs and try to get their hands up in front of Junior and say:

"Come on, Junior, do my hand!"

In order to do a hand, Junior has to hold the girl's hand in his right hand and then sign his name with a ball-point on the back of her hand.

"Junior, you got to do mine, too!"

"Put it on up here."

All the girls break into . . . smiles. Junior Johnson does a hand. Ah, sweet little cigarette-ad blonde! She says:

"Junior, why don't you ever call me up?"

"I 'spect you get plenty of calls 'thout me."

"Oh, Junior! You call me up, you hear now?"

But also a great many older people crowd in, and they say:

"Junior, you're doing a real good job out there, you're driving real good."

"Junior, when you get in that Ford, I want to see you pass that Freddie Lorenzen, you hear now?"

"Junior, you like that Ford better than that Dodge?"

And:

"Junior, here's a young man that's been waiting some time and wanting to see you—" and the man lifts up his little boy in the middle of the crowd and says: "I told you you'd see Junior Johnson. This here's Junior Johnson!"

The boy has a souvenir racing helmet on his head. He stares at Junior through a buttery face. Junior signs the program he has in his hand, and then the boy's mother says:

"Junior, I tell you right now, he's beside you all the way. He can't be moved."

And then:

"Junior, I want you to meet the meanest little girl in Wilkes County."

"She don't look mean to me."

Junior keeps signing autographs and over by the pits the other kids are all over his car, the Dodge. They start pulling off the decals, the ones saying Holly Farms Poultry and Autolite and God knows what all. They fight over the strips, the shreds of decal, as if they were totems.

All this homage to Junior Johnson lasts about forty minutes. He must be signing about 250 autographs, but he is not a happy man. By and by the crowd is thinning out, the sun is going down, wind is blowing the Coca-Cola cups around, all one can hear, mostly, is a stock car engine starting up every now and then as somebody drives it up onto a truck or something, and Junior looks around and says:

"I'd rather lead one lap and fall out of the race than stroke it and finish in the money."

"Stroking it" is driving carefully in hopes of outlasting faster and more reckless cars. The opposite of stroking it is "hard-charging." Then Junior says:

"I hate to get whipped up here in Wilkes County, North Carolina."

Wilkes County, North Carolina! Who was it tried to pin the name on Wilkes County, "The bootleg capital of America"? This fellow Vance Packard. But just a minute. . . .

The night after the race Junior and his fiancée, Flossie Clark, and myself went into North Wilkesboro to have dinner. Junior and Flossie came by Lowes Motel and picked us up in the dreamboat white Pontiac. Flossie is a bright, attractive woman, *saftig*, well-organized. She and Junior have been going together since they were in high school. They are going to get married as soon as Junior gets his new house built. Flossie has been doing the decor. Junior Johnson, in the second-highest income bracket in the United States for the past five years, is moving out of his father's white frame house in Ingle Hollow at last. About three hundred yards down the road. Overlooking a lot of good green land and Anderson's grocery. Junior shows me through the house, it is almost finished, and when we get to the front door, I ask him, "How much of this land is yours?"

Junior looks around for a minute, and then back up the hill, up past his three automated chicken houses, and then down into the hollow over the pasture where his $3100 Santa Gertrudis bull is grazing, and then he says:

"Everything that's green is mine."

Junior Johnson's house is going to be one of the handsomest homes in Wilkes County. Yes. And—such complicated problems of class and status. Junior is not only a legendary figure as a backwoods boy with guts who made good, he is also popular personally, he is still a good old boy, rich as he is. He is also respected for the sound and sober way he has invested his money. He also has one of the best business connections in town, Holly Farms Poultry. What complicates it is that half the county, anyway, reveres him as the greatest, most fabled night-road driver in the history of Southern bootlegging. There is hardly a living soul in the hollows who can conjure up two seconds' honest moral indignation over "the whiskey business." That is what they call it, "the whiskey business." The fact is, it has some positive political overtones, sort of like the I.R.A. in Ireland. The other half of the county—well, North Wilkesboro itself is a prosperous, good-looking town of 5,000, where a lot of hearty modern business burghers are making money the modern way, like everywhere else in the U.S.A., in things like banking, poultry processing, furniture, mirror, and carpet manufacture, apple growing, and so forth and so on. And one thing these men are tired of is Wilkes County's reputation as a center of moonshining. The U.S. Alcohol and Tobacco Tax agents sit over there in Wilkesboro, right next to North Wilkesboro, year in and year out, and they have been there since God knows when, like an Institution in the land, and every day that they are there, it is like a sign saying, Moonshine County. And even that is not so *bad*—it has nothing to do with it being immoral and only a little to do with it being illegal. The real thing is, it is—raw and hillbilly. And one thing thriving modern Industry is not is hillbilly. And one thing the burghers of North Wilkesboro are not about to be is hillbilly. They have split-level homes that would knock your eyes out. Also swimming pools, white Buick Snatchwagons, flagstone *terrasse*-porches enclosed with louvered glass that opens wide in the summertime, and built-in brick barbecue pits and they give parties where they wear Bermuda shorts and Jax stretch pants and serve rum collins and play twist and bossa nova records on the hi-fi and tell Shaggy Dog jokes about strange people ordering martinis. Moonshining . . . just a minute—the truth is, North Wilkesboro. . . .

So we are all having dinner at one of the fine new restaurants in North Wilkesboro, a place of suburban plate-glass elegance. The manager knows Junior and gives us the best table in the place and comes over and talks to Junior a while about the race. A couple of men get up and come over and get Junior's autograph to take home to their sons and so forth. Then toward the end of the meal a couple of North Wilkesboro businessmen come over ("Junior, how are you, Junior. You think you're going to like that fast-backed Ford?") and Junior introduces them to me.

"You're not going to do like that fellow Vance Packard did, are you?"

"Vance Packard?"

"Yeah, I think it was Vance Packard wrote it. He wrote an article and called Wilkes County the bootleg capital of America. Don't pull any of that stuff. I think it was in *American* magazine. The bootleg capital of America. Don't pull any of that stuff on us."

I looked over at Junior and Flossie. Neither one of them said anything. They didn't even change their expressions.

The next morning I met Junior down in Ingle Hollow at Anderson's Store. That's about fifteen miles out of North Wilkesboro on County Road No. 2400. Junior is known in a lot of Southern newspapers as "the wild man from Ronda" or "the lead-footed chicken farmer from Ronda," but Ronda is only his post-office-box address. His telephone exchange, with the Wilkes Telephone Membership Corporation, is Clingman, North Carolina, and that isn't really where he lives either.

Where he lives is just Ingle Hollow, and one of the communal centers of Ingle Hollow is Anderson's Store. Anderson's is not exactly a grocery store. Out front there are two gasoline pumps under an overhanging roof. Inside there are a lot of things like a soda-pop cooler filled with ice, Coca-Colas, Nehi drinks, Dr. Pepper, Double Cola, and a gumball machine, a lot of racks of Red Man chewing tobacco, Price's potato chips, OKay peanuts, cloth hats for working outdoors in, dried sausages, cigarettes, canned goods, a little bit of meal and flour, fly swatters, and I don't know what all. Inside and outside of Anderson's there are good old boys. The young ones tend to be inside, talking, and the old ones tend to be outside, sitting under the roof by the gasoline pumps, talking. And on both sides, cars; most of them new and pastel.

Junior drives up and gets out and looks up over the door where there is a row of twelve coon tails. Junior says:

"Two of them gone, ain't they?"

One of the good old boys says, "Yeah," and sighs.

A pause, and the other one says, "Somebody stole 'em."

Then the first one says, "Junior, that dog of yours ever come back?"

Junior says, "Not yet."

The second good old boy says, "You looking for her to come back?"

Junior says, "I reckon she'll come back."

The good old boy says, "I had a coon dog went off like that. They don't ever come back. I went out 'ere one day, back over yonder, and there he was, cut right from here to here. I swear if it don't look like a coon got him. Something. H'it must of turned him every way but loose."

Junior goes inside and gets a Coca-Cola and rings up the till himself, like everybody who goes into Anderson's does, it seems like. It is dead quiet in the hollow except for every now and then a car grinds over the dirt road and down the way. One coon dog missing. But he still has a lot of the black and tans, named Rock. . . .

. . . Rock, Whitey, Red, Buster are in the pen out back of the Johnson house, the old frame house. They have scars all over their faces from fighting coons. Gypsy has one huge gash in her back from fighting something. A red rooster crosses the lawn. That's a big rooster. Shirley, one of Junior's two younger sisters, pretty girls, is out by the fence in shorts, pulling weeds. Annie May is inside the house with Mrs. Johnson. Shirley has the radio outside on the porch aimed at her, The Four Seasons! "Dawn!—ahhhh, ahhhhh, ahhhhhh!" Then a lot of electronic wheeps and lulus and a screaming disc jockey, yessss! WTOB, the Vibrant Mothering Voice of Winston-Salem, North Carolina. It sounds like WABC in New York. Junior's mother, Mrs. Johnson, is a big, good-natured woman. She comes out and says, "Did you ever see anything like that in your life? Pullin' weeds listenin' to the radio." Junior's father, Robert Glenn Johnson, Sr.—he built this frame house about thirty-five years ago, up here where the gravel road ends and the woods starts. The road just peters out into the woods up a hill. The house has a living room, four bedrooms and a big kitchen. The living room is full of Junior's racing trophies, and so is the piano in Shirley's room. Junior was born and raised here with his older brothers, L. P., the oldest, and Fred, and his older sister, Ruth. Over yonder, up by that house, there's a man with a mule and a little plow. That's L. P. The Johnsons still keep that old mule around to plow the vegetable gardens. And all around, on all sides, like a rim are the ridges and the woods. Well, what about those woods, where Vance Packard said the agents come stealing over the ridges and good old boys go crashing through the underbrush to get away from the still and the women start "calling the cows" up and down the hollows as the signal *they were coming. . . .*

Junior motions his hand out toward the hills and says, "I'd say nearly everybody in a fifty-mile radius of here was in the whiskey business at one time or another. When we growed up here, everybody seemed to be more or less messing with whiskey, and myself and my two brothers did quite a bit of transporting. H'it was just a business, like any other business, far as we was concerned. H'it was a matter of survival. During the Depression here, people either had to do that or starve to death. H'it wasn't no gangster type of business or nothing. They's nobody that ever messed with it here that was ever out to hurt anybody. Even if they got caught, they never tried to shoot anybody or anything like that. Getting caught and pulling time, that was just part of it. H'it was just a business, like any other business. Me and my brothers, when we went out on the road at night, h'it was just like a milk run, far as we was concerned. They was certain deliveries to be made and. . . ."

A milk run—yes! Well, it was a business, all right. In fact, it was a regional industry, all up and down the Appalachian slopes. But never mind the Depression. It goes back a long way before that. The Scotch-Irish settled the mountains from Pennsylvania down to Alabama, and they have been making whiskey out there as long as anybody can remember. At first it was a simple matter of economics. The land had a low crop yield, compared to the lowlands, and even after a man struggled to grow his corn, or whatever, the cost of transporting it to the markets from down out of the hills was so great, it wasn't worth it. It was much more profitable to convert the corn into whiskey and sell that. The trouble started with the Federal Government on that score almost the moment the Republic was founded. Alexander Hamilton put a high excise tax on whiskey in 1791, almost as soon as the

Constitution was ratified. The "Whiskey Rebellion" broke out in the mountains of western Pennsylvania in 1794. The farmers were mad as hell over the tax. Fifteen thousand Federal troops marched out to the mountains and suppressed them. Almost at once, however, the trouble over the whiskey tax became a symbol of something bigger. This was a general enmity between the western and eastern sections of practically every seaboard state. Part of it was political. The eastern sections tended to control the legislatures, the economy and the law courts, and the western sections felt shortchanged. Part of it was cultural. Life in the western sections was rougher. Religions, codes and styles of life were sterner. Life in the eastern capitals seemed to give off the odor of Europe and decadence. Shays' Rebellion broke out in the Berkshire hills of western Massachusetts in 1786 in an attempt to shake off the yoke of Boston, which seemed as bad as George III's. To this day people in western Massachusetts make proposals, earnestly or with down-in-the-mouth humor, that they all ought to split off from "Boston." Whiskey—the mountain people went right on making it. Whole sections of the Appalachians were a whiskey belt, just as sections of Georgia, Alabama and Mississippi were a cotton belt. Nobody on either side ever had any moral delusions about why the Federal Government was against it. It was always the tax, pure and simple. Today the price of liquor is 60 per cent tax. Today, of course, with everybody gone wild over the subject of science and health, it has been much easier for the Federals to persuade people that they crack down on moonshine whiskey because it is dangerous, it poisons, kills and blinds people. The statistics are usually specious.

Moonshining was *illegal*, however, that was also the unvarnished truth. And that had a side effect in the whiskey belt. The people there were already isolated, geographically, by the mountains and had strong clan ties because they were all from the same stock, Scotch-Irish. Moonshining isolated them even more. They always had to be careful who came up there. There are plenty of hollows to this day where if you drive in and ask some good old boy where so-and-so is, he'll tell you he never heard of the fellow. Then the next minute, if you identify yourself and give some idea of why you want to see him, and he believes you, he'll suddenly say, "Aw, you're talking about *so-and-so*. I thought you said—" With all this isolation, the mountain people began to take on certain characteristics normally associated, by the diffident civilizations of today, with tribes. There was a strong sense of family, clan and honor. People would cut and shoot each other up over honor. And physical courage! They were almost like Turks that way.

In the Korean War, there were seventy-eight Medal of Honor winners. Thirty-two of them were from the South, and practically all of the thirty-two were from small towns in or near the Appalachians. The New York metropolitan area, which has more people than all these towns put together, had three Medal of Honor winners, and one of them had just moved to New York from the Appalachian region of West Virginia. Three of the Medal of Honor winners came from within fifty miles of Junior Johnson's side porch.

Detroit has discovered these pockets of courage, almost like a natural resource, in the form of Junior Johnson and about twenty other drivers. There is something exquisitely ironic about it. Detroit is now engaged in the highly sophisticated business of offering the illusion of Speed for Everyman—making their cars go 175 miles an hour on racetracks—by discovering and putting behind the wheel a breed of mountain men who are living vestiges of a degree of physical courage that became extinct in most other sections of the country by 1900. Of course, very few stock car drivers have ever had anything to do with the whiskey business. A great many always lead quiet lives off the track. But it is the same strong people among whom the whiskey business developed who produced the kind of men who could drive the stock cars. There are a few exceptions, Freddie Lorenzen, from Elmhurst, Illinois, being the most notable. But, by and large, it is the rural Southern code of honor and courage that has produced these, the most daring men in sports.

Cars and bravery! The mountain-still operators had been running white liquor with hopped-up automobiles all during the thirties. But it was during the war that the business was so hot out of Wilkes County, down to Charlotte, High Point, Greensboro, Winston-Salem, Salisbury, places like that; a night's run, by one car, would bring anywhere from $500 to $1000. People had money all of a sudden. One car could carry twenty-two to twenty-five cases of white liquor. There were twelve half-gallon fruit jars full per case, so each load would have 132 gallons or more. It would sell to the distributor in the city for about ten dollars a gallon, when the market was good, of which the driver would get two dollars, as much as $300 for the night's work.

The usual arrangement in the white liquor industry was for the elders to design the distillery, supervise the formulas and the whole distilling process and take care of the business end of the operation. The young men did the heavy work, carrying the copper and other heavy goods out into the woods, building the still, hauling in fuel—and driving. Junior and his older brothers, L. P. and Fred, worked that way with their father, Robert Glenn Johnson, Sr.

Johnson, Senior, was one of the biggest individual copper-still operators in the area. The fourth time he was arrested, the agents found a small fortune in working corn mash bubbling in the vats.

"My Daddy was always a hard worker," Junior is telling me. "He always wanted something a little bit better. A lot of people resented that and held that against him, but what he got, he always got h'it by hard work. There ain't no harder work in the world than making whiskey. I don't know of any other business that compels you to get up at all times of night and go outdoors in the snow and everything else and work. H'it's the hardest way in the world to make a living, and I don't think anybody'd do it unless they had to."

Working mash wouldn't wait for a man. It started coming to a head when it got ready to and a man had to be there to take it off, out there in the woods, in the brush, in the brambles, in the muck, in the snow. Wouldn't it have been something if you could have just set it all up inside a good old shed with a corrugated metal roof and order those parts like you want them and not have to smuggle all that copper and all that sugar and all that everything out here in the woods and be a coppersmith and a plumber and a cooper and a carpenter and a pack horse and every other goddamned thing God ever saw in this world, all at once.

And live decent hours—Junior and his brothers, about two o'clock in the morning they'd head out to the stash, the place where the liquor was hidden after it was made. Sometimes it would be somebody's house or an old shed or some place just out in the woods, and they'd make their arrangements out there, what the route was and who was getting how much liquor. There wasn't anything ever written down. Everything was cash on the spot. Different drivers liked to make the run at different times, but Junior and his brothers always liked to start out from 3 to 4 A.M. But it got so no matter when you started out you didn't have those roads to yourself.

"Some guys liked one time and some guys liked another time," Junior is saying, "but starting about midnight they'd be coming out of the woods from every direction. Some nights the whole road was full of bootleggers. It got so some nights they'd be somebody following you going just as fast as you were and you didn't know who h'it was, the law or somebody else hauling whiskey."

And it was just a business, like any other business, just like a milk route—but this funny thing was happening. In those wild-ass times, with the money flush and good old boys from all over the country running that white liquor down the road ninety miles an hour and more than that if you try to crowd them a little bit—well, the funny thing was, it got to be competitive in an almost aesthetic, a pure sporting way. The way the good old boys got to hopping up their automobiles—it got to be a science practically. Everybody was looking to build a car faster than anybody ever had before. They practically got into industrial espionage over it. They'd come up behind one another on those wild-ass nights on the highway, roaring through the black gulches between the clay cuts and the trees, pretending like they were officers, just to challenge them, test them out, race . . . *pour le sport,* you mothers, careening through the darkness, old Carolina moon. All these cars were registered in phony names. If a man had to abandon one, they would find license plates that traced back to . . . nobody at all. It wasn't anything, particularly, to go down to the Motor Vehicle Bureau and get some license plates, as long as you paid your money. Of course, it's rougher now, with compulsory insurance. You have to have your insurance before you can get your license plates, and that leads to a lot of complications. Junior doesn't know what they do about that now. Anyway, all these cars with the magnificent engines were plain on the outside, so they wouldn't attract attention, but they couldn't disguise them altogether. They were jacked up a little in the back and had 8.00 or 8.20 tires, for the heavy loads, and the sound—

"They wasn't no way you could make it sound like an ordinary car," says Junior.

God-almighty, that sound in the middle of the night, groaning, roaring, humming down into the hollows, through the clay gulches—yes! And all over the rural South, hell, all over the South, the legends of wild-driving whiskey running got started. And it wasn't just the plain excitement of it. It was something deeper, the symbolism. It brought into a modern focus the whole business, one and a half centuries old, of the country people's rebellion against the Federals, against the seaboard establishment, their independence, their defiance of the outside world. And it was like a mythology for that and for something else that was happening, the whole wild thing of the car as the symbol of liberation in the postwar South.

"They was out about every night, patrolling, the agents and the State Police was," Junior is saying, "but they seldom caught anybody. H'it was like the dogs chasing the fox. The dogs can't catch a fox, he'll just take 'em around in a circle all night long. I was never caught for transporting. We never lost but one car and the axle broke on h'it."

The fox and the dogs! Whiskey running certainly had a crazy game-like quality about it, considering that a boy might be sent up for two years or more if he were caught transporting. But these boys were just wild enough for that. There got to be a code about the chase. In Wilkes County nobody, neither the good old boys nor the agents, ever did anything that was going to hurt the other side physically. There was supposed to be some parts of the South where the boys used smoke screens and tack buckets. They had attachments in the rear of the cars, and if the agents got too close they would let loose a smoke screen to blind them or a slew of tacks to make them blow a tire. But nobody in Wilkes County ever did that because that was a good way for somebody to get killed. Part of it was that whenever an agent did get killed in the South, whole hordes of agents would come in from Washington and pretty soon they would be tramping along the ridges practically inch by inch, smoking out the stills. But mainly it was—well, the code. If you got caught, you went along peaceably, and the agents never used their guns. There were some tense times. Once was when the agents started using tack belts in Iredell County. This was a long strip of leather studded with nails that the agents would lay across the road in the dark. A man couldn't see it until it was too late and he stood a good chance of getting killed if it got his tires and spun him out. The other was the time the State Police put a roadblock down there at that damned bridge at Millersville to catch a couple of escaped convicts. Well, a couple of good old boys rode up with a load, and there was the roadblock and they were already on the bridge, so they jumped out and dove into the water. The police saw two men jump out of their car and dive in the water, so they opened fire and they shot one good old boy in the backside. As they pulled him out, he kept saying:

"What did you have to shoot at me for? What did you have to shoot at me for?"

It wasn't pain, it wasn't anguish, it wasn't anger. It was consternation. The bastards had broken the code.

Then the Federals started getting radio cars.

"The radios didn't do them any good," Junior says. "As soon as the officers got radios, then *they* got radios. They'd go out and get the same radio. H'it was an awful hard thing for them to radio them down. They'd just listen in on the radio and see where they're setting up the roadblocks and go a different way."

And such different ways. The good old boys knew back roads, dirt roads, up people's back lanes and every which way, and an agent would have to live in the North Carolina hills a lifetime to get to know them. There wasn't hardly a stretch of road on any of the routes where a good old boy couldn't duck off the road and into the backcountry if he had to. They had wild detours around practically every town and every intersection in the region. And for tight spots—the legendary devices, the "bootleg slide," the siren and the red light. . . .

It was just a matter of keeping up with the competition. You always have to have the latest equipment. It was a business thing, like any other business, you have to stay on top—"They was some guys who was more dependable, they done a better job"—and it may have been business to Junior, but it wasn't business to a generation of good old boys growing up all over the South. The Wilkes County bootleg cars started picking up popular names in a kind of folk hero worship—

"The Black Ghost," "The Grey Ghost," which were two of Junior's, "Old Mother Goose," "The Midnight Traveler," "Old Faithful."

And then one day in 1955 some agents snuck over the ridges and caught Junior Johnson at his daddy's still. Junior Johnson, the man couldn't *any*body catch!

The arrest caught Junior just as he was ready to really take off in his career as a stock car driver. Junior says he hadn't been in the whiskey business in any shape or form, hadn't run a load of whiskey for two or three years, when he was arrested. He says he didn't need to fool around with running whiskey after he got into stock car racing, he was making enough money at that. He was just out there at the still helping his daddy with some of the heavy labor, there wasn't a good old boy in Ingle Hollow who wouldn't help his daddy lug those big old cords of ash wood, it doesn't give off much smoke, out in the woods. Junior was sentenced to two years in the Federal reformatory in Chillicothe, Ohio.

"If the law felt I should have gone to jail, that's fine and dandy," Junior tells me. "But I don't think the true facts of the case justified the sentence I got. I never had been arrested in my life. I think they was punishing me for the past. People get a kick out of it because the officers can't catch somebody, and this angers them. Soon as I started getting publicity for racing, they started making it real hot for my family. I was out of the whiskey business, and they knew that, but they was just waiting to catch me on something. I got out after serving ten months and three days of the sentence, but h'it was two or three years I was set back, about half of fifty-six and every bit of fifty-seven. H'it takes a year to really get back into h'it after something like that. I think I lost the prime of my racing career. I feel that if I had been given the chance I feel I was due, rather than the sentence I got, my life would have got a real boost."

But, if anything, the arrest only made the Junior Johnson legend hotter.

And all the while Detroit kept edging the speeds up, from 150 m.p.h. in 1960 to 155 to 165 to 175 to 180 flat out on the longest straightaway, and the good old boys of Southern stock car racing stuck right with it. Any speed Detroit would give them they would take right with them into the curve, hard-charging even though they began to feel strange things such as the rubber starting to pull right off the tire casing. And God! Good old boys from all over the South roared together after the Stanchion—Speed! Guts!—pouring into Birmingham, Daytona Beach, Randleman, North Carolina; Spartanburg, South Carolina; Weaverville, Hillsboro, North Carolina; Atlanta, Hickory, Bristol, Tennessee; Augusta, Georgia; Richmond, Virginia; Asheville, North Carolina;

Charlotte, Myrtle Beach—tens of thousands of them. And still upper- and middle-class America, even in the South, keeps its eyes averted. Who cares! They kept on heading out where we all live, after all, out amongst the Drive-ins, white-enameled filling stations, concrete aprons, shopping-plaza apothecaries, show-window steak houses, Burger-Ramas, Bar-B-Cubicles and Miami aqua-swimming-pool motor inns, on out the highway . . . even outside a town like Darlington, a town of 10,000 souls, God, here they come, down route 52, up 401, on 340, 151 and 34, on through the South Carolina lespedeza fields. By Friday night already the good old boys are pulling into the infield of the Darlington raceway with those blazing pastel dreamboats stacked this way and that on the clay flat and the tubular terrace furniture and the sleeping bags and the Thermos jugs and the brown whiskey bottles coming on out. By Sunday—the race!—there are 65,000 piled into the racetrack at Darlington. The sheriff, as always, sets up the jail right there in the infield. No use trying to haul them out of there. And now —the *sound* rises up inside the raceway, and a good old boy named Ralph goes mad and starts selling chances on his Dodge. Twenty-five cents and you can take the sledge he has and smash his car anywhere you want. How they roar when the windshield breaks! The police could interfere, you know, but they are busy chasing a good old girl who is playing Lady Godiva on a hogbacked motorcycle, naked as sin, hauling around and in and out of the clay ruts.

Eyes averted, happy burghers. On Monday the ads start appearing—for Ford, for Plymouth, for Dodge—announcing that we gave it to you, speed such as you never saw. There it was! At Darlington, Daytona, Atlanta—and not merely in the Southern papers but in the albino pages of the suburban women's magazines, such as *The New Yorker*, in color—the Ford winners, such as Fireball Roberts, grinning with a cigar in his mouth in *The New Yorker* magazine. And somewhere, some Monday morning, Jim Pascal of High Point, Ned Jarrett of Boykin, Cale Yarborough of Timmonsville and Curtis Crider from Charlotte, Bobby Isaac of Catawba, E. J. Trivette of Deep Gap, Richard Petty of Randleman, Tiny Lund of Cross, South Carolina; Stick Elliott of Shelby—and from out of Ingle Hollow—

And all the while, standing by in full Shy, in alumicron suits—there is Detroit, hardly able to believe itself what it has discovered, a breed of good old boys from the fastnesses of the Appalachian hills and flats —a handful from this rare breed—who have given Detroit . . . speed . . . and the industry can present it to a whole generation as . . . yours. And the Detroit P.R. men themselves come to the tracks like folk worshipers and the millions go giddy with the thrill of speed. Only Junior Johnson goes about it as if it were . . . the usual. Junior goes on down to Atlanta for the Dixie 400 and drops by the Federal penitentiary to see his Daddy. His Daddy is in on his fifth illegal distillery conviction; in the whiskey business that's just part of it; an able craftsman, an able businessman, and the law kept hounding him, that was all. So Junior drops by and then goes on out to the track and gets in his new Ford and sets the qualifying speed record for Atlanta Dixie 400, 146.301 m.p.h.; later on he tools on back up the road to Ingle Hollow to tend to the automatic chicken houses and the road-grading operation. Yes.

Yet how can you tell that to . . . anybody . . . out on the bottom of that bowl as the motor thunder begins to lift up through him like a sigh and his eyeballs glaze over and his hands reach up and there, riding the rim of the bowl, soaring over the ridges, is Junior's yellow Ford . . . which is his white Chevrolet . . . which is a White Ghost, forever rousing the good old boys . . . hard-charging! . . up with the automobile into their America, and the hell with arteriosclerotic old boys trying to hold onto the whole pot with arms of cotton seersucker. Junior!

"I got this supervisor where I work—these middle-age people, man, they're like children. All they think about is sex and dope. He's always coming around with this little grin on his face, talking about amyl nitrite and PBD. I mean, that's what you do in the fuckin' ninth or tenth grade, man."

THE VOICES OF VILLAGE SQUARE

"Hai-ai-ai-ai-ai-ai-ai-ai-ai-ai-ai-ai-ai-ai-ai-ai-ai-ai-ai-ai-ai-ai-ai-ai-ai-ai-ai-ai-ai-ai-ai-ai-ai-ai-ai-ai-ai-ai-ai-ai-ai-ai-ai-ai-ai-ai-ai-ai-ai-ai-ai-reeeeeeeeeeeeeeeeeeeee!"

O, dear, sweet Harry, with your French gangster-movie bangs, your Ski Shop turtleneck sweater and your Army-Navy Store blue denim shirt over it, with your Bloomsbury corduroy pants you saw in the *Manchester Guardian* airmail edition and sent away for and your sly intellectual pigeon-toed libido roaming in Greenwich Village—that siren call really for you?

"Hai-ai-ai-ai-ai-ai-ai-ai-ai-ai-ai-ai-ai-aireeeeeeeeee!"

Obviously Harry thinks so. There, in the dusk, on the south side of Greenwich Avenue, near Nut Heaven, which is the intersection of Greenwich Avenue, Sixth Avenue, Eighth Street and Christopher Street, also known as Village Square, Harry stops and looks up at the great umber tower at 10 Greenwich Avenue. He can see windows but he can't see through them. He gives a shy wave and thereby becomes the eighth man in half an hour to get conned by The Voices.

Half of them, like Harry, look like the sort of kids who graduated in 1961 from Haverford, Hamilton or some other college of the genre known as Threadneedle Ivy and went to live in New York City. Here they participate in discussions denouncing our IBM civilization, the existing narcotics laws, tailfins and suburban housing developments, and announce to girls that they are Searching. Frankly, they are all lonesome and hung up on the subject of girls in New York. They all have a vision of how one day they are going to walk into some place, usually a second-hand bookstore on Bleecker Street west of Sixth Avenue, and there is going to be a girl in there with pre-Raphaelite

From *The Kandy-Kolored Tangerine-Flake Streamline Baby.* First published in *New York*, the *New York Herald Tribune*'s Sunday magazine, January 5, 1964.

hair, black leotards and a lambskin coat. Their eyes will meet, their minds will meet—you know, Searching, IBM civilization and all that, and then——

"Hai-ai-ai-ai-ai-ai-ai-ai-ai-ai-ai-ai-ai-reeeeeeeee!"

All of a sudden old Harry is waving away from down there on Greenwich Avenue, out front of the Casual-Aire shop and yelling back: "Hey! who is it?"

"Hey, Harry!" the girl yells.

"Hey, Harry!" another girl yells.

"Hey, Harry!" still another girl yells.

Four girls, five girls, six girls yell, "Hey, Harry!"

Then one of them yells, "Hai-ai-ai-ai-ai-ai-ai-ai-aireeeee! Have you got a —— —— for me?"

Then another one yells, "Hey, Harry, come on up and —— —— —— ——!"

Harry looks like a poleaxed lamb in that wobbly moment just before the cerebral cortex shuts off for good. Old Harry has been searching all right, and he has had some lubricous thoughts about what would happen after his and Dream Girl's eyes and mind met, but this laying it on the line like that, right out in the middle of Nut Heaven—it was too *gamey* or something.

So Harry walks away, west on Greenwich Avenue, with the cellblock horselaughs following him, and by now, of course, he knows he has been had.

So the girls take up new names to see if anybody will bite:

"John-n-n-n-n-n-ny!"

"Hey, Bil-l-l-l-l-l-l!"

"Frankie!"

"Hi, Honey!"

"Sammy!"

"Max!"

For some reason, a name like Max breaks everybody up, and all the girls start the cellblock horselaugh even before they find out if there is anybody down there named Max who is going to look up with the old yearning gawk.

The girls, these Sirens, these Voices, are all up in the cellblocks of the Women's House of Detention, 10 Greenwich Avenue, overlooking Village Square, and, well, what the ——, as the girls like to say, these yelling games are something to do. The percentages are in their favor. There are thousands of kids trooping through the intersection all the time, and eventually a girl is going to get somebody named Harry, Johnny, Bill, Frankie, Sammy or, affectionately, Honey.

The Women's House of Detention is, no doubt, a "hellhole," as even the Corrections Department people speak of it every time they ask for an appropriation to build a bigger one. It is a mess: 600 women in a space meant for 400. Teen-age girls, first offenders, some of them merely awaiting trial, are heaped in with "institutionalized" old puggies who feel like bigger shots inside than out. The place is filthy. It is so bad that a convicted prostitute, narcotics user and peddler, Kim Parker, combining, at age 35, the sins that land 80 per cent of the girls inside 10 Greenwich Avenue, pleaded guilty to a felony rather than a misdemeanor last October. The felony sentence might be five years at the state prison farm, which to her was a happier prospect than one year in the Women's House of Detention.

Yet there is probably not another large prison in the country that is in such intimate contact with the outside world. The building, twelve stories high, was built in 1932 as a monument to Modern Penology. The idea was to make it look not like a jail at all but like a new apartment building. There are copper facings with 1930's modern arch designs on them between the floors. In the place of bars there are windows with a heavy grillwork holding minute square panes. The panes are clouded, like cataracts. Actually, the effect is more like that of the power plant at Yale University, which was designed to resemble a Gothic cathedral, but, in any case, it does not look like a jail.

So here is a jail that looks like a Yale power plant with cataracts standing out in the middle of a community that has become a paradise for kids in New York, Greenwich Village. The girls in the House of Detention can stand up on the toilet bowl or something and look out the couple of hinged window panes they have out onto all that Life among the free kids. Right down there, off the intersection, are all the signs, Trude Heller's, the twist and bossa nova place, Burger Village, Hamburger Train, Luigi's, Lamanna Liquors, Foam Rubber City, the Captain's Table, Nedick's and the swingingest Rexall drug store in New York City. Skipping across Sixth Avenue and screaming every time the lights change are all the bouffant bohemians, with bouffants up top and stretch pants and elf shoes down below, and live guys in Slim Jims and Desert boots, and aging bohemians in Avenger boots and matching plaid poncho and slacks sets, and Modern Churchmen, painted lulus, A-trainers and twenty-eight-year-old winos who say, "All right, you don't have a quarter, but if you had a quarter would you give it to me?"

Also junkies. The same night they conned Harry—"Hey! Who is it?" —the girls could see a kid known as Fester stumbling out of the Rexall wringing one hand and holding his stomach with the other. For a while Fester had folded his sweater up into a square and knelt down in the entrance to the Rexall with his head on the sweater, moaning. Everybody just stepped around him. But then Fester jumped up and ran to the cigarette counter and with a stifled shriek clouted a total stranger in the back of the neck with his open palm. The guy just wheeled around, still holding onto his Marlboros, shocked, and Fester started wringing his hand, saying in his elfy voice, "My hand stings!" and then stumbled out, holding his gut with the other. Fester is a junky; a lot of the girls know him. There was a time when a girl could hoist a fix up into the House of Detention on a "fishing line" with the help of a guy like Fester.

Well, Fester is in bad shape, but there he is, at least, out there on the loose in Greenwich Village, where everybody goes skipping and screaming across Sixth Avenue. The girls have to yell to all that life down there. The girls in one cellblock will all start yelling down there until the girl who is the lookout gives the warning signal, sometimes "Dum-da-dum-dum" from the old Jack Webb TV show, meaning that the turnkeys are coming. The girls will even yell to somebody they have just been talking to in the visitors room on the first floor on visiting night. It is one thing to talk to somebody inside the jail. It is a better thing to know you can still talk to them when they are back out there on the street in the middle of things.

"Willie!"

It is not long after Harry has disappeared west on Greenwich Avenue, and Willie has just come out of the front door at 10 Greenwich Avenue after visiting a girl whose name one never learns. One only hears her shrieking across Greenwich Avenue from somewhere up there in the great cataracted building.

"Willie! Are you gonna sell the pants!"

There are trucks bouncing along Greenwich Avenue and Sixth Avenue and cutting across into Greenwich from Ninth Street, but she can make herself heard. Willie, on the other hand, is the last of the great shoe buyers. He has on a pair of tan triple-A's that won't quit. He is not ready for yelling across Greenwich Avenue up at the Women's House of Detention. He gives a look at all the people walking his way past Tucker's Cut Rate Florist, Hamburger Train and the Village Bake Shop.

"Are you, Willie!"

Willie tries. "I don't know where they are, I told yuh!"

"What!"

Willie puts a little lung into it this time. "I told yuh! I don't know where they are!"

"You know where they are, Willie! You gonna sell 'em or not?"

Willie wants to get out of there. He doesn't want to be yelling across Greenwich Avenue to some unseen gal in the Women's House of Detention about selling a pair of pants. So he gives the first guy who comes by a weak, smiley, conspiratorial look, as if to say, Women! But the guy just stares at him and walks slow, so he can hear more. This makes Willie mad, and so he gives the next few people the death ray look—What you looking at!—which starts his adrenaline flowing, which in turn puts him in fuller, better voice.

"Aw, I don't know where the pants are! What you bother with the pants for!"

"You gonna sell 'em, Willie!"

"All right!"

"'*All right!*'" she yells it very sarcastically. "All right, Willie, all right, you do what you want!"

"Aw, come on, honey!"

Willie wishes he hadn't yelled that. Now it seems like about a thousand nuts are scuttling through Nut Heaven laughing at him and sidling looks at him standing in his tan triple-A's yelling at a blank building.

"Naw, you do me like you did Maureen! Go on!"

"Listen—"

"Naw, you so fine, Willie!"

There is a lot of laughing from the cellblocks after that. Willie wants to vanish. All these damned faces around here gawking at him.

"All right!" Willie yells.

"You mean it!" she yells from somewhere up there. "You gonna sell the pants!"

"I told yuh!" Willie yells, right over the garbage trucks, the Vespas, the Volkswagens, the people, over the whole lumbering, flatulent mess.

"And then you coming back!"

"All right!"

"When!"

"Soon's I sell 'em!"

"They in the closet, Willie!"

"All right!" Willie yells, and then he turns and walks fast down Christopher Street.

"Willie!" she yells. "Goodbye!"

There is a kid down there wearing a big black Borsalino hat and a George Raft-style 1930's double-breasted black overcoat who has got to find out what it is all about. He runs after Willie and just asks him, straight out, and Willie blows up and suggests by means of a homey colloquialism how he can dispose of the whole subject, and selling the pants remains a private affair.

And inside the Women's House of Detention, the girls are gathering spirit. It is eventide in a holiday season. On the Sixth Avenue side, about four girls begin the old song, and then, gradually, more join in:

I'm dreaming of a white Christmas!
Just like the ones I used to know!
Where the treetops glisten!
And children listen!

To hear sleigh bells in the snow . . .

How touching are these words as they drift over Sixth Avenue from the cataracts of the Women's House of Detention! Villagers, laden with bundles, stop over there in front of the Kaiser clothing store and look up and listen, silently.

. . . with every Christmas card I write!

By now maybe twenty or thirty people have stopped on the avenue in a bunch, and they all have their heads cocked, rheumy eyes turned up in the attitude that says, I am already deeply moved and ready for more.

. . . may your days be mer-reeee and bright! . . .

How the sound rises! Every girl on the east side of the Women's House of Detention, it seems like, has joined in and taken a gulletful of air for the final line, which comes out:

. . . And may all your Christ-mases be bla-a-a-a-a-a-a-ack!

Only some of the girls don't even say black, they use adjectives such as ——, ——, —— and ——. Others have already given themselves up wholly to cellblock horselaughs, and soon they all have, and now the horselaughs come shrieking out across old Sixth Avenue to where all the obedient epopts of old-sampler sentiment are bunched in front of Kaiser's. That was a good hit! Twenty or thirty of them, free squares of New York, bunched together and all conned! gulled! faked out! put on! had! by The Voices of Village Square.

Off to a Better Place

("Ah, my dear, perhaps it's just as well. Your decorator called today. The David Hicks carpet won't be in for another six weeks, they dented the girandoles in shipping, he doesn't know what happened to the Hartman lamps, and the couch arrived but the pillows are filled with polyurethane chips instead of goose down.")

PURVEYOR OF THE PUBLIC LIFE

Up there in the office at Broadway and 52nd Street during the last days of *Confidential,* the old *Confidential* (1952–58), the most scandalous scandal magazine in the history of the world, everybody seemed to be ricocheting around amid the dolly lights and cracking up. Everybody, save one, namely, Robert Harrison himself, the publisher. Jay Breen's liver had gone into its last necrotic, cirrhotic foliation. Jay Breen used to write half the magazine, but it had gotten to the point where Breen couldn't stand to listen to the Reader anymore. Breen and his wife would come in and sit in the next room while the Reader read the stories for the next issue out loud. The Reader, whatever his name was, had a truly great voice, like Sir Ralph Richardson reading Lear soliloquies at a Bauhaus Modern lectern under a spotlight. Great diction, great resonance, etc. Harrison hired him just to read out loud. Harrison had a theory that if you read the stories out loud, every weak spot in a story would stand out. So there would be the Reader with a voice like Sir Ralph Richardson enunciating such works as "Errol Flynn and His Two-Way Mirror," "White Women Broke Up My Marriage" [to a Negro entertainer], and "How Mike Todd Made a Chump of a Movie Mogul." One of the writers would be in there muttering away because he claimed that the Reader had it in for him and was blundering over his best-turned phrases on purpose, thereby causing Harrison to throw whole stories out. But Jay Breen was long, long past all that, and presently he died, of cirrhosis of the liver. Meanwhile, Howard Rushmore, the editor, was beginning to look awful. He used to be such a

From *The Kandy-Kolored Tangerine-Flake Streamline Baby.* First published as "Public Lives: *Confidential* Magazine; Reflection in Tranquility by the Former Owner, Robert Harrison" in *Esquire,* April 1964.

big robust guy, and now he looked like a couple of eye sockets mounted on a piece of modern solder sculpture. Rushmore was an ex-Communist and a complex person. He had a talent for gossip stories, but somehow it was all wrapped up with the anti-Communist crusade he was carrying on. There came a day when Rushmore and his wife were riding in a cab on the upper East Side and he took out a revolver and shot her to death and then shot himself to death. Harrison was the publisher of *Confidential* and he remembered that day very well. He had just come into Idlewild Airport from someplace and gotten into a cab. The first he heard about Rushmore was when the cabdriver said, "Hey, did you hear that? The publisher of *Confidential* just shot himself!"

"The publisher of *Confidential*," says Harrison, the publisher of *Confidential*. "Where did the publisher of *Confidential* shoot himself?"

"In the head, in a cab," says the cabdriver. "He shot himself through the head, right in the back of a cab!"

Harrison remembers that, well, here he was, right in the back of a cab, and he didn't have the slightest inclination to pull a gun on anybody inside or outside a cab. It had been wild for a while, forty million dollars' worth of libel suits, the whole movie industry had been after him, jukebox gangsters or somebody like that had hung him upside down by his heels out his office window, Congressmen and half the newspapers in the country were crucifying him, some guy from Chicago was going to fly in and break every bone in his body, starting with his fingers and toes—but that was all pressure from outside. Inside, he wasn't drowning in his own turbulent juices like Breen or Rushmore. He was serene, and *Confidential* was beautiful. This may be a hard idea to put across—the way Harrison found *Confidential* beautiful. But the fact is, the man is an aesthete, the original *aesthete du schlock.*

At the outset all I knew about Harrison was that he was living under an assumed name in a place called the Hotel Madison. To imagine the kind of picture that brought to mind, all you have to think of was the libel suits, the outrage, all the big people who were after him in 1957 when he sold *Confidential* and dropped from view. They must have crushed him like a Phrygian sacrifice. So the picture I had of Robert Harrison, the ex-publisher of *Confidential*, in someplace called the Hotel Madison was of a skulking fifty-nine-year-old man holed up in a hotel room where the view was a close-up of the air-conditioning duct of the short-order restaurant out back, hung with heavy-duty New York lint in clots like Spanish moss. That was until I saw the Madison, Reggie, Lately Miss BMC of Canada, and Harrison's cravat.

The Madison, on East 58th Street, between Fifth and Madison, turned out to be a fairly posh and conservative old place full of big cooperative apartments and a lobby with plum and umber walls and servitors in white dickies. Harrison's sister, Helen, a polite, quiet woman with grey-blonde hair who has been his personal secretary all these years, opened the door, and there was what I later learned was the very same apartment he had lived in during the heyday of *Confidential.* It has a thirty-foot living room all buttressed with yards of faceted mirrors, a bar with Hilarious novelties on it, a pygmy tropical tree with a wooden ape hanging in the branches, ochre-colored neo-Moloch art objects, black and tan furniture, the total effect being the decorator style known as Malay Peninsula Modern. Pretty soon, out of one of the two side rooms, came Harrison, trampling through the wall-to-wall and tying the cravat.

"Have you had breakfast yet?" he says. It was one in the afternoon. "I've been on this goddamned diet. Let's go to Lindy's, I can't stand it anymore. I lost two pounds. I got to have something to eat, some of that fish or something; you know, lox."

Judging from his 1957 pictures, Harrison, now fifty-nine and grey-haired, may have a little more heft in the bags above and below the eyes, and a little more erosion in the jowls, but he is wearing his hair combed back long and on the rakish side, like Jon Hall in *The Hurricane*, and he has this silk cravat debouching like mad from the throat of his sports shirt. Furthermore, he still has a Broadway promoter's accent, the kind that seems to be created by hidden pistons, and one of those voices that come from back in the throat as if it has been Mello-cured like a Dr. Grabow pipe.

And then, from exactly where I forget, materializes Reggie, a blonde. Reggie is one of these girls who strike you as more of an ensemble, a chorus, a tableau, an opulent colonial animal, than as one person. She has great blonde bouffant hair, a coat of white fur whose locks fluff out wider than she is tall, and a dog, a toy greyhound named Tessie. Reggie and Helen get into a discussion about the dog's recent alimentary history to see if it will be safe to leave it in the apartment with Helen while Reggie, Harrison and I go off to Lindy's. The dog looks just like a racing greyhound except that it is two feet long and wears a town coat.

While they're talking, Harrison shows me a copy of his latest enterprise, a newspaper he started last year called *Inside News.*

"What do you think of it?" he says.

Obviously, from the tone he is not asking if I felt all informed by its inside news or was even entertained by it. It is an aesthetic question, as if he were showing me a Hiroshige print he just bought. The front-page headline in the newspaper is set in a great burst of red and says: "Castro's Sex Invasion of Washington." The story postulates—

that seems to be the word for it—that Castro is planning to smuggle a lot of Christine Keelers into Washington to ruin the careers of prominent officials—and features a picture of a girl in a checkerboard bikini and these odd shoes: "The Castro cutie who could change Capitol Hill into Fanny Hill. Pics smuggled from Cuba by writer," one "Marc Thorez." The picture reveals mainly that Castro has stockpiled a pair of six-inch spiked-heel shoes of the sort that turned up in the girlie magazines Harrison used to publish in the Forties.

"This is going to be bigger than *Confidential,*" says Harrison. "The keyhole stuff is dead. The big thing now is getting behind the news. This is going to be big. What's his name, the big Hollywood producer, he drives up here to the newsstand every week in a limousine just to get *Inside News.* I see him every week. He comes up in a limousine and he doesn't reach out for it. He gets out of the car and goes over and picks it up himself. Now, I think that's a goddamned compliment!"

From Harrison's face you can see that here is a man who is still trying to free his features from the sebaceous stickum of having just woke up, but he is already on the move. The old *aesthetique du schlock* is already stirred up and he is already thinking about his own story, the story about him and *Confidential.*

"I think I've got a story angle for you," he says. "The angle I like is, 'Now It Can Be Told.' You know? Of course, you guys probably have your own ideas about it, but that's the way I see it—'Now It Can Be Told.' "

And as the day wore on, you could see the first splash of red with a montage of photographs, tabloid headlines and feverish brush script over it, saying something like "Now It Can Be Told—'Inside' *Confidential!*" Harrison always liked to begin a story like that, with a layout with a big stretch of red and a lot of pictures and lettering and type faces exploding on top of it. Actually, he would probably see it not as an article but a whole one-shot. A one-shot is a magazine, or a book in magazine form, that is published just once, to capitalize on some celebrity or current event. James Dean, the movie actor, dies and a lot of one-shots come out, with titles like *The James Dean Story, The Real James Dean, James Dean Lives!* or just *James Dean.* One-shots have been among Harrison's enterprises since he sold *Confidential* in 1957. He has put out one-shots like *Menace of the Sex Deviates, New York Confidential, That Man Paar,* as well as *Naked New York.* You can almost see Harrison putting together the stories for "Now It Can Be Told." The lead piece would no doubt be called: "How *Confidential* Got Those 'Prying' Stories—from the Stars Themselves!" And there would be another big one entitled, "Why I've Started *Inside News*—To Prove I Can Do It Again!" by Bob Harrison.

And along about then Helen comes into the living room from the room they use as an office. She has a worried look on her face.

"What's wrong?" Harrison says.

"Oh, I don't know," Helen says. "Why are you bringing up all that?"

"It's all the truth, isn't it?"

"Yes, but it's all over. That's the past. It's finished. *Confidential* is over. I don't know, I just don't like to bring it all up again."

"Why not?" said Harrison. "I'm not ashamed of anything I ever did!"

Helen says in a weary voice, as if to say, That's not even the point, "But what about ________?"

"He was a nice guy," Harrison says. "I liked him."

"What do you mean, *was*," Helen says. "What is he going to say if he reads about this. You had an agreement."

"That was a long time ago," Harrison says. "Anyway, he admits it. He's writing a book and he admits I gave him his real start in his career, the publicity he got in *Confidential.* He admits it."

"What about Mike Todd, and Cohn, that was part of the agreement."

"They're both dead," says Harrison. "Besides, that was a very amusing story. Nobody got hurt."

"Still . . ." says Helen, and then she just sighs.

Then he says, "Let's go to Lindy's. You go to Lindy's much?" I had never been in there. "How long have you been in New York? You ought to start getting around to places like that. That's where everybody is."

A couple of minutes later we all—Harrison, Reggie and the dog, and myself—get into a cab, and Harrison sinks back and says, "Lindy's." The cabbie gets that bemused, Jell-O-faced look that New York cabdrivers get when they are stumped and they have to admit it.

"Let's see," he says, "where is that, again?"

"Where is Lindy's!" Harrison says in his Dr. Grabow voice. "What the hell is happening in this goddamned town!"

At Lindy's there is trouble right away about the dog. Harrison and Reggie were counting on it being Sunday and things are slow. But the maître d' at Lindy's says it is true that this is Sunday and things are slow and he still can't let any dogs in; there is a law. One trouble, I think, is that the dog has this fey grin on his face. Harrison weighs the whole thing on the scales of life and does not protest. Reggie leaves in her remarkable profusion of hair, fur and toy greyhound to take the dog back to the apartment, but she will be back. Well, that is just a setback, that is all. Harrison gets a table where he wants it, over to one side where everything is orange curves decorated with stylized emblems of such things as martinis, trombones, and pretty girls, all set at a swingy angle that reminds you of the Busy City music from the opening montage of a Fred Astaire-Ginger Rogers movie. Harrison takes a seat where he can see the door. One of the waiters comes up and says, "Mr. Harrison! How are you? You look like a million dollars!"

"I must be living right," says Harrison. "I've been on this goddamned diet. I can't stand it anymore. That's why I came over here. Has Walter been in?"

Walter hasn't been in.

"Do you know Winchell?" Harrison asks me. "No? You ought to meet him. He's a terrific guy. He's the one who really put *Confidential* over."

The waiter is saying, "Now all you need is a couple of good-looking broads and it will be just like old times."

Harrison says, "Well, you just keep your eyes open in a minute."

The great pink-orange slabs of lox, the bagels, the butter and the cups of coffee start coming, and Harrison pitches in, and to hell with the diet. Lindy's is not crowded, but people are starting to crane around to look at Harrison. A lot of people remember *Confidential*, if not Harrison himself, and in any case the word is going around the restaurant that the publisher of *Confidential* in its most notorious days is there, and everyone has a look on the face that says, in indignation or stupefaction, How did that guy get out from under the deluge and come in here to feast on all that orange-blossomy lox?

"You want to know what happened to the libel suits?" Harrison says. "Nothing happened, that's what happened." [Harrison has a tendency toward oversimplification. Some suits against *Confidential* resulted in substantial settlements.] "Forty million dollars and nothing happened. It was all a show. They loved it. I was the one who took all the responsibility. I was the one who got crucified. I was terribly condemned. And all the time some big shots were giving me the stories themselves!"

"The movie stars were giving you scandal stories about themselves?"

"That's what I'm trying to explain," Harrison says. "That's how we used to get them! From the big shots! And I was the one who always took the rap. I couldn't tell the world then, because it would jeopardize someone's standing. I'll tell you, ________ sat right there in my living room and gave me two stories about himself. We had already run one about him and an actress, I forget where we got that one. But he was up in my living room. The deal was, he would give me the stories, but 'I'll deny the whole thing,' he says.

"And Mike Todd. I knew Mike. I'll tell you a funny story about him. Mike Todd called me up from California to give me a story about Harry Cohn. Cohn was a big producer at Columbia Pictures. Mike Todd says, 'I'll meet you at the Stork Club, I'll meet you tonight,

I've got a great story for you.' So he flew all the way to New York and he gave me this story about Harry Cohn.

"There was this girl who wanted to break into the pictures, and Mike Todd wanted to help her out, but he really didn't have any use for her, so what he did was, he started raving to Cohn about this girl he'd discovered and told him he was getting ready to sign her up, but for $500 a week he'd lend her to him. So Cohn decided to outsmart Mike Todd and without saying anything he puts her under contract himself and she has her job.

"Well, you should have heard Mike Todd telling me that story. He howled! He almost died! And you know, he was so interested in that story, he came over and he worked on it with us. We almost had the story done, but we were having trouble getting a last line, and Mike Todd had to go back to Hollywood. Well, that night, in the middle of the night, he called me up from Hollywood and he said, 'I've got it! I've got that last line for you!' Here was a guy who was one of the busiest guys in Hollywood, he was doing a million things, but he called me up in the middle of the night just to get that story right. My respect for him went up a million per cent!"

There it was again! The *aesthetique du schlock!* There is only one Mike Todd in Harrison's book. More bagels, more lox, more coffee; Harrison is going strong now—names, names, names. The names *Confidential* was built on keep bubbling up. He used to meet these people in the damnedest places, he says. He was too hot to be seen with. He used to meet Lee Mortimer, a writer, in some damned telephone booth. Both of them would get right in there in the same booth and talk, and Mortimer would give him stories, for Christ's sake. "Then we'd glare at each other at some nightclub that night." Other people Harrison remembers because they were supposed to be mad as hell at him but all of a sudden were acting very friendly when they met him. Harrison tended to overestimate the world's store of goodwill for him, but the fact was that even when *Confidential* was at its most notorious peak, people would meet Harrison for the first time, brace themselves for the worst, talk to him for a while and come away telling about his "curious charm." Well, practically everybody seemed to like him in varying degrees, as Harrison recalls it, but there was only one Mike Todd. Mike Todd was not only friendly, he not only provided stories about himself, but he saw the beauty of *Confidential* as usually only Harrison could see it, he participated in it, he understood the *aesthetique du schlock!*

"I get along fine with all those people," Harrison is saying. "The only one who never liked me was ———. Did you ever read that story we did about ———, about how he ate Wheaties? That was a fabulous story. That was the best story Breen ever did. Here is this girl, and she told me the story herself. She just told it to me when we were sitting in some place, I forget the name of it, it might have been Harwyn's, that was a big place then. Anyway, in this story, here is this girl, and every time she hears the 'crunch crunch crunch' of the Wheaties, she knows ______ is coming back in the room. He thinks Wheaties are good for, you know, virility, and every time he goes out in the kitchen for the Wheaties and this girl can hear the 'crunch crunch crunch'—it was a fabulous story. You've got to read it. And that's the funny thing, he is the only one who never liked me. I ran into him one night in the Copacabana and he just looked right past me—and that was the best story we ever did!"

Yes! The *aesthetique du schlock! Schlock*, which is Yiddish for a kind of "ersatz," is the New York publishing-trade term for the sort of periodical, known academically as subliterature, in which there is a story about, say, bars where young women from Utica and Akron are lured, seduced, hooked and shanghaied as call girls, and the title is "Sin Traps for Secretaries!" and there is an illustration made up of half photograph, of models with black censor bars across their eyes and a lot of thigh and garter strap, and half superimposed drawing, of a leering devil in a silk topper, all on a layout that the editor has returned to the art department with a crayon notation that says, "Make devil red." Harrison would fret and enthuse over a *schlock* tale like the Wheaties one with the same flaming passion for art as Cardinal Newman or somebody dubbing a few oxymorons and serpentinae carminae into his third draft. Well, even *schlock* has its classics. All during the mid-fifties, the outrage was building up about *Confidential*, the sales were going up to more than four million at the newsstands per issue, the record for newsstand sales, and everybody was wondering, outraged, how such a phenomenon could crop up in the middle of the twentieth century after the lessons of the war, hate and all, and what kind of creature could be producing *Confidential*. That was because no one really knew about Harrison, the "air business," and the Cézanne, the Darwin, the Aristotle of *schlock*—the old New York *Graphic*.

Harrison's father, he was saying, had wanted him to have a trade. Like plumbing, he says, that being the worst trade Harrison can imagine on short notice. The thing was, Harrison's father had been an immigrant, from Mitau. Harrison doesn't know where that is. His father and he were as different as black and white, he was saying. His father had the Old World idea of having a trade so inculcated in him that he was suspicious about any job that wasn't a trade. Harrison says he was about fifteen or sixteen when he got a job in an advertising agency, and he was getting seventy-five bucks a week. His old man went right down to the office of the place to see what kind of funny stuff his son had gotten mixed up in. Even after he found out it was legit, he wrote it off as "air business." "This *air business,*" he kept saying.

But the air business to end all air business was the New York *Daily Graphic*. Harrison went to work for the *Graphic* as an office boy, or copy boy, when the paper was the hottest thing in New York. It was one of those Xanadus of inspired buncombe in the twenties. The *Graphic* blew up scandal and crime stories like pork bladders. When the *Graphic* wanted to do a sensational story, they had writers, photographers and composograph artists who could not only get in there and milk every gland in the human body—but do it with verve, with patent satisfaction, and, by god, celebrate it and pronounce it good with a few bawling red-eyed rounds after work. The *Graphic*'s ghost writers developed the knack of putting a story, first-person and sopping with confession, into a famous person's mouth until it seemed like the guy was lying right out there on the page like a flat-out Gulliver. And those composograph artists. The composograph was a way of developing photographs of a scene at which, unfortunately, no photographers were present. If a gal were nude when the action took place but was uncooperatively fully clothed when the *Graphic* photographers zeroed in, the composographers had a way of recollecting the heated moment in tranquillity with scissors, paste and the retouch brush. These were wild times all around. These were the days of Texas Guinan and all that kind of stuff, Harrison was saying. Harrison was only sixteen or seventeen when he went to work on the *Graphic*, and he was only an office boy, or copy boy, but this piece of air business fixed his mind like an aspic mold. Okay, it was bogus. It was ballyhoo. It was outrageous. Everybody was outraged and called the *Daily Graphic* "gutter journalism"—that's how that one got started —and the Daily Pornographic. But by god the whole thing had style. Winchell was there, developing a column called "Broadway Hearsay" that set the style for all the hot, tachycardiac gossip columns that were to follow. Even in the realm of the bogus, the *Graphic* went after bogosity with a kind of Left Bank sense of rebellious discovery. Those composographs, boy! Those confession yarns!

By 1957 people were starting to rustle through all the cerebral fretwork of Freud, Schopenhauer and Karl Menninger for an explanation of the *Confidential* phenomenon, when all the time they could have found it in some simpler, brighter stuff—that old forgotten bijou, the *aesthetique du Daily Graphic*. That was a long-faced year, 1957. Hate? Venom? Smut peddling? Scandal mongering? All those long faces floated past Harrison like a bunch of emphysematous investment counselors who had missed the train.

After his days on the *Graphic*, Harrison worked for a long time for Martin Quigley, publisher of the *Motion Picture Daily* and the *Motion Picture Herald*. Then, as he puts it, a funny thing happened. He got canned. He got canned for publishing the first of his girlie magazines, *Beauty Parade*, in Quigley's office after hours. "Quigley fired me and it was on Christmas Eve, I want you to know," says Harrison. "Yeah! Christmas Eve!" But *Beauty Parade* clicked, and by the late forties Harrison was publishing six girlie magazines, among them being *Titter*, *Wink* and *Flirt*. Harrison's first great contribution to the art, sort of like Braque coming up with the collage at a crucial point in the history of painting, was the editorial sequence. Which is to say, instead of just having a lot of unrelated girlie shots stuck into a magazine of, say, *Breezy Stories*, the way it used to be done, Harrison arranged the girlie shots in editorial sequences. A whole set of bust-and-leg pictures would be shot around the theme, "Models Discover the Sauna Baths!" Class. Harrison's second great contribution was really the brainchild of one of his editors, an educated gal who was well-versed on Krafft-Ebing. It was she who sold Harrison on the idea of fetishism, such as the six-inch spiked-heel shoes, and the eroticism of backsides or of girls all chained up and helpless, or girls whipping the hides off men and all the rest of the esoterica of the Viennese psychologists that so thoroughly pervades the girlie magazines today. She once put a volume of Krafft-Ebing on Harrison's desk, but he never read it. Apparently, life in the Harrison offices was memorable. There are commercial artists in New York today who will tell you how they would be quietly working away on some layout when a door would open and in would tramp some margarine-faced babe in a brassiere, panties and spike heels, with a six-foot length of chain over her shoulder, dragging it over the floor. Harrison, who half the time slept in the office and worked around the clock, would be just waking up and out he would charge, fighting off the sebaceous sleepers from his eyes and already setting up the day's shots, with his piston-driven Dr. Grabow voice, as if the sound of the dragging chain had been the gong of dawn.

"And then a funny thing happened," Harrison is saying, "one day my accountant calls up and asks me to meet him down at Longchamps. So I am talking to him in Longchamps and he informs me that I am broke. Broke! After making all that money! I couldn't believe what he was telling me! I think the thing was, we had six magazines, and if six magazines start losing money for a few months, you can lose hundreds of thousands of dollars and not even know what happened.

"Now, listen to this, I think this is a hell of a story. He told me I was busted, so I was looking for an idea. And that same week, I thought up *Confidential*. That same week. I think this is a hell of a story, because I'm not a rich man's son. I'm not one of these guys like

Huntington Hartford who can start one thing, and if that flops, so what, start something else.

"Anyway, we put together the first issue of *Confidential.* It must have taken about six months to do it.

"But that first issue of *Confidential* was lousy. I must have ripped that thing apart three times before I published it, and it still wasn't right. The first one went for 250,000 copies. That was in December, 1952. Those first issues were terrible. If you saw them and then you saw what we did later, you wouldn't even think it was the same magazine."

In point of fact, to the unpracticed eye they look precisely alike; but, then, the unpracticed eye does not comprehend the *aesthetique du schlock.*

"But in that second issue we had a story about Winchell, and he really liked that story. That was what really—"

And here comes Reggie. She's back, as bouffant blonde and furred out as ever, bereft only of the dog, and in Lindy's all these necks are sloshing around in the shirt fronts watching her progress to the table. Harrison is blasé about the whole thing. Reggie settles in. The dog is all right. Reggie wants some lox, too. Harrison goes on about Winchell.

"I took the magazine over to Winchell and showed it to him. We had this story called, 'Winchell Was Right About Josephine Baker.' Josephine Baker had made a scene in some club, I forget which one, she said she was being discriminated against because she was a Negro or something like that, and Winchell said she was exploiting the race thing, and there was a lot of criticism of Winchell over what he wrote. So we ran this story, 'Winchell Was Right About Josephine Baker,' and he loved it."

Just then there is a page call for Harrison to go to the telephone, so he gets up and I get to talking with Reggie. For such a visual phenomenon, she has a small voice and a quiet manner. She is telling me how she met Harrison. Her family had fled Eastern Europe after the war and had settled in Canada. Reggie had done a lot of modeling and been Miss this and that, such as Miss BMC, but she really wants to act. Anyway, a couple of years ago somebody had gotten her a job doing some modeling for something Harrison was working on.

"But as soon as I met him," Reggie says, "I wasn't interested in the job. I was interested in him. He's a very, you know, a very exciting guy."

Well, Reggie was having some problems with the immigration people over her status in the U.S.A., and one day there is a knock on the door of the apartment where she is staying with this girl friend, and it is the immigration people. They ask her all these questions about what she's doing, and then one of them tells her that she has been seen quite a bit in the company of this elderly man.

"That was Bob they were talking about!" Reggie says. She certainly does laugh at that. "I told Bob that he was The Elderly Man. He didn't like that too much, I don't think."

But everything had been straightened out and it was an exciting life. Just the other day Bob had called up Winchell's office to ask about something, and his secretary said she would take the message.

"And do you know," Reggie says, "in a little while Winchell called back himself. Bob was happy about that. They were good friends, you know. Bob comes over here to Lindy's quite a bit. He'd like to, you know, he kind of hopes he'll run into Winchell and sort of see if they're still friends. You know."

Harrison comes back to the table and says, "That was Helen."

Reggie says, "Is Tessie behaving?"

Harrison says, "Yeah." He seems a little distracted.

"I was telling him," Reggie says, "about how you were The Elderly Man."

Reggie laughs. Harrison finesses the whole subject and looks up toward the door.

"Winchell hasn't been in," Reggie says.

Harrison looks back. The cloud passes.

"Anyway," Harrison resumes, "Winchell liked that story so much, he plugged it on the air. Winchell had this program on, I forget what network, it was the hottest thing on television then. One night he held up a copy of *Confidential*, right on television. And I'm telling you, from then on, this thing flew. That was what really made *Confidential*, the publicity.

"Well, we started running a Winchell piece every issue. We'd try to figure out who Winchell didn't like and run a piece about them. One of them was 'Broadway's Biggest Double Cross.' It was about all the ingrates who Winchell had helped to start their careers who turned their backs on him and double-crossed him or something. We had one in every issue. And he kept on plugging *Confidential*. It got to the point where some days we would sit down and rack our brains trying to think of somebody else Winchell didn't like. We were running out of people, for Christ's sake!

"Pretty soon everybody believes we have a deal going with Winchell or that he owns a piece of *Confidential*. I think they called him in over at the *Mirror* and asked him about it. They thought he was investing in the magazine. But there was never anything like that. We never offered Winchell anything, and it wouldn't have been any use anyway. A lot of people tried to buy their way into his column, and they never got to first base. You can't buy Winchell. With *Confidential*, he was just crazy about the stuff we were printing, and he kept plugging it on television. Well, we had advance word once that he was going to plug one issue on television, and I happened to tell the distributor about it. And this guy sends out a notice to the dealers all over the goddamned country to stock up on a lot of this issue because Winchell is going to plug it on television. That was a stupid thing for this guy to do, because it makes it look like we have a deal with Winchell. Well, somehow, Winchell heard about this, and he really blew his stack. Luckily, none of this ever got in the papers, but by now even Winchell himself is wondering what's going on. One day he meets me in here, in Lindy's, and he sits down and says, 'Bob, you've got to tell me one thing. How the hell did I ever get involved with *Confidential*, I can't figure it out.' I had to laugh over that."

Well, the money was pouring in, Harrison is saying. *Confidential* opened a big office, about 4,000 square feet, at 1697 Broadway, but they never had more than about fifteen people on the staff.

"After we got going, people would come to us with stories about themselves, or their families, like I was telling you.

"Breen wrote half the stories himself. That guy was a fabulous writer! But you know what ruined Breen? He was making too much money, and that started him drinking. He must have been making forty or fifty thousand a year, and he never had money like that before, and he was living high and he started drinking. The trouble was, I guess, he had it too good! After a while he was drunk all the time. I remember we put out one whole issue up in Memorial Hospital, I think that was the name of it. He was in one room, for treatment, and I took the room next to it, and we put out the whole goddamned issue up there.

"Anyway we were selling five million. There's never been anything like it. And the real thing behind it was, we had a definite style. Nothing was just thrown together. Sometimes we would work on a layout for days. And those stories were beautifully written. They were *superb!* We were asked by many schools of journalism to come and lecture. Yeah! They wanted to know how we did it."

Pretty soon, though, for the *aesthetes du schlock*, life began to get too goddamned much with them.

"There was all this indignation," Harrison is saying, "and it got so the insurance companies canceled everybody's life insurance who worked for *Confidential*. We were supposed to be 'poor risks.' One of the columnists ran a story saying I had been taken for a ride by some gangsters. It was a completely phony story, but when Winchell read about it, he was mad as hell and he called up and said, 'What's the idea of not giving me that story first?' I told him there was nothing to it, it never happened, but he didn't believe it.

"Some guys did start to take me for a ride one night, though, right out here on Broadway, some gangsters, we had run some story about the jukeboxes or the garment industry, I forget which one. They pushed me in this car, and they said, 'This is it, Harrison, this is where you get yours,' or something like that, I don't remember. So I said, 'Let's get it over with. You'll be doing me a favor.' 'A favor?' this guy says. 'Yeah,' I said, 'I have cancer, it's incurable, I'm in pain all the time, I'm living on morphine, but I haven't got the guts to shoot myself. You'll be doing me a favor. I haven't got the guts.' So they throw me back out of the car on the sidewalk and this guy says, 'Let the bastard suffer!' I always had to use psychology with those guys.

"That's one thing everybody forgets about *Confidential.* We ran a lot of stories exposing the rackets, the jukebox rackets, the garment rackets, gambling, this deal where they had a regular casino going in an airplane. We drove that operation out of New York. I covered that one myself and took pictures in the airplane with a concealed camera. When those guys want to get you, that's a compliment. We ran stories exposing how children were dying from eating candy-flavored aspirin, and how boric acid was poison, and a lot of things like that. But we had to have the other stuff, the gossip, to sell the magazine, or we could have never run these stories at all. Nobody remembers that part of it, but that magazine was a goddamned public service."

Another time, Harrison was saying, somebody's goons, the jukebox mob he believes it was, came in his office and hung him out the window by his heels, head down. They wanted a retraction. He didn't remember what psychology he used then, but anyhow they pulled him back up. Another time he ran into a big mobster, he forgets what his name was, happened to be sitting at the table next to him in one of the nightclubs with his lawyer, and he tells Harrison, "One night, buddy, you're liable to find yourself in the East River with a concrete suit on, you know that, don't you?" They really talk like that, Harrison is saying. So he just tells the guy, "You know what the circulation of *Confidential* is?" The guy says, What. Six million, says Harrison. He ups it a million or so for good measure. He's right, the lawyer says. Better lay off. It would create too big a noise. Psychology.

"But the wildest thing was Izzy the Eel. One day I walk in here, in Lindy's, and here is this girl I know. She's sitting with this guy, a very well-dressed guy, and I think I know him from someplace. He looks like a garment manufacturer I knew on Seventh Avenue. 'Don't I know you?' I says to him. 'Yeah, and don't I know you?' he says. And the girl introduces us.

"So we're talking, and this guy is very friendly, he asks me where I live. So I tell him, it's the same place I live in now, the Madison. 'Oh, yeah,' the guy says, 'the Madison, a nice place, I've been in apartments in there, it's nice, where is yours in there?' So I tell him, in fact, I practically give him a blueprint of the place, how the rooms are laid out, everything. So we talk a little more, and then I leave and I don't think any more of it.

"Well, the next day I get a call from this girl, and her voice is shaking. She's really upset. 'Bob,' she says, 'I got to see you. It's urgent. You're in trouble.' So I meet her someplace and she says, 'You know who that guy was you were talking to with me yesterday?' And I say, 'Yeah.' And she says, 'That was Izzy the Eel!' 'Izzy the Eel?' I says. And she says, 'Yeah, and he's planning to kidnap you, for ransom. He thinks you and him were in Dannemora together, and now that you're making a lot of money from *Confidential*, he's going to get some of it.' 'He's out of his mind,' I said, 'I've never been in a prison in my life.'

"Well, this was one of those times I was lucky again. About a week after that I pick up the papers and Izzy the Eel has been picked up in a shooting case. Eventually they put him away for fifteen years.

"All this time I was getting all these phone calls. They'd say something like 'You're gonna get it tonight,' and hang up. Sure. I was scared, but I couldn't stay locked up in the apartment all day. So I used some psychology. I bought the biggest white Cadillac convertible they make, it was like a goddamned Caribbean yacht, and I drove all over New York, telling the world I didn't give a damn and I wasn't scared of anybody."

Well, there was that time when Harrison got shot in the Dominican Republic. But that was different. He says he was down there doing a story on a drug the Dominicans developed, called Pego-Palo, that was supposed to do great things for virility. He was out in the wilds when he got shot under "mysterious circumstances." There were headlines all over the United States saying "*Confidential* Publisher Shot."

"Anyway, that thing brought us tremendous publicity. Not long after that I was on the Mike Wallace show on television. Wallace was known as the great prosecutor then or something like that." Inquisitor? "Yeah, one of those things. There was nothing prearranged on that show. All I knew was that he would really try to let me have it. So he starts after me right away. He's very sarcastic. 'Why don't you admit it, Harrison, that so-called shooting in the Dominican Republic was a fake, a publicity stunt, wasn't it? You weren't shot at all, were you?' So I said to him, 'Would you know a bullet wound if you saw one?' He says, 'Yeah.' So I start taking off my shirt right there in front of the camera. Those guys didn't know what to do, die or play organ music. I can see the cameramen and everybody is running around the studio like crazy. Well, I have this big mole on my back, a birthmark, and the cameramen are all so excited, they think that's the bullet hole and they put the camera right on that. Well, that mole's the size of a nickel, so on television it looked like I'd been shot clean through with a cannon! That was funny. They never heard the end of it, about that show!"

All these things kept happening, Harrison said. His life was always full of this drama, it was like living in the middle of a hurricane. It finally wore him out, he is saying. "It wasn't the libel suits.

"Some of these people we wrote about would be very indignant at first, but I knew goddamned well it was a beautiful act. What they really wanted was *another* story in *Confidential*. It was great publicity for them. You couldn't put out a magazine like *Confidential* again. You know why? Because all the movie stars have started writing books about *themselves!* Look at the stuff Flynn wrote, and Zsa Zsa Gabor, and all of them. They tell all! No magazine can compete with that. That's what really finished the *Confidential* type of thing."

So Harrison retired with his soap-bubble lawsuits and his pile of money to the sedentary life of stock-market investor.

"I got into the stock market quite by accident," Harrison is saying. "This guy told me of a good stock to invest in, Fairchild Camera, so I bought a thousand shares. I made a quarter of a million dollars the first month! I said to myself, 'Where the hell has *this* business been all my life!' "

Harrison's sensational good fortune on the stock market lasted just about that long, one month.

"So I started putting out the one-shots, but there was no *continuity* in them. So then I got the idea of *Inside News*."

Suddenly Harrison's eyes are fixed on the door. There, by god, in the door is Walter Winchell. Winchell has on his snap-brim police reporter's hat, circa 1924, and an overcoat with the collar turned up. He's scanning the room, like Wild Bill Hickock entering the Crazy Legs Saloon. Harrison gives him a big smile and a huge wave. "There's Walter!" he says.

Winchell gives an abrupt wave with his left hand, keeps his lips set like bowstrings and walks off to the opposite side of Lindy's.

After a while, a waiter comes around, and Harrison says, "Who is Walter with?"

"He's with his granddaughter."

By and by Harrison, Reggie and I got up to leave, and at the door Harrison says to the maître d':

"Where's Walter?"

"He left a little while ago," the maître d' says.

"He was with his granddaughter," Harrison says.

"Oh, was that who that was," the maître d' says.

"Yeah," says Harrison. "It was his granddaughter. I didn't want to disturb them."

In the cab on the way back to the Madison Hotel Harrison says, "You know, we've got a hell of a cute story in *Inside News* about this girl who's divorcing her husband because all he does at night is watch the Johnny Carson show and then he just falls into bed and goes to sleep and won't even give her a tumble. It's a very cute story, very inoffensive.

"Well, I have an idea. I'm going to take this story and show it to Johnny Carson. I think he'll go for it. Maybe we can work out something. You know, he goes through the audience on the show, and so one night Reggie can be in the audience and she can have this copy of *Inside News* with her. When he comes by, she can get up and say, 'Mr. Carson, I see by this newspaper here, *Inside News*, that your show is breaking up happy marriages,' or something like that. And then she can hold up *Inside News* and show him the story and he can make a gag out of it. I think he'll go for it. What do you think? I think it'll be a hell of a cute stunt."

Nobody says anything for a minute, then Harrison says, sort of moodily,

"I'm not putting out *Inside News* for the money. I just want to prove —there are a lot of people say I was just a flash in the pan. I just want to prove I can do it again."

The Evolution of the Species: The Twelve-Year-Old and Her Father's Love

1951

“Poor Daddy, he doesn't even know how Oedipal this all is.”

1981

“My other daddies liked to do this, too. Hurts your freakin' ribs.”

A SUNDAY KIND OF LOVE

Love! Attar of libido in the air! It is 8:45 A.M. Thursday morning in the IRT subway station at 50th Street and Broadway and already two kids are hung up in a kind of herringbone weave of arms and legs, which proves, one has to admit, that love is not *confined* to Sunday in New York. Still, the odds! All the faces come popping in clots out of the Seventh Avenue local, past the King Size Ice Cream machine, and the turnstiles start whacking away as if the world were breaking up on the reefs. Four steps past the turnstiles everybody is already backed up haunch to paunch for the climb up the ramp and the stairs to the surface, a great funnel of flesh, wool, felt, leather, rubber and steaming alumicron, with the blood squeezing through everybody's old sclerotic arteries in hopped-up spurts from too much coffee and the effort of surfacing from the subway at the rush hour. Yet there on the landing are a boy and a girl, both about eighteen, in one of those utter, My Sin, backbreaking embraces.

He envelops her not only with his arms but with his chest, which has the American teen-ager concave shape to it. She has her head cocked at a 90-degree angle and they both have their eyes pressed shut for all they are worth and some incredibly feverish action going with each other's mouths. All round them, ten, scores, it seems like hundreds, of faces and bodies are perspiring, trooping and bellying up the stairs with arteriosclerotic grimaces past a showcase full of such novel items as Joy Buzzers, Squirting Nickels, Finger Rats, Scary Tarantulas and spoons with realistic dead flies on them, past Fred's barbershop, which is just off the landing and has glossy photographs of young men with the kind of baroque haircuts one can get in there,

From *The Kandy-Kolored Tangerine-Flake Streamline Baby*. First published in *New York*, the *New York Herald Tribune*'s Sunday magazine, February 9, 1964.

and up onto 50th Street into a madhouse of traffic and shops with weird lingerie and gray hair-dyeing displays in the windows, signs for free teacup readings and a pool-playing match between the Playboy Bunnies and Downey's Showgirls, and then everybody pounds on toward the Time-Life Building, the Brill Building or NBC.

The boy and the girl just keep on writhing in their embroilment. Her hand is sliding up the back of his neck, which he turns when her fingers wander into the intricate formal gardens of his Chicago Boxcar hairdo at the base of the skull. The turn causes his face to start to mash in the ciliated hull of her beehive hairdo, and so she rolls her head 180 degrees to the other side, using their mouths for the pivot. But aside from good hair grooming, they are oblivious to everything but each other. Everybody gives them a once-over. Disgusting! Amusing! How touching! A few kids pass by and say things like "Swing it, baby." But the great majority in that heaving funnel up the stairs seem to be as much astounded as anything else. The vision of love at rush hour cannot strike anyone exactly as romance. It is a feat, like a fat man crossing the English Channel in a barrel. It is an earnest accomplishment against the tide. It is a piece of slightly gross heroics, after the manner of those knobby, varicose old men who come out from some place in baggy shorts every year and run through the streets of Boston in the Marathon race. And somehow that is the gaffe against love all week long in New York, for everybody, not just two kids writhing under their coiffures in the 50th Street subway station; too hurried, too crowded, too hard, and no time for dalliance. Which explains why the real thing in New York is, as it says in the song, a Sunday kind of love.

There is Saturday, but Saturday is not much better than Monday through Friday. Saturday is the day for errands in New York. More millions of shoppers are pouring in to keep the place jammed up. Everybody is bobbing around, running up to Yorkville to pick up these arty cheeses for this evening, or down to Fourth Avenue to try to find this Van Vechten book, *Parties*, to complete the set for somebody, or off to the cleaner's, the dentist's, the hairdresser's, or some guy's who is going to loan you his station wagon to pick up two flush doors to make tables out of, or over to some place somebody mentioned that is supposed to have fabulous cuts of meat and the butcher wears a straw hat and arm garters and is colorfully rude.

True, there is Saturday night, and Friday night. They are fine for dates and good times in New York. But for the dalliance of love, they are just as stupefying and wound up as the rest of the week. On Friday and Saturday nights everybody is making some kind of scene. It may be a cellar cabaret in the Village where five guys from some place talk "Jamaican" and pound steel drums and the Connecticut teen-agers wear plaid ponchos and knee-high boots and drink such things as Passion Climax cocktails, which are made of apple cider with watermelon balls thrown in. Or it may be some cellar in the East 50's, a discotheque, where the alabaster kids come on in sleeveless minksides jackets, tweed evening dresses and cool-it Modernismus hairdos. But either way, it's a scene, a production, and soon the evening begins to whirl, like the whole world with the bed-spins, in a montage of taxis, slithery legs slithering in, slithery legs slithering out, worsted, piqué, grins, eye teeth, glissandos, buffoondos, tips, par lamps, doormen, lines, magenta ropes, white dickies, mirrors and bar bottles, pink men and shawl-collared coats, hatcheck girls and neon peach fingernails, taxis, keys, broken lamps and no coat hangers. . . .

And, then, an unbelievable dawning; Sunday, in New York.

George G., who writes "Z" ads for a department store, keeps saying that all it takes for him is to smell coffee being made at a certain point in the percolation. It doesn't matter where. It could be the worst death-ball hamburger dive. All he has to do is smell it, and suddenly he finds himself swimming, drowning, dissolving in his own reverie of New York's Sunday kind of love.

Anne A.'s apartment was nothing, he keeps saying, and that was the funny thing. She lived in Chelsea. It was this one room with a cameo-style carving of a bored Medusa on the facing of the mantelpiece, this one room plus a kitchen, in a brownstone sunk down behind a lot of loft buildings and truck terminals and so forth. Beautiful Chelsea. But on Sunday morning by 10:30 the sun would be hitting cleanly between two rearview buildings and making it through the old no man's land of gas effluvia ducts, restaurant vents, aerials, fire escapes, stairwell doors, clotheslines, chimneys, skylights, vestigial lightning rods, Mansard slopes, and those peculiarly bleak, filthy and misshapen backsides of New York buildings, into Anne's kitchen.

George would be sitting at this rickety little table with an oilcloth over it. How he goes on about it! The place was grimy. You couldn't keep the soot out. The place was beautiful. Anne is at the stove making coffee. The smell of the coffee being made, just the smell . . . already he is turned on. She had on a great terrycloth bathrobe with a sash belt. The way she moved around inside that bathrobe with the sun shining in the window always got him. It was the *at*mosphere of the thing. There she was, moving around in that great fluffy bathrobe with the sun hitting her hair, and they had all the time in the world. There wasn't even one flatulent truck horn out on Eighth Avenue. Nobody was clobbering their way down the stairs in high heels out in the hall at 10 minutes to 9.

Anne would make scrambled eggs, plain scrambled eggs, but it was a feast. It was incredible. She would bring out a couple of these little smoked fish with golden skin and some smoked oysters that always came in a little can with ornate lettering and royal colors and flourishes and some Kissebrot bread and black cherry preserves, and then the coffee. They had about a million cups of coffee apiece, until the warmth seemed to seep through your whole viscera. And then cigarettes. The cigarettes were like some soothing incense. The radiator was always making a hissing sound and then a clunk. The sun was shining in and the fire escapes and effluvia ducts were just silhouettes out there someplace. George would tear off another slice of Kissebrot and pile on some black cherry preserves and drink some more coffee and have another cigarette, and Anne crossed her legs under her terrycloth bathrobe and crossed her arms and drew on her cigarette, and that was the way it went.

"It was the *torpor*, boy," he says. "It was beautiful. Torpor is a beautiful, underrated thing. Torpor is a luxury. Especially in this stupid town. There in that kitchen it was like being in a perfect cocoon of love. Everything was beautiful, a perfect cocoon."

By and by they would get dressed, always in as shiftless a getup as possible. She would put on a big heavy sweater, a raincoat and a pair of faded slacks that gripped her like neoprene rubber. He would put on a pair of corduroy pants, a crew sweater with moth holes and a raincoat. Then they would go out and walk down to 14th Street for the Sunday paper.

All of a sudden it was great out there on the street in New York. All those damnable millions who come careening into Manhattan all week weren't there. The town was empty. To a man and woman shuffling along there, torpid, in the cocoon of love, it was as if all of rotten Gotham had improved overnight. Even the people looked better. There would be one of those old dolls with little flabby arms all hunched up in a coat of pastel oatmeal texture, the kind whose lumpy old legs you keep seeing as she heaves her way up the subway stairs ahead of you and holds everybody up because she is so flabby and decrepit . . . and today, Sunday, on good, clean, empty 14th Street, she just looked like a nice old lady. There was no one around to make her look slow, stupid, unfit, unhip, expendable. That was the thing about Sunday. The weasel millions were absent. And Anne walking along beside him with a thready old pair of slacks gripping her like neoprene rubber looked like possibly the most marvelous vision the world had ever come up with, and the cocoon of love was perfect. It was like having your cake and eating it, too. On the one hand, here it was, boy, the prize: New York. All the buildings, the Gotham spires, were sitting up all over the landscape in silhouette like ikons representing all that was great, glorious and triumphant in New York. And, on the other hand, there were no weasel millions bellying past you and eating crullers on the run with the crumbs flaking off the corners of their mouths as a reminder of how much *Angst* and *Welthustle* you had to put into the town to get any of that out of it for yourself. All there was was the cocoon of love, which was complete. It was like being inside a scenic Easter Egg where you look in and the Gotham spires are just standing there like a little gemlike backdrop.

By and by the two of them would be back in the apartment sprawled out on the floor rustling through the Sunday paper, all that even black ink appliquéd on big fat fronds of paper. Anne would put an E. Power Biggs organ record on the hi-fi, and pretty soon the old trammeler's bass chords would be vibrating through you as if he had clamped a diathermy machine on your solar plexus. So there they would be, sprawled out on the floor, rustling through the Sunday paper, getting bathed and massaged by E. Power Biggs' sonic waves. It was like taking peyote or something. This marvelously high feeling would come over them, as though they were psychedelic, and the most commonplace objects took on this great radiance and significance. It was like old Aldous Huxley in his drug experiments, sitting there hooking down peyote buttons and staring at a clay geranium pot on a table, which gradually became the most fabulous geranium pot in God's world. The way it curved . . . why, it curved 360 d-e-g-r-e-e-s! And the clay . . . why, it was the color of the earth itself! And the top . . . It had a r-i-m on it! George had the same feeling. Anne's apartment . . . it was hung all over the place with the usual New York working girl's modern prints, the Picasso scrawls, the Mondrians curling at the corners . . . somehow nobody ever gets even a mat for a Mondrian print . . . the Toulouse-Lautrecs with that guy with the chin kicking his silhouette leg, the Klees, that Paul Klee is cute . . . why, all of a sudden these were the most beautiful things in the whole hagiology of art . . . the way that guy with the chin k-i-c-k-s t-h-a-t l-e-g, the way that Paul Klee h-i-t-s t-h-a-t b-a-l-l . . . the way that apartment just wrapped around them like a cocoon, with lint under the couch like angel's hair, and the plum cover on the bed lying halfway on the floor in folds like the folds in a Tiepolo cherub's silks, and the bored Medusa on the mantelpiece looking like the most splendidly, gloriously b-o-r-e-d Medusa in the face of time!

"Now, that was love," says George, "and there has never been anything like it. I don't know what happens to it. Unless it's Monday. Monday sort of happens to it in New York."

The New Cookie

What are Mom & the
  Bonneville & Buddy & Sis
Up against a love like this?
That first night on
  the disco floor
She wore a pair
  of boxing trunks
While leather punks
  and painted lulus,
African queens
  and sado-zulus
Paid her court.
I grow old the 1970s way:
Deaf, but from a
  Max Q octaphonic beat,
Stroked out, but on
  my own two feet,
Disco macho!—for you,
  my New Cookie.

THE GIRL OF THE YEAR

Bangs manes bouffants beehives Beatle caps butter faces brush-on lashes decal eyes puffy sweaters French thrust bras flailing leather blue jeans stretch pants stretch jeans honeydew bottoms eclair shanks elf boots ballerinas Knight slippers, hundreds of them, these flaming little buds, bobbing and screaming, rocketing around inside the Academy of Music Theater underneath that vast old mouldering cherub dome up there—aren't they super-marvelous!

"Aren't they super-marvelous!" says Baby Jane, and then: "Hi, Isabel! Isabel! You want to sit backstage—with the Stones!"

The show hasn't even started yet, the Rolling Stones aren't even on the stage, the place is full of a great shabby mouldering dimness, and these flaming little buds.

Girls are reeling this way and that way in the aisle and through their huge black decal eyes, sagging with Tiger Tongue Lick Me brush-on eyelashes and black appliqués, sagging like display window Christmas trees, they keep staring at—her—Baby Jane—on the aisle. What the hell is this? She is gorgeous in the most outrageous way. Her hair rises up from her head in a huge hairy corona, a huge tan mane around a narrow face and two eyes opened—swock!—like umbrellas, with all that hair flowing down over a coat made of . . . *ze*bra! Those motherless stripes! Oh, damn! Here she is with her friends, looking like some kind of queen bee for all flaming little buds everywhere. She twists around to shout to one of her friends and that incredible mane swings around on her shoulders, over the zebra coat.

"Isabel!" says Baby Jane, "Isabel, hi! I just saw the Stones: They look super-divine!"

From *The Kandy-Kolored Tangerine-Flake Streamline Baby.* First published in *New York*, the *New York Herald Tribune*'s Sunday magazine, December 6, 1964.

That girl on the aisle, Baby Jane, is a fabulous girl. She comprehends what the Rolling Stones *mean.* Any columnist in New York could tell them who she is . . . a celebrity of New York's new era of Wog Hip . . . Baby Jane Holzer. Jane Holzer in *Vogue*, Jane Holzer in *Life*, Jane Holzer in Andy Warhol's underground movies, Jane Holzer in the world of High Camp, Jane Holzer at the rock and roll, Jane Holzer is—well, how can one put it into words? Jane Holzer is This Year's Girl, at least, the New Celebrity, none of your old idea of sexpots, prima donnas, romantic tragediennes, she is the girl who knows . . . The Stones, East End vitality . . .

"Isabel!" says Jane Holzer in the small, high, excited voice of hers, her Baby Jane voice, "Hi, Isabel! Hi!"

Down the row, Isabel, Isabel Eberstadt, the beautiful socialite who is Ogden Nash's daughter, has just come in. She doesn't seem to hear Jane. But she is down the row a ways. Next to Jane is some fellow in a chocolate-colored Borsalino hat, and next there is Andy Warhol, the famous pop artist.

"Isabel!" says Jane.

"What?" says Isabel.

"Hi, Isabel!" says Jane.

"Hello, Jane," says Isabel.

"You want to go backstage?" says Jane, who has to speak across everybody.

"Backstage?" says Isabel.

"With the Stones!" says Jane. "I was backstage with the Stones. They look *divine!* You know what Mick said to me? He said, 'Koom on, love, give us a kiss!' "

But Isabel has turned away to say something to somebody.

"Isabel!" says Jane.

And all around, the little buds are batting around in the rococo gloom of the Academy of Arts Theater, trying to crash into good seats or just sit in the aisle near the stage, shrieking. And in the rear the Voice of Fifteen-year-old America cries out in a post-pubertal contralto, apropos of nothing, into the mouldering void: "Yaaaagh! Yuh dirty fag!"

Well, so what; Jane laughs. Then she leans over and says to the fellow in the Borsalino hat:

"Wait'll you see the Stones! They're so sexy! They're pure sex. They're *divine!* The Beatles, well, you know, Paul McCartney—*sweet* Paul McCartney. You know what I mean. He's such a *sweet person.* I mean, the Stones are *bitter*—" the words seem to spring from her lungs like some kind of wonderful lavender-yellow Charles Kingsley bubbles "—they're all from the working class, you know? the East End. Mick Jagger—well, it's all Mick. You know what they say about his lips? They say his lips are *diabolical.* That was in one of the magazines.

"When Mick comes into the Ad Lib in London—I mean, there's nothing like the Ad Lib in New York. You can go into the Ad Lib and everybody is there. They're all young, and they're taking over, it's like a whole revolution. I mean, it's *exciting,* they're all from the lower classes, East End-sort-of-thing. There's nobody exciting from the upper classes anymore, except for Nicole and Alec Londonderry, Alec is a British marquis, the Marquis of Londonderry, and, O.K., Nicole has to put in an appearance at this country fair or something, well, O.K., she does it, but that doesn't mean—you know what I mean? Alec is so—you should see the way he walks, I could just watch him walk—*Undoes-one-ship!* They're *young.* They're all young, it's a whole new thing. It's not the Beatles. Bailey says the Beatles are *passé,* because now everybody's mum pats the Beatles on the head. The Beatles are getting fat. The Beatles—well, John Lennon's still thin, but Paul McCartney is getting a big bottom. That's all right, but I don't particularly care for that. The Stones are thin. I mean, that's why they're beautiful, they're so thin. Mick Jagger—wait'll you see Mick."

Then the show begins. An electronic blast begins, electric guitars, electric bass, enormous speakers up there on a vast yellow-gray stage. Murray the K, the D. J. and M. C., O.K.?, comes out from the wings, doing a kind of twist soft shoe, wiggling around, a stocky chap, thirty-eight years old, wearing Italian pants and a Sun Valley snow lodge sweater and a Stingy Brim straw hat. Murray the K! Girls throw balls of paper at him, and as they arc onto the stage, the stage lights explode off them and they look like falling balls of flame.

And, finally, the Stones, now—how can one express it? the Stones come on stage—

"Oh, God, Andy, aren't they *divine!*"

—and spread out over the stage, the five Rolling Stones, from England, who are modeled after the Beatles, only more lower-class-deformed. One, Brian Jones, has an enormous blonde Beatle bouffant.

"Oh, Andy, look at Mick! Isn't he *beauti*ful! Mick! Mick!"

In the center of the stage a short thin boy with a sweat shirt on, the neck of the sweat shirt almost falling over his shoulders, they are so narrow, all surmounted by this . . . enormous head . . . with the hair puffing down over the forehead and ears, this boy has exceptional lips. He has two peculiarly gross and extraordinary red lips. They hang off his face like giblets. Slowly his eyes pour over the flaming bud horde soft as Karo syrup and then close and then the lips start spreading into the most lanquid, most confidential, the wettest, most labial, most concupiscent grin imaginable. Nirvana! The buds start shrieking, pawing toward the stage.

The girls have Their Experience. They stand up on their seats. They begin to ululate, even between songs. The looks on their faces! Rapturous agony! There, right up there, under the sulphur lights, that is *them.* God, they're right there! Mick Jagger takes the microphone with his tabescent hands and puts his huge head against it, opens his giblet lips and begins to sing . . . with the voice of a bull Negro. Bo Diddley. You movung boo meb bee-uhtul, bah-bee, oh vona breemb you' honey snurks oh crim pulzy yo' mim down, and, camping again, then turning toward the shrieking girls with his wet giblet lips dissolving . . .

And, occasionally, breaking through the ululation:

"Get off the stage, you finks!"

"Maybe we ought to scream," says Jane. Then she says to the fellow in the hat: "Tell me when it's five o'clock, will you, pussycat? I have to get dressed and go see Sam Spiegel." And then Baby Jane goes: "Eeeeeeeeeeeeeeeeeeee

eeeeeeeeeeeeeeeeyes!" says Diana Vreeland, the editor of *Vogue.* "Jane Holzer is the most contemporary girl I know."

Jane Holzer at the rock and roll—

Jane Holzer in the underground movies—in Andy's studio, Andy Warhol, the famous Pop artist, experiencing the rare world of Jonas and Adolph Mekas, truth and culture in a new holy medium, underground movie-making on the lower East Side. And Jane is wearing a Jax shirt, strung like a Christmas tree with Diamonds, and they are making *Dracula,* or *Thirteen Beautiful Women* or *Soap Opera* or *Kiss* —in which Jane's lips . . . but how can one describe an underground movie? It *is* . . . avant-garde. "Andy calls everything super," says Jane. "I'm a super star, he's a super-director, we make super epics—and I mean, it's a completely new and natural way of acting. You can't imagine what really beautiful things can happen!"

Jane Holzer—with The New Artists, photographers like Jerry Schatzberg, David Bailey and Brian Duffy, and Nicky Haslam, the art director of *Show.* Bailey, Duffy and Haslam are English. Schatzberg says the photographers are the modern-day equivalents of the Impressionists in Paris around 1910, the men with a sense of New Art, the excitement of the salon, the excitement of the artistic style of life, while all the painters, the old artists, have moved uptown to West End Avenue and live in apartment buildings with Kwik-Fiks parquet floors and run around the corner to get a new cover for the ironing board before the stores close.

Jane in the world of High Camp—a world of thin young men in an environment, a decor, an atmosphere so—how can one say it?—so indefinably Yellow Book. Jane in the world of Teen Savage—Jane modeling here and there—wearing Jean Harlow dresses for *Life* and Italian fashions for *Vogue* and doing the most fabulous cover for Nicky at *Show*. David took the photograph, showing Jane barebacked wearing a little yacht cap and a pair of "World's Fair" sunglasses and holding an American flag in her teeth, so—so Beyond Pop Art, if you comprehend.

Jane Holzer at the LBJ Discotheque—where they were handing out aprons with a target design on them, and Jane Holzer put it on backward so that the target was behind and *then* did The Swim, a new dance.

Jane Holzer—well, there is no easy term available, Baby Jane has appeared constantly this year in just about every society and show business column in New York. The magazines have used her as a kind of combination of model, celebrity and socialite. And yet none of them have been able to do much more than, in effect, set down her name, Baby Jane Holzer, and surround it with a few asterisks and exploding stars, as if to say, well, here we have . . . What's Happening.

She is a socialite in the sense that she lives in a twelve-room apartment on Park Avenue with a wealthy husband, Leonard Holzer, heir to a real estate fortune, amid a lot of old Dutch and Flemish paintings, and she goes to a great many exciting parties. And yet she is not in Society the way the Good Book, the *Social Register*, thinks of Society, and the list of hostesses who have not thought of inviting Jane Holzer would be impressive. Furthermore, her stance is that she doesn't care, and she would rather be known as a friend of the Stones, anyway —and here she is at the April in Paris Ball, $150 per ticket, amid the heaving white and gold swag of the Astor Hotel ballroom, yelling to somebody: "If you aren't nice to me, I'll tell everybody you were here!"

Jane Holzer—the sum of it is glamor, of a sort very specific to New York. With her enormous corona of hair and her long straight nose, Jane Holzer can be quite beautiful, but she never comes on as A Beauty. "Some people look at my pictures and say I look very mature and sophisticated," Jane says. "Some people say I look like a child, you know, Baby Jane. And, I mean, I don't know what I look like, I guess it's just 1964 Jewish." She does not attempt to come on sexy. Her excitement is something else. It is almost pure excitement. It is the excitement of the New Style, the New Chic. The press watches Jane Holzer as if she were an exquisite piece of . . . radar. It is as if that entire ciliate corona of hers were spread out as an antenna for new waves of style. To the magazine editors, the newspaper columnists, the photographers and art directors, suddenly here is a single flamboyant girl who sums up everything new and chic in the way of fashion in the Girl of the Year.

How can one explain the Girl of the Year? The Girl of the Year is a symbolic figure the press has looked for annually in New York since World War I because of the breakdown of conventional High Society. The old establishment still holds forth, it still has its clubs, cotillions and coming-out balls, it is still basically Protestant and it still rules two enormously powerful areas of New York, finance and corporate law. But alongside it, all the while, there has existed a large and ever more dazzling society, Café Society it was called in the twenties and thirties, made up of people whose status rests not on property and ancestry but on various brilliant ephemera, show business, advertising, public relations, the arts, journalism or simply new money of various sorts, people with a great deal of ambition who have congregated in New York to satisfy it and who look for styles to symbolize it.

The establishment's own styles—well, for one thing they were too dull. And those understated clothes, dark woods, high ceilings, silversmithery, respectable nannies, and so forth and so on. For centuries their kind of power created styles—Palladian buildings, starched cravats—but with the thickening democratic façade of American life, it has degenerated to various esoteric understatements, often cryptic—Topsiders instead of tennis sneakers, calling cards with "Mr." preceding the name, the right fork.

The magazines and newspapers began looking for heroines to symbolize the Other Society, Café Society, or whatever it should be called. At first, in the twenties, they chose the more flamboyant debutantes, girls with social credentials who also moved in Café Society. But the Other Society's styles began to shift and change at a madder and madder rate, and the Flaming Deb idea no longer worked. The last of the Flaming Debs, the kind of Deb who made The Cover of *Life*, was Brenda Frazier, and Brenda Frazier and Brenda Frazierism went out with the thirties. More recently the Girl of the Year has had to be more and more exotic . . . and extraordinary. Christina Paolozzi! Her exploits! Christina Paolozzi threw a twenty-first birthday party for herself at a Puerto Rican pachanga palace, the Palladium, and after that the spinning got faster and faster until with one last grand centripetal gesture she appeared in the nude, face on, in *Harper's Bazaar*. Some became Girls of the Year because their fame suddenly shed a light on their style of life, and their style of life could be easily exhibited, such as Jackie Kennedy and Barbra Streisand.

But Baby Jane Holzer is a purer manifestation. Her style of life has created her fame—rock and roll, underground movies, decaying lofts, models, photographers, Living Pop Art, the twist, the frug, the mashed potatoes, stretch pants, pre-Raphaelite hair, Le Style Camp. All of it has a common denominator. Once it was power that created high style. But now high styles come from low places, from people who have no power, who slink away from it, in fact, who are marginal, who carve out worlds for themselves in the nether depths, in tainted "undergrounds." The Rolling Stones, like rock and roll itself and the twist—they come out of the netherworld of modern teen-age life, out of what was for years the marginal outcast corner of the world of art, photography, populated by poor boys, pretenders. "Underground" movies—a mixture of camp and Artistic Alienation, with Jonas Mekas crying out like some foggy echo from Harold Stearn's last boat for Le Havre in 1921: "You filthy bourgeois pseudo-culturati! You say you love art—then why don't you give us money to buy the films to make our masterpieces and stop blubbering about the naked asses we show?—you mucky pseuds." Teen-agers, bohos, camp culturati, photographers—they have won by default, because, after all, they *do* create styles. And now the Other Society goes to them for styles, like the decadenti of another age going down to the wharves in Rio to find those raw-vital devils, damn their potent hides, those proles, doing the tango. Yes! Oh my God, those raw-vital proles!

The ice floe is breaking, and can't one see, as Jane Holzer sees, that all these people—well, they *feel*, they are alive, and what does it mean simply to be sitting up in her Park Avenue apartment in the room with two Rubenses on the wall, worth half a million dollars, if they are firmly authenticated? It means almost nothing. One doesn't feel it.

Jane has on a "Poor" sweater, clinging to the ribs, a new fashion, with short sleeves. Her hair is up in rollers. She is wearing tight slacks. Her hips are very small. She has a boyish body. She has thin arms and long, long fingers. She sits twisted about on a couch, up in her apartment on Park Avenue, talking on the telephone.

"Oh, I know what you mean," she says, "but, I mean, couldn't you wait just two weeks? I'm expecting something to jell, it's a movie, and then you'd have a real story. You know what I mean? I mean you would have something to write about and not just Baby Jane sitting up in her Park Avenue apartment with her gotrocks. You know what I mean? . . . well, all right, but I think you'll have more of a story— . . . well, all right . . . bye, pussycat."

Then she hangs up and swings around and says, "That makes me mad. That was ——. He wants to do a story about me and do you know what he told me? 'We want to do a story about you,' he told me, 'because you're very big this year.' Do you know what that made me feel like? That made me feel like, All right, Baby Jane, we'll let you play this year, so get out there and dance, but next year, well, it's all over for you next year, Baby Jane. I mean,—! You know? I mean, I felt like telling him, 'Well, pussycat, you're the Editor of the Minute, and you know what? Your minute's up.' "

The thought leaves Jane looking excited but worried. Usually she looks excited about things but open, happy, her eyes wide open and taking it all in. Now she looks worried, as if the world could be such a simple and exhilarating place if there weren't so many old and arteriosclerotic people around to muck it up. There are two dogs on the floor at her feet, a toy poodle and a Yorkshire terrier, who rise up from time to time in some kind of secret needle-toothed fury, barking coloratura.

"Oh, ——," says Jane, and then, "You know, if you have anything at all, there are so many bitchy people just *waiting* to carve you up. I mean, I went to the opening of the Met and I wore a white mink coat, and do you know what a woman did? A woman called up a columnist and said, 'Ha, ha, Baby Jane rented that coat she went to the Met in. Baby Jane rents her clothes.' That's how bitchy they are. Well, that coat happens to be a coat my mother gave me two years ago when I was married. I mean, I don't care if somebody thinks I rent clothes. O.K. ———! Who cares?"

Inez, the maid, brings in lunch on a tray, one rare hamburger, one cheeseburger and a glass of tomato juice. Jane tastes the tomato juice.

"Oh, ——!" she says. "It's diet."

The Girl of the Year. It is as though nobody wants to give anyone credit for anything. They're only a *phenomenon*. Well, Jane Holzer did a great deal of modeling before she got married and still models, for that matter, and now some very wonderful things may be about to happen in the movies. Some of it, well, she cannot go into it exactly, because it is at that precarious stage—you know? But she has one of the best managers, a woman who manages the McGuire Sisters. And there has been talk about Baby Jane for *Who's Afraid of Virginia Woolf*, the movie, and *Candy*—

"Well, I haven't heard anything about it—but I'd *love* to play Candy."

And this afternoon, later on, she is going over to see Sam Spiegel, the producer.

"He's wonderful. He's, you know, sort of advising me on things at this point."

And somewhere out there in the apartment the dogs are loose in a midget coloratura rage amid patina-green walls and paintings by old Lowland masters. There is a great atmosphere in the apartment, an atmosphere of patina-green, faded plush and the ashy light of Park Avenue reflecting on the great black and umber slicks of the paintings. All that stretches on for twelve rooms. The apartment belongs to the Holzers, who have built a lot of New York's new apartment houses. Jane's husband, Leonard, is a slim, good-looking young man. He went to Princeton. He and Jane were married two years ago. Jane came from Florida, where her father, Carl Brookenfeld, also made a lot of money in real estate. But in a way they were from New York, too, because they were always coming to New York and her father had a place here. There was something so stimulating, so flamboyant, about New York, you know? Fine men with anointed blue jowls combed their hair straight back and had their shirts made at Sulka's or Nica-Rattner's, and their wives had copper-gold hair, real chignons and things, and heavy apricot voices that said the funniest things—"Honey, I've got news for you, you're crazy!"—things like that, and they went to El Morocco. Jane went to Cherry Lawn School in Darien, Connecticut. It was a progressive school.

And then she went to Finch Junior College:

"Oh, that was just ghastly. I wanted to flunk out and go to work. If you miss too many classes, they campus you, if you have a messy room, they campus you, they were always campusing me, and I always sneaked out. The last spring term I didn't spend one night there. I was supposed to be campused and I'd be out dancing at El Morocco. I didn't take my exams because I wanted to flunk out, but do you know what they did? They just said I was out, period. I didn't care about that, because I wanted to flunk out and go to work anyway—but the way they did it. I have a lot of good paintings to give away, and it's too bad, they're not getting any. They were not *educators*. They could have at least kept the door open. They could have said, 'You're not ready to be a serious student, but when you decide to settle down and be a serious student, the door will be open.' I mean, I had already paid for the whole term, they *had* the money. I always wanted to go there and tell them, well, ha ha, too bad, you're not getting any of the paintings. So henceforth, Princeton, which was super-marvelous, will get all the paintings."

Jane's spirits pick up over that. Princeton! Well, Jane left Finch and then she did quite a bit of modeling. Then she married Lennie, and she still did some modeling, but the real break—well the whole *thing* started in summer in London, the summer of 1963.

"Bailey is fantastic," says Jane. "Bailey created four girls that summer. He created Jean Shrimpton, he created me, he created Angela Howard and Susan Murray. There's no photographer like that in America. Avedon hasn't done that for a girl, Penn hasn't, and Bailey created four girls in one summer. He did some pictures of me for the English *Vogue*, and that was all it took."

But how does one really explain about the Stones, about Bailey, Shrimp and Mick—well, it's not so much what they *do*, that's such an old idea, what people *do*—it's what they *are*, it's a revolution, and it's the kids from the East End, Cockneys, if you want, who are making it.

"I mean today Drexel Duke sits next to Weinstein, and why shouldn't he? They both made their money the same way, you know? The furniture king sits next to the catsup king, and why shouldn't he-sort-of-thing. I mean, that's the way it was at the opening of the Met. A friend of mine was going to write an article about it.

"I mean, we don't lie to ourselves. Our mothers taught us to be pure and you'll fall in love and get married and stay in love with one man all your life. O.K. But we know it doesn't happen that way and we don't lie to ourselves about it. Maybe you won't ever find anybody you love. Or maybe you find somebody you love four minutes, maybe ten minutes. But I mean, why lie to yourself? We know we're not going to love one man all our lives. Maybe it's the Bomb—we know it could all be over tomorrow, so why try to fool yourself today. Shrimp was talking about that last night. She's here now, she'll be at the party tonight—"

The two dogs, the toy poodle and the Yorkshire terrier, are yapping, in the patina-green. Inez is looking for something besides diet. The two Rubenses hang up on the walls. A couple of horns come up through the ashy light of Park Avenue. The high wind of East End London is in the air—whhhoooooooo

oooooooooooooosh! Baby Jane blows out all the candles. It is her twenty-fourth birthday. She and everybody, Shrimp, Nicky, Jerry, everybody but Bailey, who is off in Egypt or something, they are all up in Jerry Schatzberg's . . . *pad* . . . his lavish apartment at 333 Park Avenue South, up above his studio. There is a skylight. The cook brings out the cake and Jane blows out the candles. Twenty-four! Jerry and Nicky are giving a huge party, a dance, in honor of the Stones, and already the people are coming into the studio downstairs. But it is also Jane's birthday. She is wearing a black velvet jump suit by Luis Estevez, the designer. It has huge bell-bottom pants. She puts her legs together . . . it looks like an evening dress. But she can also spread them apart, like so, and strike very Jane-like poses. This is like the Upper Room or something. Downstairs, they're all coming in for the party, all those people one sees at parties, everybody who goes to the parties in New York, but up here it is like a tableau, like a tableau of . . . Us. Shrimp is sitting there with her glorious pout and her textured white stockings, Barbara Steele, who was so terrific in *8½*, with thin black lips and wrought-iron eyelashes. Nicky Haslam is there with his Byron shirt on and his tiger skin vest and blue jeans and boots. Jerry is there with his hair flowing back in curls. Lennie, Jane's husband, is there in a British suit and a dark blue shirt he bought on 42nd Street for this party, because this is a party for the Rolling Stones. The Stones are not here yet, but here in the upper room are Goldie and the Gingerbreads, four girls in gold lamé tights who will play the rock and roll for the party. Nicky discovered them at the Wagon Wheel. Gold lamé, can you imagine? Goldie, the leader, is a young girl with a husky voice and nice kind of slightly thick—you know—glorious sort of *East End* features, only she is from New York—ah, the delicacy of mirror grossness, unabashed. The Stones' music is playing over the hi-fi.

Finally the Stones come in, in blue jeans, sweat shirts, the usual, and people get up and Mick Jagger comes in with his mouth open and his eyes down, faintly weary with success, and everybody goes downstairs to the studio, where people are now piling in, hundreds of them. Goldie and the Gingerbreads are on a stand at one end of the studio, all electric, electric guitars, electric bass, drums, loudspeakers, and a couple of spotlights exploding off the gold lamé. *Baby baby baby where did our love go.* The music suddenly fills up the room like a giant egg slicer. Sally Kirkland, Jr., a young actress, is out on the studio floor in a leopard print dress with her vast mane flying, doing the frug with Jerry Schatzberg. And then the other Girl of the Year, Caterine Milinaire, is out there in a black dress, and then Baby Jane is out there with her incredible mane and her Luis Estevez jump suit, frugging, and then everybody is out there. Suddenly it is very odd. Suddenly everybody is out there in the gloaming, bobbing up and down with the music plugged into *Baby baby baby.* The whole floor of the studio begins to bounce up and down, like a trampoline, the whole floor, some people are afraid and edge off to the side, but most keep bobbing in the gloaming, and—pow!—glasses begin to hit the floor, but every one keeps bouncing up and down, crushing the glass underfoot, while the brown whiskey slicks around. So many heads bobbing, so many bodies jiggling, so many giblets jiggling, so much anointed flesh shaking and jiggling this way and that, so many faces one wanted so desperately to see, and here they are, red the color of dried peppers in the gloaming, bouncing up and down with just a few fights, wrenching in the gloaming, until 5 A.M.—gleeeang—Goldie pulls all the electric cords out and the studio is suddenly just a dim ochre studio with broken glass all over the floor, crushed underfoot, and the sweet high smell of brown whiskey rising from the floor.

Monday's papers will record it as the Mods and Rockers Ball, as the Party of the Year, but that is Monday, a long way off. So they all decide they should go to the Brasserie. It is the only place in town where anybody would still be around. So they all get into cabs and go up to the Brasserie, up on 53rd Street between Park and Lexington. The Brasserie is the right place, all right. The Brasserie has a great entrance, elevated over the tables like a fashion show almost. There are, what?, 35 people in the Brasserie. They all look up, and as the first salmon light of dawn comes through the front window, here come . . . four teen-age girls in gold lamé tights, and a chap in a tiger skin vest and blue jeans and a gentleman in an English suit who seems to be wearing a 42nd Street hood shirt and a fellow in a sweater who has flowing curly hair . . . and then, a girl with an incredible mane, a vast tawny corona, wearing a black velvet jump suit. One never knows who is in the Brasserie at this hour—but are there any so dead in here that they do not get the point? Girl of the Year? Listen, they will *never* forget.

The Birds and the Bees

"No, no, son, that's not how it works. When you're forty-five or fifty, you'll get a new wife, a young one, a girl in her twenties."

"What happens to the old one?"

"Well, she opens up a needlepoint shop and sells yarn to her friends and joins a discussion group."

THE WOMAN WHO HAS EVERYTHING

It is a very odd, nice, fey thing. Helene can sit over here with her nylon shanks sunk in the sofa, the downy billows, and watch Jamie over there on one knee, with his back turned, fooling with a paw-foot chair. It's *only Jamie*, an interior decorator. But all right! he has a beautiful *small of the back*. Helene has an urge to pick him up by the waist like a . . . vase. This is a marvelous apartment, on 57th Street practically on Sutton Place. In fact, Helene—well, Helene is a girl who, except for a husband, has everything.

Helene was divorced three years ago. Even so! she is only twenty-five. She went to Smith. She has money, both a great deal of alimony and her own trust fund. She is beautiful. Her face—sort of a hood of thick black hair cut Sassoon fashion with two huge eyes opened within like . . . morning glories—her face is seen in *Vogue, Town & Country*, practically all the New York newspapers, modeling fashions, but with her name always in the caption, which is known as "social" modeling. She is trim, strong, lithe, she exercises. She has only one child. *Only one child*—she doesn't even mean to think that way, Kurt Jr. is three years old and *beautiful*.

Helene also has Jamie, who is her interior decorator. Here is Jamie down on one knee adjusting the detachable ebony ball under the paw-foot of one of his own chairs. He designed it. Everyone *sees* Jamie's furniture. *Oh, did Jamie do your apartment?* It is exotic but simple. You know? Black and white, a modern paw-foot, if you can imagine that, removable ebony balls——

Oh, what the hell is going on? Suddenly she feels hopeless. There are at least ten girls in New York whom she knows who are just like

From *The Kandy-Kolored Tangerine-Flake Streamline Baby*. First published in *New York*, the *New York Herald Tribune*'s Sunday magazine, February 21, 1965.

her: divorced, and young; divorced, and beautiful; divorced, and quite well off, really; divorced, and invited to every party and every this and that that one cares to be invited to; divorced, and written about in the columns by Joe Dever and everyone; divorced, a woman who has everything and, like the other ten, whose names she can tick off just like that, because she knows their cases forward and backward, great American *baronial* names, some of them, and she, and all of them, are utterly . . . utterly, utterly unable to get another husband in New York.

Of course she has tried! A great deal of good will has gone into it, hers and her friends'. The J———s invited her to dinner and set the whole thing up for no other reason than for her to meet their favorite among all the eligible young men of New York. He was beautiful, he was one of the youngest bank vice-presidents in New York, a bona-fide vice-president in this case, and a great Bermuda Racer. They talked about his strenuous life among the Wall Street studs. They talked about the things her friends had been pumping her conversation full of—Jasper Johns, *nouvelle vague*, the bogus esthetics of fashion photographers. They grimaced, mugged, smiled, picked over crab meat—and there was no "chemistry" about it all. And he took her back to East 57th Street and they stepped into an elevator with a lot of scrolly wood and a little elevator man with piping all over his uniform and the moment the door closed on them, there was practically a sound like steam in the brain that told them both, this is, yes, rather impossible; let me out.

Two weeks later the D———s invited her to dinner and Mrs. D——— met her practically as she stepped off the elevator and told her very excitedly, very confidentially, "Helene, we've put you next to absolutely our *favorite* young man in New York"—who, of course, was Bermuda Racer. Everybody's favorite. This time they just smiled, grimaced, mugged, turned the other way answering imaginary questions from the other side and picked over the melon prosciutto.

Maddening! These so-called men in New York! After a while Bermuda Racer began to look good, in retrospect. One could forget "chemistry" in time. Helene's liaisons kept falling into the same pattern; all these pampered, cautious, finicky, timid . . . vague, maddening men who wind their watches before they make love. Suddenly it would have almost been better not to be the woman who had everything. Then she could have married the stable boy, who, in New York, is usually an actor. Helene is in a . . . set whose single men are not boys. They are absorbed in careers. They don't hang around the Limelight Café with nothing more on their minds than getting New York lovelies down onto the downy billows. Somehow they don't *need* wives. They can find women when they need them, for decoration, for company, or for the downy billows, for whatever, for they are everywhere, in lavish, high-buffed plenitude.

Very ironic! It is as if Helene can see herself and all the other divorced women-with-everything in New York this afternoon, at this very moment, frozen, congealed, this afternoon, every afternoon, in a little belt of territory that runs from east to west between 46th and 72nd Streets in Manhattan. They are all there with absolutely nothing to do but make themselves irresistibly attractive to the men of New York. They are in Mr. Kenneth's, the hairdresser's, on East 54th Street, in a room hung with cloth like a huge Paisley tent or something, and a somehow Oriental woman pads in and announces, "Now let us go to the shampoo room," in the most hushed and reverent voice, as if to say, "We are doing something very *creative* here." Yet coiffures, even four hours' worth at Mr. Kenneth's, begin to seem like merely the basic process for the Woman Who Has Everything. There is so much more that must be done today, so much more has been learned. The eternal search for better eyelashes! Off to Deirdre's or some such place, on Madison Avenue—moth-cut eyelashes? square-cut eyelashes? mink eyelashes? really, mink eyelashes are a joke, too heavy, and one's lids . . . sweat; pure sweet saline eyelid perspiration. Or off to somewhere for the perfect Patti-nail application, $25 for both hands, $2.50 a finger, false fingernails—but where? Saks? Bergdorf's? Or is one to listen to some girl who comes back and says the only perfect Patti-nail place is the Beverly Hills Hotel. Or off to Kounovsky's Gym for Exercise—one means, this is 1965 and one must face, now, the fact that chocolate base and chalk can only do so much for the skin; namely, nothing; *cover* it. The important thing is what *happens* to the skin, that purple light business at Don Lee's Hair Specialist Studio, well, that is what it is about. And at Kounovsky's Gym one goes into the cloak room and checks clothes labels for a while and, eventually, runs into some girl who has found a *new* place, saying, this is my last time here. I've found a place where you *really have to take a shower* afterwards. Still—Kounovsky's. And Bene's, breaking down the water globules in the skin—and here they are all out doing nothing every day but making themselves incomparably, esoterically, smashingly lovely—for men who don't seem to *look* anyway. Incredible! Arrogant! impossible men of this city, career-clutched, selfish and drained.

So Helene sits morosely in the downy billows watching *Mr. Jamie* adjust an ebony ball on a paw-foot chair. Jamie is her interior decorator, but even before that, he had become her Token Fag, three years ago, as soon as she was divorced. She needed him. A woman is divorced in New York and for a certain period she is *radioactive* or something. No man wants to go near. She has to cool off from all that psychic toxin of the divorce. Eventually, people begin asking her for dinner or whatever, but *who* is going to escort her? She is radioactive. The Token Fag will escort her. He is a token man, a *counter* to let the game go on and everything. She can walk in with him, into anybody's coy-elegant, beveled-mirror great hall on East 73rd Street, and no one is going to start talking about her new *liaison*. There is no *liaison* except for a sort no one seems to understand. Jamie is comfortable, he is no threat. The *old business* is not going to start up again. This has nothing to do with sex. Sex! The sexual aggression was the only kind that didn't really have that *old business*, the eternal antagonisms, clashes of ego, fights for "freedom" from marriage one day and for supremacy the next, the eternal piling the load on the scapegoat. Helene's last *scene* with Kurt—Helene can tell one about that, all this improbable, ridiculous stuff in front of the movers. They had just been separated. This was long before the afternoon plane ride to El Paso and the taxi ride across the line to Juarez and the old black Mexican judge who flipped, very interested, through a new and quite ornate—arty—deck of Tarot cards under his desk the whole time. They had just separated—they were separating this particular evening. One *does* separate. One stands out in the living room in the midst of incredible heaps of cartons and duffel bags, and Kurt stands there telling *his* movers what to pick up.

"I don't mean to be picayune, Helene, but it *isn't* exactly picayune. You didn't put the Simpson tureen out here," and he starts fluttering his hand.

"The Morgetsons gave that to—they're friends of my parents."

"That isn't even the point, Helene. This is something we *agreed* on."

"You know as well as I do—"

Kurt makes a circle with his thumb and forefinger, the "O.K." sign, and thrusts it toward Helene as if he is about to say, Right, and in that very moment he says:

"Wrong!"

Oh, for godsake. Sal Mineo, or whoever it was. Somebody told Kurt once that "Sal Mineo and his set" are always putting each other on with his O.K. sign—then saying, "Wrong!"—and Kurt was so *impressed* with the Sal Mineo humor of it. Just like right now, standing out amid the packing cartons, with a couple of fat movers . . . lounging, watching. Kurt has to stand there with his hands on his hips and his thatchy head soaking up perspiration, wearing a cable-stitch tennis sweater and Topsiders. His *moving clothes*. He has to wear this corny thing, a cable-knit tennis sweater, about $42, because he is going to pick up a couple of boxes and his precious hi-fi tubes or whatever it is. They do something to these tall ironsides at Hotchkiss or some place and they never get over it. Glowering in his $42 White Shoe physical exertion sweater—the *old business*.

Kurt Jr. is out of bed, waddling into the living room and all he sees is *Daddy*, wonderful, thatchy Daddy. Children, to be honest, have *no* intuition, no insight.

"These men don't want to sit there and listen to you recite your parents' friends," says Kurt.

But they *do*, Kurt. They *are* seated, as you say yourself. Placid, reedy fat rises up around their chins like mashed potatoes. They sit on the arms of Helene's chairs and *enjoy* it, watching two wealthy young fools coming apart at the seams. Kurt Jr. apparently thinks everything Daddy says is *so funny;* he comes on, waddling in, chuckling, giggling, *Daddy!* The movers think Kurt Jr. is *so funny*—a *Baby!*—and they slosh around, chuckling in their jowls. Good spirits, and so obscene, all of it.

Jamie was at least an end to the *old business*. Most of them, Helene, all these divorcees who have everything, soon move into a second stage. Old friends of theirs, of Helene and Kurt—you know? Helene and Kurt, the Young Couple? Helene and Kurt here, Helene and Kurt there—old friends of theirs, of Kurt's, really, start taking Helene out. Fine, fat simple-minded waste of time. What do they want? It is not sex. It is nothing like that old *Redbook* warning to divorcees, that he, Mr. Not Quite Right, will say, She was married, so it is a safe bet she will play on the downy billows. In fact, practically nothing is sex madness with men in Helene's set in New York. Would that the Lord God of Hotchkiss, St. Paul's and Woodberry Forest would *let* them go mad as randy old goats—one wishes He would. Not for the sex but the madness. One longs to see them go berserk just once, sweating, puling, writhing, rolling the eyeballs around, bloating up the tongue like a black roast gizzard—anything but this . . . *vague* coolness, super-cool interest. Anyway, these old friends come around and their eyes breathe at her like gills out of the aquarium, such as that dear dappled terrier from Sullivan & Cromwell whom Kurt used to wangle invitations for, over and over. He did something on the Cotton Exchange. The Cotton Exchange! He came around with his gilly eyes breathing at her, *wondering*, beside himself with this strange delight of *Kurt's Wife* being now available for him to speculate over and breathe his gilly look at. Sweet! One day Douglas, well, Douglas is another story, but one day Douglas invited everyone to a champagne picnic in Central Park for Memorial Day, all these bottles of champagne in Skotch Koolers, huge blue and yellow woven baskets full of salmon and smoked turkey and Southside Virginia ham sandwiches prepared by André Surmain of Lutèce. Kurt's poor old dappled terrier friend from the Cotton Exchange arrived in a correct, "informal," one understands, long-sleeved polo shirt from someplace, Chipp or something, with the creases popped up in straight lines and a sheen on it. Obviously he had gone out and bought the correct thing for this champagne picnic. Poor thing! But Helene kept on going out with him. Old Terrier never made a pass. Never! He always left at 1 A.M., or whenever, with a great, wet look of rice-pudding adoration. But he was *easy*, none of the *old business*.

A terrible lesson! Soon Helene was *identified* with this placid Cotton Exchange lawyer, who still breathed unsaid longings at her through his gills. She didn't care about that. The problem was with other men. In New York there *are* no Other Men. Men in New York have no . . . confidence, whatsoever. They see a girl with a man four or five times, and she is *his*. They will not move in. Happy ever after! Helene and Terrier! Stupid! New York men would not dream of trying to break up a romance or even a relationship. That would take confidence. It would take interest. Interest—mygod, some kind of sustained interest is too much to ask.

That is why it was so absolutely marvelous when Helene saw Porfirio Rubirosa again at C———'s. She hadn't seen him for a year, but he immediately remembered and began pouring absolutely marvelous hot labial looks all over her from across the room and then came over, threading through the rubber jowls, and said:

"Helene, how do you do it! Last year, the white lace. This year, the yellow—you are . . . wonderful, what is the expression? One hundred per cent wonderful!"

And the crazy thing is, one—Helene—knows he means it because he doesn't mean it. Is that too crazy? You are a woman, he is a man. He would break up this stupid Cotton Exchange Terrier universe just to *have* you. Well, he didn't, but he would. Does one know what Helene means?

Why should Helene have to end up in these ridiculous drunk evenings with Davenport? Davenport is not a serious person. Davenport practically enters with orange banners waving, announcing that he will never get married. He is like a peteiz-cuinte paca who runs, rut-boar, all night, and if they put him in the pen, he dies, of pure childish pique. He stops breathing until the middle of his face turns blue. Dear Davenport! One morning—too much!—they overslept and Helene woke to Kurt's Nanny rattling in through the drop lock and had to make Davenport get up, skulk around, get dressed and sneak out when Nanny was in the kitchen. But little Kurt, with his idiot grin, saw him, coming out of the room. Davenport was, of course, still mugging, *pantomiming* great stealth, tiptoeing and rubber-legging around, but Kurt Jr.—incredible! what do three-year-old children think about?—he cries out, "Daddy!" Davenport is slightly shocked himself, for once, but Helene has this horrible mixed agony. She realizes right away that what has really hit her is not the cry—Daddy!—but the fact that it might bring Nanny running to see Davenport sidewinding across the wall-to-wall like a trench-coat gigolo or something.

No more Davenport! Short nights with Pierre. Pierre was a Frenchman who had come to the United States and grown wealthy from the mining industry in South America or some such thing. South America! he used to say. The slums of the United States! Helene used to rather like that. But Pierre used to wind his watch before he went to bed. A very beautiful watch. At parties, at dinner, anywhere, Pierre always grew suddenly . . . *vague,* switching off, floating away like a glider plane. He even grew vague in the downy billows. Now he is there, now he isn't. Pierre may be French but now he is thoroughly New York. In New York a man does not have to devote himself to a woman, or think about her or even pay attention to her. He can . . . glide at will. It is a man's town, because there are not fifty, not one hundred, not one thousand, beautiful, attractive, available women in New York, but *thousands* of these nubile wonders, honed, lacquered, buffed, polished—Good Lord, the spoiled, pampered worthlessness of New York men in this situation. Helene can even see the process and understand it. Why should a talented, a wealthy, even a reasonably good-looking and congenial, cultivated man in New York even feel the *need* for marriage? Unlike Cleveland, Pittsburgh, Cincinnati or practically anywhere else in America, single men are not shut out of social life in New York. Just the opposite. They are *terribly* desirable. They are invited everywhere. A mature man's social life inevitably flags a bit in New York after his marriage. A single man, if he has anything going for him, is not going to get *lonely* in New York. What does he need a wife for? What does a man need children for in New York? Well, Helene doesn't mean to even *think* that. Of course, every man has a natural desire for a son, just as she has a natural desire for a son, she *loves* Kurt Jr., he is a *beautiful* boy.

Well, this is the last straw about Pierre. Pierre winding his watch. There was enough about Pierre without this final night when he got just euphorically high enough on wine and began expanding on the metaphysics of man and woman. Some metaphysics. Some brain. It turned out Pierre had decided about ten years ago, when he was thirty-two, that he ought to get married. This was more or less a theoretical decision, one understands. It would be *fitting.* So he set out with a list of specifications for finding a wife. About so tall, with this type of figure, he even wanted a certain gently bellied look, but firm, one understands, a certain education, a certain age, not over twenty-five, a certain personality, a certain taste for decor, and on and on. It was all quite specific. He never found her, but, then, one gets the impression that he did not look all that hard and was never very disappointed about that. And so, finally, this night, with his watch wound, Pierre announced that, well, now he was forty-two years old, and he had mellowed, and life is a complex drama, and blah-blah-blah, and now he is amending his specifications to include *one child.* Not two, one understands. Two are *underfoot.* But one is all right. And what gets to Helene when she thinks about it is that for a moment there her heart leapt! Her spirits rose! She could see a breakthrough! For a second she no longer thought about the Horror number for New York divorcees—forty, age forty, after which the packing under the skin begins to dry up, wither away, Don Lee can't do a thing about it, Mr. Kenneth and Kounovsky are helpless, all that packing under the skin is drying up, withering away, until one day, they make an autopsy of the most beautiful woman in New York, in her seventy-seventh year, and they find her brain looking like a mass of dried seawood at Tokyo Sukiyaki. The packing is gone! For one moment she no longer had that vague, secret dread of the fate of the ten other divorcees she knows, all failing miserably in the only job they have, viz., finding a husband.

But—*sink*—the folded-napkin life with Pierre. Pierre's specification. Thank you for including me in your stem-winding *Weltanschauung.* So that was it with Pierre.

And now, in a few minutes, the new Buyer will be coming around, he's an editor at *Life,* not a *top* editor, one understands, but he *looks* good, he has none of that ironside Hotchkiss in him, he seems to *know* things. Helene—well, *journalists*—but Helene met him at Freddie's and it *went* well, and now he is coming around for the first time.

So Jamie is fitting the last ebony ball onto the paw feet—Jamie comes around like this at any time; it brings some kind of peace to Jamie to be down on his knees in the wall-to-wall. Or something. And, ultimately, the doorman calls up, the buzzer rings, Old Nanny fools around with the drop lock and brings him in. And—simple mind!—it happens again. Helene can almost feel her eyes rolling up and down him, inspecting him, his shoes, which are cordovan with heavy soles—how sad!—but she goes on, inspecting him, she can't stop it, sizing up every man who comes through that door as . . . Mr. Potential.

The nanny had to leave Kurt Jr.'s room to go to the door and now—oh, wonderful!—the little—boy—comes waddling out—and, like someone frozen, Helene sees that simple, widening grin on his face and knows precisely what it means and can say nothing to ward off what she knows she is going to hear. Big *Lifey* stands a little nervously, sloshing around in his cordovans, grinning stupidly at this little waddling Child in the Plot, while Kurt Jr. keeps coming and—pow!—

throws his arms around big *Lifey's* leg and looks up—idiot appeal!—and says, "Are you going to be my new Daddy?"

Ah—one thing has not changed. Helene has wheeled about, can't think up a thing to say, it doesn't really matter—and Jamie is still bent over on one knee, fooling with the chair. What would it be like with Jamie? And why not? She *can* size up Jamie. Perhaps she has been sizing up Jamie since the first time he walked through the door. There is something about Jamie. There is . . . *beauty*. It is . . . very odd, nice, fey, sick, but Jamie—never mind!—has a beautiful *small of the back,* poised, pumiced, lacquered, and it remains only for her to walk over, travel just a few feet, and put her hands upon him like a . . . vase.

The Pump House, Windansea Beach, La Jolla, 1965

THE PUMP HOUSE GANG

Our boys never hair out. The black panther has black feet. Black feet on the crumbling black panther. Pan-thuh. Mee-dah. Pam Stacy, 16 years old, a cute girl here in La Jolla, California, with a pair of orange bell-bottom hip-huggers on, sits on a step about four steps down the stairway to the beach and she can see a pair of revolting black feet without lifting her head. So she says it out loud, "The black panther."

Somebody farther down the stairs, one of the boys with the *major* hair and khaki shorts, says, "The black feet of the black panther."

"Mee-dah," says another kid. This happens to be the cry of a, well, *underground society* known as the Mac Meda Destruction Company.

"The pan-thuh."

"The poon-thuh."

All these kids, seventeen of them, members of the Pump House crowd, are lollygagging around the stairs down to Windansea Beach, La Jolla, California, about 11 a.m., and they all look at the black feet, which are a woman's pair of black street shoes, out of which stick a pair of old veiny white ankles, which lead up like a senile cone to a fudge of tallowy, edematous flesh, her thighs, squeezing out of her bathing suit, with old faded yellow bruises on them, which she probably got from running eight feet to catch a bus or something. She is standing with her old work-a-hubby, who has on *san*dals: you know, a pair of navy-blue anklet socks and these sandals with big, wide, new-smelling tan straps going this way and that, *for keeps*. Man, they look like orthopedic sandals, if one can imagine that. Obviously,

From *The Pump House Gang*. First published as "The Pump House Gang Meets the Black Panthers—or Silver Threads Among the Gold in Surf City" and "The Pump House Gang Faces Life" in *New York*, the *World Journal Tribune*'s Sunday magazine, February 13 and 20, 1966.

these people come from Tucson or Albuquerque or one of those hincty adobe towns. All these hincty, crumbling black feet come to La Jolla-by-the-sea from the adobe towns for the weekend. They even drive in cars all full of thermos bottles and mayonnaisey sandwiches and some kind of latticework wooden-back support for the old crock who drives and Venetian blinds on the back window.

"The black panther."

"Pan-thuh."

"Poon-thuh."

"Mee-dah."

Nobody says it to the two old crocks directly. God, they must be practically 50 years old. Naturally, they're carrying every piece of garbage imaginable: the folding aluminum chairs, the newspapers, the lending-library book with the clear plastic wrapper on it, the sunglasses, the sun ointment, about a vat of goo—

It is a Mexican standoff. In a Mexican standoff, both parties narrow their eyes and glare but nobody throws a punch. Of course, nobody in the Pump House crowd would ever even jostle these people or say anything right to them; they are too cool for that.

Everybody in the Pump House crowd looks over, even Tom Coman, who is a cool person. Tom Coman, 16 years old, got thrown out of his garage last night. He is sitting up on top of the railing, near the stairs, up over the beach, with his legs apart. Some nice long willowy girl in yellow slacks is standing on the sidewalk but leaning into him with her arms around his body, just resting. Neale Jones, 16, a boy with great lank perfect surfer's hair, is standing nearby with a Band-Aid on his upper lip, where the sun has burnt it raw. Little Vicki Ballard is up on the sidewalk. Her older sister, Liz, is down the stairs by the Pump House itself, a concrete block, 15 feet high, full of machinery for the La Jolla water system. Liz is wearing her great "Liz" styles, a hulking rabbit-fur vest and black-leather boots over her Levi's, even though it is about 85 out here and the sun is plugged in up there like God's own dentist lamp and the Pacific is heaving in with some fair-to-middling surf. Kit Tilden is lollygagging around, and Tom Jones, Connie Carter, Roger Johnson, Sharon Sandquist, Mary Beth White, Rupert Fellows, Glenn Jackson, Dan Watson from San Diego, they are all out here, and everybody takes a look at the panthers.

The old guy, one means, you know, he must be practically 50 years old, he says to his wife, "Come on, let's go farther up," and he takes her by her fat upper arm as if to wheel her around and aim her away from here.

But she says, "No! We have just as much right to be here as they do."

"That's *not the point*—"

"Are you going to—"

"*Mrs. Roberts,*" the work-a-hubby says, calling his own wife by her official married name, as if to say she took a vow once and his word is law, even if he is not testing it with the blond kids here—"farther up, *Mrs. Roberts.*"

They start to walk up the sidewalk, but one kid won't move his feet, and, oh, god, her work-a-hubby breaks into a terrible shaking Jell-O smile as she steps over them, as if to say, Excuse me, sir, I don't mean to make trouble, please, and don't you and your colleagues rise up and jump me, screaming *Gotcha*—

Mee-dah!

Some old bastard took Tom Coman's garage away from him, and that means eight or nine surfers are out of a place to stay.

"I went by there this morning, you ought to see the guy," Tom Coman says. Yellow Stretch Pants doesn't move. She has him around the waist. "He was out there painting and he had this brush and about a thousand gallons of ammonia. He was really going to scrub me out of there."

"What did he do with the furniture?"

"I don't know. He threw it out."

"What are you going to do?"

"I don't know."

"Where are you going to stay?"

"I don't know. I'll stay on the beach. It wouldn't be the first time. I haven't had a place to stay for three years, so I'm not going to start worrying now."

Everybody thinks that over awhile. Yellow Stretch just hangs on and smiles. Tom Coman, 16 years old, piping fate again. One of the girls says, "You can stay at my place, Tom."

"Um. Who's got a cigarette?"

Pam Stacy says, "You can have these."

Tom Coman lights a cigarette and says, "Let's have a destructo." A destructo is what can happen in a garage after eight or ten surfers are kicked out of it.

"Mee-dah!"

"Wouldn't that be bitchen?" says Tom Coman. Bitchen is a surfer's term that means "great," usually.

"Bitchen!"

"Mee-dah!"

It's incredible—that old guy out there trying to scour the whole surfing life out of that garage. He's a pathetic figure. His shoulders are hunched over and he's dousing and scrubbing away and the sun doesn't give him a tan, it gives him these . . . *mottles* on the back of his neck. But never mind! The hell with destructo. One only has a destructo spontaneously, a Dionysian . . . *bursting out,* like those holes through the wall during the Mac Meda Destruction Company Convention at Manhattan Beach—Mee-dah!

Something will pan out. It's a magic economy—yes!—all up and down the coast from Los Angeles to Baja California they take off from home and get to the beach, and if they need a place to stay, well, somebody rents a garage for twenty bucks a month and everybody moves in, girls and boys. Furniture—it's like, one means, you know, one *appropriates* furniture from here and there. It's like the Volkswagen buses a lot of kids now use as beach wagons instead of woodies. Woodies are old station wagons, usually Fords, with wooden bodies, from back before 1953. One of the great things about a Volkswagen bus is that one can . . . *exchange* motors in about three minutes. A good VW motor exchanger can go up to a parked Volkswagen, and a few ratchets of the old wrench here and it's up and out and he has a new motor. There must be a few nice old black panthers around wondering why their nice hubby-mommy VWs don't run so good anymore—but—then—they—are—probably—puzzled—about—a—lot of things. Yes.

Cash—it's practically in the air. Around the beach in La Jolla a guy can walk right out in the street and stand there, stop cars and make the candid move. Mister, I've got a quarter, how about 50 cents so I can get a *large* draft. Or, I need some after-ski boots. And the panthers give one a Jell-O smile and hand it over. Or a guy who knows how to do it can get $40 from a single night digging clams, and it's nice out there. Or he can go around and take up a collection for a keg party, a keg of beer. Man, anybody who won't kick in a quarter for a keg is a jerk. A couple of good keg collections—that's a trip to Hawaii, which is the surfer's version of a trip to Europe: there is a great surf and great everything there. Neale spent three weeks in Hawaii last year. He got $30 from a girl friend, he scrounged a little here and there and got $70 more and he headed off for Hawaii with $100.02, that being the exact plane fare, and borrowed 25 cents when he got there to . . . blast the place up. He spent the 25 cents in a photo booth, showed the photos to the people on the set of *Hawaii* and got a job in the movie. What's the big orgy about money? It's warm, nobody even wears shoes, nobody is starving.

All right, Mother gets worried about all this, but it is limited worry, as John Shine says. Mainly, Mother says, *Sayonara*, you all, and you head off for the beach.

The thing is, everybody, practically everybody, comes from a good family. Everyone has been . . . *reared well,* as they say. Everybody is very upper-middle, if you want to bring it down to that. It's just that this is a new order. Why hang around in the hubby-mommy household with everybody getting neurotic hang-ups with each other and slamming doors and saying, Why can't they have some privacy? Or, it doesn't mean anything that I have to work for a living, does it? It doesn't mean a thing to you. All of you just lie around here sitting in the big orange easy chair smoking cigarettes. I'd hate for you to have to smoke standing up, you'd probably get phlebitis from it—Listen to me, Sarah—

—why go through all that? It's a good life out here. Nobody is mugging everybody for money and affection. There are a lot of bright people out here, and there are a lot of interesting things. One night there was a toga party in a garage, and everybody dressed in sheets, like togas, boys and girls and they put on the appropriated television set to an old Deanna Durbin movie and turned off the sound and put on Rolling Stones records, and you should have seen Deanna Durbin opening her puckered kumquat mouth with Mick Jagger's voice bawling out, *I cain't get no satisfaction.* Of course, finally everybody started pulling the togas off each other, but that is another thing. And one time they had a keg party down on the beach in Mission Bay and the lights from the amusement park were reflected all over the water and that, the whole design of the thing, those nutty lights, that was part of the party. Liz put out the fire throwing a "sand potion" or something on it. One can laugh at Liz and her potions, her necromancy and everything, but there is a lot of thought going into it, a lot of, well, mysticism.

You can even laugh at mysticism if you want to, but there is a kid like Larry Alderson, who spent two years with a monk, and he learned a lot of stuff, and Artie Nelander is going to spend next summer with some Outer Mongolian tribe; he really means to do that. Maybe the "mysterioso" stuff is a lot of garbage, but still, it is interesting. The surfers around the Pump House use that word, mysterioso, quite a lot. It refers to the mystery of the Oh Mighty Hulking Pacific Ocean and everything. Sometimes a guy will stare at the surf and say, "Mysterioso." They keep telling the story of Bob Simmons' wipeout, and somebody will say "mysterioso."

Simmons was a fantastic surfer. He was fantastic even though he had a bad leg. He rode the really big waves. One day he got wiped out at Windansea. When a big wave overtakes a surfer, it drives him right to the bottom. The board came in but he never came up and they never found his body. Very mysterioso. The black panthers all talked about what happened to "the Simmons boy." But the mysterioso thing was how he could have died at all. If he had been one of the old pan-thuhs, hell, sure he could have got killed. But Simmons was, well, one's own age, he was the kind of guy who could have been in the Pump House gang, he was . . . *immune*, he was plugged into the whole pattern, he could feel the whole Oh Mighty Hulking Sea, he didn't have to think it out step by step. But he got wiped out and killed. Very mysterioso.

Immune! If one is in the Pump House gang and really keyed in to this whole thing, it's—well, one is . . . *immune*, one is not full of black pan-thuh panic. Two kids, a 14-year-old girl and a 16-year-old boy, go out to Windansea at dawn, in the middle of winter, cold as hell, and take on 12-foot waves all by themselves. The girl, Jackie Haddad, daughter of a certified public accountant, wrote a composition about it, just for herself, called "My Ultimate Journey":

"It was six o'clock in the morning, damp, foggy and cold. We could feel the bitter air biting at our cheeks. The night before, my friend Tommy and I had seen one of the greatest surf films, *Surf Classics.* The film had excited us so much we made up our minds to go surfing the following morning. That is what brought us down on the cold, wet, soggy sand of Windansea early on a December morning.

"We were the first surfers on the beach. The sets were rolling in at eight to ten, filled with occasional 12-footers. We waxed up and waited for a break in the waves. The break came, neither of us said a word, but instantly grabbed our boards and ran into the water. The paddle out was difficult, not being used to the freezing water.

"We barely made it over the first wave of the set, a large set. Suddenly Tommy put on a burst of speed and shot past me. He cleared the biggest wave of the set. It didn't hit me hard as I rolled under it. It dragged me almost 20 yards before exhausting its strength. I climbed on my board gasping for air. I paddled out to where Tommy was resting. He laughed at me for being wet already. I almost hit him but I began laughing, too. We rested a few minutes and then lined up our position with a well known spot on the shore.

"I took off first. I bottom-turned hard and started climbing up the wave. A radical cut-back caught me off balance and I fell, barely hanging onto my board. I recovered in time to see Tommy go straight over the falls on a 10-footer. His board shot nearly 30 feet in the air. Luckily, I could get it before the next set came in, so Tommy didn't have to make the long swim in. I pushed it to him and then laughed. All of a sudden Tommy yelled, 'Outside!'

"Both of us paddled furiously. We barely made it up to the last wave, it was a monster. In precision timing we wheeled around and I took off. I cut left in reverse stance, then cut back, driving hard toward the famous Windansea bowl. As I crouched, a huge wall of energy came down over me, covering me up. I moved toward the nose to gain more speed and shot out of the fast-flowing suction just in time to kick out as the wave closed out.

"As I turned around I saw Tommy make a beautiful drop-in, then the wave peaked and fell all at once. Miraculously he beat the suction. He cut back and did a spinner, which followed with a reverse kick-up.

"Our last wave was the biggest. When we got to shore, we rested, neither of us saying a word, but each lost in his own private world of thoughts. After we had rested, we began to walk home. We were about half way and the rain came pouring down. That night we both had bad colds, but we agreed it was worth having them after the thrill and satisfaction of an extra good day of surfing."

John Shine and Artie Nelander are out there right now. They are just "outside," about one fifth of a mile out from the shore, beyond where the waves start breaking. They are straddling their surfboards with their backs to the shore, looking out toward the horizon, waiting for a good set. Their backs look like some kind of salmon-colored porcelain shells, a couple of tiny shells bobbing up and down as the swells roll under them, staring out to sea like Phrygian sacristans looking for a sign.

John and Artie! They are—they are what one means when one talks about the surfing life. It's like, you know, one means, they have this life all of their own; it's like a glass-bottom boat, and it floats over the "real" world, or the square world or whatever one wants to call it. They are not exactly off in a world of their own, they are and they aren't. What it is, they float right through the real world, but it can't touch them. They do these things, like the time they went to Malibu, and there was this party in some guy's apartment, and there wasn't enough *legal* parking space for everybody, and so somebody went out and painted the red curbs white and everybody parked. Then the cops came. Everybody ran out. Artie and John took an airport bus to the Los Angeles Airport, just like they were going to take a plane, in khaki shorts and T-shirts with Mac Meda Destruction Company stenciled on them. Then they took a helicopter to Disneyland. At Disneyland crazy Ditch had his big raincoat on and a lot of flasks strapped onto his body underneath, Scotch, bourbon, all kinds of stuff. He had plastic tubes from the flasks sticking out of the flyfront of his raincoat and everybody was sipping whiskey through the tubes—

—Ooooo-eeee—Mee-dah! They chant this chant, Mee-dah, in a real fakey deep voice, and it *really bugs people*. They don't know what the hell it is. It is the cry of the Mac Meda Destruction Company. The Mac Meda Destruction Company is . . . an *underground* society that started in La Jolla about three years ago. Nobody can remember exactly how; they have arguments about it. Anyhow, it is mainly something to *bug* people with and organize huge beer orgies with. They have their own complete, bogus phone number in La Jolla. They have Mac Meda Destruction Company decals. They stick them on phone booths, on cars, anyplace. Some mommy-hubby will come out of the shopping plaza and walk up to his Mustang, which is supposed to make him a hell of a tiger now, and he'll see a sticker on the side of it saying, "Mac Meda Destruction Company," and for about two days or something he'll think the sky is going to fall in.

But the big thing is the parties, the "conventions." Anybody can join, any kid, anybody can come, as long as they've heard about it, and they can only hear about it by word of mouth. One was in the Sorrento Valley, in the gulches and arroyos, and the fuzz came, and so the older guys put the young ones and the basket cases, the ones just too stoned out of their gourds, into the tule grass, and the cops shined their searchlights and all they saw was tule grass, while the basket cases moaned scarlet and oozed on their bellies like reptiles and everybody else ran down the arroyos, yelling Mee-dah.

The last one was at Manhattan Beach, inside somebody's poor hulking house. The party got *very Dionysian* that night and somebody put a hole through one wall, and everybody else decided to see if they could make it bigger. Everybody was stoned out of their hulking gourds, and it got to be about 3:30 a.m. and everybody decided to go see the riots. These were the riots in Watts. The Los Angeles *Times* and the San Diego *Union* were all saying, WATTS NO-MAN'S-LAND and STAY WAY FROM WATTS YOU GET YO SE'F KILLED, but naturally nobody believed that. Watts was a blast, and the Pump House gang was immune to the trembling gourd panic rattles of the L. A. *Times* black pan-thuhs. Immune!

So John Shine, Artie Nelander and Jerry Sterncorb got in John's VW bus, known as the Hog of Steel, and they went to Watts. Gary Wickham and some other guys ran into an old man at a bar who said he owned a house in Watts and had been driven out by the drunk niggers. So they drove in a car to save the old guy's house from the drunk niggers. Artie and John had a tape recorder and decided they were going to make a record called "Random Sounds from the Watts Riots." They drove right into Watts in the Hog of Steel and there was blood on the streets and roofs blowing off the stores and all these apricot flames and drunk Negroes falling through the busted plate glass of the liquor stores. Artie got a nice recording of a lot of Negroes chanting "Burn, baby, burn." They all got out and talked to some Negro kids in a gang going into a furniture store, and the Negro kids didn't say Kill Whitey or Geed'um or any of that. They just said, Come on, man, it's a party and it's free. After they had been in there for about three hours talking to Negroes and watching drunks collapse in the liquor stores, some cop with a helmet on came roaring up and said, "Get the hell out of here, you kids, we cannot and will not provide protection."

Meantime, Gary Wickham and his friends drove in in a car with the old guy, and a car full of Negroes *did* stop them and say, Whitey, Geed'um, and all that stuff, but one of the guys in Gary's car just draped a pistol he had out the window and the colored guys drove off. Gary and everybody drove the old guy to his house and they all walked in and had a great raunchy time drinking beer and raising hell. A couple of Negroes, the old guy's neighbors, came over and told the old guy to cut out the racket. There were flames in the sky and ashes coming down with little rims of fire on them, like apricot crescents. The old guy got very cocky about all his "protection" and went out on the front porch about dawn and started yelling at some Negroes across the street, telling them "No more drunk niggers in Watts" and a lot of other unwise slogans. So Gary Wickham got up and everybody left. They were there about four hours altogether and when they drove out, they had to go through a National Guard checkpoint, and a lieutenant from the San Fernando Valley told them he could not and would not provide protection.

But exactly! Watts just happened to be what was going on at the time, as far as the netherworld of La Jolla surfing was concerned, and so one goes there and sees what is happening and comes back and tells everybody about it and laughs at the L.A. *Times*. That is what makes it so weird when all these black pan-thuhs come around to pick up "surfing styles," like the clothing manufacturers. They don't know what any of it means. It's like archaeologists discovering hieroglyphics or something, and they say, god, that's neat—Egypt!—but they don't know what the hell it is. They don't know anything about . . . *The Life*. It's great to think of a lot of old emphysematous pan-thuhs in the Garment District in New York City struggling in off the street against a gummy 15-mile-an-hour wind full of soot and coffee-brown snow and gasping in the elevator to clear their old nicotine-phlegm tubes on the way upstairs to make out the invoices on a lot of surfer stuff for 1966, the big nylon windbreakers with the wide, white horizontal competition stripes, nylon swimming trunks with competition stripes, bell-bottom slacks for girls, the big hairy sleeveless jackets, vests, the blue "tennies," meaning tennis shoes, and the . . . *look*, the Major Hair, all this long lank blond hair, the plain face kind of tanned and bleached out at the same time, but with big eyes. It all starts in a few places, a few strategic groups, the Pump House gang being one of them, and then it moves up the beach, to places like Newport Beach and as far up as Malibu.

Pretty soon the California littoral will be littered with these guys, stroked out on the beach like beached white whales, and girls, too, who can't give up the mystique, the mysterioso mystique, Oh Mighty Hulking Sea, who can't *conceive* of living any other life. It is pathetic when they are edged out of groups like the Pump House gang. Already there are some guys who hang around with the older crowd around the Shack who are stagnating on the beach. Some of the older guys, like Gary Wickham, who is 24, are still in *The Life*, they still have it, but even Gary Wickham will be 25 one day and then 26 and then . . . and then even pan-thuh age. Is one really going to be pan-thuh age one day? Watch those black feet go. And Tom Coman still snuggles with Yellow Slacks, and Liz still roosts moodily in her rabbit fur at the bottom of the Pump House and Pam still sits on the steps contemplating the mysterioso mysteries of Pump House ascension and John and Artie still bob, tiny pink porcelain shells, way out there waiting for godsown bitchen *set*, and godsown sun is still turned on like a dentist's lamp and so far—

—the panthers scrape on up the sidewalk. They are at just about the point Leonard Anderson and Donna Blanchard got that day, December 6, 1964, when Leonard said, Pipe it, and fired two shots, one at her and one at himself. Leonard was 18 and Donna was 21—21! —god, for a girl in the Pump House gang that is almost the horror line right there. But it was all so mysterioso. Leonard was just lying down on the beach at the foot of the Pump House, near the stairs, just talking to John K. Weldon down there, and then Donna appeared at the top of the stairs and Leonard got up and went up the stairs to meet her, and they didn't say anything, they weren't *angry* over anything, they never had been, although the police said they had, they just turned and went a few feet down the sidewalk, away from the Pump House and—blam blam!—these two shots. Leonard fell dead on the sidewalk and Donna died that afternoon in Scripps Memorial Hospital. Nobody knew what to think. But one thing it seemed like—well, it seemed like Donna and Leonard thought they had lived *The Life* as far as it would go and now it was running out. All that was left to do was—but that is an *insane* idea. It can't be like that, *The Life* can't run out, people can't change all that much just because godsown chronometer runs on and the body packing starts deteriorating and the fudgy tallow shows up at the thighs where they squeeze out of the bathing suit—

Tom, boy! John, boy! Gary, boy! Neale, boy! Artie, boy! Pam, Liz, Vicki, Jackie Haddad! After all this—just a pair of bitchen black panther bunions inching down the sidewalk away from the old Pump House stairs?

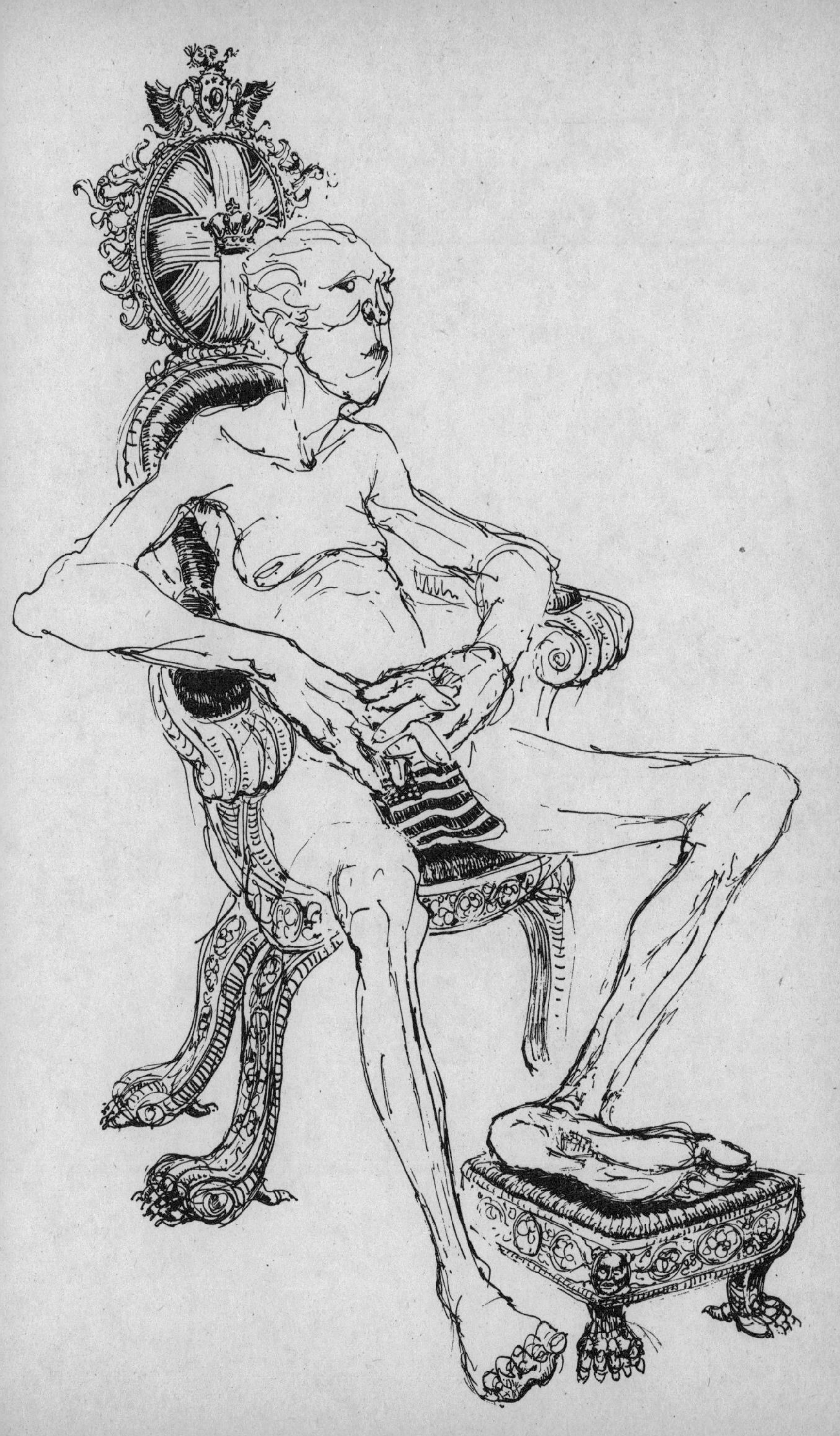

THE MID-ATLANTIC MAN

Roger! Have you met George? Cyril! Have you met George? Keith! Have you met George? Brian! Have you met George? Tony! Have you met George! Nigel! Have you—

—oh god, he's doing a hell of a job of it, introducing everybody by their first names, first-naming the hell out of everybody, introducing them to George, who just arrived from New York: George is an American and the key man in the Fabrilex account. A hell of a job of introductions he is doing. He has everybody from the firm, plus a lot of other people, English and American, all calculated to impress and flatter American George, all piled into this sort of library-reception room upstairs at the —— Club amid the lyre-splat chairs, bullion-fringe curtains, old blacky Raeburn-style portraits, fabulously junky glass-and-ormolu chandeliers, paw-foot chiffoniers, teapoys, ingenious library steps leading resolutely up into thin air, a wonderful dark world of dark wood, dark rugs, candy-box covings, moldings, flutings, pilasters, all red as table wine, brown as boots, made to look like it has been steeped a hundred years in expensive tobacco, roast beef, horse-radish sauce and dim puddings.

The Americans really lap this Club stuff up, but that is not the point, the point is that—Christ, Americans are childish in many ways and about as subtle as a Wimpy bender: but in the long run it doesn't make any difference. They just turn on the power. They have the power, they just move in and take it, introducing people by their first names as they go, people they've never laid eyes on, *pals*, and who gives a damn. They didn't go to Cambridge and learn to envy people

From *The Pump House Gang*. First published in the London *Weekend Telegraph*; appeared subsequently in *New York*, the *World Journal Tribune*'s Sunday magazine, November 27, 1966.

who belonged to the Pitt Club and commit the incredible gaffe of walking into the Pitt Club with a Cambridge scarf on. They just turn on the money or whatever it takes, and they take it, and the grinning first names shall inherit the earth, their lie-down crewcuts as firm and pure as Fabrilex—and—

—he has had a couple of highballs. Highballs! That is what they call whisky-and-sodas. And now he is exhilarated with the absolute *baldness* of putting on his glistening ceramic grin and introducing all of these faces to George by their first names, good old George, cleaned-and-pressed old George, big-blucher-shoed old George, popped-out-of-the-Fabrilex-mold old George—the delicious baldness of it!—

Karl! Have you met George? Alec! Have you met George? John! Have you met George? George, predictably, has a super-ingratiating and deferential grin on his face, shaking hands, pumping away, even with people who don't put their hands out at first—Mark! shake hands with George, he wants to say—and as George shakes hands he always lowers his head slightly and grins in panic and looks up from under his eyebrows, deferentially, this kind of unconscious deference because he . . . is meeting *Englishmen* . . .

Still! Why should George give a damn? He can throw away points like this right and left. That's the way Americans are. They can make the wrong gesture, make the most horrible malapropisms, use so many wrong forks it drives the waiter up the wall; demonstrate themselves to be, palpably, social hydrocephalics, total casualties of gaucherie and humiliation—and yet afterwards they don't give a damn. They are right back the next morning as if nothing had happened, smashing on, good-humored, hard-grabbing, winning, taking, clutching. George can scrape and bobble his eyeballs under his eyebrows all day and he will still make his £20,000 a year and buy and sell every bastard in this room—

Nicholas! Have you met George?

Harold! Have you met George?

Freddie! Have you met George?

"Pe-t-e-r . . ."

. . . Oh Christ . . . the second syllable of the name just dribbles off his lips.

With Peter—suddenly he can't go through with it. He can't do the first name thing with Peter, he can't hail him over and introduce him to this American—Peter!—George!—as if of course they're pals, *pals*. Peter? A pal? Peter is on precisely his level in the hierarchy of the firm, the same age, 33, yet . . . in another hierarchy—class, to call it by its right name—

Peter's fine yet languid face, his casual yet inviolate wavy thatchy hair—that old, ancient thing, class, now has him and he can't introduce

Peter by his first name. It is as if into the room has burst the policeman, the arresting officer, from . . . that world, the entire world of nannies, *cottages ornées* in Devonshire, honeysuckle iron balustrades, sailor suits, hoops and sticks, lolly Eton collars, deb parties, introductions to rich old men, clubs, cliques, horn-handled cigar cutters—in short, the ancient, ineradicable anxiety of class in England—and he knows already the look of patient, tolerant disgust that will begin to slide over Peter's face within the next half second as he looks at him and his American friends and his ceramic grin and his euphoria and his *highballs*. In that instant, confronted by the power of the future on the one hand—George's eyeballs begin to bobble under the eyebrows—and the power of the past on the other—Peter's lips begin to curdle—he realizes what has happened to himself. He has become a Mid-Atlantic Man.

He meets them all the time in London now. They are Englishmen who have reversed the usual process and . . . gone American. The usual process has been that Americans have gone to England and . . . gone English. Woodrow Wilson appoints Walter Hines Page ambassador to the Court of St. James's and tells him: "Just one word of advice, don't become an Englishman." Page says, "Sure, O.K.," but, of course, he does, he becomes so much an Englishman he can't see straight. The usual pattern is, he begins using his knife and fork Continental style, holding the fork in the left hand. He goes to a tailor who puts that nice English belly into the lapels of his coat and builds up suits made of marvelous and arcane layers and layers of worsted, welts, darts, pleats, double-stitches, linings, buttons, pockets, incredible numbers of pockets, and so many buttons to button and unbutton, and he combs his hair into wings over the ears, and he puts a certain nice drag in his voice and learns to walk like he is recovering from a broken back. But one knows about all that. The American has always gone English in order to endow himself with the mystique of the English upper classes. The Englishman today goes American, becomes a Mid-Atlantic Man, to achieve the opposite. He wants to get out from under the domination of the English upper classes by . . . going classless. And he goes classless by taking on the style of life, or part of the style of life, of a foreigner who cannot be fitted into the English class system, the modern, successful, powerful American.

The most obvious example of the Mid-Atlantic Man is the young English show-business figure, a singer, musician, manager, producer, impresario, who goes American in a big way. A singer, for example, sings American rhythm and blues songs, in an American accent, becomes a . . . *pal* of American entertainers, studs his conversation with American slang, like, I mean you know, man, that's where it's at, baby, and, finally, begins to talk with an American accent in an attempt to remove the curse of a working-class accent. But the typical Mid-Atlantic Man is middle class and works in one of the newer industries, advertising, public relations, chemical engineering, consulting for this and that, television, credit cards, agentry, industrial design, commercial art, motion pictures, the whole world of brokerage, persuasion, savantry and shows that has grown up beyond the ancient divisions of landowning, moneylending and the production of dry goods.

He is vaguely aware—he may try to keep it out of his mind—that his background is irrevocably middle class and that everybody in England is immediately aware of it and that this has held him back. This may even be why he has gravitated into one of the newer fields, but still the ancient drag of class in England drags him, drags him, drags him. . . .

They happen to be watching television one night and some perfectly urbane and polished person like Kenneth Allsop comes on the screen and after three or four sentences somebody has to observe, poor Kenneth Allsop, listen to the way he says practically, he will never get the Midlands out of his voice, he breaks it all up, into prac-ti-cally . . . and he laughs, but grimly, because he knows there must be at least fifty things like that to mark him as hopelessly middle class and he has none of Allsop's fame to take the curse off.

He first began to understand all this as far back as his first month at Cambridge. Cambridge!—which was supposed to turn him into one of those inviolate, superior persons who rule England and destiny. Cambridge was going to be a kind of finishing school. His parents had a very definite idea of it that way, a picture of him serving sherry to some smart friends in his chambers, wearing a jacket that seems to have worn and mellowed like a 90-year-old Persian rug. Even he himself had a vague notion of how Cambridge was going to transform him from a bright and mousy comprehensive schoolboy into one of those young men with spread collars and pale silk ties who just . . . *assumes* he is in control, at restaurants, in clubs, at parties, with women, in careers, in life, on rural weekends, and thereby is.

And then the very first month this thing happened with the Pitt Club and the Cambridge scarf. His first move on the road to having smart people over to his chambers for sherry, and Cuban tobacco—Cuban tobacco was also included in this vision—was to buy a Cambridge scarf, a nice long thing with confident colors that would wrap around the neck and the lower tip of his chin and flow in the wind. So he would put on his scarf and amble around the streets, by the colleges, peeking in at the Indian restaurants, which always seemed to be closed, and thinking, Well, here I am, a Cambridge man.

. . .

One day he came upon this place and a glow came from inside, red as wine, brown as boots, smart people, sherry-sherry, and so he stepped inside—and suddenly a lot of white faces turned his way, like a universe erupting with eggs Benedict, faces in the foyer, faces from the dining tables farther in. A porter with chipped-beef jowls stepped up and looked him up and down once, dubious as hell, and said:

"Are you a member, sir?"

Such a voice! It was obvious that he knew immediately that he was not a member and the question was merely, witheringly, rhetorical and really said, Why does a hopeless little nit like you insist on wandering in where you don't belong, and all the eggs Benedict faces turned toward him were an echo of the same thing. They all knew immediately! And it was as if their eyes had fastened immediately upon his jugular vein—no!—upon the Cambridge scarf.

He mumbled and turned his head . . . there in the ancient woody brown of the place was a long coat rack, and hanging on it was every kind of undergraduate garment a *right* mind could think of, greatcoats, riding macs, cloaks, capes, gowns, mantles, even ponchos, mufflers, checked mufflers, Danish mufflers, camel-tan mufflers, ratty old aunt-knitty mufflers—everything and anything in the whole woofy English goddamn universe of cotton, wool, rubber and leather . . . except for a Cambridge scarf. This place turned out to be the Pitt Club, watering trough of the incomparables, the Cambridge elite. Wearing a Cambridge scarf in here was far, far worse than having no insignia at all. In a complex Cambridge hierarchy of colleges and clubs—if all one had was an insignia that said merely that one had been admitted to the university—that was as much as saying, well, he's here and that's all one can say about him, other than that he is a hopeless fool.

He did not throw the Cambridge scarf away, strangely enough. He folded it up into a square and tucked it way back in the bottom of his bottom drawer, along with the family Bible his grandfather had given him. From that day on he was possessed by the feeling that there were two worlds, the eggs Benedict faces and his, and never, in four years, did he invite a single smart person over for sherry. Or for Cuban tobacco. He smoked English cigarettes that stained his teeth.

Even years later, in fact, he held no tremendous hopes for the advertising business until one day he was in New York—one day!—with all Mid-Atlantic Men it seems to start one day in New York.

Practically always they have started flying to New York more and more on business. He started flying over on the Fabrilex account. Fabrilex was going to run a big campaign in England. So he began flying to New York and getting gradually into the New York advertising life, which turned out to be a strangely . . . *stimulating*—all Mid-Atlantic Men come back with that word for New York, stimulating

. . . strangely stimulating aura of sheer money, drive, conniving, hard work, self-indulgence, glamour, childishness, cynicism.

Beginning with the reception room of the —— Agency. It was decorated with the most incredible black leather sofas, quilted and stuffed to the gullet, with the leather gushing and heaving over the edge of the arms, the back and everywhere. There was wall-to-wall carpet, not like a Wilton but so thick one could break one's ankle in it, and quite vermilion, to go with the vermilion walls and all sorts of inexplicable polished brass objects set in niches, candelabra, busts, pastille-burners, vases, etc., and a receptionist who seemed to be made of polished Fabrilex topped with spun brass back-combed hair. She didn't sit at a desk but at a delicate *secretaire* faced with exotic wood veneers, tulipwood, satinwood, harewood. She also operated a switchboard, which was made to look, however, like the keyboard of a harpsichord. There was one large painting, apparently by the last painter in Elizabeth, New Jersey, to copy Franz Kline. Three different members of the firm, Americans, told him the reception room looked like "a San Francisco whorehouse." Three of them used that same simile, a San Francisco whorehouse. This was not said in derision, however. They thought it was crazy but they were proud of it. New York!

One of them told him the reception room looked like a San Francisco whorehouse while having his shoes shined at his desk in his office. They were both sitting there talking, the usual, except that a Negro, about 50, was squatted down over a portable shoeshine stand shining the American's shoes. But he kept right on talking about the San Francisco whorehouse and Fabrilex as if all he had done was turn on an air-conditioner. He also had an "executive telephone." This was some sort of amplified microphone and speaker connected to the telephone, so that he didn't have to actually pick up a telephone, none of that smalltime stuff. All he had to do was talk in the general direction of the desk. But of course! The delicious . . . *baldness* of it! Who gives a damn about subtlety? Just win, like, that's the name of the game, and the —— Agency had £70 million in accounts last year.

They always took him to lunch at places like the Four Seasons, and if it came to £16 for four people, for lunch, that was nothing. There are expensive places where businessmen eat lunch in London, but they always have some kind of coy atmosphere, trattorias, chez this or that, or old places with swiney, pebbly English surnames, Craw's, Grouse's, Scob's, Clot's. But the Four Seasons! The place practically exudes an air-conditioned sweat of pure huge expensive-account . . . *money*. Everybody sits there in this huge bald smooth-slab Mies-van-der-Rohe-style black-onyx executive suite atmosphere taking massive infusions of exotic American cocktails, Margaritas, Gibsons, Bloody Marys, Rob Roys, Screwdrivers, Pisco Sours, and French wines and French brandies, while the blood vessels dilate and the ego dilates and Leonard Lyons, the columnist, comes in to look around and see who is there, and everyone watches these ingenious copper-chain curtains rippling over the plate glass, rippling up, up, it is an optical illusion but it looks like they are rippling, rippling, rippling, rippling up this cliff of plate glass like a waterfall gone into reverse.

And some guy at the table is letting everybody in on this deliciously child-cynical American secret, namely, that a lot of the cigarette advertising currently is based on motivational research into people's reactions to the cancer scare. For example, the ones that always show blue grass and blue streams and blond, blue-eyed young people with picnic baskets, and gallons of prime-of-life hormones gushing through their Diet-Rite loins, are actually aimed at hypochondriacs who need constant reassurance that they aren't dying of cancer. On the other hand, the ones that say "I'd rather fight than switch" really mean "I'd rather get cancer than give up smoking"—New York!—the copper curtains ripple up. . . .

One interesting, rather nice thing he notices, however, is that they are tremendously anxious to please him. They are apparently impressed by him, even though he comes there very much as the beggar. They are the parent firm. Whatever they say about the Fabrilex campaign in England goes, in the long run. If they want to aim it at hypochondriac masochists who fear cancer of the skin, then that's it. Yet they treat him as a partner, no, as slightly superior. Then he gets it. It is because he is English. They keep staring at his suit, which is from Huntsman and has 12-inch side vents. They watch his table manners and then . . . glorious! *im*itate him. Old George! He used to say to waiters, "*Would* you please bring some water" or whatever it was, whereas he always said, "*Could* you bring the cheese now, please?" or whatever it was—the thing is, the Americans say *would*, which implies that the waiter is doing one a favor by granting this wish, whereas the Englishman—class!—says *could*, which assumes that since the waiter is a servant, he will if he can.

And old George got that distinction right off! That's it with these Americans. They're incurable children, they're incurable nouveaux, they spell *finesse* with a *ph* to give it more *tone*—but they sense the status distinctions. And so by the second time old George is saying "Could you bring me some water, do you think?" and running do-you-think together into an upper-class blur over the top of his sopping glottis just . . . like a real Englishman.

So all of a sudden *he* began to sense that he had it both ways. He had the American thing and the English thing. They emerge from the Four Seasons, out on to 52nd Street—kheew!—the sun blasts them in the eyes and there it is, wild, childish, bald, overpowering Park Avenue in the Fifties, huge cliffs of plate glass and steel frames, like a mountain of telephone booths. Hundreds of, jaysus, millions of dollars' worth of shimmering junk, with so many sheets of plate glass the buildings all reflect each other in marine greens and blues, like a 25-cent postcard from Sarasota, Florida—not a good building in the lot, but, jaysus, the sheer incredible yah!—we've-got-it money and power it represents. The Rome of the twentieth century—and because wealth and power are here, everything else follows, and it is useless for old England to continue to harp on form, because it is all based on the wealth and power England had 150 years ago. The platter of the world's goodie sweets tilts . . . to New York, girls, for one thing, all these young lithe girls with flamingo legs come pouring into New York and come popping up out of the armpit-steaming sewer tunnels of the New York subways, out of those screeching sewers, dressed to the eyeballs, lathed, polished, linked, lacquered, coiffed with spun brass.

Ah, and *they* loved Englishmen, too. He found a brass-topped beauty and he will never forget following her up the stairs to her flat that first night. The front door was worn and rickety but heavy and had an air hinge on it that made it close and lock immediately, automatically—against those ravenous, adrenal New York animals *out there;* even New York's criminals are more animal, basic savage, Roman, *criminal* —he never remembered a block of flats in London with an air hinge on the front door—and he followed her up the stairs, a few steps behind her, and watched the muscles in her calves contract and the hamstring ligaments spring out at the backs of her knees, oh young taut healthy New York girl flamingo legs, and it was all so . . . tender and brave.

Precisely! Her walk-up flat was so essentially dreary, way over in the East Eighties, an upper floor of somebody's old townhouse that had been cut up and jerry-built into flats just slightly better than a bed-sitter, with the bedroom about the size of a good healthy wardrobe closet and a so-called Pullman kitchen in the living room, some fiercely, meanly efficient uni-unit, a little sink, refrigerator and stove all welded together behind shutters at one end, and a bathroom with no window, just some sort of air duct in there with the slits grimed and hanging, booga, with some sort of gray compost of lint, sludge, carbon particles and noxious gases. And the toilet barely worked, just a lazy spiral current of water down the hole after one pulled down that stubby little handle they have. The floor tilted slightly, but—brave and tender!

Somehow she had managed to make it all look beautiful, Japanese globe lamps made of balsa strips and paper, greenery, great lush fronds of some kind of plant, several prints on the wall, one an insanely erotic water-color nude by Egon Schiele, various hangings, coverings, drapings of primitive textiles, monk's cloth, homespuns, a little vase full of violet paper flowers, a bookcase, painted white, full of heavyweight, or middleweight, paperback books, *The Lonely Crowd, The Confessions of Felix Krull, African Genesis*—brave and tender!—all of these lithe young girls living in dreadful walk-up flats, alone, with a cat, and the faint odor of cat feces in the Kitty Litter, and an oily wooden salad bowl on the table, and a cockroach silhouetted on the rim of the salad bowl—and yet there was something touching about it, *haunting*, he wanted to say, the desperate fight to stay in New York amid the excitement of money and power, the Big Apple, and for days, if he is to be honest about it, he had the most inexplicably tender memory of—all right!—the poor sad way the water had lazed down in the toilet bowl. That poor, marvelous, erotic girl. At one point she had told him she had learned to put a diaphragm on in 15 seconds. She just said it, out of thin air. So bald.

Early the next morning he took a cab back to his hotel to change for the day and the driver tried to project the thing in manic bursts through the rush-hour traffic, lurches of acceleration, sudden braking, skids, screeches, all the while shouting out the window, cursing and then demanding support from him—"Dja see that! Guy got his head up his ass. Am I right?"—and strangely, he found himself having a thoroughly American reaction, actually answering these stupid questions because he wanted to be approved of by this poor bastard trying to hurtle through the money-and-power traffic, answering a cab driver who said, "Guy got his head up his ass, am I right"—because suddenly he found himself close to the source, he understood this thing—the hell with scarves, Pitt Clubs and pale silk ties, and watch out England, you got your head up your ass, and here comes a Mid-Atlantic Man.

His career back with the —— Agency in London picked up brilliantly for Mid-Atlantic Man. His momentum was tremendous when he came back. London was a torpid little town on a river. He began to cultivate the American members of the firm. Certain things about the advertising business that he had never been able to stomach, really, but nevertheless swallowed silently—suddenly he began to realize that what it was, these things were American, bald and cynical, only now he . . . *understood*. Yea-saying!

There was one American woman in the firm, and in the most unconcerned way she would talk about the opening of a big new American hotel that had gone up in London and how the invitation list was divided into (1) Celebrities, (2) VIPs, (3) CIPs and (4) just

Guests. Things like that used to make his flesh crawl, but now—now—the beautiful part was the CIPs—Commercially Important People, people important to the hotel for business reasons but whose names meant nothing in terms of publicity, however. Marvelous!

He got to be a good friend of hers. One day they went out to lunch, and there were a lot of people on the footpaths, and suddenly she spotted a woman about 20 feet away and said, "Look at her! The perfect C-1." One of the innovations, for the purpose of surveys and aiming campaigns accurately, had been to break down consumers into four categories: A, B, C-1 and C-2. A was upper class, B was middle class, C-1 was upper working class or lower middle class, in that range, and C-2 was plain working class.

"The perfect C-1!" she said.

"The perfect C-1?"

"Yes! Look. She's done her hair herself. She's wearing a Marks & Spencer knitted dress. She bought her shoes at Lotus. She's carrying a shopping basket"—with this she moved right up next to the woman and looked in the shopping basket—"she's bought pre-cut wrapped bread"—she only barely turns back to him to announce all this out loud—"she's bought a box of Wiz detergent with five free plastic daffodils inside"—and the poor woman wheels her head around resentfully—but he wants to shout for joy: Bald! Delicious! A running commentary on a London street about a perfect C-1!

That night he took her to the —— Trattoria, underneath those inevitable white plaster arches and black metal cylinder lamps. He came on breezy, first-naming the waiters as he walked in, like . . . a pal. Over the avocado vinaigrette he told her, conspiratorially, that the Agency was still hopelessly backward because it was run, in England, by the kind of Englishmen who think a successful business is one where you can get educated men to work for you for £2,000 a year and come to work dressed as if they make £10,000. After the wine he told her: "I've got the neuroses of New York and the decadence of London."

She thought that was—god!—great. So he sprang it, spontaneously as he could manage it, on many occasions thereafter. He also took to wearing black knit ties. Somehow they have become the insignia of Mid-Atlantic Man. He got the idea from David Frost, who always wore one.

Instead of using Cockney or Liverpool slang for humorous effect, narked, knickers-job and all that, he began using American hip-lower-class slang, like, I mean, you know, baby, and a little late Madison Avenue. "Why, don't we throw it—" he would be speaking of somebody's idea—"and see if it skips across the pond." He always brought the latest American rock 'n' roll records back with him from New York, plus a lot of news of discothèques, underground movies, and people like Andy, Jane, Borden, Olivier. He always made a big point of telling everyone that he was expecting a call from New York, from *David*—and everyone knew this was a big New York advertising man—David!—David!—New York! New York!—hot line to the source! —land of flamingo legs and glass cliffs!—mine! mine!—

But then there were a few disquieting developments. The waiters at the —— Trattoria began *treating* him like an American. He would come on all pally—and they would do things like this: He would order some esoteric wine, Château whateveritwas, and they would bring him a bottle and pour out a little in his glass and he would taste it and pronounce it good and then one of his . . . *pals*, a waiter, would say, right out loud, in front of the girl he was with: We didn't have any more Château whateveritwas, sir, so I brought you Château thing, I hope it's all right, sir. All he can do is sit there and nod like a fool, because he has already tasted it and pronounced it good Château whateveritwas—oh Christ.

And then, at the Agency, the Americans began to treat him as one of them. There was this stupid moment when A—, an American who ranged just above him, was going off on holiday, and he said to him, very solemnly, in front of several Englishmen:

"Think about Pube-Glo for me while I'm gone."

Not "think about the Pube-Glo account" or "work on the Pube-Glo campaign," but think about Pube-Glo, with that pure, simple American double-think loyalty to the product itself. He had to stand there, in front of other Englishmen, and solemnly agree to think about Pube-Glo. What was worse, he would have to show some evidence of having thought about Pube-Glo when A— came back, which meant he would actually have to spend time out of his life thinking about this vile fake-erotic concoction named Pube-Glo.

The hell of it was, he gradually found himself thinking English, not necessarily wisely, but rather fundamentally. Two New York Italians came over to take over—"hype up" was the term transmitted from New York—the art department, and he looked at them. They were dressed in flash clothes, sort of Sy Devore of Hollywood style, wearing tight pants like a chubby hairdresser, and right away they began changing this and that, like some sort of colonial inspector generals. They were creeps even by New York standards. Even? Where was his love of that delicious, cynical . . . baldness . . .

Part of it was back in New York trampled to death. Jaysus, he didn't want to say anything, but the more he went to New York . . . sometimes the whole . . . attitude in New York was hard to take. He was in New York, staying at George's big apartment on East 57th

Street, and he had to get out to the airport. He had two huge heavy bags because it was just before Christmas and he was bringing back all sorts of things. So he half trundled them out to the elevator, and at length it arrived and he said to the elevator man: "Could you give me a hand with these, please?"

"I'm sorry, Mac," the elevator man said, "I can't leave this elevator. My job is running this elevator. It's against the law, I can't leave a running elevator," and so forth and so on, even after he had dragged the bags on himself, a lecture all the way down.

At the ground floor the doorman opened the door for him but looked at the bags as if they were covered with flies. Outside it was slushy and rainy, and there was a pond of slush out from the curb. So he said to the doorman—this time summoning up the ancient accent of British command:

"Could you get me a cab, please."

"No, I couldn't," the man says, with just a hint of mockery. "I would, Buddy, but I can't. I can't get no cab on a night like this. You'll have to take your best shot."

Finally he flags down a cab, and both the doorman and the driver watch, with great logistic interest, as he navigates the bags through the pond of slush, getting his shoes and socks wet. In the cab he tells the man he wants to go to the airport, and he answers, in a hideous impersonation of a Cockney accent:

"Ow-kay, guv."

Then he turns up the car radio very loud to WQXR, the classical music station, apparently to impress him. The piece is something horribly morose by that old fraud Stravinsky.

Back in London he learns that a few changes have taken place. The Hon. ——, a melon-jawed ball of fire who is 31 and once had a job doing whatever it was, somewhere, has been brought in at a high level as a "consultant," and so has young Lady ——. Meantime, Peter ——, an Etonian, an Oxonian, first cousin of Lord ——, has suddenly been elevated to his level after ten months with the firm. And gradually it becomes obvious. Advertising may be a new industry, it may be an American art, it may be a triumph of the New World, but in the competition for new accounts, the clients—English new money as well as foreign clients—they want to be dealing with an upper-class Englishman, want to feel they are buying upper-class treatment for their £20,000 or whatever, want to let their blood vessels dilate and their egos dilate over lunch at the Connaught with upper-class Englishmen—

—but wait a minute, it can't *all* go back to that, he will hang in there, try to get that inviolable feeling again, the best of both worlds, and here amid the lyre-splat chairs, the bullion-fringe curtains, the old blacky Raeburn-style portraits, Roger! Have you met George? Cyril! Have you met George? Keith! Have you—

—and Peter. Pe-t-e-r . . . he watches Peter's lip curdle. It is as if it is taking forever, as in a Cocteau film, old George's eyes are frozen in the panic-grinning bobble, and—oh God of Fabrilex!—none of these smart bastards are coming over for sherry after all, are they, ever, ever.

On Parents Day

"Puh-leeze, Mummy, nobody wants to hear about coke, Acapulco, or Fleetwood Mac."

ON THE BUS

I couldn't tell you for sure which of the Merry Pranksters got the idea for the bus, but it had the Babbs touch. It was a superprank, in any case. The original fantasy, here in the spring of 1964, had been that Kesey and four or five others would get a station wagon and drive to New York for the New York World's Fair. On the way they could shoot some film, make some tapes, freak out on the Fair and see what happened. They would also be on hand, in New York, for the publication of Kesey's second novel, *Sometimes a Great Notion*, early in July. So went the original fantasy.

Then somebody—Babbs?—saw a classified ad for a 1939 International Harvester school bus. The bus belonged to a man in Menlo Park. He had a big house and a lot of grounds and a nice set of tweeds and flannels and eleven children. He had rigged out the bus for the children. It had bunks and benches and a refrigerator and a sink for washing dishes and cabinets and shelves and a lot of other nice features for living on the road. Kesey bought it for $1,500—in the name of Intrepid Trips, Inc.

Kesey gave the word and the Pranksters set upon it one afternoon. They started painting it and wiring it for sound and cutting a hole in the roof and fixing up the top of the bus so you could sit up there in the open air and play music, even a set of drums and electric guitars and electric bass and so forth, or just ride. Sandy went to work on the wiring and rigged up a system with which they could broadcast from inside the bus, with tapes or over microphones, and it would blast outside over powerful speakers on top of the bus. There were also microphones outside that would pick up sounds along the road and

From *The Electric Kool-Aid Acid Test*, chapters 6 and 7 (New York: Farrar, Straus and Giroux, 1968).

broadcast them inside the bus. There was also a sound system inside the bus so you could broadcast to one another over the roar of the engine and the road. You could also broadcast over a tape mechanism so that you said something, then heard your own voice a second later in variable lag and could rap off of that if you wanted to. Or you could put on earphones and rap simultaneously off sounds from outside, coming in one ear, and sounds from inside, your own sounds, coming in the other ear. There was going to be no goddamn sound on that whole trip, outside the bus, inside the bus, or inside your own freaking larynx, that you couldn't tune in on and rap off of.

The painting job, meanwhile, with everybody pitching in in a frenzy of primary colors, yellows, oranges, blues, reds, was sloppy as hell, except for the parts Roy Seburn did, which were nice manic mandalas. Well, it was sloppy, but one thing you had to say for it; it was freaking lurid. The manifest, the destination sign in the front, read: "Furthur," with two *u*'s.

They took a test run up into northern California and right away this wild-looking thing with wild-looking people was great for stirring up consternation and vague befuddling resentment among the citizens. The Pranksters were now out among them, and it was exhilarating—look at the mothers staring!—and there was going to be holy terror in the land. But there would also be people who would look up out of their poor work-a-daddy lives in some town, some old guy, somebody's stenographer, and see this bus and register . . . delight, or just pure open-invitation wonder. Either way, the Intrepid Travelers figured, there was hope for these people. They weren't totally turned off. The bus also had great possibilities for altering the usual order of things. For example, there were the cops.

One afternoon the Pranksters were on a test run in the bus going through the woods up north and a forest fire had started. There was smoke beginning to pour out of the woods and everything. Everybody on the bus had taken acid and they were zonked. The acid was in some orange juice in the refrigerator and you drank a paper cup full of it and you were zonked. Cassady was driving and barreling through the burning woods wrenching the steering wheel this way and that way to his inner-wired beat, with a siren wailing and sailing through the rhythm.

A *siren?* It's a highway patrolman, which immediately seems like the funniest thing in the history of the world. Smoke is pouring out of the woods and they are all sailing through leaf explosions in the sky, but the cop is bugged about this freaking bus. The cop yanks the bus over to the side and he starts going through a kind of traffic-safety inspection of the big gross bus, while more and more of the smoke is billowing out of the woods. Man, the license plate is on wrong and there's no light over the license plate and this turn signal looks bad and how about the brakes, let's see that hand brake there. Cassady, the driver, is already into a long monologue for the guy, only he is throwing in all kinds of sirs: "Well, yes sir, this is a Hammond bi-valve serrated brake, you understand, sir, had it put on in a truck ro-de-o in Springfield, Oregon, had to back through a slalom course of baby's bottles and yellow nappies, in the existential culmination of Oregon, lots of outhouse freaks up there, you understand, sir, a punctual sort of a state, sir, yes, sir, holds to 28,000 pounds, 28,000 pounds, you just look right here, sir, tested by a pure-blooded Shell Station attendant in Springfield, Oregon, winter of '62, his gumball boots never froze, you understand, sir, 28,000 pounds hold, right here—" Whereupon he yanks back on the hand-brake handle as if it's attached to something, which it isn't, it is just dangling there, and jams his foot on the regular brake, and the bus shudders as if the hand brake has a hell of a bite, but the cop is thoroughly befuddled now, anyway, because Cassady's monologue has confused him, for one thing, and what the hell are these . . . *people* doing. By this time everybody is off the bus rolling in the brown grass by the shoulder, laughing, giggling, yahooing, zonked to the skies on acid, because, mon, the woods are burning, the whole world is on fire, and a Cassady monologue on automotive safety is rising up from out of his throat like weenie smoke, as if the great god Speed were frying in his innards, and the cop, representative of the people of California in this total freaking situation, is all hung up on a hand brake that doesn't exist in the first place. And the cop, all he can see is a bunch of crazies in screaming orange and green costumes, masks, boys and girls, men and women, twelve or fourteen of them, lying in the grass and making hideously crazy sounds—christ almighty, why the hell does he have to contend with . . . So he wheels around and says, "What are you, uh—show people?"

"That's right, officer," Kesey says. "We're show people. It's been a long row to hoe, I can tell you, and it's *gonna* be a long row to hoe, but that's the business."

"Well," says the cop, "you fix up those things and . . ." He starts backing off toward his car, cutting one last look at the crazies. ". . . And watch it next time . . ." And he guns on off.

That was it! How can you give a traffic ticket to a bunch of people rolling in the brown grass wearing Day-Glo masks, practically Greek masques, only with Rat phosphorescent *élan*, giggling, keening in their costumes and private world while the god Speed sizzles like a short-order French fry in the gut of some guy who doesn't even stop talking to breathe. A traffic ticket? The Pranksters felt more immune than ever. There was no more reason for them to remain in isolation while the ovoid eyes of La Honda suppurated. They could go through the face of America muddling people's minds, but it's a momentary high, and the bus would be gone, and all the Fab foam in their heads would settle back down into their brain pans.

So the Hieronymus Bosch bus headed out of Kesey's place with the destination sign in front reading "Furthur" and a sign in the back saying "Caution: Weird Load." It was weird, all right, but it was euphoria on board, barreling through all that warm California sun in July, on the road, and everything they had been working on at Kesey's was on board and heading on Furthur. Besides, the joints were going around, and it was nice and high out here on the road in America. As they headed out, Cassady was at the wheel, and there was Kesey, Babbs, Page Browning, George Walker, Sandy, Jane Burton, Mike Hagen, Hassler, Kesey's brother Chuck and his cousin Dale, a guy known as Brother John, and three newcomers who were just along for the ride or just wanted to go to New York.

One of them was a young, quite handsome kid—looked sort of like the early, thin Michael Caine in *Zulu*—named Steve Lambrecht. He was the brother-in-law of Kesey's lawyer, Paul Robertson, and he was just riding to New York to see a girl he knew named Kathy. Another was a girl named Paula Sundsten. She was young, plump, ebullient, and very sexy. Kesey knew her from Oregon. Another one was some girl Hagen of the Screw Shack had picked up in San Francisco, on North Beach. She was the opposite of Paula Sundsten. She was thin, had long dark hair, and would be moody and silent one minute and nervous and carrying on the next. She was good-looking like a TV witch.

By the time they hit San Jose, barely 30 miles down the road, a lot of the atmosphere of the trip was already established. It was nighttime and many souls were high and the bus had broken down. They pulled into a service station and pretty soon one of the help has his nose down in under the hood looking at the engine while Cassady races the motor and the fluorescent stanchion lights around the station hit the bus in weird phosphorescent splashes, the car lights stream by on the highway, Cassady guns the engine some more, and from out of the bus comes a lot of weird wailing, over the speakers or just out the windows. Paula Sundsten has gotten hold of a microphone with the variable-lag setup and has found out she can make weird radio-spook laughing ghoul sounds with it, wailing like a banshee and screaming "How was your stay-ay-ay-ay . . . in San Ho-zay-ay-ay-ay-ay," with the variable lag picking up the ay-ay-ay-ays and doubling them, quadrupling them, octupling them. An endless ricocheting echo—and all the while this weird, slightly hysterical laugh and a desperate little plunking mandolin sail through it all, coming from Hagen's girl friend, who is lying back on a bench inside, plunking a mandolin and laughing—in what way . . .

Outside, some character, some local, has come over to the bus, but the trouble is, he is not at all impressed with the bus, he just has to do the American Man thing of when somebody's car is broken down you got to come over and make your diagnosis.

And he is saying to Kesey and Cassady, "You know what I'd say you need? I'd say you need a good mechanic. Now, I'm not a good mechanic, but I—" And naturally he proceeds to give his diagnosis, while Paula wails, making spook-house effects, and the Beauty Witch keens and goons—and—

"—like I say, what you need is a good mechanic, and I'm not a good mechanic, but—"

And—of course!—the Non-people. The whole freaking world was full of people who were bound to tell you they weren't qualified to do this or that but they were determined to go ahead and do just that thing anyway. Kesey decided he was the Non-navigator. Babbs was the Non-doctor. The bus trip was already becoming an allegory of life.

Before heading east, out across the country, they stopped at Babbs's place in San Juan Capistrano, down below Los Angeles. Babbs and his wife Anita had a place down there. They pulled the bus into Babbs's garage and sat around for one final big briefing before taking off to the east.

Kesey starts talking in the old soft Oregon drawl and everybody is quiet.

"Here's what I hope will happen on this trip," he says. "What I hope will continue to happen, because it's already starting to happen. All of us are beginning to do our thing, and we're going to keep doing it, right out front, and none of us are going to deny what other people are doing."

"Bullshit," says Jane Burton.

This brings Kesey up short for a moment, but he just rolls with it.

"That's Jane," he says. "And she's doing her thing. Bullshit. That's her thing and she's doing it.

"None of us are going to deny what other people are doing. If saying bullshit is somebody's thing, then he says bullshit. If somebody is an ass-kicker, then that's what he's going to do on this trip, kick asses. He's going to do it right out front and nobody is going to have anything to get pissed off about. He can just say, 'I'm sorry I kicked you in the ass, but I'm not sorry I'm an ass-kicker. That's what I do, I kick people in the ass.' Everybody is going to be what they are, and whatever they are, there's not going to be anything to apologize about. What we are, we're going to wail with on this whole trip."

Haul ass, and what we are, out across the Southwest, and all of it on film and on tape. Refrigerator, stove, a sink, bunk racks, blankets, acid, speed, grass—with Hagen handling the movie camera and everybody on microphones and the music blaring out over the roar of the bus, rock 'n' roll, Jimmy Smith. Cassady is revved up like they've never seen him before, with his shirt off, a straw version of a cowboy hat on his head, bouncing up and down on the driver's seat, shifting gears—doubledy-clutch, doubledy-clutch, blamming on the steering wheel and the gearshift box, rapping over the microphone rigged up by his seat like a manic tour guide, describing every car going by,

"—there's a barber going down the highway cutting his hair at 500 miles an hour, you understand—"

"So remember those expressions, sacrifice, glorious and in vain!" Babbs says.

"Food! Food! Food!" Hagen says.

"Get out the de-glom ointment, sergeant!" says Babbs, rapping at Steve Lambrecht. "The only cure for joint glom, gets the joint off the lip in instant De-Glom—"

—and so on, because Steve always has a joint glommed onto his lip and, in fact, gets higher than any man alive, on any and all things one throws his way, and picks up the name Zonker on this trip—

"—De-Glom for the Zonker!—"

—and then Babbs parodies Cassady—

"—and there's a Cadillac with Marie Antoinette—"

—and the speakers wail, and the mandolin wails and the weird laugh wails, and the variable lag wails-ails-ails-ails-ails-ails, and somebody—who?—hell, *every*body wails.

"—we're finally beginning to move, after three fucking days!"

On the second day they reached Wikieup, an old Wild West oasis out in the Arizona desert along Route 60. It was all gray-brown desert and sun and this lake, which was like a huge slimy kelpy pond, but the air was fantastic. Sandy felt great. Then Kesey held the second briefing. They were going to take their first acid of the trip here and have their first major movie production. He and Babbs and the gorgeous sexy Paula Sundsten were going to take acid—*Wikieup!*—and the others were going to record what happened. Hagen and Walker were going to film it, Sandy was going to handle the sound, and Ron Bevirt was going to take photographs.

Sandy feels his first twinge of—what? Like . . . there is going to be

Authorized Acid only. And like . . . they are going to be separated into performers and workers, stars and backstage. Like . . . there is an inner circle and an outer circle. This was illogical, because Hagen and Walker, certainly, were closer to Kesey than any other Pranksters besides Babbs, and they were "workers," too, but that was the way he feels. But he doesn't say anything. Not . . . out front.

Kesey and Babbs and Paula hook down some acid orange juice from the refrigerator and wait for the vibrations. Paula is in a hell of a great mood. She has never taken LSD before, but she looks fearless and immune and ready for all, and she hooks down a good slug of it. They wait for the vibrations . . . and here they come.

Babbs has a big cane, a walking stick, and he is waving it around in the air, and the three of them, Babbs, Kesey and Paula, go running and kicking and screaming toward the lake and she dives in—and comes up with her head covered in muck and great kelpy strands of green pond slime—and beaming in a way that practically radiates out over the face of the lake and the desert. She has surfaced euphoric—

"Oooooh! It sparkles!"

—pulling her long strands of slime-slithering hair outward with her hands and grokking and freaking over it—

"Oooooooh! It sparkles!"

—the beads of water on her slime strands are like diamonds to her, and everybody feels her feeling at once, even Sandy—

"Ooooooooh! It sparkles!"

—surfaced euphoric! euphorically garlanded in long greasy garlands of pond slime, the happiest slime freak in the West—

—and Babbs is euphoric for her—

"Gretchen Fetchin the Slime Queen!" he yells and waves his cane at the sky.

"Oooooooh! It sparkles!"

"Gretchen Fetchin the Slime Queen!"

"It sparkles!"

"Gretchen Fetchin!"

And it is beautiful. Everybody goes manic and euphoric like a vast contact high, like they have all suddenly taken acid themselves. Kesey is in an athletic romp, tackling the ferns and other slimy greenery in the lake. Babbs and Paula—Gretchen Fetchin!—are yahooing at the sky. Hagen is feverishly filming it all, Sandy has a set of huge cables stretched out to the very edge of the lake, picking up the sound, Ron Bevirt is banging away with his camera. Babbs and Paula—Gretchen Fetchin!—and Kesey keep plunging out into the mucky innards of the lake.

"Come back!" Hagen the cameraman starts yelling. "You're out of range!"

But Babbs and Paula and Kesey can't hear him. They are cartwheeling further and further out into the paradise muck—

"It sparkles!"

"Gretchen Fetchin—Queen of the Slime!"

But meanwhile Hagen's Beauty Witch, in the contagion of the moment, has slipped to the refrigerator and taken some acid, and now she is outside the bus on the desert sand wearing a black snakeskin blouse and a black mantle, with her long black hair coming down over it like a pre-Raphaelite painting and a cosmic grin on her witch-white face, lying down on the desert, striking poses and declaiming in couplets. She's zonked out of her nut, but it's all in wild manic Elizabethan couplets:

"Methinks you need a gulp of grass
And so it quickly came to pass
You fell to earth with eely shrieking,
Wooing my heart, freely freaking!"

—and so forth. Well, she wins Hagen's manic heart right away, and soon he has wandered off from the Lake of the Slime Euphoria and is in a wide-legged stance over her with the camera as she lies declaiming on the desert floor, camera zeroed in on her like she is Maria Montez in a love scene—and now the Beauty Witch is off on her trip for good . . .

Back on the bus and off for Phoenix in the slime-euphoric certitude that they and the movie—The Movie!—many allegories of life—that they could not miss now. Hagen pressed on with the film, hour after hour in the bouncing innards of the bus. There were moments in the History of Film that broke everybody up. One was when they reached Phoenix. This was during the 1964 election excitement and they were in Barry Goldwater's home town, so they put a streamer on the bus reading: "A Vote for Barry is a Vote for Fun." And they put American flags up on the bus and Cassady drove the bus backward down the main drag of Phoenix while Hagen recorded it on film and the flags flew backward in the windstream. The citizens were suitably startled, outraged, delighted, nonplused, and would wheel around and stare or else try to keep their cool by sidling glances like they weren't going to be impressed by any *weird shit*—and a few smiled in a frank way as if to say, I am with you—if only I could be with you!

The fact that they were all high on speed or grass, or so many combinations thereof that they couldn't keep track, made it seem like a great secret life. It was a great secret life. The befuddled citizens could only see the outward manifestations of the incredible stuff going on inside their skulls. They were all now characters in their own movies or the Big Movie. They took on new names and used them.

Steve Lambrecht was Zonker. Cassady was Speed Limit. Kesey was Swashbuckler. Babbs was Intrepid Traveler. Hagen, bouncing along with the big camera, soaring even while the bus roared, was Mal Function. Ron Bevirt had charge of all the equipment, the tools, wires, jacks, and stuff, and became known as Equipment Hassler, and then just Hassler. George Walker was Hardly Visible. And Paula Sundsten became . . . Gretchen Fetchin the Slime Queen, of course . . .

A notebook!—for each of the new characters in The Movie, a plain child's notebook, and each character in this here movie can write in his notebook himself or other people can pick up the notebook and write in it—who knows who wrote what?—and in Gretchen Fetchin's it says:

Bury them in slime!
She cried, flailing about the garden—
With a sprig of parsley clutched in
her hands—which had always been
clamped in her hands.
　　This is strange business,
Gets weirder all the time,
She said, wrapping some around
her finger, for we are always
moist in her hand . . . "Naturally," she
said, "The roots are deep."
　　That was no surprise, but she
was mildly curious to
know what the hell is

　　　　　　　THAT
　　Whereupon he got very
clumsy, giggled confidentially,
and tripped over her shadow,
carrying them both into
an unaccountable adventure.

Barely a week out and already beautiful ebullient sexy Gretchen Fetchin the Slime Queen, Gretch, is *synched* in. Kesey, the very Swashbuckler himself, makes a play for her, and that should be that, but she looks at—Babbs—who tripped over her shadow?—Hmmmm-mmmm? So many shadows and shafts of Southwest sun bouncing in through the windows and all over the floor, over the benches over the bunk uprights bouncing out of the freaking roar of the engine bouncing two sets of Gretch eyes two sets of Babbs eyes, four sets of Gretch eyes four sets of Babbs eyes eight sets of Gretch eyes eight sets of Babbs eyes all grinning vibrating bouncing in among one another carrying them both into an unaccountable adventure, you understand. Kesey sulks a bit—Kesey himself—but the sulk bounces and breaks up into Southwestern sunballs. *Drivin' on dirt in Utah, a '46 Plymouth with an overhead cam*, says Cassady. The refrigerator door squeaks open, gurgle gurgle, this acid O.J. makes a body plumb smack his lips, Hagen and his Black Witch girl friend hook down a cup of acid orange juice apiece and Hagen's sweet face spirals, turning sweet Christian boy clockwise and sweet sly Screw Shack counterclockwise, back and forth, and they disappear, bouncing, up the ladder, up through the turret hole and onto the roof where, under the mightily hulking sun of the Southwest and 70 miles an hour—Pretty soon Hagen is climbing back down the ladder and heading for the refrigerator and hooking down another cup of orange juice and smiling for all, Christian boy and Screw Shack sly, spiraling this way and that way —and climbing back up top the bus in order to—

MAL FUNCTION!

If only I had $10, then we
could split ½ a Ritalin order
with Margo—I eat
Ritalin like aspirin
Now, let's charm Brooks Brothers—
impressed?

At night the goddamn bus still bouncing and the Southwest silvery blue coming in not exactly bouncing but slipping and sliding in shafts, sickly shit, and car beams and long crazy shadows from car beams sliding in weird bends over the inside, over the love bunk. The love bunk'll get you if you don't wash out. One shelf on the bunk has a sleeping bag on it and into this sleeping bag crawl whoever wants to make it, do your thing, bub, and right out front, and wail with it, and Sandy looks over and he can see a human . . . bobbing up and down in the sleeping bag with the car beams sliding over it and the motor roaring, the fabulous love bunk, and everyone—*synch*—can see that sleeping bag veritably filling up with sperm, the little devils swimming like mad in there in the muck, oozing into the cheap hairy shit they quilt the bag with, millions billions trillions of them, darting around, crafty little flagellants, looking to *score*, which is natural, and if any certified virgin on the face of the earth crawled into that sleeping bag for a nap after lunch she would be a hulking knocked-up miracle inside of three minutes—but won't this goddamn *bouncing* ever stop—

This being a school bus, and not a Greyhound, the springs and the shock absorbers are terrible and the freaking grinding straining motor shakes it to pieces and hulking vibrations synched in to no creature on earth keep batting everybody around on the benches and the bunks. It is almost impossible to sleep and the days and nights have their own sickly cycle, blinding sun all day and the weird car beams and shadows sliding sick and slow at night and all the time the noise. Jane Burton is nauseous practically the whole time. Nobody can sleep so they keep taking more speed to keep going, psychic energizers like Ritalin, anything, and then smoke more grass to take the goddamn tachycardiac edge off the speed, and acid to make the whole thing turn into something else. Then it all starts swinging back and forth between grueling battering lurching flogging along the highway—and unaccountable delays, stopped, unendurable frustration by the side of the road in the middle of nowhere while the feeling of no-sleep starts turning the body and the skull into a dried-out husk inside with a sour greasy smoke like a tenement fire curdling in the brainpan. They have to pull into gasoline stations to go to the bathroom, cop a urination or an egestion—keep regular, friends—but 12—how many, 14?—did we lose somebody—did we pick up somebody—climbing out of this bus, which is weird-looking for a start, but all these weird people are too much, clambering out—the service station attendant and his Number One Boy stare at this—Negro music is blaring out of the speakers and these weird people clamber out, half of them in costume, lurid shirts with red and white stripes, some of them with weird paint on their faces, like comic-book Indians, with huge circles under their eyes, eyes red, noses not blue, not nearly blue enough, but eyes red—all trooping out toward the Clean Rest Rooms, already queuing up, practically—

"Wait a minute," the guy says. "What do you think you're doing?"

"Fill 'er up!" says Kesey, very soft and pleasant. "Yes, sir, she's a big bus and she takes a lotta gas. Yep."

"I mean what are *they* doing?"

"Them? I 'spect they're going to the bathroom. Ay-yuh, that big old thing's the worst gas-eater you ever saw"—all the time motioning to Hagen to go get the movie camera and the microphone.

"Well, can't all those people use the bathrooms."

"All they want to do is go to the bathroom"—and now Kesey takes the microphone and Hagen starts shooting the film—*whirrrrrrrrrrrrrrrrr*—but all very casual as if, well, sure, don't *you* record it all, every last morsel of friendly confrontation whenever you stop on the great American highway to cop a urination or two? or a dozen?

"Well, now, listen! You ain't using the bathrooms! You hear me, now! You see that motel back there? I own that motel, too, and we got one septic tank here, for here and there, and you're not gonna overflow it for me. Now git that thing out of my face!"

—Kesey has the microphone in the guy's face, like this is all for the six o'clock news, and then he brings the microphone back to his face, just like the TV interview shows, and says,

"You see that bus out there? Every time we stop to fill 'er up we have to lay a *whole lot* of money on somebody, and we'd like it to be you, on account of your hospitality."

"It's an unaccountable adventure in consumer spending," says Babbs.

"Get those cameras and microphones out of here," the guy says. "I'm not afraid of you!"

"I should hope not," says Kesey, still talking soft and down-home. "All that money that big baby's gonna drink up. Whew!"

Sheerooooooo—all this time the toilets are flushing, this side and that side and the noise of it roars and gurgles right through the cinder block walls until it sounds like there's nothing in the whole wide open U. S. of A. except for Clean Rest Room toilets and Day-Glo crazies and cameras and microphones from out of nowhere, and the guy just caves in under it. He can't fit it into his movie of Doughty American Entrepreneur—*not no kind of way*—

"Well, they better make it fast or there's going to be trouble around here." And he goes out to fill 'er up, this goddamn country is going down the drain.

But they don't speed it up. Walker is over to the coin telephone putting in a call to Faye back in La Honda. Babbs is clowning around out on the concrete apron of the gas station with Gretchen Fetchin. Jane Burton feels bilious—the idea is to go to New York, isn't it? even on a 1939 school bus it could be done better than this. What are we waiting, waiting, waiting, waiting for, playing games with old crocks at gas stations. Well, we're waiting for Sandy, for one thing. Where in the hell is Sandy. But Sandy—he hasn't slept in days and he has an unspecific urge to *get off the bus*—but not to sleep, just to get off—for—what?—before:::::what? And Sandy is back over at the motel, inspecting this electro-pink slab out in the middle of nowhere—somebody finally finds him and brings him back. Sandy is given the name Dis-mount in the great movie.

"There are going to be times," says Kesey, "when we can't wait for somebody. Now, you're either on the bus or off the bus. If you're on the bus, and you get left behind, then you'll find it again. If you're off the bus in the first place—then it won't make a damn." And nobody had to have it spelled out for them. Everything was becoming allegorical, understood by the group mind, and especially this: "You're either on the bus . . . or off the bus."

Except for Hagen's girl, the Beauty Witch. It seems like she never even gets off the bus to cop a urination. She's sitting back in the back of the bus with nothing on, just a blanket over her lap and her legs wedged back into the corner, her and her little bare breasts, silent, looking exceedingly witch-like. Is she on the bus or off the bus? She has taken to wearing nothing but the blanket and she sheds that when she feels like it. Maybe that is her thing and she is doing her thing and *wailing with it* and the bus barrels on off, heading for Houston, Texas, and she becomes Stark Naked in the great movie, one moment all conked out, but with her eyes open, staring, the next laughing and coming on, a lively Stark Naked, and they are all trying to just snap their fingers to it but now she is getting looks that have nothing to do with the fact that she has not a thing on, hell, big deal, but she is now waxing extremely freaking ESP. She keeps coming up to somebody who isn't saying a goddamn thing and looking into his eyes with the all-embracing look of total acid understanding, our brains are one brain, so let's *visit,* you and I, and she says: "Ooooooooh, you really *think* that, *I* know what you mean, but do you-u-u-u-u-u-u-ueeeeee-eeeeeeeeeeeeeeee"—finishing off in a sailing tremolo laugh as if she has just read your brain and it is the weirdest of the weird shit ever, your brain eeeeeeeeeeeeeeeeeeeeeeeeeeeeeeeeee—

STARK NAKED!

in a black blanket—
        Reaching out for herself,
she woke up one morning to
find herself accosted on all
sides by   LARGE
              MEN
surrounding her threatening her
with their voices, their presence, their always
desire reaching inside herself
and touching her obscenely upon her
desire and causing her to laugh
and
LAUGH
              with the utter
              ridiculousness
              of it . . .

—but no one denied her a moment of it, neither the conked-out bug-eyed paranoia nor the manic keening coming on, nobody denied her, and she could wail, nobody tried to cool that inflamed brain that was now seeping out Stark Naked into the bouncing goddamn—*stop it!*—currents of the bus throgging and roaring 70 miles an hour into Texas, for it was like it had been ordained, by Kesey himself, back in San Juan Capistrano, like there was to be a reaction scale in here, from negative to positive, and no one was to rise up negative about anything, one was to go positive with everything—*go with the flow*—everyone's cool was to be tested, and to shout No, no matter what happened, was to fail. And hadn't Kesey passed the test first of all? Hadn't Babbs taken Gretchen Fetchin, and did he come back at either one of them uptight over that? And wasn't it Walker who was calling La Honda from the Servicenters of America? All true, and go with the flow. And they went with the flow, the whole goddamn flow of America. The bus barrels into the superhighway toll stations and the microphones on top of the bus pick up all the clacking and ringing and the mumbling by the toll-station attendant and the brakes squeaking and the gears shifting, all the sounds of the true America that are screened out everywhere else, it all came amplified back inside the bus, while Hagen's camera picked up the faces, the faces in Phoenix, the cops, the service-station owners, the stragglers and the strugglers of America, all laboring in their movie, and it was all captured and kept, piling up, inside the bus. Barreling across America with the microphones picking it all up, the whole roar, and microphone up top gets eerie in a great rush and then *skakkkkkkkkkkkkkk* it is ripping and roaring over asphalt and *thok* it's gone, no sound at all. The microphone has somehow ripped loose on top of the bus and hit the roadway and dragged along until it snapped off entirely—and Sandy can't believe it. He keeps waiting for somebody to tell Cassady to stop and go back and get the microphone, because this was something Sandy had rigged up with great love and time, it was his *thing*, his part of the power—but instead they are all rapping and grokking over the sound it made—"Wowwwwwwwww! Did you—wowwwwwww" —as if they had synched into a never-before-heard thing, a unique thing, the sound of an object, a microphone, hitting the American asphalt, the open road at 70 miles an hour, like if it was all there on tape they would have the instant, the moment, of anything, *anyone* ripped out of the flow and hitting the Great Superhighway at 70 miles an hour—and they *had* it on tape—and played it back in variable lag skakkkkkk-akkk-akkkk-akkkooooooooooo.

oooooooooooooooooooooooo—Stark Naked waxing weirder and weirder, huddled in the black blanket shivering, then out, bobbing wraith, her little deep red areolae bobbing in the crazed vibrations—

finally they pull into Houston and head for Larry McMurtry's house. They pull up to McMurtry's house, in the suburbs, and the door of the house opens and out comes McMurtry, a slight, slightly wan, kindly-looking shy-looking guy, ambling out, with his little boy, his son, and Cassady opens the door of the bus so everybody can get off, and suddenly Stark Naked shrieks out: "Frankie! Frankie! Frankie! Frankie!" —this being the name of her own divorced-off little boy—and she whips off the blanket and leaps off the bus and out into the suburbs of Houston, Texas, stark naked, and rushes up to McMurtry's little boy and scoops him up and presses him to her skinny breast, crying and shrieking, "Frankie! oh Frankie! my little Frankie! oh! oh! oh!"—while McMurtry doesn't know what in the name of hell to do, reaching tentatively toward her stark-naked shoulder and saying, "Ma'am! Ma'am! Just a minute, ma'am"—

—while the Pranksters, spilling out of the bus—stop. The bus is stopped. No roar, no crazed bounce or vibrations, no crazed car beams, no tapes, no microphones. Only Stark Naked, with somebody else's little boy in her arms, is bouncing and vibrating.

And there, amid the peaceful Houston elms on Quenby Road, it dawned on them all that this woman—which one of us even knows her?—had completed her trip. She had gone with the flow. She had gone stark raving mad.

Stark Naked; Stark Naked; silence; but, well . . . That this or a couple of other crackups in the experience of the Pranksters had anything to do with that goofy baboon, Dope, was something that didn't cross the minds of the Pranksters at that point. *Craziness* was not an absolute. They had all voluntarily embarked upon a trip and a state of consciousness that was "crazy" by ordinary standards. The trip, in fact the whole deal, was a risk-all balls-out plunge into the unknown, and it was assumed merely that more and more of what was already inside a person would come out and expand, gloriously or otherwise. Stark Naked had done her thing. She roared off into the void and was picked up by the cops by and by, and the doors closed in the County psychiatric ward, and that was that, for the Pranksters were long gone.

The trip had started out as a great bursting forth out of the forest fastness of La Honda, out into an unsuspecting America. And for Sandy, anyway, that was when the trip went best, when the Pranksters were out among them, and the citizens of the land were gawking and struggling to summon up the proper emotion for this—what in the name of God are the ninnies *doing*. But the opposite was happening, too. On those long stretches of American superhighway between performances the bus was like a pressure cooker, a crucible, like one of those chambers in which the early atomic scientists used to compress heavy water, drive the molecules closer and closer together until the very atoms exploded. On the bus all traces of freakiness or competition or bitterness or whatever were intensified. They were right out front, for sure.

Jane Burton, who was now known as Generally Famished, and Sandy—Dis-mount—took to going off whenever they could, like in Houston, for a square meal. Square on every level, Tonto. They would just go right into one of those Square American steak houses with the big plate-glass window with the corny little plastic windmill in the window advertising Heineken's Beer and the Diners Club and American Express stickers on the plate-glass door and go in and have a square steak and square French fries and boiled bland peas and carrots and A-1 sauce. Jane, now ravaged from lack of sleep, and ravenously hungry, generally famished, or slightly bilious the whole time, wondering what the hell they were now doing on the southern rim of the United States when New York was way up there. Sandy—with this subliminal urge to get off the bus, and yet be *on the bus*—on *that* level—and neither of them knowing what to make of Kesey—always Kesey . . .

And the heat. From Houston they headed east through the Deep South, and the Deep South in July was . . . lava. The air rushing into the open windows of the bus came in hot and gritty like invisible smoke, and when they stopped, it just rolled over them, pure lava. The rest in Houston didn't do too much good, because the heat just started it all again, nobody slept, and it was like all you could do to cut through the lava with speed and grass and acid.

New Orleans was a relief, because they got out and walked around the French Quarter and down by the docks in their red and white striped shirts and Day-Glo stuff and the people freaked over them. And the cops came while they were down by the docks, which was just comic relief, because by now the cops were a piece of cake. The city cops were no more able to keep their Cop Movie going than the country cops. Hassler talked sweet to them like the college valedictorian and Kesey talked sweet and down-home and Hagen filmed it all like this was some crazed adventure in cinema verité and the cops skedaddled in a herd of new Ford cruisers with revolving turret lights. Sayonara, you all.

They just kept walking around New Orleans in their striped shirts and wearing shorts, and they could all see Kesey's big muscular legs, like a football player's, striding on up ahead like he owned the place, like they all owned the place, and everybody's spirits picked up. So they head out to Lake Pontchartrain, on the northern edge of New Orleans. They all took acid, but a small dose, about 75 micrograms—everybody happy and high on acid, and rock 'n' roll records blaring, Martha and the Vandellas and Shirley Ellis, all that old stuff pounding away. Lake Pontchartrain is like a great big beautiful spacious—space! —park on the water. They pull the bus up in a parking area and there are nice trees round and all that endless nice water and they put on their bathing suits. Walker, who has a hell of a build, puts on a pair of red, yellow, and black trunks, and Kesey, who has a hell of a build, puts on a pair of blue and white trunks, and Zonker, who has a hell of a build, only leaner, puts on a pair of orange trunks, and the blue of the water and the scorched-out green of the grass and the leaves and—a little breeze?—it is all swimming in front of their old acid eyes like a molten postcard—water! What they don't know is, it is a segregated beach, for Negroes only. The spades all sitting there on benches sit there staring at these white crazies coming out of a weird bus and heading for New Or-leans 30th-parallel Deep South segregated water. Zonker is really zonked this time, and burning up with the heat, about 100 degrees, and he dives in and swims out a ways and pretty soon he sees he is surrounded by deep orange men, Negroes, all treading water around him and giving him rotten looks. One of them has a gold tooth in the front with a star cut out in it, so that a white enamel star shows in the middle of the gold, and the gold starts flashing out at him in the sun—*cheeeakkk*—in time with his heartbeat which is getting faster all the time, these goddamn flashes of gold and white star after-images, and the Golden Mouth says, "Man, there sure is a lotta trash in the water today."

"You ain't shittin', man," says another one of them.

"Lotta fuckin' trash, man," says another one, and so on.

Suddenly Golden Mouth is speaking straight to Zonker: "What's all this trash doing in the water, man?"

Zonker is very nonplused, partly because the whole day has turned orange on him, because of the acid—orange trunks, orange water, orange sky, orange menacing spades.

"Boy, what you doing here!" Golden Mouth says very sharp all of a sudden. Orange and big and orange hulking fat back big as an orange mantra ray. "Boy, you know what we gonna do? We gonna cut yo' little balls off. We gonna take you up on that beach and *wail* with you!"

"Heh-hehhhhhhhhhhhh!" The others start this wailing moaning laugh.

For some reason, however, this makes Zonker smile. He can feel it spreading across his face, like a big orange slice of orange sugar-jelly candy and he is suspended there treading water and grinning while the Golden Mouth flashes and flashes and flashes.

Then the Golden Mouth says, "Well, it sure is *some kinda trash,*" and starts laughing, only amiably this time, and they all laugh, and Zonker laughs and swims back to shore.

By this time a big crowd of Negroes has gathered around the mad bus. Funky music is blasting off the speakers, a Jimmy Smith record. Zonker gets on the bus. It seems like thousands of Negroes are dancing around the bus, doing rock dances and the dirty boogie. Everything is orange and then he looks at the writhing mass of Negroes, out every window, nothing but writhing Negroes mashed in around the bus and writhing, and it all starts turning from orange to brown. Zonker starts getting the feeling he is inside an enormous intestine and it is going into peristaltic contractions. He can feel the whole trip turning into a horrible bummer. Even Kesey, who isn't afraid of anything, looks worried. "We better get out of here," Kesey says. But squeezed out? —in bummer brown peristaltic contractions? Luckily for Zonker, maybe for everyone, the white cops turn up at that point and break up the crowd and tell the white crazies to drive on, this is a segregated beach, and for once they don't pile out and try to break up the Cop Movie. They go with the Cop Movie and get their movie out of there.

On into the flatlands of Mississippi and Alabama, Biloxi, Mobile, U.S. Route 90, the flatlands and the fields and the heat doesn't let up ever. They are heading for Florida. Sandy hasn't slept in days:::::how many:::::like total insomnia and everything is *bend*ing in curvy curdling lines. Sun and flatlands. So damned hot—and everything is getting torn into opposites. The dead-still heat-stroked summertime deep Southland—and Sandy's heart racing at a constant tachycardia and his brain racing and reeling out and so essential to . . . *keep moving, Cassady!* . . . but there are two Cassadys. One minute Cassady looks 58 and crazy—*speed!*—and the next, 28 and peaceful—*acid*—and Sandy can tell the peaceful Cassady in an instant, because his nose becomes . . . long and smooth and almost patrician, whereas the wild Cassady looks beat-up. And Kesey—*always Kesey!* Sandy looks . . . and Kesey is old and haggard and his face is lopsided . . . and then Sandy looks and Kesey is young, serene, and his face is lineless, and round and smooth as a baby's as he sits for hours on end reading comic books, absorbed in the plunging purple Steve Ditko shadows of Dr. Strange attired in capes and chiaroscuro, saying: "How could they have known that this gem was merely a device to bridge DIMENSIONS! It was a means to enter the dread PURPLE DIMENSION—from our own world!" Sandy may wander . . . off the bus, but it remains all Kesey. Dr. Strange! Always seeing two Keseys. Kesey the Prankster and Kesey the organizer. Going through the steams of southern Alabama in late June and Kesey rises up from out of the comic books and becomes Captain Flag. He puts on a pink kilt, like a miniskirt, and pink socks and patent-leather shoes and pink sunglasses and wraps an American flag around his head like a big turban and holds it in place with an arrow through the back of it and gets up on top of the bus roaring through Alabama and starts playing the flute at people passing by. The Alabamans drawn into the PINK DIMENSION do a double-freak take for sure and it is *Too Much!* as George Walker always says, too mullyfogging much. They pull into a gas station in Mobile and half the Pranksters jump out of the bus, blazing red and white stripes and throwing red rubber balls around in a crazed way like a manic ballet of slick Servicenter flutter decoration while the guy fills up the tank, and he looks from them to Captain Flag to the bus itself, and after he collects for the gas he looks through the window at Cassady in the driver's seat and shakes his head and says:

"No wonder you're so nigger-heavy in California."

FORNIA-FORNIA-FORNIA-FORNIA-FORNIA-FORNIA-FORNIA-FORNIA as it is picked up inside the bus in variable lag, and that breaks everybody up.

That was when it was good . . . grinding on through Alabama, and then suddenly, to Sandy, Kesey is old and haggard and the organizer. Sandy can see him descending the ladder down from the roof of the bus and glowering at him, and he knows—intersubjectivity!—that Kesey is thinking, You're too detached, Sandy, you're not out front, you may be sitting right here grinding and roaring through Alabama but you're . . . off the bus . . . And he approaches Sandy, hunched over under the low ceiling of the bus, and to Sandy he looks like an ape with his mighty arms dangling, like The Incredible Hulk, and suddenly Sandy jumps up and crouches into an ape position, dangling his arms and mimicking him—and Kesey breaks into a big grin and throws his arms around Sandy and hugs him—

He approves! Kesey approves of me! At last I have re*sponded* to something, brought it all out front, even if it is resentment, *done* something, done my thing—and in that very action, just as he taught, it is gone, the resentment . . . and I am back on the bus again, synched in . . .

Always Kesey! And in that surge of euphoria—*Kesey approves!*—Sandy knew that Kesey was the key to whatever was going right and whatever was going wrong on this trip, and nobody, not one of them who ever took this trip, got in this movie, would ever have even the will to walk up to Kesey and announce irrevocably: I am off the bus. It would be like saying, I am off this . . . Unspoken Thing we are into . . .

• • •

Pensacola, Florida. 110 degrees. A friend of Babbs has a little house near the ocean, and they pull in there, but the ocean doesn't help at all. The heat makes waves in the air, like over a radiator. Most of the Pranksters are in the house or out in the yard. Some of the girls are outside the bus barbecuing some meat. Sandy is by himself inside the bus, in the shade. The insomnia is killing him. He has got to get some sleep or keep moving. He can't stand it in here stranded in between with his heart pounding. He goes to the refrigerator and takes out the orange juice. The acid in New Orleans, the 75 micrograms, wasn't enough. It's like he hasn't had a good high the whole trip, nothing . . . blissful. So he hooks down a big slug of Unauthorized Acid and sits back.

He would like something nice and peaceful, closed in softly alone on the bus. He puts on a set of earphones. The left earphone is hooked into a microphone inside the house and picks up Kesey's Cousin Dale playing the piano. Dale, for all his country ways, has studied music a long time and plays well and the notes come in like liquid drops of amethyst vibrating endlessly in the . . . acid . . . atmosphere and it is very nice. The right earphone is hooked into a microphone picking up the sounds outside the house, mainly the barbecue fires crackling. So Dale concerto and fire crackle in these big padded earphones closed in about his head . . . only the sounds are somehow sliding out of control. There is no synch. It is as if the two are fighting for his head. The barbecue crackles and bubbles in his head and the amethyst droplets crystallize into broken glass, and then tin, a tin piano. The earphones seem to get bigger and bigger, huge padded shells about to enclose his whole head, his face, his nose—amok sound overpowering him, as if it is all going to end right here inside this padded globe —*panic*—he leaps up from the seat, bolts a few feet with the earphones still clamped on his skull, then rips them off and jumps out of the bus—Pranksters everywhere in the afternoon sun in red and white striped shirts. Babbs has the power and is directing the movie and is trying to shoot something—Acid Piper. Sandy looks about. Nobody he can tell it to, that he has taken acid by himself and it is turning into a bummer, he can't bring this out front . . . He runs into the house, the walls keep jumping up so goddamn close and all the angles are under extreme stress, as if they could break. Jane Burton is sitting alone in the house, feeling bilious. Jane is the only person he can tell.

"Jane," he says, "I took some acid . . . and it's really weird . . ." But it is such an effort to talk . . .

The heat waves are solidifying in the air like the waves in a child's marble and the perspectives are all berserk, walls rushing up then sinking way back like a Titian banquet hall. And the heat—Sandy has to do something to pull himself together, so he takes a shower. He undresses and gets in the shower and . . . flute music, Babbs! flute music comes spraying out of the nozzle and the heat is inside of him, it is like he can look down and see it burning there and he looks down, two bare legs, a torso rising up at him and like he is just noticing them for the first time. They exist apart from, like another human being's, such odd turns and angles they take amid the flute streams, swells and bony processes, like he has never seen any of this before, this flesh, this stranger. He groks over that—only it isn't a stranger, it is his . . . mother . . . and suddenly he is back in this body, only it is his mother's body—and then his father's—he has become his mother and his father. No difference between I and Thou inside this shower of flutes on the Florida littoral. He wrenches the water off, and it stops, the flute. He is himself again—hide from the panic—no, *gotcha*—and he pulls on his clothes and goes back out in the living room. Jane is still sitting there. Talk, christ, to somebody—Jane!—but the room goes into the *zooms*, wild lurches of perspective, a whole side of the room zooming right up in front of his face, then zooming back to where it was—Jane!—Jane in front of his face, a foot away, then way back over there on the sofa, then zooming up again, all of it rocketing back and forth in the hulking heat—"Sandy!"—somebody is in the house looking for him, Hagen? who is it?—seems Babbs wants him in the movie. Red-and-white striped Pranksters burning in the sun. Seems Babbs has an idea for a section of the movie. In this scene Babbs is the Pied Piper, tootling on a flute, and all the red and white striped children are running after him in colorful dances. They hand Sandy a Prankster shirt, which he doesn't want. It is miles too big. It hangs on him in this sick loose way like he is desiccating in the sun. Into the sun—the shirt starts flashing under his face in the sun in explosive beams of sunball red and sunball silver-white as if he is moving through an aura of violent beams. Babbs gives him his cue and he starts doing a crazy dance out by a clothesline while the camera whirrs away. He can feel the crazy look come over his face and feel his eyeballs turning up and white with just vague flashes of red and silver-white exploding in under his eyelids . . . and the freaking heat, dancing like a crazy in the sun, and he goes reeling off to one side.

It becomes very important that nobody know he has taken Unauthorized Acid. He can trust Jane . . . This is not very out front, but he must remain very cool. Chuck Kesey is marching around the yard blowing a tuba, going *boop boop a boop boop* very deep and loud, then he comes by Sandy and looks at him and smiles over the mouthpiece and goes *bup bup a bup bup,* very tender and soft and—intersubjectivity!—he *knows* and *understands*—and that is nice because Chuck is one of the nicest people in the world and Sandy can trust him. If only he can remain cool . . .

There is a half pound of grass in a tin can by the bus and Sandy gets down on all fours to help and starts digging his playing in the sun, and he somehow kicks over the can and the grass spills all over this silty brown dirt. Everybody is upset and Hagen gets down to try to separate the grass from the dirt, and Sandy gets down on all fours to help and starts digging his fingers into the dirt to try to dig out the grass, only as he starts digging, the dirt gets browner and browner as he digs, and he starts grooving over the brownness of it, so brown, so deep, so rich, until he is digging way past the grass, on down into the ground, and Hagen says,

"Hey! What the hell's the matter with you?"

And Sandy knows he should just come out with it and say, I'm stoned, man, and this brown is a groove, and then it would be all out front and over with. But he can't bring himself to do it, he can't bring himself all the way out front. Instead, it gets worse.

Kesey comes over with a football and a spray can of Day-Glo. He wants Sandy to spray it Day-Glo, and then he and Babbs and some others are going to take it out near the water at dusk and pass the Day-Glo ball around, and Sandy starts spraying it, only it's all one thing, the ball and Kesey's arm, and he is spraying Kesey's arm in the most dedicated, cool way, and Kesey says:

"Hey! What the hell's the matter with you—"

And as soon as he says it, he *knows,* which is suddenly very bad.

"I'm . . . stoned," says Sandy. "I took some acid, and I . . . took too much and it's going very bad."

"We wanted to save that acid for the trip back," Kesey says. "We wanted to have some for the Rockies."

"I didn't take *that much*"—he's trying to explain it, but now a Beatles record is playing over the loudspeaker of the bus and it's raining into his head like needles—"but it's bad."

Kesey looks exasperated, but he tries some condolence. "Look—just stay with it. Listen to the music—"

"Listen to the *music!*" Sandy yells. "Christ! Try and stop me!"

Kesey says very softly: "I know how you feel, Sandy. I've been there myself. But you just have to stay with it"—which makes Sandy feel good: *he's with me*. But then Kesey says, "But if you think I'm going to be your guide for this trip, you're sadly mistaken." And he walks off.

Sandy starts feeling very paranoid. He walks off, away from the house, and comes upon some sort of greeny glade in the woods. Babbs and Gretchen Fetchin are lying on the ground in the shade, just lazing on it, but Babbs's legs shift and his arms move and Gretch's legs shift, and Sandy sees . . . Babbs and Gretch in a *pond,* swimming languidly. He knows they are on ground, and yet they are *in the water*—and he says,

"How is it?"

"Wet!" says Babbs.

—and—marvelous—it is very nice—as if Babbs knows exactly what is in his mind—*synch*—and is going to swing with it. We are all one brain out here and we are all on the bus, after all. And suddenly there in the Florida glade it is like the best of the whole Prankster thing all over again.

He came back to the house at dark, into the yard, and there were a million stars in the sky, like tiny neon bulbs, and you could see them between the leaves of the trees, and the trees seemed to be covered with a million tiny neon bulbs, and the bus, it broke up into a sculpture of neon bulbs, millions of them massed together to make a bus, like a whole nighttime of neon dust, with every particle a neon bulb, and they all vibrated like a huge friendly neon cicada universe.

He goes down to the water where the Pranksters all are, a little inlet, and it is dark and placid and he gets in and wades out until the water laps almost even with his mouth, which makes it very secure and warm and calm and nice and he looks at the stars and then at a bridge in the distance. All he can see of the bridge is the lights on it, swooping strands of lights, rising, rising, rising—and just then Chuck Kesey comes gliding toward him through the water, smiling, like a great friendly fish. Chuck *knows* and it is very nice—and the lights of the bridge keep rising, rising, until they merge with the stars, until there is a bridge leading right up into heaven.

A Problem in Etiquette

In which the guest of honor, the famous architect, asked if he could "bring someone," and the host and hostess try to decide if they dare seat Someone between Chuck Brassbender of Morgan Guaranty and Harmsden Grousestalker of Sullivan & Cromwell, as originally planned.

THESE RADICAL CHIC EVENINGS

At 2 or 3 or 4 a.m., somewhere along in there, on August 25, 1966, his forty-eighth birthday, in fact, Leonard Bernstein woke up in the dark in a state of wild alarm. That had happened before. It was one of the forms his insomnia took. So he did the usual. He got up and walked around a bit. He felt groggy. Suddenly he had a vision, an inspiration. He could see himself, Leonard Bernstein, the *egregio maestro*, walking out on stage in white tie and tails in front of a full orchestra. On one side of the conductor's podium is a piano. On the other is a chair with a guitar leaning against it. He sits in the chair and picks up the guitar. A guitar! One of those halfwitted instruments, like the accordion, that are made for the Learn-To-Play-in-Eight-Days E-Z-Diagram 110-IQ fourteen-year-olds of Levittown! But there's a reason. He has an anti-war message to deliver to this great starched white-throated audience in the symphony hall. He announces to them: "I love." Just that. The effect is mortifying. All at once a Negro rises up from out of the curve of the grand piano and starts saying things like, "The audience is curiously embarrassed." Lenny tries to start again, plays some quick numbers on the piano, says, "I love. *Amo ergo sum.*" The Negro rises again and says, "The audience thinks he ought to get up and walk out. The audience thinks, 'I am ashamed even to nudge my neighbor.'" Finally, Lenny gets off a heartfelt anti-war speech and exits.

For a moment, sitting there alone in his home in the small hours of the morning, Lenny thought it might just work and he jotted the idea

From *Radical Chic & Mau-Mauing the Flak Catchers*, pp. 3–31 (New York: Farrar, Straus and Giroux, 1970). First published as "Radical Chic: That Party at Lenny's" in *New York Magazine*, June 8, 1970.

down. Think of the headlines: BERNSTEIN ELECTRIFIES CONCERT AUDIENCE WITH ANTI-WAR APPEAL. But then his enthusiasm collapsed. He lost heart. Who the hell was this Negro rising up from the piano and informing the world what an ass Leonard Bernstein was making of himself? It didn't make sense, this superego Negro by the concert grand.

Mmmmmmmmmmmmmmmm. These are nice. Little Roquefort cheese morsels rolled in crushed nuts. Very tasty. Very subtle. It's the way the dry sackiness of the nuts tiptoes up against the dour savor of the cheese that is so nice, so subtle. Wonder what the Black Panthers eat here on the hors d'oeuvre trail? Do the Panthers like little Roquefort cheese morsels rolled in crushed nuts this way, and asparagus tips in mayonnaise dabs, and *meatballs petites au Coq Hardi*, all of which are at this very moment being offered to them on gadrooned silver platters by maids in black uniforms with hand-ironed white aprons . . . The butler will bring them their drinks . . . Deny it if you wish to, but such are the *pensées métaphysiques* that rush through one's head on these Radical Chic evenings just now in New York. For example, does that huge Black Panther there in the hallway, the one shaking hands with Felicia Bernstein herself, the one with the black leather coat and the dark glasses and the absolutely unbelievable Afro, Fuzzy-Wuzzy-scale, in fact—is he, a Black Panther, going on to pick up a Roquefort cheese morsel rolled in crushed nuts from off the tray, from a maid in uniform, and just pop it down the gullet without so much as missing a beat of Felicia's perfect Mary Astor voice . . .

Felicia is remarkable. She is beautiful, with that rare burnished beauty that lasts through the years. Her hair is pale blond and set just so. She has a voice that is "theatrical," to use a term from her youth. She greets the Black Panthers with the same bend of the wrist, the same tilt of the head, the same perfect Mary Astor voice with which she greets people like Jason, John and D.D., Adolph, Betty, Gian-Carlo, Schuyler, and Goddard, during those *après*-concert suppers she and Lenny are so famous for. What evenings! She lights the candles over the dining-room table, and in the Gotham gloaming the little tremulous tips of flame are reflected in the mirrored surface of the table, a bottomless blackness with a thousand stars, and it is that moment that Lenny loves. There seem to be a thousand stars above and a thousand stars below, a room full of stars, a penthouse duplex full of stars, a Manhattan tower full of stars, with marvelous people drifting through the heavens, Jason Robards, John and D. D. Ryan, Gian-Carlo Menotti, Schuyler Chapin, Goddard Lieberson, Mike Nichols, Lillian Hellman, Larry Rivers, Aaron Copland, Richard Avedon, Milton and

Amy Greene, Lukas Foss, Jennie Tourel, Samuel Barber, Jerome Robbins, Steve Sondheim, Adolph and Phyllis Green, Betty Comden, and the Patrick O'Neals . . .

. . . and now, in the season of Radical Chic, the Black Panthers. That huge Panther there, the one Felicia is smiling her tango smile at, is Robert Bay, who just forty-one hours ago was arrested in an altercation with the police, supposedly over a .38-caliber revolver that someone had, in a parked car in Queens at Northern Boulevard and 104th Street or some such unbelievable place, and taken to jail on a most unusual charge called "criminal facilitation." And now he is out on bail and walking into Leonard and Felicia Bernstein's thirteen-room penthouse duplex on Park Avenue. Harassment & Hassles, Guns & Pigs, Jail & Bail—they're *real*, these Black Panthers. The very idea of them, these real revolutionaries, who actually put their lives on the line, runs through Lenny's duplex like a rogue hormone. Everyone casts a glance, or stares, or tries a smile, and then sizes up the house for the somehow delicious counterpoint . . . Deny it if you want to! but one *does* end up making such sweet furtive comparisons in this season of Radical Chic . . . There's Otto Preminger in the library and Jean vanden Heuvel in the hall, and Peter and Cheray Duchin in the living room, and Frank and Domna Stanton, Gail Lumet, Sheldon Harnick, Cynthia Phipps, Burton Lane, Mrs. August Heckscher, Roger Wilkins, Barbara Walters, Bob Silvers, Mrs. Richard Avedon, Mrs. Arthur Penn, Julie Belafonte, Harold Taylor, and scores more, including Charlotte Curtis, women's news editor of *The New York Times*, America's foremost chronicler of Society, a lean woman in black, with her notebook out, standing near Felicia and big Robert Bay, and talking to Cheray Duchin.

Cheray tells her: "I've never met a Panther—this is a first for me!" . . . never dreaming that within forty-eight hours her words will be on the desk of the President of the United States . . .

This is a first for me. But she is not alone in her thrill as the Black Panthers come trucking on in, into Lenny's house, Robert Bay, Don Cox the Panthers' Field Marshal from Oakland, Henry Miller the Harlem Panther defense captain, the Panther women—Christ, if the Panthers don't know how to get it all together, as they say, the tight pants, the tight black turtlenecks, the leather coats, Cuban shades, Afros. But real Afros, not the ones that have been shaped and trimmed like a topiary hedge and sprayed until they have a sheen like acrylic wall-to-wall—but like funky, natural, scraggly . . . wild . . .

These are no civil-rights Negroes *wearing gray suits three sizes too big—*

—no more interminable Urban League banquets in hotel ballrooms where they try to alternate the blacks and whites around the tables as if they were stringing Arapaho beads—

—*these are* real men!

Shoot-outs, revolutions, pictures in *Life* magazine of policemen grabbing Black Panthers like they were Vietcong—somehow it all runs together in the head with the whole thing of how *beautiful* they are. *Sharp as a blade.* The Panther women—there are three or four of them on hand, wives of the Panther 21 defendants, and they are so lean, so *lithe*, as they say, with tight pants and Yoruba-style headdresses, almost like turbans, as if they'd stepped out of the pages of *Vogue*, although no doubt *Vogue* got it from them. All at once every woman in the room knows exactly what Amanda Burden meant when she said she was now anti-fashion because "the sophistication of the baby blacks made me rethink my attitudes." God knows the Panther women don't spend thirty minutes in front of the mirror in the morning shoring up their eye holes with contact lenses, eyeliner, eye shadow, eyebrow pencil, occipital rim brush, false eyelashes, mascara, Shadow-Ban for undereye and Eterna Creme for the corners . . . And here they are, right in front of you, trucking on into the Bernsteins' Chinese yellow duplex, amid the sconces, silver bowls full of white and lavender anemones, and uniformed servants serving drinks and Roquefort cheese morsels rolled in crushed nuts—

But it's all right. They're *white* servants, not Claude and Maude, but white South Americans. Lenny and Felicia are geniuses. After a while, it all comes down to servants. They are the cutting edge in Radical Chic. Obviously, if you are giving a party for the Black Panthers, as Lenny and Felicia are this evening, or as Sidney and Gail Lumet did last week, or as John Simon of Random House and Richard Baron, the publisher, did before that; or for the Chicago Eight, such as the party Jean vanden Heuvel gave; or for the grape workers or Bernadette Devlin, such as the parties Andrew Stein gave; or for the Young Lords, such as the party Ellie Guggenheimer is giving next week in *her* Park Avenue duplex; or for the Indians or the SDS or the G.I. coffee shops or even for the Friends of the Earth—well, then, obviously you can't have a Negro butler and maid, Claude and Maude, in uniform, circulating through the living room, the library, and the main hall serving drinks and canapés. Plenty of people have tried to think it out. They try to picture the Panthers or whoever walking in bristling with electric hair and Cuban shades and leather pieces and the rest of it, and they try to picture Claude and Maude with the black uniforms coming up and saying, "Would you care for a drink, sir?" They close their eyes and try to picture it *some way*, but there *is* no way. One simply cannot see that moment. So the current wave of Radical Chic has touched off the most desperate search for white servants. Carter and Amanda Burden have white servants. Sidney Lumet and his wife Gail, who is Lena Horne's daughter, have three white servants, including a Scottish nurse. Everybody has white servants. And Lenny and Felicia—they had it worked out before Radical Chic even started. Felicia grew up in Chile. Her father, Roy Elwood Cohn, an engineer from San Francisco, worked for the American Smelting and Refining Co. in Santiago. As Felicia Montealegre (her mother's maiden name), she became an actress in New York and won the *Motion Picture Daily* critics' award as the best new television actress of 1949. Anyway, they have a house staff of three white South American servants, including a Chilean cook, plus Lenny's English chauffeur and dresser, who is also white, of course. Can one comprehend how perfect that is, given . . . the times? Well, many of their friends can, and they ring up the Bernsteins and ask them to get South American servants for them, and the Bernsteins are so generous about it, so obliging, that people refer to them, good-naturedly and gratefully, as "the Spic and Span Employment Agency," with an easygoing ethnic humor, of course.

The only other thing to do is what Ellie Guggenheimer is doing next week with her party for the Young Lords in her duplex on Park Avenue at 89th Street, just ten blocks up from Lenny and Felicia. She is giving her party on a Sunday, which is the day off for the maid and the cleaning woman. "Two friends of mine"—she confides on the telephone—"two friends of mine who happen to be . . . not white —that's what I hate about the times we live in, the *terms*—well, they've agreed to be butler and maid . . . and I'm going to be a maid myself!"

Just at this point some well-meaning soul is going to say, Why not do without servants altogether if the matter creates such unbearable tension and one truly believes in equality? Well, even to raise the question is to reveal the most fundamental ignorance of life in the great co-ops and townhouses of the East Side in the age of Radical Chic. Why, my God! servants are not a mere convenience, they're an absolute psychological necessity. Once one is into that life, truly into it, with the morning workout on the velvet swings at Kounovsky's and the late mornings on the telephone, and lunch at the Running Footman, which is now regarded as really better than La Grenouille, Lutèce, Lafayette, La Caravelle, and the rest of the general Frog Pond, less ostentatious, more of the David Hicks feeling, less of the Parish-Hadley look, and then—well, then, the idea of not having servants is unthinkable. But even that does not say it all. It makes it sound like a matter of convenience, when actually it is a sheer and fundamental matter of—*having servants*. Does one comprehend?

God, what a flood of taboo thoughts runs through one's head at these Radical Chic events . . . But it's delicious. It is as if one's nerve endings were on red alert to the most intimate nuances of status. Deny it if you want to! Nevertheless, it runs through every soul here. It is the matter of the marvelous contradictions on all sides. It is like the delicious shudder you get when you try to force the prongs of two horseshoe magnets together . . . *them* and *us* . . .

For example, one's own servants, although white, are generally no problem. A discreet, euphemistic word about what sort of party it is going to be, and they will generally be models of correctness. The euphemisms are not always an easy matter, however. When talking to one's white servants, one doesn't really know whether to refer to blacks as *blacks, Negroes*, or *colored people*. When talking to other . . . well, *cultivated* persons, one says *blacks*, of course. It is the only word, currently, that implicitly shows one's awareness of the dignity of the black race. But somehow when you start to say the word to your own white servants, you hesitate. You can't get it out of your throat. Why? *Counter-guilt!* You realize that you are about to utter one of those touchstone words that divide the cultivated from the uncultivated, the attuned from the unattuned, the *hip* from the dreary. As soon as the word comes out of your mouth—you know it before the first vocable pops on your lips—your own servant is going to size you up as one of those *limousine liberals*, or whatever epithet they use, who are busy pouring white soul all over the black movement, and would you do as much for the white lower class, for the domestics of the East Side, for example, fat chance, sahib. Deny it if you want to! but such are the delicious little agonies of Radical Chic. So one settles for *Negro*, with the hope that the great god Culturatus has laid the ledger aside for the moment . . . In any case, if one is able to make that small compromise, one's own servants are no real problem. But the elevator man and the doorman—the death rays they begin projecting, the curt responses, as soon as they see it is going to be one of *those* parties! Of course, they're all from Queens, and so forth, and one has to allow for that. For some reason the elevator men tend to be worse about it than the doormen, even; less sense of *politesse*, perhaps.

Or—what does one wear to these parties for the Panthers or the Young Lords or the grape workers? What does a woman wear? Obviously one does not want to wear something frivolously and pompously expensive, such as a Gerard Pipart party dress. On the other hand one does not want to arrive "poormouthing it" in some outrageous turtleneck and West Eighth Street bell-jean combination, as if one is "funky" and of "the people." Frankly, Jean vanden Heuvel —that's Jean there in the hallway giving everyone her famous smile, in which her eyes narrow down to f/16—frankly, Jean tends too much toward the funky fallacy. Jean, who is the daughter of Jules Stein, one of the wealthiest men in the country, is wearing some sort of rust-red snap-around suede skirt, the sort that English working girls pick up on Saturday afternoons in those absolutely *berserk* London boutiques like Bus Stop or Biba, where everything looks chic and yet skimpy and raw and vital. Felicia Bernstein seems to understand the whole thing better. Look at Felicia. She is wearing the simplest little black frock imaginable, with absolutely no ornamentation save for a plain gold necklace. It is perfect. It has dignity without any overt class symbolism.

Lenny? Lenny himself has been in the living room all this time, talking to old friends like the Duchins and the Stantons and the Lanes. Lenny is wearing a black turtleneck, navy blazer, Black Watch plaid trousers and a necklace with a pendant hanging down to his sternum. His tailor comes here to the apartment to take the measurements and do the fittings. Lenny is a short, trim man, and yet he always seems tall. It is his head. He has a noble head, with a face that is at once sensitive and rugged, and a full stand of iron-gray hair, with sideburns, all set off nicely by the Chinese yellow of the room. His success radiates from his eyes and his smile with a charm that illustrates Lord Jersey's adage that "contrary to what the Methodists tell us, money and success are good for the soul." Lenny may be fifty-one, but he is still the *Wunderkind* of American music. Everyone says so. He is not only one of the world's outstanding conductors, but a more than competent composer and pianist as well. He is the man who more than any other has broken down the wall between elite music and popular tastes, with *West Side Story* and his children's concerts on television. How natural that he should stand here in his own home radiating the charm and grace that make him an easy host for leaders of the oppressed. How ironic that the next hour should prove so shattering for this *egregio maestro!* How curious that the Negro by the piano should emerge tonight!

A bell rang, a dinner-table bell, by the sound of it, the sort one summons the maid out of the kitchen with, and the party shifted from out of the hall and into the living room. Felicia led the way, Felicia and a small gray man, with gray hair, a gray face, a gray suit, and a pair of Groovy but gray sideburns. A little gray man, in short, who would be popping up at key moments . . . to keep the freight train of history on the track, as it were . . .

Felicia was down at the far end of the living room trying to coax everybody in.

"Lenny!" she said. "Tell the fringes to come on in!" Lenny was still in the back of the living room, near the hall. "Fringes!" said Lenny. "Come on in!"

In the living room most of the furniture, the couches, easy chairs, side tables, side chairs, and so on, had been pushed toward the walls, and thirty or forty folding chairs were set up in the middle of the floor. It was a big, wide room with Chinese yellow walls and white moldings, sconces, pier-glass mirrors, a portrait of Felicia reclining on a summer chaise, and at the far end, where Felicia was standing, a pair of grand pianos. A pair of them; the two pianos were standing back to back, with the tops down and their bellies swooping out. On top of both pianos was a regular flotilla of family photographs in silver frames, the kind of pictures that stand straight up thanks to little velvet- or moiré-covered buttresses in the back, the kind that decorators in New York recommend to give a living room a homelike lived-in touch. "The million-dollar *chatchka* look," they call it. In a way it was perfect for Radical Chic. The nice part was that with Lenny it was instinctive; with Felicia, too. The whole place looked as if the inspiration had been to spend a couple of hundred thousand on the interior without looking pretentious, although that is no great sum for a thirteen-room co-op, of course . . . Imagine explaining all that to the Black Panthers. It was another delicious thought . . . The sofas, for example, were covered in the fashionable splashy prints on a white background covering deep downy cushions, in the Bill Baldwin or Margaret Owen tradition—without it looking like Billy or Margaret had been in there fussing about with teapoys and japanned chairs. *Gemütlich* . . . Old Vienna when Grandpa was alive . . . That was the ticket . . .

Once Lenny got "the fringes" moving in, the room filled up rapidly. It was jammed, in fact. People were sitting on sofas and easy chairs along the sides, as well as on the folding chairs, and were standing in the back, where Lenny was. Otto Preminger was sitting on a sofa down by the pianos, where the speakers were going to stand. The Panther wives were sitting in the first two rows with their Yoruba headdresses on, along with Henry Mitchell and Julie Belafonte, Harry Belafonte's wife. Julie is white, but they all greeted her warmly as "Sister." Behind her was sitting Barbara Walters, hostess of the *Today Show* on television, wearing a checked pants suit with a great fluffy fur collar on the coat. Harold Taylor, the former "Boy President" of Sarah Lawrence, now fifty-five and silver-haired, but still youthful-looking, came walking down toward the front and gave a hug and a big social kiss to Gail Lumet. Robert Bay settled down in the middle of the folding chairs. Jean vanden Heuvel stood in the back and sought to focus . . . f/16 . . . on the pianos . . . Charlotte Curtis stood beside the door, taking notes.

And then Felicia stood up beside the pianos and said: "I want to thank you all very, very much for coming. I'm very, very glad to see so many of you here." Everything was fine. Her voice was rich as a woodwind. She introduced a man named Leon Quat, a lawyer involved in raising funds for the Panther 21, twenty-one Black Panthers who had been arrested on a charge of conspiring to blow up five New York department stores, New Haven Railroad facilities, a police station, and the Bronx Botanical Gardens.

Leon Quat, oddly enough, had the general look of those fifty-two-year-old men who run a combination law office, real estate, and insurance operation on the second floor of a two-story taxpayer out on Queens Boulevard. And yet that wasn't the kind of man Leon Quat really was. He had the sideburns. Quite a pair. They didn't come down just to the intertragic notch, which is that little notch in the lower rim of the ear, and which so many tentative Swingers aim their sideburns toward. No, on top of this complete Queens Boulevard insurance-agent look, he had real sideburns, to the bottom of the lobe, virtual mutton-chops, which somehow have become the mark of the Movement.

Leon Quat rose up smiling: "We are very grateful to Mrs. Bernstein"—only he pronounced it "steen."

"STEIN!"—a great smoke-cured voice booming out from the rear of the room! It's Lenny! Leon Quat and the Black Panthers will have a chance to hear from Lenny. That much is sure. He is on the case. Leon Quat must be the only man in the room who does not know about Lenny and the Mental Jotto at 3 a.m. . . . For years, twenty at the least, Lenny has insisted on *-stein* not *-steen*, as if to say, I am not one of those 1921 Jews who try to tone down their Jewishness by watering their names down with a bad soft English pronunciation. Lenny has made such a point of *-stein* not *-steen*, in fact, that some people in this room think at once of the story of how someone approached Larry Rivers, the artist, and said, "What's this I hear about you and Leonard Bernstein"—*steen*, he pronounced it—"not speaking to each other any more?"—to which Rivers said, "*STEIN!*"

"We are very grateful . . . for her marvelous hospitality," says Quat, apparently not wanting to try the name again right away.

Then he beams toward the crowd: "I assume we are all just an effete clique of snobs and intellectuals in this room . . . I am referring to the words of Vice-President Agnew, of course, who can't be with us today because he is in the South Pacific explaining the Nixon doctrine to the Australians. All vice-presidents suffer from the Avis complex—they're second best, so they try harder, like General Ky or Hubert Humphrey . . ." He keeps waiting for the grins and chuckles after each of these mots, but all the celebrities and culturati are nonplussed. They give him a kind of dumb attention. They came here for the Panthers and Radical Chic, and here is Old Queens Boulevard Real Estate Man with sideburns on telling them Agnew jokes. But Quat is too deep into his weird hole to get out. "Whatever respect I have had for Lester Maddox, I lost it when I saw Humphrey put his arm around his shoulder . . ." and somehow Quat begins disappearing down a hole bunging Hubert Humphrey with lumps of old Shelley Berman material. Slowly he climbs back out. He starts telling about the oppression of the Panther 21. They have been in jail since February 2, 1969, awaiting trial on ludicrous charges such as conspiring to blow up the Bronx Botanical Gardens. Their bail has been a preposterous $100,000 per person, which has in effect denied them the right to bail. They have been kept split up and moved from jail to jail. For all intents and purposes they have been denied the right to confer with their lawyers to prepare a defense. They have been subjected to inhuman treatment in jail—such as the case of Lee Berry, an epileptic, who was snatched out of a hospital bed and thrown in jail and kept in solitary confinement with a light bulb burning over his head night and day. The Panthers who have not been thrown in jail or killed, like Fred Hampton, are being stalked and harassed everywhere they go. "One of the few higher officials who is still . . . in the clear"—Quat smiles—"is here today. Don Cox, Field Marshal of the Black Panther Party."

"Right on," a voice says to Leon Quat, rather softly. And a tall black man rises from behind one of Lenny's grand pianos . . . *The Negro by the piano* . . .

The Field Marshal of the Black Panther Party has been sitting in a chair between the piano and the wall. He rises up; he has the hard-rock look, all right; he is a big tall man with brown skin and an Afro and a goatee and a black turtleneck much like Lenny's, and he stands up beside the piano, next to Lenny's million-dollar *chatchka* flotilla of family photographs. In fact, there is a certain perfection as the first Black Panther rises within a Park Avenue living room to lay the Panthers' ten-point program on New York Society in the age of Radical Chic. Cox is silhouetted—well, about nineteen feet behind him is a white silk shade with an Empire scallop over one of the windows overlooking Park Avenue. Or maybe it isn't silk, but a Jack Lenor Larsen mercerized cotton, something like that, lustrous but more subtle than silk. The whole image, the white shade and the Negro by the piano silhouetted against it, is framed by a pair of bottle-green velvet curtains, pulled back.

And does it begin now?—but this Cox is a cool number. He doesn't come on with the street epithets and interjections and the rest of the rhetoric and red eyes used for mau-mauing the white liberals, as it is called.

"The Black Panther Party," he starts off, "stands for a ten-point program that was handed down in October 1966 by our Minister of Defense, Huey P. Newton . . ." and he starts going through the ten points . . . "We want an educational system that expresses the true nature of this decadent society" . . . "We want all black men exempt from military service" . . . "We want all black men who are in jail to be set free. We want them to be set free because they have not had fair trials. We've been tried by predominantly middle-class, all-white juries" . . . "And most important of all, we want peace . . . see . . . We want peace, but there can be no peace as long as a society is racist and one part of society engages in systematic oppression of another" . . . "We want a plebiscite by the United Nations to be held in black communities, so that we can control our own destiny" . . .

Everyone in the room, of course, is drinking in his performance like tiger's milk, for the . . . Soul, as it were. All love the tone of his voice, which is Confidential Hip. And yet his delivery falls into strangely formal patterns. What are these block phrases, such as "our Minister of Defense, Huey P. Newton"—

"Some people think that we are racist, because the news media find it useful to create that impression in order to support the power structure, which we have nothing to do with . . . see . . . They like for the Black Panther Party to be made to look like a racist organization, because that camouflages the true class nature of the struggle. But they find it harder and harder to keep up that camouflage and are driven to campaigns of harassment and violence to try to eliminate the Black Panther Party. Here in New York twenty-one members of the Black Panther Party were indicted last April on ridiculous charges of conspiring to blow up department stores and flower gardens. They've had twenty-seven bail hearings since last April . . . see . . ."

—But everyone in here loves the *sees* and the *you knows*. They are so, somehow . . . *black* . . . so *funky* . . . so metrical . . . Without ever bringing it fully into consciousness everyone responds—communes over—the fact that he uses them not for emphasis but for punctuation, metrically, much like the *uhs* favored by High Church Episcopal ministers, as in, "And bless, uh, these gifts, uh, to Thy use and us to, uh, Thy service"—

". . . they've had twenty-seven bail hearings since last April . . . see . . . and every time the judge has refused to lower the bail from $100,000 . . . Yet a group of whites accused of actually bombing buildings—they were able to get bail. So that clearly demonstrates the racist nature of the campaign against the Black Panther Party. We don't say 'bail' any more, we say 'ransom,' for such repressive bail can only be called ransom.

"The situation here in New York is very explosive, as you can see, with people stacked up on top of each other. They can hardly deal with them when they're *un*organized, so that when a group comes along like the Black Panthers, they want to eliminate that group by any means . . . see . . . and so that stand has been embraced by J. Edgar Hoover, who feels that we are the greatest threat to the power structure. They try to create the impression that we are engaged in criminal activities. What are these 'criminal activities'? We have instituted a breakfast program, to address ourselves to the needs of the community. We feed hungry children every morning before they go to school. So far this program is on a small scale. We're only feeding fifty thousand children nationwide, but the only money we have for this program is donations from the merchants in the neighborhoods. We have a program to establish clinics in the black communities and in other ways also we are addressing ourselves to the needs of the community . . . see . . . So the people know the power structure is lying when they say we are engaged in criminal activities. So the pigs are driven to desperate acts, like the murder of our deputy chairman, Fred Hampton, in his bed . . . see . . . in his sleep . . . But when they got desperate and took off their camouflage and murdered Fred Hampton, in his bed, in his sleep, see, that kind of shook people up, because they saw the tactics of the power structure for what they were . . .

"We relate to a phrase coined by Malcolm X: 'By any means necessary' . . . you see . . . 'By any means necessary' . . . and by that we mean that we recognize that if you're attacked, you have the right to defend yourself. The pigs, they say the Black Panthers are armed, the Black Panthers have weapons . . . see . . . and therefore they have the right to break in and murder us in our beds. I don't think there's anybody in here who wouldn't defend themselves if somebody came in and attacked them or their families . . . see . . . I don't think there's anybody in here who wouldn't defend themselves . . ."

—and every woman in the room thinks of her husband . . . with his cocoa-butter jowls and Dior Men's Boutique pajamas . . . ducking into the bathroom and locking the door and turning the shower on, so he can say later that he didn't hear a thing—

"We call them pigs, and rightly so," says Don Cox, "because they have the way of making the victim look like the criminal, and the criminal look like the victim. So every Panther must be ready to defend himself. That was handed down by our Minister of Defense, Huey P. Newton: Everybody who does not have the means to defend himself in his home, or if he does have the means and he does not defend himself—we expel *that man* . . . see . . . As our Minister of Defense, Huey P. Newton, says, 'Any unarmed people are slaves, or are slaves in the real meaning of the word' . . . We recognize that this country is the most oppressive country in the world, maybe in the history of the world. The pigs have the weapons and they are ready to use them on the people, and we recognize this as being very bad. They are ready to commit genocide against those who stand up against them, and we recognize this as being very bad.

"All we want is the good life, the same as you. To live in peace and lead the good life, that's all we want . . . see . . . But right now there's no way we can do that. I want to read something to you:

" 'When in the course of human events, it becomes necessary for one people to dissolve the political bands which have connected them with another, and . . ." He reads straight through it, every word. ". . . and, accordingly, all experience hath shown, that mankind are more disposed to suffer, while evils are sufferable, than to right themselves by abolishing the forms to which they are accustomed. But when a long train of abuses and usurpations, pursuing invariably the same object, evinces a design to reduce them under absolute despotism, it is their right, it is their duty, to throw off such government, and to provide new guards for their future security.'

"You know what that's from?"—and he looks out at everyone and hesitates before laying this gasper on them—"That's from the Declaration of Independence, the American Declaration of Independence. And we will defend ourselves and do like it says . . . you know? . . . and that's about it."

The "that's about it" part seems so casual, so funky, so right, after the rhetoric of what he has been saying. And then he sits down and sinks out of sight behind one of the grand pianos.

The thing is beginning to move. And—hell, yes, the *Reichstag fire!* Another man gets up, a white named Gerald Lefcourt, who is chief counsel for the Panther 21, a young man with thick black hair and the muttonchops of the Movement and that great motor inside of him that young courtroom lawyers ought to have. He lays the Reichstag fire on them. He reviews the Panther case and then he says:

"I believe that this odious situation could be compared to the Reichstag fire attempt"—he's talking about the way the Nazis used the burning of the Reichstag as the pretext for first turning loose the Gestapo and exterminating all political opposition in Germany—"and I believe that this trial could also be compared to the Reichstag trial . . . in many ways . . . and that opened an era that this country could be heading for. That could be the outcome of this case, an era of the Right, and the only thing that can stop it is for people like ourselves to make a noise and make a noise now."

. . . and not be Krupps, Junkers, or Good Germans . . .

". . . We had an opportunity to question the Grand Jury, and we found out some interesting things. They all have net worths averaging $300,000, and they all come from this neighborhood," says Lefcourt, nodding as if to take in the whole Upper East Side. And suddenly everyone feels, really *feels*, that there are two breeds of mankind in the great co-ops of Park Avenue, the blue-jowled rep-tied Brook Club Junker reactionaries in the surrounding buildings . . . and the few *attuned* souls here in Lenny's penthouse. ". . . They all have annual incomes in the area of $35,000 . . . And you're supposed to have a 'jury of your peers' . . . They were shocked at the questions we were asking them. They shouldn't have to answer such questions, that was the idea. They all belong to the Grand Jury Association. They're somewhat like a club. They have lunch together once in a while. A lot of them went to school together. They have no more understanding of the Black Panthers than President Nixon."

The Junkers! Leon Quat says: "Fascism always begins by persecuting the least powerful and least popular movement. It will be the Panthers today, the students tomorrow—and then . . . the Jews and other troublesome minorities! . . . What price civil liberties! . . . Now let's start this off with the gifts in four figures. Who is ready to make a contribution of a thousand dollars or more?"

All at once—nothing. But the little gray man sitting next to Felicia, the gray man with the sideburns, pops up and hands a piece of paper to Quat and says: "Mr. Clarence Jones asked me to say—he couldn't be here, but he's contributing $7,500 to the defense fund!"

"Oh! That's marvelous!" says Felicia.

Then the voice of Lenny from the back of the room: "As a guest of my wife"—he smiles—"I'll give my fee for the next performance of *Cavalleria Rusticana*." Comradely laughter. Applause. "I *hope* that will be four figures!"

Things are moving again. Otto Preminger speaks up from the sofa down front: "I geeve a t'ousand dollars!"

Right on. Quat says: "I can't assure you that it's tax deductible." He smiles. "I wish I could, but I can't." Well, the man looks brighter and brighter every minute. He knows a Radical Chic audience when he sees one. Those words are magic in the age of Radical Chic: it's *not* tax deductible.

The contributions start coming faster, only $250 or $300 at a clip, but faster . . . Sheldon Harnick . . . Bernie and Hilda Fishman . . . Judith Bernstein . . . Mr. and Mrs. Burton Lane . . .

"I know some of you are caught with your Dow-Jones averages down," says Quat, "but come on—"

Quat says: "We have a $300 contribution from Harry Belafonte!"

"No, no," says Julie Belafonte.

"I'm sorry," says Quat, "it's Julie's private money! I apologize. After all, there's a women's liberation movement sweeping the country, and I want this marked down as a gift from *Mrs.* Belafonte!" Then he says: "I know you want to get to the question period, but I know there's more gold in this mine. I think we've reached the point where we can pass out the blank checks."

More contributions . . . $100 from Mrs. August Heckscher . . .

"We'll take *any*thing!" says Quat. "We'll take it all!" . . . He's high on the momentum of his fund-raiser voice . . . "You'll leave here with nothing!"

But finally he wraps it up. A beautiful ash-blond girl with the most perfect Miss Porter's face speaks up. She's wearing a leather and tweed dress. She looks like a Junior Leaguer graduating to the Ungaro Boutique.

"I'd like to ask Mr. Cox a question," she says. Cox is standing up again, by the grand piano. "Besides the breakfast program," she says, "do you have any other community programs, and what are they like?"

Cox starts to tell about a Black Panther program to set up medical clinics in the ghettos, and so on, but soon he is talking about a Panther demand that police be required to live in the community they patrol. "If you police the community, you must live there . . . see . . . Because if he lives in the community, he's going to think twice before he brutalizes us, because we can deal with him when he comes home at night . . . see . . . We are also working to start liberation schools for black children, and these liberation schools will actually teach them about their environment, because the way they are now taught, they are taught not to see their real environment . . . see . . . They get Donald Duck and Mother Goose and all that lame happy jive . . . you know . . . We'd like to take kids on tours of the white suburbs, like Scarsdale, and like that, and let them see how their oppressors live . . . you know . . . but so far we don't have the money to carry out these programs to meet the real needs of the community. The only money we have is what we get from the merchants in the black community when we ask them for donations, which they *should give*, because they are the exploiters of the black community"—

—and *shee-ut*. What the hell is Cox getting into that for? Quat and the little gray man are ready to spring in at any lonesome split second. For God's sake, Cox, don't open that can of worms. Even in this bunch of upholstered skulls there are people who can figure out just *who* those merchants are, what group, and just how they are *asked* for donations, and we've been free of that little issue all evening, man —don't bring out *that* ball-breaker—

But the moment is saved. Suddenly there is a much more urgent question from the rear: "Who do you call to give a party? Who do you call to give a party?"

Every head spins around . . . Quite a sight . . . It's a slender blond man who has pushed his way up to the front ranks of the standees. He's wearing a tuxedo. He's wearing black-frame glasses and his blond hair is combed back straight in the Eaton Square manner. He looks like the intense Yale man from out of one of those 1927 Frigidaire ads in *The Saturday Evening Post*, when the way to sell anything was to show Harry Yale in the background, in a tuxedo, with his pageboy-bobbed young lovely, heading off to dinner at the New Haven Lawn Club. The man still has his hand up in the air like the star student of the junior class.

"I won't be able to stay for everything you have to say," he says, "but who do you call to give a party?"

In fact, it is Richard Feigen, owner of the Feigen Gallery, 79th near Madison. He arrived on the art scene and the social scene from Chicago three years ago . . . He's been moving up hand over hand ever since . . . like a champion . . . Tonight—the tuxedo—tonight there is a reception at the Museum of Modern Art . . . right on . . . a "contributing members'" reception, a private viewing not open to mere "members" . . . But before the museum reception itself, which is at 8:30, there are private dinners . . . right? . . . which are the *real* openings . . . in the homes of great collectors or great climbers or the old Protestant elite, marvelous dinner parties, the real thing, black tie, and these dinners are the only true certification of where one stands in this whole realm of Art & Society . . . The whole game depends on whose home one is invited to before the opening . . . And the game ends as the host gathers everyone up about 8:45 for the trek to the museum itself, and the guests say, almost ritually, "God! I wish we could see the show from here! It's too delightful! I simply don't want to *move!*" . . . And of course, they mean it! Absolutely! For them, the opening is already over, the hand is played . . . And Richard Feigen, man of the hour, replica 1927 Yale man, black tie and Eaton Square hair, has dropped in, on the way, *en passant*, to the Bernsteins', to take in the other end of the Culture tandem, Radical Chic . . . and the rightness of it, the exhilaration, seems to sweep through him, and he thrusts his hand into the air, and somehow Radical Chic reaches its highest, purest state in that moment . . . as Richard Feigen, in his tuxedo, breaks in to ask, from the bottom of his heart, "Who do you call to give a party?"

Pedagogy

"Go ahead. Try me. The next one of you peckerwoods who sprays burning lighter fluid into my locker, boosts the tape deck out of my car or pees on the upholstery, hits me in the back of the head in the hallway with a johnny-mop canister or a urinal puck, tries any mackin' or jackin' in the back of the class, seals up this room with Krazy Glue so I can't get out, makes goomba-goomba sounds and asks the substitute teacher if she's got life insurance, or refers to me as 'you mollyfoggin' lamehead,' is gonna get a new hole in his nose."

MAU-MAUING THE FLAK CATCHERS

Going downtown to mau-mau the bureaucrats got to be the routine practice in San Francisco. The poverty program *encouraged* you to go in for mau-mauing. They wouldn't have known what to do without it. The bureaucrats at City Hall and in the Office of Economic Opportunity talked "ghetto" all the time, but they didn't know any more about what was going on in the Western Addition, Hunters Point, Potrero Hill, the Mission, Chinatown, or south of Market Street than they did about Zanzibar. They didn't know where to look. They didn't even know who to ask. So what could they do? Well . . . they used the Ethnic Catering Service . . . right . . . They sat back and waited for you to come rolling in with your certified angry militants, your guaranteed frustrated ghetto youth, looking like a bunch of wild men. Then you had your test confrontation. If you were outrageous enough, if you could shake up the bureaucrats so bad that their eyes froze into iceballs and their mouths twisted up into smiles of sheer physical panic, into shit-eating grins, so to speak—then they knew you were the real goods. They knew you were the right studs to give the poverty grants and community organizing jobs to. Otherwise they wouldn't know.

There was one genius in the art of confrontation who had mau-mauing down to what you could term a laboratory science. He had it figured out so he didn't even have to bring his boys downtown in person. He would just show up with a crocus sack full of revolvers, ice picks, fish knives, switchblades, hatchets, blackjacks, gravity knives, straight razors, hand grenades, blow guns, bazookas, Molotov cocktails, tank rippers, unbelievable stuff, and he'd dump it all out on somebody's shiny walnut conference table. He'd say "These are some

---

From *Radical Chic & Mau-Mauing the Flak Catchers.*

of the things I took off my boys last night . . . I don't know, man . . . Thirty minutes ago I talked a Panther out of busting up a cop . . ." And they would lay money on this man's ghetto youth patrol like it was now or never . . . The Ethnic Catering Service . . . Once they hired the Ethnic Catering Service, the bureaucrats felt like it was all *real.* They'd say to themselves, "We've given jobs to a hundred of the toughest hard-core youth in Hunters Point. The problem is on the way to being solved." They never inquired if the bloods they were giving the jobs to were the same ones who were causing the trouble. They'd say to themselves, "We don't have to find *them.* They find *us*" . . . Once the Ethnic Catering Service was on the case, they felt like they were reaching all those hard-to-reach hard-to-hold hard-core hardrock blackrage badass furious funky ghetto youth.

There were people in the Western Addition who practically gave classes in mau-mauing. There was one man called Chaser. Chaser would get his boys together and he would give them a briefing like the U.S. Air Force wing commander gives his pilots in Thailand before they make the raid over North Vietnam, the kind of briefing where everybody is supposed to picture the whole mission like a film in their heads, the landmarks, the Red River, the approach pattern, the bombing run, every twist and turn, the SAM missile sites, the getaway, everything. In the same way Chaser would picture the room you would be heading into. It might be a meeting of the Economic Opportunity Council, which was the San Francisco poverty-program agency, or the National Alliance of Businessmen, which was offering jobs for the hard core, or the Western Regional Office of the Office of Economic Opportunity, or whatever, and he'd say:

"Now don't forget. When you go downtown, y'all wear your *ghetto rags* . . . see . . . Don't go down there with your Italian silk jerseys on and your brown suède and green alligator shoes and your Harry Belafonte shirts looking like some supercool toothpick-noddin' fool . . . you know . . . Don't nobody give a damn how pretty you can look . . . You wear your *combat* fatigues and your leather *pieces* and your shades . . . your *ghetto rags* . . . see . . . And don't go down there with your hair all done up nice in your curly Afro like you're messing around. You go down with your hair *stickin' out* . . . and *sittin' up!* Lookin' wild! I want to see you down there looking like a bunch of *wild niggers!*"

This Chaser was a talker. He used to be in vaudeville. At least that was what everybody said. That was how he learned to be such a beautiful talker. When the poverty program started, he organized his own group in the Western Addition, the Youth Coalition. Chaser was about forty, and he wasn't big. He was small, physically. But he knew how to make all those young aces of his take care of business. Chaser was black with a kind of brown hue. He had high cheekbones, like an Indian. He always wore a dashiki, over some ordinary pants and a Ban-lon shirt. He had two of these Ban-lon shirts and he alternated them. Anyway, he always wore the dashiki and a beret. He must not have had much hair on top of his head, because on the sides his hair stuck out like a natural, but the beret always laid flat. If he had as much hair on the top of his head as he had sticking out on the sides, that beret would have been sitting up in the air like the star on a Christmas tree. When everybody started wearing the Afros, it was hard on a lot of older men who were losing their hair. They would grow it long on the sides anyway and they would end up looking like that super-Tom on the Uncle Ben Rice box, or Bozo the Clown. Sometimes Chaser would wear a big heavy overcoat, one of those big long heavy double-breasted triple-button quadruple-lapel numbers like you see the old men wearing in Foster's Cafeteria. When you saw Chaser with that big coat on, over top of the dashiki, you'd have to smile, because then you knew Chaser wasn't in anybody's bag. Chaser was in Chaser's bag. That was all right, because you don't meet many men like Chaser. If there is any such thing as a born leader, he was one of them.

"Now, you women," he'd say. "I don't want you women to be macking with the brothers if they ain't tending to business. You women make your men get out of the house and get to work for the Youth Coalition. Don't you be macking around with nobody who ain't out working for the Youth Coalition. If he ain't man enough to be out on the street working for the people, then he ain't man enough for you to be macking around with."

This worked like a charm with the women and with the men, too. Chaser kept saying "You women," but he was really talking to the men. He was challenging their masculinity. A lot of these young aces knew that their women thought they weren't man enough to stand up and make something out of themselves. And the women liked what he was saying, too, because he was including them in on the whole thing.

Then Chaser would say, "Now when we get there, I want you to come down front and stare at the man and don't say nothing. You just glare. No matter what he says. He'll try to get you to agree with him. He'll say, 'Ain't that right?' and 'You know what I mean?' and he wants you to say yes or nod your head . . . see . . . It's part of his psychological jiveass. But you don't say nothing. You just glare . . . see . . . Then some of the other brothers will get up on that stage behind him, like there's no more room or like they just gathering around. Then you brothers up there behind him, you start letting him have it . . . He starts thinking, 'Oh, good God! Those bad cats are in front of me, they all *around* me, they *behind* me. I'm sur*round*ed.' That shakes 'em up.

"And then when one of the brothers is up talking, another brother comes up and whispers something in his ear, like this," and Chaser cups his hand around his mouth like he's whispering something. "And the brother stops talking, like he's listening, and the man thinks, 'What's he saying? What kind of unbelievable shit are they planning now?' The brother, he's not saying anything. He's just moving his lips. It's a tactic . . . you know . . . And at the end I'll slap my hand down on the desk—*whop*—and everybody gets up, like one man, and walks out of there. And that really shakes 'em up. They see that the people are unified, and disciplined, and mad, and tired of talking and ready for walking, and that shakes 'em up."

Chaser had his two main men, James Jones and Louis Downs. Downs was Chaser's showpiece. He was sharp. He was young and had a very athletic build. He had a haircut of the intellectual-natural variety and a pair of José Feliciano sunglasses and a black leather dashiki, and he'd have on a pair of A-1 racer pants. The A-1 racers are not just narrow, they're like a stovepipe, with the 16½-inch cuffs. And he'd have on either a pair of Vietnam combat boots with the green webbing or a pair of tennis shoes, but a really expensive kind of tennis shoe. You look at them and you know he really had to look especially hard to find that pair. He'd always be bracing his hands in front of him, pressing the heels of his hands together, which made the muscles pop up around his neck and his shoulders. James Jones was Chaser's philosopher. He was a talker, too. He'd come on like a Southern Christian Leadership preacher, giving all the reasons why, and then Downs would come on hard and really sharp. Between the three of them, Chaser and Downs and James Jones, they were like the Three Musketeers. They were beautiful to behold.

Chaser was funny. Just like he had everything planned out on his side, right down to the last detail, he thought the Man must have it planned out that far, too. Chaser had a kind of security paranoia. At a demonstration or something you'd see Chaser giving instructions to his boys with his hand over his mouth. He'd always be talking with his hand over his mouth, mumbling into his fingers, and he'd tell his boys to talk that way, too. Chaser was convinced that the Man had electronic eavesdropping devices trained on them. He'd tell you about the "parabolic earphones" and the deaf-mutes. He believed that the Man had trained a corps of deaf-mutes to read lips for crowd control. He'd have you believing it, too. It was like, What would *you* do if you were a deaf-mute and shuffling and shitkicking through life and the government comes along and offers to pay you money for reading lips and playing C.I.A. . . . Chaser didn't blame them any more than he'd blame a dog . . . They were being exploited like all the other Toms that didn't know any better . . .

Brothers like Chaser were the ones who perfected mau-mauing, but before long everybody in the so-called Third World was into it. Everybody was out mau-mauing up a storm, to see if they could win the victories the blacks had won. San Francisco, being the main port of entry for immigrants from all over the Pacific, had as many colored minorities as New York City. Maybe more. Blacks, Chicanos, Latinos, Chinese, Japanese, Filipinos, American Indians, Samoans—everybody was circling around the poverty program. By the end of 1968 there were eighty-seven different groups getting into the militant thing, getting into mau-mauing.

Nobody kept records on the confrontations, which is too bad. There must have been hundreds of them in San Francisco alone. Across the country there must have been thousands. When the confrontations touched the white middle class in a big way, like when black students started strikes and disruptions at San Francisco State, Columbia, Cornell, or Yale, or when somebody like James Forman came walking up to the pulpit of the Riverside Church carrying a four-pound cane the size of the shillelagh the Fool Killer used to lug around to the State Fair to kill fools with—when Forman got up there with that hickory stick like he was going to swat all undeserving affluent white Christians over the bean unless they paid five hundred million dollars in reparations—then the media described it blow by blow. But what went on in the colleges and churches was just a part of it. Bad dudes were out mau-mauing at all the poverty agencies, at boards of education, at city halls, hospitals, conventions, foundations, schools, charities, civic organizations, all sorts of places. It got to be an American custom, like talk shows, Face the Nation, marriage counseling, marathon encounters, or zoning hearings.

That was certainly the way the message came down to the youth of the Third World in areas like the Mission, Chinatown, and Japan Town. Mau-mauing was the ticket. The confrontation route was the only road. So the Chinese, the Japanese, the Chicanos, the Indians picked up on mau-mauing from the bloods. Not only that, they would try to do it exactly *like* the bloods. They'd talk like the bloods, dress like the bloods, try to wear naturals like the bloods, even if their hair was too straight to do it. There were Spanish and Oriental dudes who washed their hair every day with Borax to make it fluff up and sit out.

When anybody other than black people went in for mau-mauing, however, they ran into problems, because the white man had a different set of fear reflexes for each race he was dealing with.

Whites didn't have too much fear of the Mexican-American, the

Chicano. The notion was that he was small, placid, slow, no particular physical threat—until he grew his hair Afro-style, talked like a blood or otherwise managed to seem "black" enough to raise hell. Then it was a different story.

The whites' physical fear of the Chinese was nearly zero. The white man pictured the Chinese as small, quiet, restrained little fellows. He had a certain deep-down voodoo fear of their powers of Evil in the Dark . . . the Hatchet Men . . . the Fangs of the Tong . . . but it wasn't a live fear. For that matter, the young Chinese themselves weren't ready for the age of mau-mauing. It wasn't that they feared the white man, the way black people had. It was more that they didn't fear or resent white people enough. They looked down on whites as childish and uncultivated. They also found it somewhat shameful to present themselves as poor and oppressed, on the same level with Negroes and Mexican-Americans. It wasn't until 1969 that militants really got into confrontations in Chinatown.

Every now and then, after the poverty scene got going, and the confrontations became a regular thing, whites would run into an ethnic group they drew a total blank on, like the Indians or the Samoans. Well, with the Samoans they didn't draw a blank for long, not once they actually came up against them. The Samoans on the poverty scene favored the direct approach. They did not fool around. They were like the original unknown terrors. In fact, they were unknown terrors and a half.

Why so few people in San Francisco know about the Samoans is a mystery. All you have to do is see a couple of those Polynesian studs walking through the Mission, minding their own business, and you won't forget it soon. Have you ever by any chance seen professional football players in person, like on the street? The thing you notice is not just that they're big but that they are *so* big, it's weird. Everything about them is gigantic, even their heads. They'll have a skull the size of a watermelon, with a couple of little squinty eyes and a little mouth and a couple of nose holes stuck in, and no neck at all. From the ears down, the big yoyos are just one solid welded hulk, the size of an oil burner. You get the feeling that football players come from a whole other species of human, they're so big. Well, that will give you some idea of the Samoans, because they're bigger. The average Samoan makes Bubba Smith of the Colts look like a shrimp. They start out at about 300 pounds and from there they just get *wider*. They are big huge giants. Everything about them is wide and smooth. They have big wide faces and smooth features. They're a dark brown, with a smooth cast.

Anyway, the word got around among the groups in the Mission that the poverty program was going to cut down on summer jobs, and the

Mission was going to be on the short end. So a bunch of the groups in the Mission got together and decided to go downtown to the poverty office and do some mau-mauing in behalf of the Mission before the bureaucrats made up their minds. There were blacks, Chicanos, Filipinos, and about ten Samoans.

The poverty office was on the first floor and had a big anteroom; only it's almost bare, nothing in it but a lot of wooden chairs. It looks like a union hall minus the spittoons, or one of those lobbies where they swear in new citizens. It's like they want to impress the poor that they don't have leather-top desks . . . All our money goes to you . . .

So the young aces from the Mission come trooping in, and they want to see the head man. The word comes out that the No. 1 man is out of town, but the No. 2 man is coming out to talk to the people.

This man comes out, and he has that sloppy Irish look like Ed McMahon on TV, only with a longer nose. In case you'd like the local viewpoint, whites really have the noses . . . enormous, you might say . . . a whole bag full . . . long and pointed like carrots, goobered up like green peppers, hooked like a squash, hanging off the face like cucumbers . . . This man has a nose that is just on the verge of hooking over, but it doesn't quite make it.

"Have a seat, gentlemen," he says, and he motions toward the wooden chairs.

But he doesn't have to open his mouth. All you have to do is look at him and you get the picture. The man's a lifer. He's stone civil service. He has it all down from the wheatcolor Hush Puppies to the wash'n' dry semi-tab-collar shortsleeves white shirt. Those wheatcolor Hush Puppies must be like some kind of fraternal garb among the civil-service employees, because they all wear them. They cost about $4.99, and the second time you move your toes, the seams split and the tops come away from the soles. But they all wear them. The man's shirt looks like he bought it at the August end-of-summer sale at the White Front. It is one of those shirts with pockets on both sides. Sticking out of the pockets and running across his chest he has a lineup of ball-point pens, felt nibs, lead pencils, wax markers, such as you wouldn't believe, Paper-mates, Pentels, Scriptos, Eberhard Faber Mongol 482's, Dri-Marks, Bic PM-29's, everything. They are lined up across his chest like campaign ribbons.

He pulls up one of the wooden chairs and sits down on it. Only he sits down on it backwards, straddling the seat and hooking his arms and his chin over the back of the chair, like the head foreman in the bunkhouse. It's like saying, "We don't stand on ceremony around here. This is a shirtsleeve operation."

"I'm sorry that Mr. Johnson isn't here today," he says, "but he's not in the city. He's back in Washington meeting some important project deadlines. He's very concerned, and he would want to meet with you people if he were here, but right now I know you'll understand that the most important thing he can do for you is to push these projects through in Washington."

The man keeps his arms and his head hung over the back of his chair, but he swings his hands up in the air from time to time to emphasize a point, first one hand and then the other. It looks like he's giving wig-wag signals to the typing pool. The way he hangs himself over the back of the chair—that keeps up the funky shirtsleeve-operation number. And throwing his hands around—that's dy*nam*ic . . . It says, "We're hacking our way through the red tape just as fast as we can."

"Now I'm here to try to answer any questions I can," he says, "but you have to understand that I'm only speaking as an individual, and so naturally none of my comments are binding, but I'll answer any questions I can, and if I can't answer them, I'll do what I can to get the answers for you."

And then it dawns on you, and you wonder why it took so long for you to realize it. This man is the flak catcher. His job is to catch the flak for the No. 1 man. He's like the professional mourners you can hire in Chinatown. They have certified wailers, professional mourners, in Chinatown, and when your loved one dies, you can hire the professional mourners to wail at the funeral and show what a great loss to the community the departed is. In the same way this lifer is ready to catch whatever flak you're sending up. It doesn't matter what bureau they put him in. It's all the same. Poverty, Japanese imports, valley fever, tomato-crop parity, partial disability, home loans, second-probate accounting, the Interstate 90 detour change order, lockouts, secondary boycotts, G.I. alimony, the Pakistani quota, cinch mites, Tularemic Loa loa, veterans' dental benefits, workmen's compensation, suspended excise rebates—whatever you're angry about, it doesn't matter, he's there to catch the flak. He's a lifer.

Everybody knows the scene is a shuck, but you can't just walk out and leave. You can't get it on and bring thirty-five people walking all the way from the Mission to 100 McAllister and then just turn around and go back. So . . . might as well get into the number . . .

One of the Chicanos starts it off by asking the straight question, which is about how many summer jobs the Mission groups are going to get. This is the opening phase, the straight-face phase, in the art of mau-mauing.

"Well," says the Flak Catcher—and he gives it a twist of the head and a fling of the hand and the ingratiating smile—"It's hard for me to answer that the way I'd like to answer it, and the way I know you'd like for me to answer it, because that's precisely what we're working on back in Washington. But I can tell you this. At this point I see no reason why our project allocation should be any less, if all we're looking at is the urban-factor numbers for this area, because that should remain the same. Of course, if there's been any substantial pre-funding, in Washington, for the fixed-asset part of our program, like Head Start or the community health centers, that could alter the picture. But we're very hopeful, and as soon as we have the figures, I can tell you that you people will be the first to know."

It goes on like this for a while. He keeps saying things like, "I don't know the answer to that right now, but I'll do everything I can to find out." The way he says it, you can tell he thinks you're going to be impressed with how honest he is about what he doesn't know. Or he says, "I wish we could give *everybody* jobs. Believe me, I would like nothing better, both personally and as a representative of this Office."

So one of the bloods says, "Man, why do you sit there shining us with this bureaucratic rhetoric, when you said yourself that ain't nothing you say that means a goddam thing?"

Ba-ram-ba-ram-ba-ram-ba-ram—a bunch of the aces start banging on the floor in unison. It sounds like they have sledge hammers.

"Ha-unnnnh," says the Flak Catcher. It is one of those laughs that starts out as a laugh but ends up like he got hit in the stomach halfway through. It's the first assault on his dignity. So he breaks into his shit-eating grin, which is always phase two. Why do so many bureaucrats, deans, preachers, college presidents, try to smile when the mau-mauing starts? It's fatal, this smiling. When some bad dude is challenging your manhood, your smile just proves that he is right and you are chickenshit—unless you are a bad man yourself with so much heart that you can make that smile say, "Just keep on talking, sucker, because I'm gonna count to ten and then *squash* you."

"Well," says the Flak Catcher, "I can't promise you jobs if the jobs aren't available yet"—and then he looks up as if for the first time he is really focusing on the thirty-five ghetto hot dogs he is now facing, by way of sizing up the threat, now that the shit has started. The blacks and the Chicanos he has no doubt seen before, or people just like them, but then he takes in the Filipinos. There are about eight of them, and they are all wearing the Day-Glo yellow and hot-green sweaters and lemon-colored pants and Italian-style socks. But it's the headgear that does the trick. They've all got on Rap Brown shades and Russian Cossack hats made of frosted-gray Dynel. They look *bad*. Then the man takes in the Samoans, and they look worse. There's about ten of them, but they fill up half the room. They've got on Island shirts with designs in streaks and blooms of red, only it's a really raw shade of red, like that red they paint the floor with in the tool and die works. They're glaring at him out of those big dark wide brown faces. The monsters have tight curly hair, but it grows in long strands, and they comb it back flat, in long curly strands, with a Duke pomade job. They've got huge feet, and they're wearing sandals. The straps on the sandals look like they were made from the reins on the Budweiser draft horses. But what really gets the Flak Catcher, besides the sheer size of the brutes, is their Tiki canes. These are like Polynesian scepters. They're the size of sawed-off pool cues, only they're carved all over in Polynesian Tiki Village designs. When they wrap their fists around these sticks, every knuckle on their hands pops out the size of a walnut. Anything they hear that they like, like the part about the "bureaucratic rhetoric," they bang on the floor in unison with the ends of the Tiki sticks—*ba-ram-ba-ram-ba-ram-ba-ram*—although some of them press one end of the stick onto the sole of their sandal between their first two toes and raise their foot up and down with the stick to cushion the blow on the floor. They don't want to scuff up the Tiki cane.

The Flak Catcher is still staring at them, and his shit-eating grin is getting worse. It's like he *knows* the worst is yet to come . . . Goddamn . . . that one in front there . . . that Pineapple Brute . . .

"Hey, Brudda," the main man says. He has a really heavy accent. "Hey, Brudda, how much you make?"

"Me?" says the Flak Catcher. "How much do I make?"

"Yeah, Brudda, you. How much money you make?"

Now the man is trying to think in eight directions at once. He tries out a new smile. He tries it out on the bloods, the Chicanos, and the Filipinos, as if to say, "As one intelligent creature to another, what do you do with dumb people like this?" But all he gets is the glares, and his mouth shimmies back into the terrible sickening grin, and then you can see that there are a whole lot of little muscles all around the human mouth, and his are beginning to squirm and tremble . . . He's fighting for control of himself . . . It's a lost cause . . .

"How much, Brudda?"

Ba-ram-ba-ram-ba-ram-ba-ram—they keep beating on the floor.

"Well," says the Flak Catcher, "I make $1,100 a month."

"How come you make so much?"

"Wellllll"—the grin, the last bid for clemency . . . and now the poor man's eyes are freezing into little round iceballs, and his mouth is getting dry—

Ba-ram-ba-ram-ba-ram-ba-ram

"How come you make so much? My fadda and mudda both work and they only make six hundred and fifty."

Oh shit, the cat kind of blew it there. That's way over the poverty line, about double, in fact. It's even above the guideline for a family of twelve. You can see that fact register with the Flak Catcher, and he's trying to work up the nerve to make the devastating comeback. But he's not about to talk back to these giants.

"Listen, Brudda. Why don't you give up your paycheck for summer jobs? You ain't doing shit."

"Wellll"—the Flak Catcher grins, he sweats, he hangs over the back of the chair—

Ba-ram-ba-ram-ba-ram-ba-ram—"Yeah, Brudda! Give us your paycheck!"

There it is . . . the ultimate horror . . . He can see it now, he can hear it . . . Fifteen tons of it . . . It's horrible . . . it's possible . . . It's so obscene, it just might happen . . . Huge Polynesian monsters marching down to his office every payday . . . Hand it over, Brudda . . . ripping it out of his very fingers . . . eternally . . . He wrings his hands . . . the little muscles around his mouth are going haywire. He tries to recapture his grin, but those little amok muscles pull his lips up into an O, like they were drawstrings.

"I'd gladly give up my salary," says the Flak Catcher. "I'd *glad*ly do it, if it would do any good. But can't you see, gentlemen, it would be just a drop in the bucket . . . just *a drop in the bucket!*" This phrase *a drop in the bucket* seems to give him heart . . . it's something to hang onto . . . an answer . . . a reprieve . . . "Just consider what we have to do in this city alone, gentlemen! All of us! It's just *a drop in the bucket!*"

The Samoans can't come up with any answer to this, so the Flak Catcher keeps going

"Look, gentlemen," he says, "you tell me what to do and I'll do it. Of *course* you want more summer jobs, and we want you to have them. That's what we're here for. I wish I could give everybody a job. You tell me how to get more jobs, and we'll get them. We're doing all we can. If we can do more, you tell me how, and I'll gladly do it."

One of the bloods says, "Man, if you don't *know how,* then we don't *need* you."

"Dat's right, Brudda! Whadda we need you for!" You can tell the Samoans wish they had thought of that shoot-down line themselves—*Ba-ram-ba-ram-ba-ram-ba-ram*—they clobber the hell out of the floor.

"Man," says the blood, "you just taking up space and killing time and drawing pay!"

"Dat's right, Brudda! You just drawing pay!" *Ba-ram-ba-ram-ba-ram-ba-ram*

"Man," says the blood, "if you don't know nothing and you can't do nothing and you can't say nothing, why don't you tell your boss what we want!"

"Dat's right, Brudda! Tell the man!" *Ba-ram-ba-ram-ba-ram-ba-ram*

"As I've already told you, he's in Washington trying to meet the deadlines for *your* projects!"

"You talk to the man, don't you? He'll let you talk to him, won't he?"

"Yes . . ."

"Send him a telegram, man!"

"Well, all right—"

"Shit, pick up the telephone, man!"

"Dat's right, Brudda! Pick up the telephone!" *Ba-ram-ba-ram-ba-ram-ba-ram*

"Please, gentlemen! That's pointless! It's already after six o'clock in Washington. The office is closed!"

"Then call him in the morning, man," says the blood. "We coming back here in the morning and we gonna *watch* you call the man! We gonna stand right on *top* of you so you won't forget to make that call!"

"Dat's right, Brudda! On *top* of you!" *Ba-ram-ba-ram-ba-ram-ba-ram*

"All right, gentlemen . . . all right," says the Flak Catcher. He slaps his hands against his thighs and gets up off the chair. "I'll tell you what . . ." The way he says it, you can tell the man is trying to get back a little corner of his manhood. He tries to take a tone that says, "You haven't really been in here for the past fifteen minutes intimidating me and burying my nuts in the sand and humiliating me . . . We've really been having a discussion about the proper procedures, and I am willing to grant that you have a point."

"If that's what you want," he says, "I'm certainly willing to put in a telephone call."

"If we *want!* If you *willing!* Ain't no want or willing *about* it, man! You *gonna* make that call! We gonna be here and *see* you make it!"

"Dat's right, Brudda! We be seeing you"—*Ba-ram-ba-ram-ba-ram*—"We coming *back!*"

And the Flak Catcher is standing there with his mouth playing bad tricks on him again, and the Samoans hoist their Tiki sticks, and the aces all leave, and they're thinking . . . We've done it again. We've mau-maued the goddamn white man, scared him until he's singing a duet with his sphincter, and the people sure do have power. Did you see the look on his face? Did you see the sucker trembling? Did you see the sucker trying to lick his lips? He was *scared*, man! That's the last time that sucker is gonna try to *urban-factor* and *pre-fund* and *fix-asset* with us! He's gonna go home to his house in Diamond Heights and he's gonna say, "Honey, fix me a drink! Those mother-fuckers were ready to kill me!" That sucker was some kind of *petrified* . . . He could see eight kinds of Tiki sticks up side his head . . .

Of course, the next day nobody shows up at the poverty office to make sure the sucker makes the telephone call. Somehow it always seems to happen that way. Nobody ever follows it up. You can get everything together once, for the demonstration, for the confrontation, to go downtown and mau-mau, for the fun, for the big show, for the beano, for the main event, to see the people bury some gray cat's nuts and make him crawl and whine and sink in his own terrible grin. But nobody ever follows it up. You just sleep it off until somebody tells you there's going to be another big show.

And then later on you think about it and you say, "What really happened that day? Well, another flak catcher lost his manhood, that's what happened." Hmmmmmm . . . like maybe the bureaucracy isn't so dumb after all . . . All they did was sacrifice one flak catcher, and they've got hundreds, thousands . . . They've got replaceable parts. They threw this sacrifice to you, and you went away pleased with yourself. And even the Flak Catcher himself wasn't losing much. He wasn't losing his manhood. He gave that up a long time ago, the day he became a lifer . . . Just who is fucking over who? . . . You did your number and he did his number, and they didn't even have to stop the music . . . The band played on . . . *Still*—did you see the *look* on his face? That sucker—

When black people first started using the confrontation tactic, they made a secret discovery. There was an extra dividend to this tactic. There was a creamy dessert. It wasn't just that you registered your protest and showed the white man that you meant business and weakened his resolve to keep up the walls of oppression. It wasn't just that you got poverty money and influence. There was something sweet that happened right there on the spot. You made the white man quake. You brought *fear* into his face.

Black people began to realize for the first time that the white man, particularly the educated white man, the leadership, had a deep dark Tarzan mumbo jungle voodoo fear of the black man's masculinity. This was a revelation. For two hundred years, wherever black people lived, north or south, mothers had been raising their sons to be meek, to be mild, to check their manhood at the front door in all things that had to do with white people, for fear of incurring the wrath of the Man. The *Man* was the white man. He was the only *man*. And now, when you got him up close and growled, this all-powerful superior animal turned out to be terrified. You could read it in his face. He had the same fear in his face as some good-doing boy who has just moved onto the block and is hiding behind his mama and the moving man and the sofa while the bad dudes on the block size him up.

So for the black man mau-mauing was a beautiful trip. It not only stood to bring you certain practical gains like money and power. It also energized your batteries. It recharged your masculinity. You no longer had to play it cool and go in for pseudo-ignorant malingering and put your head into that Ofay Pig Latin catacomb code style of protest. Mau-mauing brought you respect in its cash forms: namely, fear and envy.

This was the difference between a confrontation and a demonstration. A demonstration, like the civil-rights march on Washington in 1963, could frighten the white leadership, but it was a general fear, an external fear, like being afraid of a hurricane. But in a confrontation, in mau-mauing, the idea was to frighten white men personally, face to face. The idea was to separate the man from all the power and props of his office. Either he had enough heart to deal with the situation or he didn't. It was like saying, "You—yes, you right there on the platform—we're not talking about the *gov*ernment, we're not talking about the *Of*fice of Economic Oppor*tun*ity—we're talking about *you*, you up there with your hands shaking in your pile of papers . . ." If this worked, it created a personal, internal fear. The internal fear was, "I'm afraid I'm not man enough to deal with these bad niggers!"

That may sound like a simple case of black people being good at terrifying whites and whites being quick to run scared. But it was more than that. The strange thing was that the confrontation ritual was built into the poverty program from the beginning. The poverty bureaucrats depended on confrontations in order to know what to do.

Whites were still in the dark about the ghettos. They had been studying the "urban Negro" in every way they could think of for fifteen years, but they found out they didn't know any more about the ghettos than when they started. Every time there was a riot, whites would call on "Negro leaders" to try to cool it, only to find out that the Negro leaders didn't have any followers. They sent Martin Luther King into Chicago and the people ignored him. They sent Dick Gregory into Watts and the people hooted at him and threw beer cans. During the riot in Hunters Point, the mayor of San Francisco, John Shelley, went into Hunters Point with the only black member of the Board of Supervisors, and the brothers threw rocks at both of them. They sent in the middle-class black members of the Human Rights Commission, and the brothers laughed at them and called them Toms. Then they figured the leadership of the riot was "the gangs," so they sent in the "ex-gang leaders" from groups like Youth for Service to make a "liaison with the key gang leaders." What they didn't know was that Hunters Point and a lot of ghettos were so disorganized, there weren't even any "key gangs," much less "key gang leaders," in there. That riot finally just burnt itself out after five days, that was all.

But the idea that the real leadership in the ghetto might be the *gangs* hung on with the poverty-youth-welfare establishment. It was considered a very sophisticated insight. The youth gangs weren't petty criminals . . . they were "social bandits," primitive revolutionaries . . . Of course, they were hidden from public view. That was why the true nature of ghetto leadership had eluded everyone for so long . . . So the poverty professionals were always on the lookout for the bad-acting dudes who were the "real leaders," the "natural leaders," the "charismatic figures" in the ghetto jungle. These were the kind of people the social-welfare professionals in the Kennedy Administration had in mind when they planned the poverty program in the first place. It was a truly adventurous and experimental approach they had. Instead of handing out alms, which never seemed to change anything, they would encourage the people in the ghettos to organize. They would help them become powerful enough to force the Establishment to give them what they needed. From the beginning the poverty program was aimed at helping ghetto people rise up against their oppressors. It was a scene in which the federal government came into the ghetto and said, "Here is some money and some field advisors. Now you organize your own pressure groups." It was no accident that Huey Newton and Bobby Seale drew up the ten-point program of the Black Panther Party one night in the offices of the North Oakland Poverty Center.

To sell the poverty program, its backers had to give it the protective coloration of "jobs" and "education," the Job Corps and Operation Head Start, things like that, things the country as a whole could accept. "Jobs" and "education" were things everybody could agree on. They were part of the free-enterprise ethic. They weren't uncomfortable subjects like racism and the class structure—and giving the poor the money and the tools to fight City Hall. But from the first that was what the lion's share of the poverty budget went into. It went into "community organizing," which was the bureaucratic term for "power to the people," the term for finding the real leaders of the ghetto and helping them organize the poor.

And how could they find out the identity of these leaders of the people? Simple. In their righteous wrath they would rise up and *confront* you. It was a beautiful piece of circular reasoning. The real leaders of the ghetto will rise up and confront you . . . Therefore, when somebody rises up in the ghetto and confronts you, then you know he's a leader of the people. So the poverty program not only encouraged mau-mauing it, it practically *demanded* it. Subconsciously, for administrators in the poverty establishment, public and private, confrontations became a ritual. That was the way the system worked. By 1968 it was standard operating procedure. To get a job in the post office, you filled out forms and took the civil-service exam. To get into the poverty scene, you did some mau-mauing. If you could make the flak catchers lose control of the muscles around their mouths, if you could bring fear into their faces, your application was approved.

Ninety-nine percent of the time whites were in no physical danger whatsoever during mau-mauing. The brothers understood through and through that it was a tactic, a procedure, a game. If you actually hurt or endangered somebody at one of these sessions, you were only cutting yourself off from whatever was being handed out, the jobs, the money, the influence. The idea was to terrify but don't touch. The term *mau-mauing* itself expressed this game-like quality. It expressed the put-on side of it. In public you used the same term the whites used, namely, "confrontation." The term *mau-mauing* was a source of amusement in private. The term *mau-mauing* said, "The white man has a voodoo fear of us, because deep down he still thinks we're savages. Right? So we're going to do that Savage number for him." It was like a practical joke at the expense of the white man's superstitiousness.

Almost every time that mau-mauing actually led to violence, you would find a revolutionary core to the organization that was doing it. If an organization was truly committed to revolution, then the poverty program, or the university, or whatever, was only something to hitch a ride on in the first place. Like at San Francisco State when the Black Students Union beat up the editor of the school newspaper, *The Gater*, and roughed up a lot of people during the strike. The BSU was allied with the Black Panthers. Stokely Carmichael, when he was with the Panthers, had come over to State and worked with the BSU, and given a speech that fired up the brothers for action. The willingness to be violent was a way of saying we are serious, we intend to go all the way, this *is* a revolution.

But this was a long way from the notion that all black militants in the ghetto were ready to be violent, to be revolutionaries. They weren't. A lot of whites seemed to think all the angry young men in the ghettos were ready to rise up and follow the Black Panthers at a moment's notice. Actually the Panthers had a complicated status in the ghettos in San Francisco. You talked to almost any young ace on the street, and he admired the Panthers. He looked up to them. The Panthers were stone courageous. They ripped off the white man and blew his mind and fucked him around like nobody has *ever* done it. And so on. And yet as an organization the Panthers hardly got a toehold in the ghettos in San Francisco, even though their national headquarters were just over the Bay Bridge in Oakland. Whites always seemed to think they had the ghetto's leaders identified and catalogued, and they were always wrong.

Like one time in an English class at San Francisco State there was a teacher who decided to read aloud to the class from *Soul on Ice* by Eldridge Cleaver. This teacher was a white woman. She was one of those Peter, Paul, and Mary-type intellectuals. She didn't wear nylons, she didn't wear make-up, she had bangs and long straight brown hair down to below her shoulders. You see a lot of middle-class white intellectual women like that in California. They have a look that is sort of Pioneer Hip or Salt of the Earth Hip, with flat-heeled shoes and big Honest Calves. Most of the students in her class were middle-class whites. They were the average English Literature students. Most of them hadn't even reached the Save the Earth stage, but they dressed Revolutionary Street Fighter. After the strike at State, middle-class students didn't show up on campus any more in letter sweaters or those back-to-school items like you see in the McGregor ads. They dressed righteous and "with the people." They would have on guerrilla gear that was so righteous that Che Guevara would have had to turn in his beret and get bucked down to company chaplain if he had come up against it. They would have on berets and hair down to the shoulders, 1958 Sierra Maestra style, and raggedy field jackets and combat boots and jeans, but not Levi's or Slim Jims or Farahs or Wranglers or any of those tailored hip-hugging jeans, but jeans of the people, the black Can't Bust 'Em brand, hod-carrier jeans that have an emblem on the back of a hairy gorilla, real *funky* jeans, and woolly green socks, the kind that you get at the Army surplus at two pair for twenty-nine cents. Or else they would go for those checked lumberjack shirts that are so heavy and woolly that you can wear them like a jacket. It's like the Revolution has nostalgia for the proletariat of about 1910, the Miners with Dirty Faces era, because today the oppressed, the hard-core youth in the ghetto—they aren't into the Can't Bust 'Ems with the gorilla and the Army surplus socks. They're into the James Brown look. They're into the ruffled shirts, the black belted leather pieces from Boyd's on Market Street, the bell-cuff herringbones, all that stuff, looking sharp. If you tried to put one of those lumpy lumberjack shirts on them, they'd vomit. Anyway, most of the students in this woman's English literature class were white middle class, but there were two or three students from the ghettos.

She starts reading aloud from *Soul on Ice*, and she's deep into it. She's got the whole class into Eldridge Cleaver's cellblock in San Quentin, and Cleaver is telling about his spiritual awakening and how he discovered the important revolutionary thinkers. She goes on and on, a long passage, and she has a pure serene tone going. When she finishes, she looks up in the most soulful way, with her chin up and her eyes shining, and she closes the book very softly under her chin, the way a preacher closes the Bible.

Naturally all of the white kids are wiped out. They're sitting there looking at each other and saying, "Far out" . . . "Too much" . . . "Wow, that's heavy" . . . They're shaking their heads and looking very solemn. It's obvious that they just assume that Eldridge Cleaver speaks for all the black people and that what we need is a revolution . . . That's the only thing that will change this rotten system . . . In their minds they're now in the San Francisco State cellblock, and the only thing that is going to alter this shit is the Big Bust-out . . .

The teacher lets all this sink in, and then she says: "I'd like to hear some comments."

One of the ghetto brothers raises his hand, and she turns to him with the most radiant brotherly smile the human mind can imagine and says, "Yes?"

And this student, a funky character with electric hair, says: "You know what? Ghetto people would laugh if they heard what you just read. That book wasn't written for the ghettos. It was written for the white middle class. They published it and they read it. What is this 'having previously dabbled in the themes and writings of Rousseau, Thomas Paine, and Voltaire' that he's laying down in there? You try coming down in the Fillmore doing some *previously dabbling* and talking about Albert Camus and James Baldwin. They'd laugh you off the block. That book was written to give a thrill to white women in Palo Alto and Marin County. That book is the best su*burb*an jive I ever heard. I don't think he even wrote it. Eldridge Cleaver wouldn't write something like that. I think his wife wrote it . . . *Pre-vi-ously dab-bled* . . . I mean like don't dabble the people no previouslies and don't previous the people no dabblies and don't preevy-dabble the people with no split-level Palo Alto white bourgeois housewife Buick Estate Wagon backseat rape fantasies . . . you know? . . ."

As you can see, the man goes completely off his bean on this subject. He's saying every outrageous thing that bubbles up into his brain, because he wants to blow the minds of the whites in the room. They're all staring at him with congealed faces, like they just gotted sapped in the back of the neck. They hardly had a chance to get down into the creamy pudding of their romantic Black Hero trip, when this dude comes along and unloads on them. But they don't dare say a word against him, because he's hard-core, and he has that ghetto patter. He's the one who must know . . .

So mostly the fellow is trying to blow their minds because they are being so smug and knowing about The Black Man. He's saying, Don't try to tell *us* who our leaders are, because you don't know. And that's the truth. The Panthers were righteous brothers, but there were a lot of militants in the ghettos of San Francisco who had their own numbers going. There were the Mission Rebels, the Cortland Progressives, the New Society, the United Council for Black Dignity, the Young Adults, the New Thang, the Young Men for Action . . . it was a list with no end . . . By the time you completed a list of all the organizations that existed at any given time, some new ones would have already started . . . Everybody had his own angle and his own way of looking at black power. The Panthers were on a very special trip. The Panthers were fighting The Pig. And the Pig was fighting the Panthers. If you joined the Panthers, you had to be ready to fight the police, because that was the trip you'd be on. One of the main things you stood to get out of it was a club up side your head, or a bullet. If you were a man who had really been worked over by the police, then you could relate to that and you were ready for that fight. The Panthers were like the Muslims in that respect. But as bad as things were in the ghettos, there weren't but so many aces who were ready to play it all-or-nothing that way.

The ghettos were full of "individualists" . . . in the sense the Russian revolutionaries used to use that word about the lumpenproletariat of Russia. The lumpenproletariat—the "underclass," as they say today—used to drive the Russian revolutionaries up the wall. Someone like Nikolai Bukharin would end up talking about them like he was some cracker judge from the year 1911: ". . . shiftlessness, lack of discipline, hatred of the old, but impotence to construct or organize anything new, an individualistic declassed 'personality,' whose actions are based only on foolish caprices . . ." He sounded like some Grand Kloogle on the bedsheet circuit.

In the ghettos the brothers grew up with their own outlook, their own status system. Near the top of the heap was the pimp style. In all the commission reports and studies and syllabuses you won't see anything about the pimp style. And yet there it was. In areas like Hunters Point boys didn't grow up looking up to the man who had a solid job working for some company or for the city, because there weren't enough people who had such jobs. It seemed like nobody was going to make it *by* working, so the king was the man who made out best by *not* working, by *not* sitting all day under the Man's bitch box. And on the street the king was the pimp. Sixty years ago Thorstein Veblen wrote that at the very bottom of the class system, down below the "working class" and the "honest poor," there was a "spurious aristocracy," a leisure class of bottom dogs devoted to luxury and aristocratic poses. And there you have him, the pimp. The pimp is the dude who wears the $150 Sly Stone-style vest and pants outfit from the haberdasheries on Polk and the $35 Lester Chambers-style four-inch-brim black beaver fedora and the thin nylon socks with the vertical stripes and drives the customized sun-roof Eldorado with the Jaguar radiator cap. The pimp was the artistocrat of the street hustle. But there were other lines of work that the "spurious aristocrats" might be into. They might be into gambling, dealing drugs, dealing in stolen goods or almost anything else. They would truck around in the pimp style, too. Everything was the street hustle. When a boy was growing up, it might take the form of getting into gangs or into a crowd that used drugs. There were plenty of good-doing boys who grew up under the shadows of their mothers and were aiming toward a straight life. But they were out of it in their own community. The status system on the block would be running against them, and they wouldn't "come out," meaning come out of the house and be on their own, until their late teens.

The pimp style was a supercool style that was much admired or envied. You would see some dude, just some brother from down the hall, walking down the street with his Rollo shirt on, and his black worsted bells with a three-button fly at the bell bottom of each pants leg, giving a spats effect, and he is walking with that rolling gait like he's got a set of ball-bearing discs in his shoulders and his hips, and you can say to the dude, "Hey, Pimp!" and he's not offended. He'll chuckle and say, "How you doing, baby." He's smiling and pleased with himself, because you're pulling his leg but at the same time you're saying that he's looking cool, looking sharp, looking good.

Sometimes a group of buddies who ran together, who were "stone pimp," as the phrase went, would move straight into the poverty program. They would do some fabulous, awesome, inspired mau-mauing, and the first thing you knew, they would be hanging out in the poverty scene. The middle-class bureaucrats, black and white, would never know what to make of an organization like this. They couldn't figure them out. There was one organization in a city just outside of San Francisco, in the kind of section that catches the bums, the winos, the prostitutes with the biscuits & gravy skin, the gay boys, the flaming lulus, the bike riders, the porno shops, peep shows, $8-a-week hotels with the ripped window shades flapping out. This area had everything you needed for a successful application for a poverty-program grant except for the one thing you need the most, namely, the militant youth. So that was when a remarkable ace known as Dudley showed up with a couple of dozen bonafide spurious aristocrats . . . his Ethnic Catering Service for skid row . . . There wasn't one of them that looked much under thirty, and nobody had ever heard of any black youth in that area before anyway, but they could mau-mau as if they had been trained by the great Chaser himself . . . They got a grant of nearly $100,000.

Every now and then the poverty bureaucrats from the Economic Opportunity Council or from City Hall would hold an area executive board meeting or some other kind of session at their clubhouse, and it was always a bear. A group of poverty workers and administrators would walk in there for the first time, and you could tell from the looks on their faces that something had hit them as different . . . and weird . . . They *felt* it . . . they *sensed* it . . . without knowing what it was. Actually it was a simple thing. The pimp-style aristocrats would be sitting around like a bunch of secretary birds.

There would be Dudley and the boys . . . Dudley, with his Fuzzy-Wuzzy natural and his welts. Dudley was a powerful man with big slabs of muscle like Sonny Liston and these long welts, like the welted seams on top of a pair of moccasins, on his cheeks, his neck, on the backs of his fists. These welts were like a historical map of fifteen years of Saturday night knife-fighting in the Bay Area. And Dudley's Afro . . . the brother had grown the rankest natural of all times. It wasn't shaped or anything close to it. It was growing like a clump of rumpus weed by the side of the road. It was growing every which way, and it wasn't even all one color. There was a lot of gray in it. It looked superfunky. It looked like he'd taken the stuffing out of the seat of one of those old ripped-up chairs you see out on the sidewalk with its insides spilling out after a fire on Webster Street—it looked like he'd taken the stuffing out of one of those chairs and packed it all over his head. Dudley was the fiercest looking man in the Bay Area, but there would be him and all his boys sitting around like a covey of secretary birds.

That was the pimp look, the look of hip and supercool and so fine. The white bureaucrats, and the black ones, too, walked in trying to look as earthy and rugged as they could, in order to be "with the people." They tried to walk in like football players, like they had a keg of beer between their legs. They rounded their shoulders over so it made their necks look bigger. They thickened up their voices and threw a few "mans" and "likes" and "digs" into their conversations. When they sat down, they gave it that Honcho wide-open spread when they crossed their legs, putting the right foot, encased in a cordovan brogue with a sole sticking out like a rock ledge, on the left knee, as if the muscles in their thighs were so big and stud-like that they couldn't cross their legs all the way if they tried. But the pimp-style aristocrats had taken the manhood thing through so many numbers that it was beginning to come out through the other side. To them, by now, being hip was striking poses that were so cool, so languid, they were almost feminine. It was like saying, "We've got masculinity to spare." We've been through so much shit, we're so confident of our manhood, we're so hip and so suave and wise in the ways of the street, that we can afford to be *refined* and not sit around here trying to look like a bunch of stud brawlers. So they would not only cross their legs, they'd cross them further than a woman would. They would cross them so far, it looked like one leg was wrapped around the other one three or four times. One leg would seem to wrap around the other one and disappear in the back of the knee socket. And they'd be leaning forward in the chair with their heads cocked to one side and their chins hooked over their collarbones and their shades riding low on their noses, and they'd be peering out over the upper rim of the shades. And they'd have one hand cocked in front of their chins, hanging limp at the wrist with the forefinger sticking out like some kind of curved beak. They would look like one of those supercool secretary birds that stand around on one long A-1 racer leg with everything drawn up into a beautiful supercool little bunch of fluffy feathers at the top.

They liked to run a meeting like everything else, namely, very cool. Dudley was conducting the meeting when in through the back door comes one of his boys, a tall dude with the cool rolling gait and his hands stuck in his pants pockets, which are the high Western-style pockets. The door he came in leads up a short flight of stairs and out onto an alley. This is a commercial district, and the alley is one of those dead-end slits they use for deliveries. It's always full of corrugated boxes and excelsior and baling wire and industrial wrapping paper and other debris. It's the kind of alley that has a little half sidewalk on one side and there are always a couple of cars parked lopsided with two wheels up on the sidewalk and two on the alley. Anyway, the dude comes lollygagging in, as cool as you please, and walks over to where Dudley is sitting like a secretary bird and leans over and whispers something to him. Even the way he leans over is stone pimp-style. His legs don't bend and his back doesn't bend. It's like he's been cleaned, pressed, and Perma-creased at hip level, right where his hand fits into his Western pocket, and he just jackknifes at the desired angle where the crease is. He keeps his hand in the pocket when he bends over. He just lets the hand bend backward at the wrist. It looks like his fingers are caught in his appendix.

"Say *what*, man?" says Dudley. "Don't you see I'm trying to hold a con-fer-ence in here?"

"But like man," says the Dude, "this is ve-ry im-por-tant."

"What the hell you into that's so im-por-tant, sucker?"

"Well, man, just wait a *min*-ute and let me tell you. You know that wino, Half and Half, that hangs out in the alley?"

"Yeah, I know him."

"Well, man, he's out there in the alley trying to burn down the buil-ding."

Dudley doesn't even move at first. He just peers out over his shades at his boys and at all the bureaucrats from downtown, and then he cocks his head and cocks his index finger in front of his chin and says,

"We gonna have a tem-po-rary re-cess. The brother ask me to take care some business."

Then Dudley unwinds very casually and stands up, and he and the brother start walking toward the back door, but so cool and so slow, with the whole rolling gait, that it looks like Marcel Marceau doing one of those walks where he doesn't actually move off the spot he started on. They open the door like they're going out to check out the weather, but once they're on the other side—*whoosh!*—it's like somebody lit their after-burners. They're up those stairs like a rocket and out into the alley and on top of the wino, Half and Half, in just under one half a second.

This Half and Half is one of those stone winos who hang around there, one of those winos whose face is so weather-beaten it looks like a pebble-grain full-brogue oxblood shoe. He has white hair, but a full head of white hair, so thick it looks like every hair he ever had in his head was nailed in for good. All that boozing and drinking half-and-half, which is half sherry and half port, must do righteous things for the hair, because there are no old men in the world who have hair like the winos. This Half and Half is such a stone wino that the only clothes he has left are the green KP fatigues they hand out in the hospitals and the jails, because the rest have been ripped up, vomited on, or stolen. He has on the fatigues and a pair of black street shoes with thin white hospital socks. He has pushed the socks way down into the heels of the shoes because his ankles are swollen and covered with skin ulcers, which he swabs with paper towels he cops from out the public toilets. The old crock hates these black studs who have turned up down on his skid-row cul-de-sac, and he keeps trying to burn up the building. He has a big pile of paper and excelsior and other stuff shoved up against the wall and he has it smoldering in a kind of fogged-in wino way, trying to in-cin-e-rate the mother.

All of that is going on outside in the alley. From inside the clubhouse at first there's nothing: silence. Then you start to hear a sound that sounds like there is a paddlewheel from off a Mississippi steamboat out there in the alley, and to every paddle is attached a size 12E motorcycle boot, and as the wheel goes around every one of these boots hits the wino . . . *thunk . . . thunk . . . whop . . . whump . . . thunk . . . thunk . . . whop . . . whump . . .*

The white bureaucrats and the black bureaucrats look at Dudley's boys, and Dudley's boys just stare back over the top of their shades and sit there wound and cocked as coolly as the secretary bird . . .

thunk . . . thunk . . . whop . . . whump . . . thunk . . . thunk . . . whop . . . whump . . .

And then the white bureaucrats look at the black bureaucrats and the black bureaucrats look at the white bureaucrats, and one of the bureaucrats who is dressed in the Roos-Atkins Ivy League clothes and the cordovan shoes starts going "Unh, unh, unh." The thing is, the man thinks he doesn't have any more middle-class Uncle Tom mannerisms and attributes, but he just can't help going into the old preachery "Unh, unh, unh."

thunk . . . thunk . . . whop . . . whump . . .

"Unh, unh, unh."

thunk . . . thunk . . . whop . . . whump . . .

"Unh, unh, unh."

Then it stops and the door opens again, and Dudley and the Dude come walking back in even slower and more cool except for the fact that they're breathing hard, and they take their seats and cross their legs and get wound back up and cocked and perched, and Dudley peers out over his shades and says, "The meeting is resumed."

Brothers from down the hall like Dudley got down to the heart of the poverty program very rapidly. It took them no time at all to see that the poverty program's big projects, like manpower training, in which you would get some job counseling and some training so you would be able to apply for a job in the bank or on the assembly line—everybody with a brain in his head knew that this was the usual bureaucratic shuck. Eventually the government's own statistics bore out the truth of this conclusion. The ghetto youth who completed the manpower training didn't get any more jobs or earn any more money than the people who never took any such training at all. Everybody but the most hopeless lames knew that the only job you wanted out of the poverty program was a job *in* the program itself. Get on the payroll, that was the idea. Never mind *getting* some job counseling. *You* be the job counselor. You be the "neighborhood organizer." As a job counselor or a neighborhood organizer you stood to make six or seven hundred dollars a month, and you were still your own man. Like if you were a "neighborhood organizer," all you had to do was go out and get the names and addresses of people in the ghetto who wanted to relate to the services of the poverty center. That was a very flexible arrangement. You were still on the street, and you got paid for it. You could still run with the same buddies you always ran with. There was nobody looking over your shoulder. You didn't have to act like a convert, like the wino who has to sing hymns at the mission before he can get his dinner, to get something out of the poverty scene. In fact, the more outrageous you were, the better. That was the only way they knew you were a real leader. It was true that middle-class people who happened to live in the target areas got the top jobs, but there was still room for street types.

You'd run into some ace on the corner and you'd say, "Hey, man, what you doing?"

And he'd say, "Nothing, man, what you doing?"

And you'd say, "I'm a neighborhood organizer," or "I'm a job counselor, man" . . . and that gave you status, because it was well known that there were some righteous brothers in on the poverty program.

Some of the main heroes in the ghetto, on a par with the Panthers even, were the Blackstone Rangers in Chicago. The Rangers were so bad, the Rangers so terrified the whole youth welfare poverty establishment, that in one year, 1968, they got a $937,000 grant from the Office of Economic Opportunity in Washington. The Ranger leaders became job counselors in the manpower training project, even though most of them never had a job before and weren't about to be looking for one. This wasn't a case of the Blackstone Rangers putting some huge prank over on the poverty bureaucrats, however. It was in keeping with the poverty program's principle of trying to work through the "real leaders" of the black community. And if they had to give it the protective coloration of "manpower training," then that was the way it would have to be done. Certainly there was no one who could doubt that the Blackstone Rangers were the most powerful group in the Woodlawn area of Chicago. They had the whole place terrified. The Rangers were too much. They were champions. In San Francisco the champions were the Mission Rebels. The Rebels got every kind of grant you could think of, from the government, the foundations, the churches, individual sugar daddies, from everywhere, plus a headquarters building and poverty jobs all over the place.

The police would argue that in giving all that money to gangs like the Blackstone Rangers the poverty bureaucrats were financing criminal elements and helping to destroy the community. The poverty bureaucrats would argue that they were doing just the opposite. They were bringing the gangs into the system. Back in 1911 Robert Michels, a German sociologist, wrote that the bureaucracy provides the state with a great technique for self-preservation. The bureaucracy has the instinct to expand in any direction. The bureaucracy has the instinct to get all the discontented elements of the society involved and entangled in the bureaucracy itself. In the late 1960's it looked like he might be right. By the end of 1968 there were no more gangs in San Francisco in the old sense of the "fighting gangs." Everybody was into black power, brown power, yellow power, and the poverty program in one way or another. This didn't mean that crime decreased or that a man discontinued his particular hustles. But it did mean he had a different feeling about himself. He wasn't a hustler or a hood. He was a fighter for the people, a ghetto warrior. In the long run it may turn out that the greatest impact of the poverty program, like some of the WPA projects of the Depression, was not on poverty but on morale, on the status system on the streets. Some day the government may look back and wish it had given the Flak Catchers Distinguished Service medals, like the astronauts.

The poverty program, the confrontations, the mau-mauing, brought some of the talented aces something more. It brought them celebrity, overnight. You'd turn on the TV, and there would be some dude you had last seen just hanging out on the corner with the porkpie hat scrunched down over his eyes and the toothpick nodding on his lips—and there he was now on the screen, a leader, a "black spokesman," with whites in the round-shouldered suits and striped neckties holding microphones up to his mouth and waiting for The Word to fall from his lips.

But whatever you wanted to achieve, for your people, for the community, or for yourself and your buddies—the competition was getting rough. Every day there were new organizations coming out of the woodwork. To get your organization in on the poverty program, you had to get recognized by some official agency, and to get recognized you had to do some mau-mauing in most cases. Once you got recognition, then you had the bureaucrats working full-time for you, drawing up the statistics and prospectuses, knocking on the right doors, and making the applications for the "funding," the money that was available from the government, the foundations, or the churches.

But it didn't end there. Just like you were trying to put the pressure on the bureaucrats, the brothers in your organization would be putting the pressure on you. They'd be waiting on your doorstep to see if you were getting anything for the brothers, to see if you really had any class. That was one reason why Summer Jobs was such a big deal. That was what the whole session between Samoans and the Flak Catcher was over, summer jobs. The jobs themselves were nothing. They were supposed to be for teenagers from poor families. It was an O.E.O. program, and you got $1.35 an hour and ended up as a file clerk or stock-room boy in some federal office or some foundation—hell, they didn't even need one half the people they already had working for them, and so all you learned was how to make work, fake work, and malinger out by the Xerox machine. It is true that you learned those skills from experts in the field, but it was a depressing field to be in.

Nevertheless, there was some fierce mau-mauing that went on over summer jobs, especially in 1969, when the O.E.O. started cutting back funds and the squeeze was on. Half of it was sheer status. There were supposed to be strict impartial guidelines determining who got the summer jobs—but the plain fact was that half the jobs were handed out organization by organization, according to how heavy your organization was. If you could get twenty summer jobs for your organization, when the next organization only got five, then you were four times the aces they were . . . no lie . . . But there were so many groups out mau-mauing, it was hard to make yourself heard over the uproar. You practically had to stand in line. It was a situation that called for a show of class. You had to show some style, some imagination, some ingenuity.

It brought out the genius in seemingly plain people. Like there was one man with a kind of common name like Bill Jackson. He and some of his buddies had created a poverty organization, the Youth of the Future, and had gotten recognition from one of the E.O.C. area boards. But when it came to summer jobs, the Youth of the Future was out of it, like a lot of organizations. Apparently some people thought that was all the Youth of the Future was, just another organization on the poverty scene, just this Bill Jackson and his buddies from off the block.

So one morning about eleven o'clock a flamboyant black man in a dashiki turns up at City Hall. And this flamboyant black man, the Dashiki Chieftain, isn't running with any brothers from off the block. He is at the head of an army of about sixty young boys and girls from the ghetto. And even his dashiki—it's no ordinary dashiki. This number is *elegant*. It's made of the creamiest black and red wool with great leopard-fur cuffs on the sleeves and leopard-fur patch pockets on the front . . . and a belt. You don't see a dashiki with a belt every day. And he has one of those leopard-fur African fez numbers on his head, and around his neck he has a necklace with beads and tiger teeth leading down to a kind of African carved head pendant. He comes marching up the stairs of City Hall and through those golden doors in his Somaliland dashiki, leading the children's army. And these kids are not marching in any kind of formation, either. They are swinging very free, with high spirits and good voices. The Dashiki Chief has distributed among them all the greatest grandest sweetest creamiest and most luscious mess of all-American pop drinks, sweets, and fried food ever brought together in one place. Sixty strong, sixty loud, sixty wild, they come swinging into the great plush gold-and-marble lobby of the San Francisco City Hall with their hot dogs, tacos, Whammies, Frostees, Fudgsicles, french fries, Eskimo Pies, Awful-Awfuls, Sugar-Daddies, Sugar-Mommies, Sugar-Babies, chocolate-covered frozen bananas, malted milks, Yoo-Hoos, berry pies, bubble gums, cotton candy, Space Food sticks, Frescas, Baskin-Robbins boysenberry-cheesecake ice-cream cones, Milky Ways, M&Ms, Tootsie Pops, Slurpees, Drumsticks, jelly doughnuts, taffy apples, buttered

Karamel Korn, root-beer floats, Hi-C punches, large Cokes, 7-Ups, Three Musketeer bars, frozen Kool-Aids—with the Dashiki Chief in the vanguard.

In no time at all the man's dashiki is practically flapping in the breeze from the hurricane of little bodies swirling around him, roaring about with their creamy wavy gravy food and drink held up in the air like the torches of freedom, pitching and rolling at the most perilous angles, a billow of root-beer float here . . . a Yoo-Hoo typhoon there . . . The kids have discovered the glories of the City Hall lobby. Such echoes! Their voices ricochet off the marble in the most groovy way. Screams work best, screams and great hollow shrieks . . . and the most high-toned clatter of sixty pairs of little feet running at top speed . . . This place is Heaven off-the-rack!

The lobby is officially known as the great central court, and it's like some Central American opera house, marble, arches, domes, acanthus leaves and Indian sandstone, quirks and galleries, and gilt filigrees, like Bourbon Louis curlicues of gold in every corner, along every molding, every flute, every cusp, every water-leaf and cartouche, a veritable angels' choir of gold, a veritable obsession of gold . . . and all kept polished as if for the commemoration of the Generalissimo's birthday . . . and busts of great and glorious mayors of San Francisco, perched on top of pedestals in their business suits with their bald marble skulls reflecting the lacy gold of the place . . . Angelo Rossi . . . James Rolph . . . cenotaphs, pediments, baroque balusters, and everywhere marble, marble, marble, gold, gold, gold . . . and through this Golden Whore's Dream of Paradise rush the children of the Youth of the Future.

By now the guards are asking the Dashiki Chief what he thinks he's doing. City Hall functionaries are asking him what he wants. The Dashiki Chief informs them that his name is Jomo Yarumba, and the Youth of the Future are now here, and he wants to see Mayor Joseph Alioto.

Meanwhile, the childstorm is intensifying. A little girl carrying a soft-top beer-style container of Fresca is about to collide with a little boy holding a double-dip Baskin-Robbins strawberry rhubarb sherbet cone, and the City Hall lifers can envision it already: a liver-red blob of sherbet sailing over the marble expanse of the City Hall lobby on a foaming bile-green sea of Fresca, and the kids who are trying to rip the damned paper off the ice cream in the Drumstick popsicles, which always end up inextricable messes of crabbed paper and molten milk fat, mixing it up with the kids whose frozen Kool-Aids are leaking horrible streaks of fuchsia and tubercular blue into the napkins they have wrapped around them in their palms and mashing it all onto the marble bean of Mayor Angelo Rossi . . . and now Jomo Yarumba and his childstorm are swooping up the great marble stairs of the great central court toward the first gallery and the outer office of the Mayor himself, and the City Hall functionaries are beginning to confer in alarm. By and by a young man from the Mayor's office comes out and explains to Jomo Yarumba that the Mayor regrets he has a very tight schedule today and can't possibly see him.

"We'll wait for the cat to get through," says the Dashiki Chief.

"But he's completely tied up, all day."

"Hell, man, we'll stay here all night. We'll see the cat in the morning."

"All night?"

"That's right. We ain't budging, man. We're here to tend to business."

The young guy from the Mayor's office retreats . . . Much consternation and concern in the lobby of City Hall . . . the hurricane could get worse. The little devils start screaming, wailing, ululating, belching, moaning, giggling, making spook-show sounds . . . filling the very air with a hurricane of malted milk, an orange blizzard of crushed ice from the Slurpees, with acid red horrors like the red from the taffy apples and the jelly from the jelly doughnuts, with globs of ice cream in purple sheets of root beer, with plastic straws and huge bilious waxed cups and punch cans and sprinkles of Winkles, with mustard from off the hot dogs and little lettuce shreds from off the tacos, with things that splash and things that plop and things that ooze and stick, that filthy sugar moss from off the cotton candy, and the Karamel Korn and the butterscotch daddy figures from off the Sugar-Daddies and the butterscotch babies from off the Sugar-Babies, sugar, water, goo, fried fat, droplets, driplets, shreds, bits, lumps, gums, gobs, smears, from the most itchy molecular Winkle to the most warm moist emetic mass of Three Musketeer bar and every gradation of solubility and liquidity known to syrup—filling the air, choking it, getting trapped gurgling and spluttering in every glottis—

And it was here that Bill Jackson proved himself to be a brilliant man and a true artist, a rare artist, of the mau-mau. One of the few things that could stir every bureaucrat in City Hall, make every bureaucrat rev up his adrenaline and quicken his pulse and cut the red tape and bypass the normal channels and get it together by word of mouth, by jungle drum, by hoot and holler from floor to floor, was just what Bill Jackson was doing now. Even an armed attack wouldn't have done so much. There's already an 84-page contingency paper for armed attack, emergency guidelines, action memos, with all the channels laid down in black and white for bucking the news up the chain . . . But this! Sixty black hellions and some kind of crazy in a dashiki wreaking creamy wavy gravy through the grand central court of City Hall . . . This lacerated the soul of every lifer, every line bureaucrat, every flak catcher in the municipal government . . . There are those who may think that the bureaucrats and functionaries of City Hall are merely time servers, with no other lookout than filling out their forms, drawing their pay, keeping the boat from rocking and dreaming of their pension like the lid on an orderly life. But bureaucrats, especially in City Halls, have a hidden heart, a hidden well of joy, a low-dosage euphoria that courses through their bodies like thyroxin . . . Because they have a secret: each, in his own way, is hooked into The Power. The Government is the Power, and they are the Government, and the symbol of the Government is the golden dome of City Hall, and the greatest glory of City Hall is the gold-and-marble lobby, gleaming and serene, cool and massive, studded with the glistening busts of bald-headed men now as anonymous as themselves but touched and blessed forever by The Power . . . And in an age of torrid sensations, of lust, gluttony, stroke-house movies, fellatio-lipped young buds jiggling down the street with their hard little nipples doing the new boogaloo through their translucent nylon jerseys, an age of marijuana, LSD, THC, MDA, cocaine, methedrine, and motels where the acrid electric ozone of the central air conditioning mixes with the sickly sweet secretions oozing from every aperture—in the midst of such cheap thrills and vibrating nerve ends, who is left to record the secret, tender, subtle, and ineffable joys of the line bureaucrat savoring the satin cushion of City Hall? Who else is left to understand the secret bliss of the coffee break at 10:30 a.m., the walk with one's fellows through the majesty of the gold-and-marble lobby and out across the grass and the great white walkways of City Hall Plaza, past the Ionic columns and Italian Renaissance façade of the Public Library on the opposite side and down McAllister Street a few steps to the cafeteria, where you say hello to Jerry as he flips the white enamel handle on the urn and pours you a smoking china mug of coffee and you sit down at a Formica table and let coffee and cigarette smoke seep through you amid the Spanish burble of the bus boys, knowing that it is all set and cushioned, solid and yet lined with velvet, all waiting for you, as long as you want it, somewhere below your consciousness, the Bourbon Louis baroque hulk and the golden dome of City Hall, waiting for you on the walk back, through the Plaza and up the steps and into the great central court, and you stop and talk with your good buddy by the door to the Registrar's or by the bust of Mayor Angelo Rossi, both of you in your shirtsleeves but with your ties held down smoothly by a small-bar tie clip, rocking back on the heels of your Hush Puppies, talking with an insider's chuckles of how that crazy messenger, the one with the glass eye, got caught trying to run football-pool cards off on the Xerox machine because he couldn't see the Viper standing there on his blind side for five minutes with his arms folded, just watching him . . . while your eyes play over the lobby and all the hopeless wondering mendicants who wander in off the street, looking this way and that for some sign of where the Assessor's office is, or the Board of Supervisors', or the Tax Collector's, probably taking their first plunge into the endless intricate mysteries of The Power, which they no more understand than they could understand the comradely majesty of this place, this temple, this nave and crossing of the euphoria of The Power—and suddenly here are these black ragamuffins! neither timorous nor bewildered! On the contrary—sportive, scornful, berserk, filling the air, the very sanctum, with far-flung creamy wavy gravy, with their noise, their insolence, their pagan vulgarity and other shitfire and abuse! And no one can lay a hand on them! No one can call in the Tac Squad to disperse sixty black children having a cotton-candy and M&M riot for themselves . . . The infidels are immune . . .

The incredible news was now sweeping through City Hall. The Mayor's number-three man came out and took a look and disappeared. The Mayor's number-two man came out and took a look and disappeared. The Mayor's press secretary came out and took a look . . . it was rumored that The Media were heading over . . . and the press secretary disappeared, and the kids dervished through it all, spinning their inspired typhoon up to the very architraves, and Bill Jackson orchestrated the madness in his whirling dashiki . . .

And in no time at all here was the Man himself, Mayor Joseph Alioto, advancing into their midst, attended by the number-four man, the number-three man, the number-two man, and the press secretary, and with his bald head gleaming as gloriously as Angelo Rossi's or James Rolph's, heading toward Jomo Yarumba with his broad smile beaming as if he had known the famous youth leader all his life, as if nothing in the world had been weighing more on his mind this morning than getting downstairs promptly to meet the inspiring Youth of the Future . . . And as the Mayor shook hands with Jomo Yarumba—there! it was done in a flash!—the Youth of the Future were now home safe . . .

Thereafter Bill Jackson could get down to the serious business, which was to use his official recognition to raise money for the sewing machines for his organization's dashiki factory . . . black-designed, black-made, black-worn dashikis to be manufactured by the youth themselves . . . There were no two ways about it. Bill Jackson and his group were looking good. That particular scene gave a lot of people heart. It wasn't long before an enterprising brother named Ronnie started his own group. The New Thang.

"The New *Thang?*" said Mayor Alioto, after they had put in their own unique and confounding appearance at City Hall.

"That's right, The New Thang."

The Mayor looked wigged out, as if the lights had gone out in his skull.

"Thang," said Ronnie. "That's Thing in African."

"Oh," said the Mayor. There wasn't even the faintest shade of meaning in his voice.

Lillian Carter

THE TRUEST SPORT: JOUSTING WITH SAM AND CHARLIE

Down a perfectly green tunnel, as cool and quiet as you can possibly imagine—no, it's not a tunnel, it's more like a hall of mirrors—but they're not mirrors, those aren't reflections, they're openings, one after another, on and on—just a minute! it's very familiar!—out of this cool green memory comes a steward, a tiny man, in uniform, a white jacket, perfectly starched and folded and creased like an envelope over his crisp little bones. Who doesn't know him! Here comes Bye Borty-bibe—

"Bye borty-bibe!"

He's saying it!

Dowd wakes up and it's 5:45 on the button, as always, and he looks across the stateroom at the steward. The steward is a little Filipino in a white jacket who hesitates, so as to make sure Dowd actually wakes up at bye borty-bibe, as he always pronounces it, and then he disappears down the passageway.

There is something eccentric in the way the day begins. It's terribly genteel!—having a little servant in a white jacket come by and respectfully summon you into consciousness so you can go hang your hide out for human skeet and sweat horribly. More servants will come in after Dowd leaves and make up his bed and clean up the stateroom and dust off the TV and the safe and clean off the desk and take out the laundry. *Only your laundryman knows for sure!* That was the usual joke, but there were some men who came aboard for the first time, and after a couple of hops north they would actually wonder whether it could get so bad—whether a man could get so frightened that he would literally lose control—*only your laundryman knows for sure!*—

From *Mauve Gloves & Madmen, Clutter & Vine* (New York: Farrar, Straus and Giroux, 1976). First published in *Esquire*, October 1975.

and whether later, in the bowels of the ship, in the laundry room, there might actually be some little laundry humper, some sweatback, some bye-bye steward of the soul, who would, in fact, *know*.

In the first moments, when you wake up, it's as if you're furiously scanning, painting all the stray trash on the screen, although usually that begins to fade as soon as you're on your feet. In a moment Dowd would be out in the good green passageway. The passageway is a very cool and immaculate green, not luxurious, you understand—in fact, every twenty feet there is a hatchway with a kneeknocker you have to step over, and as you look on and on through these hatchways, one after the other, it's like a hall of mirrors—but it is green and generally pleasing to the nervous system. Actually . . . that is not all there is to it. It is also good because, if the truth be known, being on this good green passageway means that you are traveling first-class, sleeping in a stateroom, with only one roommate, and you have the aforesaid servants standing by. It is not even a subject that one thinks about in so many words. And yet the ship is constructed in such an obvious fashion, in layers, that one can't help but know that down below . . . they are living in quite another way, in compartments, with thirty to forty souls to a compartment, and they wake up to a loudspeaker and make up their own bunks and run along to a loudspeaker through gray-and-beige tunnels and eat in a gray-and-beige galley off trays with scullion gullies stamped into them, instead of in a wardroom.

A wardroom!—also genteel in its way. Like the rest of them, Dowd is usually doing well if he gets up in time to make it to breakfast with his guy-in-back, Garth Flint, in the smaller wardroom, where they eat cafeteria-style. More than once he hasn't even managed that and has departed with nothing in his gullet but a couple of cups of coffee, notwithstanding all the lectures about the evil consequences this has for your blood-sugar level. But when they come back, Dowd and Flint and the others can enjoy the offerings of a proper wardroom, the formal one. They can take off the reeking zoom-bags, get dressed, sit down at a table with a white tablecloth on it, write out their orders on club slips, after the fashion of a men's club in New York or London, and more little Filipino stewards in white jackets will pick up the orders and serve dinner on china plates. The china has a certain dignity: it's white with a band of blue about the rim and a blue crest in the center. The silverware—now, that's rather nice! It's ornamental and heavy, it has curlicues and a noble gravity, the sort of silverware one used to see in the dining room of the good hotel near the railroad station. So they have dinner on a field of white and silver, while little stewards in white jackets move about the edges. The bulkheads (as the walls are known here) are paneled with walnut rectangles framed with more walnut; not actual wood, which is forbidden because it is inflammable, but similar enough to fool the eye. Off to the side are clusters of lounge chairs upholstered in leather and some acey-deucey tables. Silver and heavy glass wink out of a manly backdrop, rich as burled wood and Manila cigars; for here in the wardrooms of the *Coral Sea* the Navy has done everything that interior decoration and white mess jackets can do to live up to the idea of Officers & Gentlemen, within the natural limits of going to war on the high seas.

The notion often crosses Dowd's mind: *It's like jousting.*

Every day they touch the napkins to their mouths, depart this gently stewarded place, and go forth, observing a checklist of written and unwritten rules of good form, to test their mettle, to go forth to battle, to hang their hides out over the skeet shooters of Hanoi-Haiphong . . . thence to return, after no more than two hours . . . to this linenfold club and its crisp starched white servitors.

One thing it is not good to think about is the fact that it would be even thus on the day when, finally, as has already happened to 799 other American aviators, radar-intercept officers, and helicopter crewmen, your hide is blown out of the sky. That day, too, would begin within this same gentlemanly envelope.

Fliers with premonitions are not healthy people. They are known as accidents waiting to happen. Now, John Dowd and Garth Flint are not given to premonitions, which is fortunate and a good sign; except that it won't make a great deal of difference today, because this is that day.

To get up on the flight deck of the *Coral Sea*, Dowd and Flint usually went out through a hatch onto a catwalk. The catwalk hung out over the side of the ship just below the level of the deck. At about midships they climbed a few feet up a ladder and they would be on the deck itself. A simple, if slightly old-fashioned, procedure, and by now second nature—

—but what a marvelous low-volt amusement was available if you were on the *Coral Sea* and you saw another mortal, some visitor, some summer reservist, whoever, make his first excursion out onto that deck. He takes a step out onto the catwalk, and right away the burglar alarm sounds in his central nervous system. Listen, Skipper!—the integrity of the circuit has been violated somewhere! He looks out over the railing of the catwalk, and it might as well be the railing of the goddamned Golden Gate Bridge. It's a sixty-foot drop to the sea below, which is water—but what conceivable difference does that make? From this height the water looks like steel where it picks up reflections of the hull of the carrier, except that it ripples and breaks up into queasy facets—and in fact the horizon itself is pitching up and down . . . The whole freaking Golden Gate Bridge is pitching up and down . . . the big wallowing monster can't hold still . . . Christ, let's get up on the deck, away from the edge—but it's only when he reaches the deck itself and stands with both feet planted flat that the full red alert takes over.

This flight deck—in the movie or the training film the flight deck is a grand piece of gray geometry, perilous, to be sure, but an amazing abstract shape dominating the middle of the ocean as we look down upon it on the screen—and yet, once the newcomer's two feet are on it—ge*om*etry—my God, man, this is a . . . skillet! It *heaves*, it moves up and down underneath his feet, it pitches up, it pitches down, as the ship moves into the wind and, therefore, into the waves, and the wind keeps sweeping across, sixty feet up in the air out in the open sea, and there are no railings whatsoever—and no way whatsoever to cry out to another living soul for a helping hand, because on top of everything else the newcomer realizes that his sense of hearing has been *amputated entirely* and his voice is useless. This is a *skillet!*—a frying pan!—a short-order grill!—not gray but black, smeared with skid marks from one end to the other and glistening with pools of hydraulic fluid and the occasional jet-fuel slick, all of it still hot, sticky, greasy, runny, virulent from God knows what traumas—still ablaze!—consumed in detonations, explosions, flames, combustion, roars, shrieks, whines, blasts, cyclones, dust storms, horrible shudders, fracturing impacts, all of it taking place out on the very edge of control, if in fact it can be contained at all, which seems extremely doubtful, because the whole scorched skillet is still *heaving* up and down the horizon and little men in screaming red and yellow and purple and green shirts with black Mickey Mouse helmets over their ears are skittering about on the surface as if for their very lives (you've said it now!), clustering about twin-engine F-4 fighter planes like little bees about the queen, rolling them up a stripe toward the catapult slot, which runs through the deck like the slot in the back of a piggy bank, hooking their bellies on to the shuttle that comes up through the slot and then running for cover as the two jet engines go into their shriek and a huge deflection plate rises up behind the plane because it is about to go into its explosion and quite enough gets blown—quite enough!—quite enough gets blown off this heaving grill as it is, and then they explode—both engines explode into full afterburn, 37,000 pounds of force, and a very storm of flame, heat, crazed winds, and a billion blown steely particles—a very storm engulfs the deck, followed by an unbelievable shudder—*kaboom!*—that pounds through the skillet and destroys whatever may be left of the neophyte's vestibular system, and the howling monster is flung up the deck like something out of a red-mad slingshot, and the F-4 is launched, dropping off the lip of the deck tail down with black smoke pouring out of both engines in its furious struggle to gain altitude—and already *another* plane is ready on the *second* catapult and the screams and explosions have started again and the little screaming-yellow men with their Mouseketeer ears are running once more—

—and yet this flaming bazooka assembly line will, in the newcomer's memory, seem orderly, sublimely well controlled, compared to the procedure he will witness as the F-4's, F-8's, A-4's, A-6's return to the ship for what in the engineering stoicisms of the military is known as recovery and arrest. To say that an F-4 is coming back onto this heaving barbecue from out of the sky at a speed of 135 knots . . . that may be the truth on paper, but it doesn't begin to get across the idea of what a man sees from the deck itself, because it perhaps creates the notion that the plane is *gliding* in. On the deck one knows different! As the aircraft comes closer and the carrier heaves on into the waves and the plane's speed does *not* diminish—one experiences a neural alarm he has never in his wildest fears imagined before: This is not an *air*plane coming toward me, it's a brick, and it is not *gliding*, it's *falling*, a fifty-thousand-pound brick, headed not for a stripe on the deck, but for *me*—and with a horrible *smash!* it hits the skillet, and with a blur of momentum as big as a freight train's it hurtles toward the far end of the deck—another blinding storm!—another roar as the pilot pushes the throttle up to full military power and another smear of rubber screams out over the skillet—and this is normal!—quite okay!—a wire stretched across the deck has grabbed the hook on the end of the plane as it hit the deck tail down, and the smash was the rest of the twenty-five-ton brute slamming onto the deck, as if tripped up, so that it is now straining against the wire at full throttle, in case it hadn't held and the plane had "boltered" off the end of the deck and had to struggle up into the air again. And already the Mickey Mouse helmets are running toward their fiery monster . . .

The obvious dangers of the flight deck were the setting, the backdrop, the mental decor, the emotional scenery against which all that happened on the carrier was played out, and the aviator was he who lived in the very eye of the firestorm. This grill was *his* scenery. Its terrors rose out of his great moments: the launch and recovery. For that reason some crewmen liked to check out the demeanor of the aviators during these events, just as they might have in the heyday of the chivalric code.

When John Dowd and Garth Flint came out on deck in their green flight suits, carrying their helmets and their knee-boards, they were an unmistakable pair. Dowd was the tallest pilot on the ship, almost six feet five. Six years ago he was captain of the Yale basketball team. He was so tall, he had to slump his way through the physicals in order to get into flight training, where six four was the upper limit. He looked like a basketball player. His face, his Adam's apple, his shoulders, his elbows—he was a tower of sharp angles. Flint was Dowd's radar-intercept officer. He was five eight and rather solidly built. He was not small, but next to Dowd he looked like a little jockey.

Today they were to go out on a two-ship formation, with Dowd's roommate, Dick Brent, flying a second F-4B. Dowd's would be the lead ship; Brent's the wing. The usual monsoon overcast was down within about five hundred feet of the deck. It was another day inside the gray pearl: the ship, a tight circle of the waters of the Gulf of Tonkin around it, a dome of clouds, fog, mist, which was God's great gift to the North Vietnamese.

They climb aboard and Dowd eases the power on to taxi the ship toward the catapult, while the aircraft directors nurse it onto the slot. The catapult officer is out there on the deck with his Mousketeer ear baffles on and his yellow jersey flapping in the wind. Assuming the preliminary stages have been completed correctly, the catapult officer is supposed to hold up five fingers to show the pilot that all looks good for launch. If the gauges look okay, the pilot then shows that he is ready for his little slide-for-life . . . by saluting. At this point three things are supposed to happen in a very rapid sequence: the catapult officer drops to one knee (to avoid having his head removed by the wing) and throws his hand forward like a cheerleader doing the "locomotive"; the pilot cuts on full afterburn; and a seaman on a catwalk across the deck presses a black rubber button and throws both hands up in the air. This somewhat hopeless-looking gesture says: "It's done! We've fired the catapult! You're on your way! There's no stopping it!"

To Dowd this is another eccentric note. This man who fires the slingshot—or who seems to—actually he's signaling the steam-catapult crew below deck—this man, who appears to flick you into the sky or the sea with his finger, according to how things work out, is some little swabbo making seventy-eight dollars a month or whatever it is. Somehow this fact puts just that much more edge on the demeanor of the pilot's salute, because what that salute says is: "I hereby commit my hide to your miserable care, sir, to you and your sailor with the button and your motherless catapult. I'm a human cannonball, and it's your cannon."

So it is that today, just before he cuts on full afterburn and sets off the full 37,000-pound explosion and consumes the skillet in the firestorm and braces the stick so he won't lose control in the bad lurch of the slingshot, just before the big ride, in the key moment of knightly correctness, Dowd rolls his salute off his helmet with a languid swivel of his wrist, like Adolphe Menjou doffing his hat . . . a raffish gesture, you might say, with a roll to it that borders on irony . . . but a friendly note all the same . . . For this is a good day! They are flying again! There is no bomb load—therefore less weight, therefore an easy launch! . . . a good day—otherwise he might have, or would have been entitled to, according to the unwritten and unspoken rules (especially since he has more than one hundred missions behind him)—he might have ended that cool rolling salute by leaving his middle finger sticking up in the air, in an accepted fashion that tells one and all: "You're only giving me the grand goose. Why should I salute? (Here's one for you.)"

But this is a good day!—and Dowd surrenders to the catapult without even an ironic protest, and he feels a tremendous compression, so great that the surface of his eyeballs flattens and his vision blurs, and the F-4B shrieks, and he and Flint hurtle down the stripe and off the bow of the ship, half blind and riding a shrieking beast, into the gray pearl. It couldn't have been a smoother launch; it was absolutely nominal.

Dowd heads on through the pearl, through the overcast, with Brent's plane about five hundred yards back. The ride to the coast of North Vietnam will take them about twenty minutes. Just how high the cloud cover will be up around Haiphong is impossible to say, which means that the game of high-low may be a trifle too interesting. The weather has been so bad, nobody has been up there. Well . . . now somebody's going up there. Already, without any doubt, the Russian trawlers in the gulf have painted the two aircraft on their radar screens. *Painted!* Such a nice word for it! The phosphorescent images come sliding onto the screen, as if a brush were doing it. And with those two delicate little strokes on a Russian radar screen somewhere out there in the muck, the game is on again.

American pilots in Vietnam often ran through their side of the action ahead of time as if it were a movie in the mind . . . trying to picture every landmark on the way to the Red River delta, every razorback green ridge, all that tropical hardscrabble down below, every jut in the coast, every wretched misty snake bend in the Red River, every bridge around Haiphong harbor, every change of course, the angle of every bomb run from the assigned altitude . . . But just try to imagine the enemy's side of it. Try to imagine your own aircraft (encasing your own hide) sliding onto their screens like a ghost stroke (observed by what Russian?) and the trawler signaling the coast and the cannon crews and SAM battalions cranking up in the delta and devising (saying what exactly?) their black trash for the day, which could be inexplicably varied.

One day flying over Haiphong would be "a walk in Haiphong Park," as Dowd would put it. The next day the place would erupt with the wildest storms of ground fire since the bombing of Berlin, Merseburg, and Magdeburg in the Second World War, absolute sheets of 37-millimeter, 57-millimeter, and 85-millimeter cannon fire, plus the SAM's. The antiaircraft cannons now had sights that computed the leads instantly and automatically, and they were more accurate than anything ever dreamed of in the Second World War or the Korean war. But it was the SAM's that were the great equalizer. It was SAM's that made aerial combat in Vietnam something different from what the aces of wars gone by—admirable innocent fellows!—had ever known.

Dowd used to say to himself: "The SAM's come up, and the boys go down." One way or the other! The SAM's, the Russian surface-to-air missiles, were aimed and guided by radar. They climbed at about Mach 3, which was likely to be at least three times as fast as your own ship was going when you heard the warning over your radio ("I have a valid launch!"). The SAM's were not fired at random—each had a radar lock on your aircraft or somebody else's. The only way to evade a SAM was to dive for the deck, i.e., the ground. The SAM's own G-forces were so great they couldn't make the loop and come back down. "The SAM's come up, and the boys go down." And the merriment has just begun. The dive brings you down so low, you are now down into the skeet range of that insidiously well-aimed flak! This, as they say, put you between a rock and a hard place. Sometimes the North Vietnamese also sent up the Mig-21's. But they were canny about it. The Migs went up mainly to harass the bombers, the F-105's, A-4's, and A-6's, to force them to jettison their bomb loads (in order to gain speed to evade the Migs) before they reached the target. But occasionally the F-4's got a chance to tangle with them. What a luxury! How sporting! How nice to have a mere Mig to deal with instead of the accursed SAM's! Of course, you just might have both to contend with at the same time. The North Vietnamese were so SAM-crazy, once in a while they'd fire them up in the middle of a hassle and hit their own planes.

Dowd saw his first SAM last year when he was on a flak-suppression run. Other aviators had always told him they looked like "flying telephone poles," but the only thing he saw at first was a shower of sparks, like the sparks from a Roman candle. That was the rocket tail. And then he could make out the shaft—all of this happening in an instant—and it was, in fact, like a pale-gray telephone pole, moving sideways through the sky as if skidding on its tail, which meant the ship it was after had already dived for the deck and the SAM was trying to overcome its own momentum and make the loop. You were always reassured with the statement, "If you can see it"—meaning a SAM—"you can evade it"—but there were some pilots who were so egotistical they believed that the one they saw was the one that had their name on it. A fatal delusion in many cases!—for the SAM's came up in fans of six or eight, fired from different sites and different angles. "The SAM's come up, and the boys go down"—and Dowd and his whole formation hit the deck and got out of there. Not long after that, Dowd and Flint were hit by ground fire for the first time—it was to happen four more times—in the same sort of situation. They had just come down out of the dive when they took hits in the port ramp and intake duct. Fortunately it was 14.5-millimeter fire, instead of one of the big cannons, and they made it on back to the ship.

High-low! In what?—ten minutes?—Dowd will have to start playing the same game again this morning. Soon he will have to decide whether to go above the overcast or right on the deck. Above the overcast they will be safe from the gunners, who need visual sightings in order to use their automatic lead mechanisms. But right above the overcast is where SAM rules like a snake. More aviators have been wiped out by SAM's popping out of the clouds they're sitting on than any other way. Rather than contend with that automated blind beast, some pilots prefer to come in low over the terrain in the eternal attempt to get in "under the radar." But what is it really, a strategic defense or a psychological defense?

Such was the nature of the game that Dowd and every other pilot here had to play. Many of the pilots who flew over Vietnam had been trained by instructors who had flown in the Korean war. What tigers those old Korea jocks were! What glorious memories they had! What visions those aces could fill your skull with! What a tangy taste they gave to the idea of aerial combat over Southeast Asia! The Korean war brought on the first air-to-air combat between jet fighters, but it turned out to be dogfighting of the conventional sort nonetheless, American F-86's versus Soviet-built Mig-15's mainly—and it was a picnic . . . a field day . . . a duck shoot . . . American pilots, flying F-86's in all but a few dozen cases, shot down 839 Korean and Chinese Mig-15's. Only fifty-six F-86's were lost. Quite a carnival it was. Morale among American ground troops in Korea slid like the mud, but the pilots were in Fighter Jock Heaven. The Air Force was producing aces—fighter pilots who had shot down five planes or more—as fast as the Communists could get the Migs up in the air. By the time the war stopped, there were thirty-eight Air Force aces, and between them they had accounted for a total of 299.5 kills. High spirits these lads had. They chronicled their adventures with a good creamy romanticism such as nobody in flying had dared treat himself to since the days of Lufbery, Frank Luke, and Von Richthofen in the First World War. Why hold back! Jousting is jousting, and a knight's a knight. Colonel Harrison R. Thyng, who shot down five Migs in Korea (and eight German and Japanese planes in the Second World War), glowed like Excalibur when he described his Fourth Fighter-Interceptor Wing: "Like olden knights the F-86 pilots ride up over North Korea to the Yalu River, the sun glinting off silver aircraft, contrails streaming behind, as they challenge the numerically superior enemy to come on up and fight." Lances and plumes! Come on up and fight! Now there was a man having a wonderful time!

In Vietnam, however, the jousting was of a kind the good colonel and his knights never dreamed of. The fighter plane that the Air Force and the Navy were now using instead of the F-86—namely, the F-4—was competing with the new generation of Migs and was winning by a ratio of two to one, according to the air-to-air combat scoreboards, regular league standings, that were kept in various military publications. That was nothing like the fifteen-to-one ratio in Korea, of course—but more than that, it was not even the main event any longer. Not even the heroic word "ace" carried the old wallop. The studs-of-all-the-studs in Vietnam were not the pilots in air-to-air combat but the men who operated in that evil space between the rock and the hard place, between the SAM's and the automatic cannon fire.

In the past three years—1965, 1966, and the year just ending for John Dowd, 1967—the losses had been more brutal than the Air Force or the Navy had ever admitted. Jack Broughton, an Air Force colonel and commander of a wing of F-105's flying over Hanoi-Haiphong from out of Thailand, described the losses as "astronomical and unacceptable," and they were increasing sharply each year. What made the North Vietnamese game of high-low—SAM's and ground fire—so effective was a set of restrictions such as no combat pilots had ever had to contend with before.

Flying out over Hanoi and Haiphong was like playing on some small and sharply defined court. These two cities were by far the major targets in North Vietnam, and so there was very little element of surprise along the lines of switching targets. They could only be approached down a ridge of mountains ("Thud Ridge") from the west, out of Thailand, which would be the Air Force attacking with F-105 fighter-bombers, or across a wide-open delta (perfect for radar defenses) from the east, which would be the Navy attacking from carriers in the gulf. The North Vietnamese and the Russians packed so much artillery in around these two cities that pilots would come back saying, "It was like trying to fly through a rainstorm without hitting a drop."

God knows how many planes and pilots were lost just trying to knock out the North Vietnamese ground fire. The Air Force had Wild Weasel or Iron Hand units made up of pilots in F-105's who offered themselves as living SAM bait. They would deliberately try to provoke launches by the SAM battalions so that other ships could get a radar lock on the SAM sites and hit them with cluster-bomb strikes. This became the ultimate game of radar chess. If the SAM battalions beamed up at the Wild Weasels and committed too early, they stood to get obliterated, which would also allow the main strike force to get through to its target. On the other hand, if they refused to go for the bait, recognizing it for what it was, and shut down their beams—that might give the strike force just enough time to slip through unchallenged. So they'd keep shutting on and off, as in some lethal game of "one finger, two fingers." Their risk was nothing, however, compared to that of the Wild Weasel pilots, who were the first in and the last out, who hung around in the evil space far too long and stood to get snuffed any way the game went.

Navy pilots, Dowd among them, were sent out day after day for "flak suppression." The North Vietnamese could move their flak sites around overnight, so that the only way to find them was by leading with your head, as it were, flying over the target area until you saw them fire the cannons. This you could detect by the rather pretty peach-pink sparkles, which were the muzzle explosions. The cannons made no sound at all (way up here) and seemed tiny and merely decorative . . . with their little delicate peach-pink sparkles amid the bitter green of the scrabble. Dowd and his comrades could not unload on these flak sites just anywhere they found them, however. As if to make the game a little more hazardous, the Pentagon had declared certain areas bomb-free zones. A pilot could hit only "military targets," which meant he couldn't hit villages, hospitals, churches, or Haiphong harbor if there was a "third-party" ship there. So, naturally, being no fools, the North Vietnamese loaded the villages up with flak sites, loaded the churches up with munitions, put SAM sites behind the hospitals, and "welded a third-party ship to the dock" in Haiphong harbor, as Garth Flint put it. There always seemed to be some neutral flag in port there, with one of North Vietnam's best customers being our friends the British. One day one of Dowd's *Coral Sea* comrades came in for a run on a railroad freight depot, pickled his bombs too soon, went long, and hit a church—whereupon the bitter-green landscape rocked with secondary and tertiary explosions and a succession of fireballs. The place had gone up like an arsenal, which of course it was. Every now and then Dowd would be involved in a strike aimed at "cutting off" Haiphong harbor. This was not to be done, however, by mining the harbor or blowing the docking facilities out of the water or in any other obvious and easy manner. No, this had to be accomplished by surgically severing the bridges that connected the port with the mainland. This required bomb runs through the eye of a needle, and even if the bridges were knocked out, the North Vietnamese simply moved everything across by barge until the bridges were back.

If you were a pilot being flung out every day between the rock and the hard place, these complicated proscriptions took on an eerie diffidence, finally. They were like an unaccountable display of delicate manners. In fact, it was the Johnson Administration's attempt to fight a "humane" war and look good in the eyes of the world. There was something out-to-lunch about it, however. The eyes of the world did not flutter for a second. Stories of American atrocities were believed by whoever wanted to believe them, no matter what actually occurred, and the lacy patterns that American bombing missions had to follow across Hanoi-Haiphong never impressed a soul, except for the pilots and radar-intercept officers who knew what a difficult and dangerous game it was.

If the United States was seriously trying to win the battle of world opinion—well, then, here you had a real bush-league operation. The North Vietnamese were the uncontested aces, once you got into this arena. One of the most galling things a pilot had to endure in Vietnam was seeing the North Vietnamese pull propaganda coup after propaganda coup, often with the help, unwitting or otherwise, of Americans. There was not merely a sense of humiliation about it. The North Vietnamese talent in this direction often had direct strategic results.

For example, the missions over N—— D——. Now, here was one time, in Dowd's estimation, when they had gotten the go-ahead to do the job right. N—— D—— was an important transportation center in the Iron Triangle area. For two days they softened the place up, working on the flak sites and SAM sites in the most methodical way. On the third day they massed the bomb strike itself. They tore the place apart. They ripped open its gullet. They put it out of the transport business. It had been a model operation. But the North Vietnamese now are blessed with a weapon that no military device known to America could ever get a lock on. As if by magic . . . in Hanoi . . . appears . . . Harrison Salisbury! Harrison Salisbury—writing in *The New York Times* about the atrocious American bombing of the hardscrabble folk of North Vietnam in the Iron Triangle! If you had real sporting blood in you, you had to hand it to the North Vietnamese. They were champions at this sort of thing. It was beautiful to watch. To Americans who knew the air war in the North firsthand, it seemed as if the North Vietnamese were playing Mr. Harrison Salisbury of *The New York Times* like an ocarina, as if they were blowing smoke up his pipe and the finger work was just right and the song was coming forth better than they could have played it themselves.

Before you knew it, massive operations like the one at N—— D—— were no longer being carried out. It was back to threading needles. And yet it couldn't simply be blamed on Salisbury. No series of articles by anyone, no matter what the publication, could have had such an immediate strategic effect if there weren't some sort of strange collapse of will power taking place back in the States. One night, after a couple of hops, Dowd sank back into an easy chair in the wardroom of the *Coral Sea* and picked up a copy of some newspaper that was lying around. There on the first page was William Sloane Coffin, the Yale University chaplain, leading a student antiwar protest. Not only that, there was Kingman Brewster, the president of Yale, standing by, offering tacit support . . . or at least not demurring in any way. It gave Dowd a very strange feeling. Out in the Gulf of Tonkin, on a carrier, one was not engulfed in news from stateside. A report like this came like a remote slice of something—but a slice of something how big? Coffin, who had been at Yale when Dowd was there—Coffin was one thing. But the president of Yale? There was Kingman Brewster with his square-cut face—but looked at another way, it was a strong face gone flaccid, plump as a piece of chicken Kiev. Six years before, when Dowd was a senior at Yale and had his picture taken on the Yale Fence as captain of the basketball team . . . any such Yale scene as was now in this newspaper would have been impossible to contemplate.

The collapse of morale, or weakening of resolve, or whatever it should be called—this was all taking place in the States at the very moment when the losses were beginning to mount in both the Navy and the Air Force. Aviators were getting shot down by the hundreds. Sometimes, at night, after dinner, after the little stewards in white had cleared away the last of the silver from off the white line, after playing a few rounds of acey-deucey in the lounge or just sinking into the leather billows of the easy chairs, after a movie in the wardroom, after a couple of unauthorized but unofficially tolerated whiskeys in somebody's stateroom—after the usual, in short, when he was back in his own quarters, Dowd would take out his mimeographed flight schedule for the day just completed and turn it over to the blank side and use it to keep a journal. In 1966 and 1967 more and more of these entries would make terse note of the toll of friends: "We lost Paul Schultz & Sully—presumably captured immediately on landing in parachute. Direct hit from SAM coming out of clouds—site near Kien An." Or: "Bill C. got it over Ha Tinh today—body seen bloody on ground."

Or they were about how John Dowd hadn't gotten his: "The Lord giveth and the Lord taketh away. I think today was a *give* day. 8 SAM's or so fired from multiple sites and it looked like a few had my no. on them. However they missed their mark & so this entry is made . . . Doc H. presented those who participated in the 'A' strike with a little vial of J. W. Dant cough medicine."

In light of all that, it may be of interest to note one fact concerning the mission to Haiphong and points north that Dowd has just headed off on: he did not merely volunteer for it—he thought it up!

For four days, which is to say, ever since Christmas Day, the coastal ports of Haiphong, Cam Pha, and Hon Gay have been socked in with bad weather. Dowd suggested and volunteered for a weather-reconnaissance hop to find out how bad it actually was, to see if the soup was moving at all, to see if the harbors were by any chance clear of third-party ships and therefore eligible for bombing, and so on. If anyone had asked, Dowd would have merely said that anything was better than sitting around the ship for days on end, doing make-work.

But *any*thing—even playing high-low with SAM over the North?

The answer to that question perhaps leads to the answer to a broader one: How was it that despite their own fearsome losses in 1965, 1966 and 1967, despite hobbling restrictions and dubious strategies set by the Pentagon, despite the spectacle of the antiwar movement building back home—how was it that, in the face of all this, American fliers in Vietnam persisted in virtuoso performances and amazing displays of *esprit* throughout the war? Somehow it got down to something that is encoded in the phrase "a great hop."

The last time Dowd and Garth Flint were out was four days ago, Christmas Day, during the American Christmas cease-fire; and what a little tourist excursion that was. They flew a photo run over Route 1A in North Vietnam, came in under the cloud cover, right down on top of the "Drive-In," as it was called, fifty feet from the ground, with Garth taking pictures, and the Charlies were down there using Christmas Day and the cease-fire for all it was worth. The traffic jam at the Phun Cat ferry, going south to the Ho Chi Minh Trail, was so enormous that they couldn't have budged even if they thought Dowd was going to open up on them. They craned their heads back and stared up at him. He was down so low, it was as if he could have chucked them under their chins. Several old geezers, in the inevitable pantaloons, looked up without even taking their hands off the drafts of the wagons they were pulling. It was as if they were harnessed to them. The wagons were so full of artillery shells, it was hard to see how one man, particularly so spindly a creature, could possibly pull one, but there they were in the middle of the general jam-up, in with the trucks, bicycles, motorcycles, old cars, rigs of every sort, anything that would roll.

Now, that was a good hop—and Dowd so recorded it in his journal—an interesting hop, a nice slice of the war, something to talk about, but merely a photo hop . . . and not *a great hop*. There was such a thing as a great hop, and it was quite something else.

Sometimes, at night, when Dowd would write on the back of his flight schedule, he'd make such entries as:

"Great hop! Went to Nam Dinh and hosed down the flak sites around that city. Migs joined in the caper, but no one got a tally. Think I lucked out in a last-minute bomb run & racked up a flak site pretty well."

The atmosphere of the great hop had something about it that was *warlike* only in the sense that it was, literally, a part of combat. A word that comes closer is *sporting*. Throughout his tour of duty on the *Coral Sea*, no matter how bearish the missions became, Dowd seemed to maintain an almost athletic regard for form. Even on days he spent diving from SAM's and running the flak gauntlets, even on days when he was hit by flak, he would wind up his journal entries with a note about how well (or how poorly) he drove his F-4 back down onto the carrier, and often with a playful tone: "2nd pass was a beauty but only received an OK—which was an unfortunate misjudgment on the part of the LSO [landing signal officer]." Or: "Went to Haiphong Barracks. 3 SAM's launched—one appeared to be directed at yours truly—however with skill & cunning we managed to avoid it, although it cost us our first bombing run, which was in question due to lack of a target—no flak to suppress. After whifferdilling around we rolled in on a preplanned secondary target. What deleterious havoc this bombing caused the enemy is questionable. However the overall mission was quite successful . . . RTB good approach except for last ¼ mile. Received *cut*-1 for my efforts."

A great hop! *With skill & cunning we managed to avoid* . . . death, to call it by its right name. But pilots never mentioned death in the abstract. In fact, the word itself was taboo in conversation. So were the words "bravery" and "fear" and their synonyms. Which is to say, pilots never mentioned the three questions that were uppermost in the minds of all of them: Will I live or die? Will I be brave, whatever happens? Will I show my fear? By now, 1967, with more than a hundred combat missions behind him, Dowd existed in a mental atmosphere that was very nearly mystical. Pilots who had survived that many games of high-low over North Vietnam were like the preacher in *Moby Dick* who ascends to the pulpit on a rope ladder and then pulls the ladder up behind him.

Friends, near ones and dear ones, the loved ones back home, often wondered just what was on the minds of the fliers as the casualties began to increase at a fearsome rate in 1966 and 1967. Does a flier lie on his back in bed at night with his eyes wide open, staring holes through the ceiling and the flight deck and into outer space, thinking of the little ones, Jeffrey and Jennifer, or of his wife, Sandy, and of the soft lost look she has when she first wakes in the morning or of Mom and Dad and Christmas and of little things like how he used to click the toggles on his rubber boots into place before he went out into the snow when he was eight? No, my dear ones back home—I'm afraid not! The lads did not lie in their staterooms on the *Coral Sea* thinking of these things—not even on Christmas Eve, a few days ago!

Well . . . what was on their minds?

(Hmmmm . . . How to put it into words . . . Should it be called the "inner room"?)

Dowd, for one, had entered the Navy in 1961 without the slightest thought of flying or of going to war. The Navy had no such designs for him, either. Quite the contrary. All they asked was that he keep playing basketball! At Yale, Dowd had been an aggressive player, the sort who was matched up against other college stars, such as Dave De Busschere of the University of Detroit (later of the New York Knicks). At the end of his last season, 1961, Dowd was drafted by the Cleveland entry in the new American Basketball Association. He had his naval R.O.T.C. obligation to serve out, however, and the Navy sent him to Hawaii to play ball for the fleet. This he did; his team won the All-Navy championship in 1962. There was nothing to stop him from playing basketball for the rest of his service stint . . . just putting the ball in the hoop for Uncle Sam in heavy-lidded Hawaii.

Now that he was in the military, however, Dowd, like many service athletes, began to get a funny feeling. It had to do with the intangible thing that made sports so alluring when you were in school or college, the intangible summed up in the phrase "where the action is." At Yale, as at other colleges, playing sports was *where the action was*—or where the applause, the stardom, and the honor were, to be more exact. But now that he was in the Navy, something about sports, something he had never thought about, became obvious. Namely, all team sports were play-acting versions of military combat.

It is no mere coincidence that the college sport where there is the greatest risk of injury—football—is also the most prestigious. But the very risk of injury in football is itself but a mild play-acting version of the real thing: the risk of death in military action. So a service athlete was like a dilettante. He was play-acting inside the arena of the real thing. The real thing was always available, any time one had the stomach for it, even in peacetime. There were plenty of ways to hang your side out over the edge in the service, even without going to war. Quite unconsciously, the service athlete always felt mocked by that unspoken challenge. And in the Navy there was no question but that *the* action-of-all-actions was flying fighter planes off carriers.

In his last year at Yale, Dowd had married a girl named Wendy Harter from his home town, Rockville Centre, Long Island. About a year and a half later they had a son, John Jr. And then, out in Hawaii, on those hot liquid evenings when the boy couldn't go to sleep, they would drive him out to Hickam Field to watch the airplanes. Both commercial liners and military fighters came into Hickam. By and by Dowd was taking his wife and his son out there even when the boy was practically asleep in his tracks. One night they were out at Hickam, and Wendy surprised Dowd by reading his mind out loud for him.

"If you like them so much," she said, "why don't you fly them?"

So he started training . . . with a vague feeling of *pour le sport.* This was 1963, when the possibility of an American war in Vietnam was not even talked about.

A man may go into military flight training believing that he is entering some sort of technical school where he is simply going to acquire a certain set of skills. Instead, he finds himself enclosed in the walls of a fraternity. That was the first big surprise for every student. Flying was not a craft but a fraternity. Not only that, the activities of this particular brotherhood began to consume all of a man's waking hours.

But why? And why was it so obsessive? Ahhhhh—*we don't talk about that!* Nevertheless, the explanation was: flying required not merely talent but one of the grandest gambles of manhood. Flying, particularly in the military, involved an abnormal risk of death at every stage. Being a military flight instructor was a more hazardous occupation than deep-sea diving. For that matter, simply taking off in a single-engine jet fighter, such as an F-102, or any other of the military's marvelous bricks with fins on them, presented a man, on a perfectly sunny day, with more ways to get himself killed than his wife and children could possibly imagine. Within the fraternity of men who did this sort of thing day in and day out—within the flying fraternity, that is—mankind appeared to be sheerly divided into those who have it and those who don't—although just what *it* was . . . was never explained. Moreover, the very subject was taboo. *It* somehow seemed to be the transcendent solution to the binary problem of Death/Glory, but since not even the *terminology* could be uttered, speculating on the answer became doubly taboo.

For Dowd, like every other military pilot, the flying fraternity turned out to be the sort that had outer and inner chambers. No sooner did the novitiate demonstrate his capabilities in the outermost chamber and gain entrance to the next . . . than he discovered that he was once again a novitiate insofar as entry through the *next* door was concerned . . . and on and on the series goes. Moreover, in carrier training the tests confronted the candidate, the eternal novitiate, in more rapid succession than in any other form of flying.

He first had to learn to fly a propeller-driven airplane. Perhaps a quarter of an entering class might be eliminated, washed out, at this stage. Then came jet training and formation flight. As many as 50 percent of those left might wash out at these stages. But in naval flying, on top of everything else, there was the inevitable matter of . . . the heaving greasy skillet. That slab of metal was always waiting out in the middle of the ocean. The trainees first practiced touching down on the shape of a flight deck painted on an airfield. They'd touch down and then gun right off. This was safe enough—the shape didn't move, at least—but it could do terrible things to, let us say, the gyroscope of the soul. *That shape—it's so damned small!* And more novitiates washed out. Then came the day, without warning, when they were sent out over the ocean for the first of many days of reckoning with the skillet. The first day was always a clear day with little wind and a calm sea. The carrier was so steady it seemed to be resting on pilings—but what a bear that day was!

When Dowd was in training, aviators learned to land on the flight deck with the aid of a device that bore the horrible, appropriate name of the "meatball." This was a big mirror set up on the deck with a searchlight shining into it at a 3-degree angle—the angle of the flight deck—so that it reflected at the same angle. The aviator was to guide himself onto the deck by keeping the great burst of light, the meatball, visible in the center of the mirror. And many, many good souls washed out as they dropped like a brick toward the deck and tried to deal with that blazing meatball. Those who survived that test perhaps thought for a brief moment that at last they were regulars in Gideon's Army. But then came night landings. The sky was black, and the sea was black, and now that hellish meatball bobbed like a single sagging star in outer space. Many good men "bingoed" and washed out at this juncture. The novitiate was given three chances to land on the deck. If he didn't come in on his first or second approach and flew by instead, then he had to make it on his third, or the word "bingo!" would sound over his earphones—and over the entire flight deck, as he well knew—meaning that he would have to fly back to shore and land on a nice, safe immovable airfield . . . where everyone likewise knew he was a poor sad Bingo coming in from the carrier. It didn't take many bingos to add up to a washout.

One night, when Dowd had just started night training, the sea and the wind seemed to be higher, the clouds seemed lower, the night blacker than he thought possible. From up in the air the meatball seemed to bob and dart around in a crazy fashion, like a BB under glass in one of those roll-'em-in-the-hole games you hold in the palm of your hand. He made two passes and leveled off a good two hundred feet above the ship each time. On the third time around . . . it suddenly seemed of supreme, decisive, eternal importance that the word "bingo" not sound over *his* earphones. He fought the meatball all the way down in a succession of jerks, shudders, lurches, and whifferdills, then drove his plane onto the deck through sheer will, practically like a nail. The fourth and last deck wire caught him, and he kept the throttle pushed forward into the "full military power" position, figuring he was on the verge of boltering off the end and would have to regain altitude instantaneously. He had his head down and his hand thrust forward, with his engine roaring—for how long? —God knows—before it dawned on him that he was actually down safe and could get out. The whole flight deck was waiting for him to shut off his damned engine. As he climbed down from the aircraft, he heard the skipper's voice boom out over the speaker system:

"How do you like flying now, Lieutenant?"

He noted with some satisfaction, however, that they then closed down the deck because of the weather. And was he *now* in the fraternity at last? . . . Hardly. He was just *beginning*. Everything he had learned to do so far became merely the routine. He was now expected to perform such incredible stunts day in and day out, under conditions of fleet operations and combat.

Being a carrier pilot was like being a paratrooper in that it took a while to learn how many different ways you could be killed in the course of an ordinary operation. A fellow F-4 jock, a friend, an experienced aviator, comes in one night low on fuel, not sure he has enough for a second pass, touches down long, bolters, tries to regain altitude, can't, careens off the far end of the deck, fifty thousand pounds of metal and tubes, and sinks without a trace. It all happens in a matter of seconds, *just like that*. Another friend, with even more experience, a combat veteran, *gets his* without moving a muscle. He's in his F-4, in the flight line, waiting for his turn on the catapult, when the ship up ahead somehow turns at the wrong angle, throttles up without a deflection shield behind it, and the whole fifteen tons of thrust hits his F-4, and the man and his guy-in-back and the ship are blown off the deck like a candy wrapper and are gone forever—in an instant, a snap of the fingers, *just like that.*

Yet once an aviator was in combat, all that, too, became simply the given, the hazards of everyday life on the job, a mere backdrop. From now on one found new doors, new tests, coming up with a mad rapidity. Your first day in combat . . . your first bombing run . . . first strafing run . . . the first time you're shot at . . . the first time you see a SAM . . . which also means the first time you dive for the deck straight into the maw of the flak cannons . . . the first time your ship gets dinged by flak . . . and the first time you *see someone else* in your own formation blown out of the sky over the North—and in many ways what an aviator saw with his own eyes was more terrible than the sudden unseen things happening to himself.

For Dowd and Garth Flint this came one day during a bombing run near the Iron Triangle. They were closing in on the target, barreling through the eternal cloud cover, unable to see even the ships in their own wing, when all at once a great livid ghost came drifting straight across their path, from left to right. It was an F-4. It had taken a direct hit, and smoke was pouring out of the cockpit. The smoke enveloped the fuselage in the most ghostly fashion. The pilot had cobbed it to starboard in a furious effort to reach the water, the gulf, to try to bail out where Navy rescue planes could reach them. In the blink of an eye the ghastly cartridge disappeared, swallowed up by the clouds. They would never make it. Dowd and Flint plowed on to the target, following their wing command, even though the gunners below obviously had dead range on the formation. To have done anything else would have been unthinkable.

Unthinkable, to be sure. By late 1967 thinkable/unthinkable played on a very narrow band. The options had been cut back sharply. Both Navy and Air Force fliers were *getting theirs* at a rate that was "astronomical and unacceptable," by ordinary logic, as Jack Broughton had said. But fliers with a hundred missions over the North were people who by now had pulled the rope ladder up into the pulpit. Somehow they had removed their ties with the ordinary earth. They no longer lived on it. Home and hearth, loved ones and dear ones—it wasn't that they had consciously lost their love or dear regard for such folks and such things . . . it was just that the dear folks back home were . . . so far away, back there through such an incalculable number of chambers and doors. The fliers over the North now lived in, or near, the fraternity's innermost room. Or, at the very least, they now knew *who it was*, finally, who had access to that room. It was not merely he who could be called "brave." No, it was he who was able to put his hide on the line in combat and then had the moxie, the reflexes, the experience, the coolness to pull it back in the last yawning moment—and then was able to go out again *the next day*, and the next day, and every next day, and do it all over again, even if the series proved infinite. It was the *daily routine* of risking one's hide while operating a hurtling piece of machinery that separated military flying from all other forms of soldiering and sailoring known to history.

Even *without going into combat* career Navy fighter pilots stood one chance in four of dying in an accident before their twenty years were up, and one chance in two of having to punch out, eject by parachute, at some point. In combat, especially in Vietnam, God knew what the figures were. The Pentagon was not saying. No, the Pentagon itself seemed bent on raising the ante to ridiculous heights, imposing restrictions that every aviator knew to be absurd. And "the nation"? "our country"? "the folks back home"? They seemed to have lost heart for the battle. But even that realization seemed . . . so far away, back through so many doors. Finally, there was only the business of the fraternity and the inner room.

All of the foregoing was out-of-bounds in conversation. Nevertheless, there it was. The closest aviators came to talking about it was when they used the term "professionalism." Many extraordinary things were done in the name of professionalism. And when everything else went wrong, this professionalism existed like an envelope, in the sense that each airplane was said to have a certain "performance envelope." Inside, inside that space, the aviators remained one another's relentless judges right up to the end, when not a hell of a lot of people outside seemed to care any longer. They were like casebook proof of something an English doctor, Lord Moran, had written forty years before. Moran had been a doctor treating soldiers in the trenches during the First World War, and he wrote one of the few analytical studies ever addressed specifically to the subject of bravery: *The Anatomy of Courage*. In the wars of the future, he said, aerial combat, not soldiering, would have "first call on adventurous youth." But the bravery of these adventurers, he said, would have a curiously detached quality. For the pilot, "love of the sport—success at the game—rather than sense of duty makes him go on."

The unspoken things! *Bye borty-bibe* . . . every morning when he woke up and rolled out of bed in his stateroom, the components of the game of high-low lit up in every aviator's brain, and he would all too literally calculate the state of his soul that morning by the composition of his bowel movement, with diarrhea being the worst sign of all. Well, not quite the worst; for occasionally one would hear some poor soul in another cubicle of the head . . . vomiting. One would be curious . . . but in another way one would just as soon not know who it was. (After all, he might be in my wing.) Since none of this could be spoken, demeanor was everything. (*Only your laundryman knows for sure!*) It *was* like jousting! One *did* return to the carrier like a knight! . . . or as near to knightly status as was likely to be possible in an age of mimeographed flight assignments and mandatory debriefings.

The most beautiful possible moments came when you brought your aircraft back to the deck from battle half shot up. Just a few weeks ago Dowd and Garth Flint came back with an 85-millimeter shell hole shot clear through a rear stabilizer wing. It looked as if you could put your arm through it, and it was no more than a yard from the fuselage. Dowd and Flint had scarcely opened the cockpit before the Mouseketeers, the deckhands, were gaping at the damage. Dowd climbed down to the deck, took off his helmet, and started walking away. Then, as if he'd just remembered something, he turned about and said to the onlookers: "Check that stabilizer, will you? Think maybe we caught a little flak."

How gloriously bored! The unspoken, unspeakable things! All the gagged taboos!

No doubt that was what made American airmen, while on leave, the most notorious bar patrons in the Philippines, Japan, and Thailand during the Vietnam years. In keeping with a tradition as old as the First World War, drink and drunkenness gave pilots their only license to *let it out*. Not to talk about the unspoken things—not to break the taboo—but to set free all the strangled roars, screams, bawls, sighs, and raving yahoos. Emotion displayed while drunk didn't count. Everybody knew that. One night Dowd was drinking at a bar at Cubi Point with an A-4 pilot named Starbird. It was getting to that hour of the night when you're so drunk you can't hear any more. Your skull itself is roaring and your screams and songs get beaten back by the gale. The bartender announces that the bar is now closed. He slides a brass pole under the handles on the tops of the big beer coolers behind the bar and locks them shut. Starbird reaches across the bar and grabs the brass pole and emits a roar of sheer gorilla fury and pulls it up out of its mooring, until it's looped in the middle like a piece of spaghetti, and announces: "The bar just reopened."

After a long season of such affronts by many roaring souls, Navy bars and officers' clubs in Subic Bay began ruling themselves off limits to pilots returning from tours in the North (Yankee Station). Then came a gesture from on high that Dowd would never forget. Admiral Red Hyland himself sent out a directive to all clubs and pubs within the purview of the Fleet, saying: It has come to my attention that the cocktail lounge conduct of aviators returning from Yankee Station has occasioned some negative responses. This is to inform all hands that the combat conduct of these men has been exemplary, despite the most trying conditions, and now hear this: THEY WILL BE ACCORDED THE FULL PRIVILEGES OF OFFICERS AND GENTLEMEN! (For you I bend the brass! The bars just reopened!)

At last!—someone had come close to saying it! to putting it into words! to giving a tiny corner of the world some actual inkling that they just might have . . . the ineffable . . . *it!*

That memo, like all memos, soon vanished down the memory hole. Yet it meant more to Dowd than any medal he ever got.

High or low? The weather doesn't get any better as they pull closer to Haiphong, and Dowd decides to play it low. It looks like the kind of overcast the SAM's like best, high and solid. Dowd, with Brent off his wing, comes into Haiphong at about two hundred feet at close to Mach 1. Suddenly they break out of the mist and they're over the harbor. They bank for one turn around it, which immediately cuts their speed down to about 450 knots. It's peaceful, just another inexplicable stroll in Haiphong Park. The overcast is down to four hundred feet, meaning it's hopeless so far as a bombing strike is concerned. Besides, the inevitable third-party ships are welded in . . .

The weather is so bad, it's as if the enemy has decided to take a holiday from the war, knowing no bombers will be coming in. There's no sense loitering, however, and Dowd heads out for a look at Cam Pha and Hon Gay, two ports north of Haiphong. High or low . . . Dowd stays down low. There's nothing below but a smattering of islands.

All at once Dowd sees a streak of orange shoot up over the nose on the port side. Garth Flint, in the back seat, sees another streak come up under the nose on the starboard . . . They both know at once: tracer bullets . . . *They go to school with the tracer bullets* . . . The tracers show the gunners whether or not they're near the mark . . . and without any doubt they're near the mark. Then they hear a sound like *twack* . . . It sounds like nothing more than a good-size rock hitting an automobile . . . the shot hit the bottom of the nose section . . . Dowd immediately cobs it, gives it full power in a furious bid to get up into the cloud cover and out over the gulf. Every warning light on the panel is lit up red, but he still has control of the plane. Smoke starts pouring into the cockpit. The heat is so intense he can barely touch sections of the panel. It's so hot he can hardly hold the controls. The fire seems to be in the hydraulics system of the wheel well. He tries to vent the cockpit, but the vent doesn't work. Then he blows the canopy off to try to clear the smoke, but the smoke pours out so heavily he still can't see. Everything metal is becoming fiercely hot. He wonders if the ejection mechanism will still work. He can hardly hold the stick.

For Garth Flint, in back, with the canopy gone, it's as if a hurricane has hit, a hurricane plus smoke. Maps are blowing all over the place, and smoke is pouring back. It's chaos. They're going about 350 knots, and the rush of air is so furious Flint can no longer hear anything on the radio, not even from Dowd. He wonders: Can we possibly get back onto the carrier if the smoke is this bad and Dowd can't hear radio communications? Oddly, all his worries center on this one problem. An explosion right in front of him! In the roiling smoke, where Dowd used to be, there's a metal pole sticking up in the air. It's made of sections, like a telescope. It's something Flint's never seen before . . . the fully sprung underpinning of an F-4 ejection system, sticking up in the air as they hurtle over the Gulf of Tonkin. This spastic pole sticking up in the front seat is now his only companion in this stricken ship going 350 knots. Dowd has punched out!

Flint stares at the pole for perhaps two or three seconds, then pulls the ring under his seat. He's blasted out of the ship, with such force that he can't see.

Meanwhile, Dowd's furious ride is jerked to a halt by his parachute opening. He assumes Garth is floating down ahead of him. In fact, Dowd had yelled over the radio for Garth to eject and assumed he was on his way, not knowing Garth couldn't hear a word he said. Considering the way he had cobbed the engine and turned the plane to starboard and out over the gulf, Dowd expects to see water as he comes down through the clouds. Instead, little islands—and the live possibility of capture—are rising up toward him.

Reprieve! The wind carries him about a quarter mile from shore. Just the way the survival training told you, he prepares to shuck his parachute before he hits the water, at the same time keeping his life raft uninflated so the people onshore can't spot him so easily. He hits the water . . . it's surprisingly cold . . . he inflates the flotation device he's wearing—but feels himself being dragged under. The water, which looked so calm from above, is running five- to seven-foot swells. It pitches up and down in front of him and beneath him, and he's being dragged under. He can't comprehend it—the parachute, which he thought he had so skillfully abandoned at the textbook-proper second, has somehow wrapped around his right leg in the slosh of the swells and he's going under. He pulls out the knife that they're issued for just such a situation. But the nylon cords are wet and the damned knife won't cut them. He's going under. For the first time since the flak hit, the jaws of the Halusian Gulp have opened. *I'm going to die.* At first it's an incredible notion. Then it's infuriating. To die by drowning out in this squalid pond after a ten-cent shootdown on a weather-recce mission—it's humiliating! Another fly-boy disappears into the Cosmic Yawn! He's swept by a wave of the purest self-pity. It's actually about to happen—*his death*—the erasure of John Dowd from human existence—in a few seconds—*just like that!* The ineffable talent, the mystical power—*it!*—that let him hang his hide out over the Jaws and always pull it back—he *doesn't* have it, after all!—he is no more special than the hundreds of other pilots who have already been swallowed up over the North! It's pathetic. It's a miserable and colossal affront. His whole life does not roll before his eyes—only the miserable pity of the here and now. He does not think of home and hearth. He does not think of Mom at the shuttling sewing machine late at night or the poignancy of seeing one's own child daydreaming. No, there is only the here and now and the sum total of this total affront to all that comprises John Dowd—being dragged down in a fish pond by a parachute, holding in his hand a knife that the Navy issued for a task that it won't perform—it's utterly piteous and pathetic! . . . *Jesus! How I pity myself now!* . . . And that makes him furious. He gives the parachute a ferocious yank. Whuh?—in that very explosion of the final anger he discovers something: the damned thing is caught—not around his leg but on his knee-board! . . . The board is attached to his flight suit so he can jot down figures, keep charts handy, whatever . . . one last breath! Now he's completely underwater . . . He can't see . . . He grabs the knee-board and rips it off his flight suit . . . a miracle! . . . he's free! . . . The parachute is gone . . . the death anchor . . . He bobs back to the surface . . . Christ! . . . the hell with the colossal affront of fate . . . There's only *now!* . . . Never mind! . . . He inflates the raft, as it says in the manual . . . He's on the side of the manual now! . . . Oh yes! . . . Navy-issue! . . . Why not! . . . He climbs on the raft . . . He's not drowning anymore, he's on his belly on a raft swooping up and down with the swells of the gulf . . . Never mind the past! . . . He scans the water and the nearby island . . . Not miserable Fate, but islanders with guns . . . That's what he's looking for . . . Is that one of them? . . . But on the water . . . there's Garth! . . . Flint is on a raft about two hundred yards away, bobbing in and out of Dowd's line of vision . . . It's all shaping up . . . Never mind Fate! The hell with colossal affronts! He's pulled it back after all—out of the Jaws . . .

Meanwhile, Dick Brent, in the other F-4B, has seen Dowd and

Flint eject. After about fifteen minutes of diving and fishing down through the clouds, Brent spots them on the water below and radios the position. Brent sees a few people on the shore of an island, looking out toward the two men, but the islanders don't seem to be making any attempt to go out by boat to retrieve Garth and Dowd, which also means capture them. (In fact, the islanders had long since learned to leave well enough alone. American pilots in the water were often followed by screaming rescue aircraft that blew every boat out of the tub.)

After about another thirty minutes Spads are coming in low over the water. To Garth Flint it appears as if the Spad pilots don't see him, only Dowd. Over his emergency radio Flint says: "If you see two pilots, rock your wings." One of the Spads rocks its wings. The Spads call in a helicopter known as a Big Mother. The helicopter, too, heads straight for Dowd. A morose thought crosses Flint's mind: "He's a lieutenant, I'm only a lieutenant (j.g.)—so they're picking him up first."

Then it dawns on him that they're going after Dowd because he's in closer to shore and therefore more vulnerable to gunfire or capture. Hell, it's going to be okay.

Back on the *Coral Sea* Dowd and Flint were debriefed in the ready room. They drank coffee and tried to warm up. The china had a certain dignity. It was white with bands of blue about the rims and blue crests here and there. The silverware—now, that was rather nice. It was ornamental and heavy. The questions came, one after the other, and they went through everything that happened. Yet during this debriefing the two men were waiting for *something else*. Surely, they would mention *something else*. But they didn't. It was a debriefing much like *every* debriefing. Just the facts! No quarter given! No slack in the line! Then the commander of their squadron said, with a note of accusation: "Why were you flying so low?"

Now, that was really too much! Why . . . you *bastard!* But they said nothing except the usual. What they wanted to say . . . well, how could they have put it into words? How, within the inner room, does one say: "My God, man, we've just been into the Jaws!—about as far into the goddamned Jaws as you can go and still come back again!—and you want to know why we flew so low! We've just been *there!* at the lost end of the equation! where it drops off the end of the known world! Ask us about . . . *the last things*, you bastard, and we will enlighten you!" There were no words in the chivalric code for such thoughts, however.

But all at once the skipper of the *Coral Sea*, the maximum leader, a former combat pilot himself, appeared—and he smiled! And that smile was like an emission of radio waves.

"We're glad to have you back, men."

That was all he said. But he smiled again! Such ethereal waves! Invisible but comprehensible, they said, "I know. I've been there myself." Just that!—not a sound!—and yet a doxology for all the unspoken things. How full my heart, O Lord!

Flint took one day off before going out on his next mission, on New Year's Eve. Dowd had suffered a back injury in the ejection from the F-4B, and so it was another two days before he climbed back into the metal slingshot, got slung off the skillet, and went flying over North Vietnam again.

The Lord's Work

". . . and his lord answered and said unto the servant who had buried his talent, his piece of gold, in the ground: 'Thou *wick*ed and *sloth*ful *ser*vant! Thou *knew*est that I reap where I sowed not and gather where I have not strewed. Thou oughtest therefore to have put my money to the exchangers, and *then* at my coming I should have received my *own* . . . *with interest!*' Now, friends, if you've got your money lying around in a passbook savings account down at the bank . . . *you* . . . are like that *wick*ed *ser*vant! *You* . . . have got your *gold* . . . *stuck* in the *ground!* Wouldn't you rather be able to answer, in the Final Hour, when the Last Questions are asked: 'Oh, *yes*, Lord! I took *my gold* . . . *out* of the passbook savings account! I put *my gold* . . . *into* the Gospel Money Market Fund! Fourteen-point-five percent per annum as of June 15! Interest *com*pounded daily! Withdrawals in part or in full . . . at *any* time! Check-writing privileges . . . *of* course! Bank by wire . . . *a*vailable! Call me tonight, toll free—the Reverend Bob Lee Boyd, Gospel Money Market Fund, *In*corporated—and wake up to*mor*row . . . on the *side* . . . of the *An*gels! This is not an offering, which can be made by formal prospectus only."

THE ME DECADE AND THE THIRD GREAT AWAKENING

1. *Me and my hemorrhoids*

The trainer said, "Take your finger off the repress button." Everybody was supposed to let go, let all the vile stuff come up and gush out. They even provided vomit bags, like the ones on a 747, in case you literally let it *gush out*! Then the trainer told everybody to think of "the one thing you would most like to eliminate from your life." And so what does our girl blurt over the microphone?

"*Hemorrhoids!*"

Just so!

That was how she ended up in her present state . . . stretched out on the wall-to-wall carpet of a banquet hall in the Ambassador Hotel in Los Angeles with her eyes closed and her face pressed into the stubble of the carpet, which is a thick commercial weave and feels like clothesbrush bristles against her face and smells a bit *high* from cleaning solvent. That was how she ended up lying here concentrating on her hemorrhoids.

Eyes shut! deep in her own space! her hemorrhoids! the grisly peanut—

Many others are stretched out on the carpet all around her; some 249 other souls, in fact. They're all strewn across the floor of the banquet hall with their eyes closed, just as she is. But, Christ, the others are concentrating on things that sound serious and deep when you talk about them. And how they had talked about them! They had

From *Mauve Gloves & Madmen, Clutter & Vine*. First published in *New York Magazine* and *New West Magazine*, August 23, 1976. Portions of this piece appeared, in an earlier version as "The Third Great Awakening," in *The Critic*, May/June 1973.

all marched right up to the microphone and "shared," as the trainer called it. What did they want to eliminate from their lives? Why, they took their fingers right off the old repress button and told the whole room. My husband! my wife! my homosexuality! my inability to communicate, my self-hatred, self-destructiveness, craven fears, puling weaknesses, primordial horrors, premature ejaculation, impotence, frigidity, rigidity, subservience, laziness, alcoholism, major vices, minor vices, grim habits, twisted psyches, tortured souls—and then it had been her turn, and she had said, "Hemorrhoids."

You can imagine what that sounded like. That broke the place up. The trainer looked like a cocky little bastard up there on the podium, with his deep tan, white tennis shirt, and peach-colored sweater, a dynamite color combination, all very casual and spontaneous—after about two hours of trying on different outfits in front of a mirror, *that* kind of casual and spontaneous, if her guess was right. And yet she found him attractive. *Commanding* was the word. He probably wondered if she was playing the wiseacre, with her "hemorrhoids," but he rolled with it. Maybe she *was* being playful. Just looking at him made her feel mischievous. In any event, *hemorrhoids* was what had bubbled up into her brain.

Then the trainer had told them to stack their folding chairs in the back of the banquet hall and lie down on the floor and close their eyes and get deep into their own spaces and concentrate on that one item they wanted to get rid of most—and really feel it and let the feeling gush out.

So now she's lying here concentrating on her hemorrhoids. The strange thing is . . . it's no joke after all! She begins to feel her hemorrhoids in all their morbid presence. She can actually *feel* them. The sieges always began with her having the sensation that a peanut was caught in her anal sphincter. That meant a section of swollen varicose vein had pushed its way out of her intestines and was actually coming out of her bottom. It was as hard as a peanut and felt bigger and grislier than a peanut. Well—for God's sake!—in her daily life, even at work, *especially* at work, and she works for a movie distributor, her whole picture of herself was of her . . . *seductive physical presence.* She was not the most successful businesswoman in Los Angeles, but she was certainly successful enough, and quite in addition to that, she was . . . *the main sexual presence in the office.* When she walked into the office each morning, everyone, women as well as men, checked her out. She *knew* that. She could feel her sexual presence go through the place like an invisible chemical, like a hormone, a scent, a universal solvent.

The most beautiful moments came when she was in her office or in a conference room or at Mr. Chow's taking a meeting—nobody "had" meetings any more, they "took" them—with two or three men, men she had never met before or barely knew. The overt subject was, inevitably, eternally, "the deal." She always said there should be only one credit line up on the screen for any movie: "Deal by . . ." But the meeting would also have a subplot. The overt plot would be "The Deal." The subplot would be "The Men Get Turned On by Me." Pretty soon, even though the conversation had not strayed overtly from "the deal," the men would be swaying in unison like dune grass at the beach. And she was the wind, of course. And then one of the men would say something and smile and at the same time reach over and touch her . . . on top of the hand or on the side of the arm . . . as if it meant nothing . . . as if it were just a gesture for emphasis . . . *but, in fact, a man is usually deathly afraid of reaching out and touching a woman he doesn't know* . . . and she knew it meant she had hypnotized him sexually . . .

Well—for God's sake!—at just that sublime moment, likely as not, the goddamn peanut would be popping out of her tail! As she smiled sublimely at her conquest, she also had to sit in her chair lopsided, with one cheek of her buttocks higher than the other, as if she were about to crepitate, because it hurt to sit squarely on the peanut. If for any reason she had to stand up at that point and walk, she would have to walk as if her hip joints were rusted out, as if she were sixty-five years old, because a normal stride pressed the peanut, and the pain would start up, and the bleeding, too, very likely. Or if she couldn't get up and had to sit there for a while and keep her smile and her hot hormonal squinted eyes pinned on the men before her, the peanut would start itching or burning, and she would start double-tracking, as if her mind were a tape deck with two channels going at once. In one she's the sexual princess, the Circe, taking a meeting and clouding men's minds . . . and in the other she's a poor bitch who wants nothing more in this world than to go down the corridor to the ladies' room and get some Kleenex and some Vaseline and push the peanut back up into her intestines with her finger.

And even if she's able to get away and do that, she will spend the rest of that day and the next, and the next, with a *deep worry* in the back of her brain, the sort of worry that always stays on the edge of your consciousness, no matter how hard you think of something else. She will be wondering at all times what the next bowel movement will be like, how solid and compact the bolus will be, trying to think back and remember if she's had any milk, cream, chocolate, or any other binding substance in the last twenty-four hours, or any nuts or fibrous vegetables like broccoli. Is she really *in for it* this time—

The Sexual Princess! On the outside she has on her fireproof grin and her Fiorio scarf, as if to say she lives in a world of Sevilles and

450SL's and dinner last night at Dominick's, a movie business restaurant on Beverly Boulevard that's so exclusive, Dominick keeps his neon sign (*Dominick's*) turned off at night to make the wimps think it's closed, but *she* (Hi, Dominick!) can get a table—while inside her it's all the battle between the bolus and the peanut—

—and is it too late to leave the office and go get some mineral oil and let some of that vile glop roll down her gullet or get a refill on the softener tablets or eat some prunes or drink some coffee or do something else to avoid one of those horrible hard-clay boluses that will come grinding out of her, crushing the peanut and starting not only the bleeding but . . . *the pain!* . . . a horrible humiliating pain that feels like she's getting a paper cut in her anus, like the pain you feel when the edge of a piece of bond paper slices your finger, plus a horrible hellish purple bloody varicose pressure, but lasting not for an instant, like a paper cut, but for an eternity, prolonged until the tears are rolling down her face as she sits in the cubicle, and she wants to cry out, to scream until it's over, to make the screams of fear, fury, and humiliation obliterate the pain. But someone would hear! No doubt they'd come bursting right into the ladies' room to save her! and feed and water their morbid curiosities! And what could she possibly say? And so she had simply held that feeling in all these years, with her eyes on fire and her entire pelvic saddle a great purple tub of pain. She had repressed the whole squalid horror of it—*the searing peanut*—until now. The trainer had said, "Take your finger off the repress button!" Let it gush up and pour out!

And now, as she lies here on the floor of the banquet hall of the Ambassador Hotel with 249 other souls, she knows exactly what he meant. She can feel it *all*, all of the pain, and on top of the pain all the humiliation, and for the first time in her life she has permission from the Management, from herself and everyone around her, to let the feeling gush forth. So she starts moaning.

"Ooooooooooooooooooooooohhhhhhhhhhhhhhhhh!"

And when she starts moaning, the most incredible and exhilarating thing begins to happen. A wave of moans spreads through the people lying around her, as if her energy were radiating out like a radar pulse.

"Oooooooooooooooooooooohhhhhhhhh!"

So she lets her moan rise into a keening sound.

"Ooooooooooooooooooohhhhhhhhhheeeeeeeeeeeeeeeeeeeeeeee!"

And when she begins to keen, the souls near her begin keening, even while the moans are still spreading to the prostrate folks farther from her, on the edges of the room.

"Eeeeeeeeeeeeeooooooohhhhhhhhhheeeeeeeeeeeeeeeooooooooh!"

So she lets her keening sound rise up into a real scream.

"Eeeeeeeeeeeeeeeeeeaiaiaiaiaiaiaiaiaiaiaiaiaiaiai!"

And this rolls out in a wave, too, first through those near her, and then toward the far edges.

"Aiaiaiaiaiaiaiaiaiaiaieeeeeeeeeeeeeeeeeeeeohhhhhhhhheeeeeaiaiai!"

And so she turns it all the way up, into a scream such as she has never allowed herself in her entire life.

"AiaiaiaiaiaiaiaiaaaAAAAAAAAAAAAAAAARRRRRRRGGGGGG-HHHHHH!"

And her full scream spreads from soul to soul, over the top of the keens and fading moans—

"AAAAAAARRRRRGGGGHHHaiaiaiaiaieeeeeeeeeeeoooooohhheeee-eeaiaiaiaiaaaaAAAAAAAAAARRRRRRRGGGGGHHHHHHHHHH!"

—until at last the entire room is consumed in her scream, as if there are no longer 250 separate souls but one noösphere of souls united in some incorporeal way by her scream—

"AAAAAAAAARRRRRRRGGGGGGHHHHHHH!"

—which is not simply *her* scream any longer . . . but the world's! Each soul is concentrated on its own burning item—my husband! my wife! my homosexuality! my inability to communicate, my self-hatred, self-destruction, craven fears, puling weaknesses, primordial horrors, premature ejaculation, impotence, frigidity, rigidity, subservience, laziness, alcoholism, major vices, minor vices, grim habits, twisted psyches, tortured souls—and yet each unique item has been raised to a cosmic level and united with every other until there is but one piercing moment of release and liberation at last!—a whole world of anguish set free by—

My hemorrhoids.

"Me and My Hemorrhoids Star at the Ambassador" . . . during a three-day Erhard Seminars Training (est) course in the banquet hall. The truly odd part, however, is yet to come. In her experience lies the explanation of certain grand puzzles of the 1970's, a period that will come to be known as the Me Decade.

2. *The holy roll*

In 1972 a farsighted caricaturist did this drawing of Teddy Kennedy, entitled "President Kennedy campaigning for reelection in 1980 . . . courting the so-called Awakened vote." The picture shows Kennedy ostentatiously wearing not only a crucifix but also (if one looks just above the cross) a pendant of the Bleeding Heart of Jesus. The crucifix is the symbol of Christianity in general, but the Bleeding Heart is the symbol of some of Christianity's most ecstatic, non-rational,

holy-rolling cults. I should point out that the artist's prediction lacked certain refinements. For one thing, Kennedy may be campaigning to be President in 1980, but he is not terribly likely to be the incumbent. For another, the odd spectacle of politicians using ecstatic, non-rational, holy-rolling religion in Presidential campaigning was to appear first not in 1980 but in 1976.

The two most popular new figures in the 1976 campaign, Jimmy Carter and Jerry Brown, are men who rose up from state politics . . . absolutely aglow with mystical religious streaks. Carter turned out to be an evangelical Baptist who had recently been "born again" and "saved," who had "accepted Jesus Christ as my personal Savior"—i.e., he was of the Missionary lectern-pounding Amen ten-finger C-major-chord Sister-Martha-at-the-Yamaha-keyboard loblolly piney-woods Baptist faith in which the members of the congregation stand up and "give witness" and "share it, Brother" and "share it, Sister" and "praise God!" during the service.* Jerry Brown turned out to be the Zen Jesuit, a former Jesuit seminarian who went about like a hairshirt Catholic monk, but one who happened to believe also in the Gautama Buddha, and who got off koans in an offhand but confident manner, even on political issues, as to how it is not the right answer that matters but the right question, and so forth.

Newspaper columnists and news-magazine writers continually referred to the two men's "enigmatic appeal." Which is to say, they couldn't explain it. Nevertheless, they tried. They theorized that the war in Vietnam, Watergate, the FBI and CIA scandals, had left the electorate shell-shocked and disillusioned and that in their despair the citizens were groping no longer for specific remedies but for sheer faith, something, anything (even holy rolling), to believe in. This was in keeping with the current fashion of interpreting all new political phenomena in terms of recent disasters, frustration, protest, the decline of civilization . . . the Grim Slide. But when *The New York Times* and CBS employed a polling organization to try to find out just what great gusher of "frustration" and "protest" Carter had hit, the results were baffling. A Harvard political scientist, William Schneider,

* Carter is not, however, a member of the most down-home and ecstatic of the Baptist sects, which is a back-country branch known as the Primitive Baptist Church. In the Primitive Baptist churches men and women sit on different sides of the room, no musical instruments are allowed, and there is a good deal of foot-washing and other rituals drawn from passages in the Bible. The Progressive Primitives, another group, differ from the Primitives chiefly in that they allow a piano or organ in the church. The Missionary Baptists, Carter's branch, are a step up socially (not necessarily divinely) but would not be a safe bet for an ambitious member of an in-town country club. The In-town Baptists, found in communities of 25,000 or more, are too respectable, socially, to be called ecstatic and succeed in being almost as tame as the Episcopalians, Presbyterians, and Methodists.

concluded for the Los Angeles *Times* that "the Carter protest" was a new kind of protest, "a protest of good feelings." That was a new kind, sure enough: a protest that wasn't a protest.

In fact, both Carter and Brown had stumbled upon a fabulous terrain for which there are no words in current political language. A couple of politicians had finally wandered into the Me Decade.

3. Him?—the new man?

The saga of the Me Decade begins with one of those facts that are so big and so obvious (like the Big Dipper) no one ever comments on them any more. Namely: the thirty-year boom. Wartime spending in the United States in the 1940's touched off a boom that has continued for more than thirty years. It has pumped money into every class level of the population on a scale without parallel in any country in history. True, nothing has solved the plight of those at the very bottom, the chronically unemployed of the slums. Nevertheless, in the city of Compton, California, it is possible for a family of four at the very lowest class level, which is known in America today as "on welfare," to draw an income of $8,000 a year entirely from public sources. This is more than most British newspaper columnists and Italian factory foremen make, even allowing for differences in living costs. In America truck drivers, mechanics, factory workers, policemen, firemen, and garbagemen make so much money—$15,000 to $20,000 (or more) per year is not uncommon—that the word "proletarian" can no longer be used in this country with a straight face. So one now says "lower middle class." One can't even call workingmen "blue collar" any longer. They all have on collars like Joe Namath's or Johnny Bench's or Walt Frazier's. They all have on $35 superstar Qiana sport shirts with elephant collars and 1940's Airbrush Wallpaper Flowers Buncha Grapes & Seashell designs all over them.

Well, my God, the old utopian socialists of the nineteenth century—such as Saint-Simon, Owen, Fourier, and Marx—*lived* for the day of the liberated workingman. They foresaw a day when industrialism (Saint-Simon coined the word) would give the common man the things he needed in order to realize his potential as a human being: surplus (discretionary) income, political freedom, free time (leisure), and freedom from grinding drudgery. Some of them, notably Owen and Fourier, thought all this might come to pass first in the United States. So they set up communes here: Owen's New Harmony commune in Indiana and thirty-four Fourier-style "phalanx" settlements—socialist communes, because the new freedom was supposed to be possible only under socialism. The old boys never dreamed that it would come to pass instead as the result of a Go-Getter Bourgeois business boom such as began in the U.S. in the 1940's. Nor would they have liked it if they had seen it. For one thing, the *homo novus,* the new man, the liberated man, the first common man in the history of the world with the much-dreamed-of combination of money, freedom, and free time—this American workingman—didn't *look* right. The Joe Namath–Johnny Bench–Walt Frazier superstar Qiana wallpaper sports shirts, for a start.

He didn't look right . . . and he wouldn't . . . *do right*! I can remember what brave plans visionary architects at Yale and Harvard still had for *the common man* in the early 1950's. (They actually used the term "the common man.") They had brought the utopian socialist dream forward into the twentieth century. They had things figured out for the workingman down to truly minute details, such as lamp switches. The new liberated workingman would live as the Cultivated Ascetic. He would be modeled on the B.A.-degree Greenwich Village bohemian of the late 1940's—dark wool Hudson Bay shirts, tweed jackets, flannel trousers, briarwood pipes, good books, sandals and simplicity—except that he would live in a Worker Housing project. All Yale and Harvard architects worshipped Bauhaus principles and had the Bauhaus vision of Worker Housing. The Bauhaus movement absolutely hypnotized American architects, once its leaders, such as Walter Gropius and Ludwig Mies van der Rohe, came to the United States from Germany in the 1930's. Worker Housing in America would have pure beige rooms, stripped, freed, purged of all moldings, cornices, and overhangs—which Gropius regarded as symbolic "crowns" and therefore loathsome. Worker Housing would be liberated from all wallpaper, "drapes," Wilton rugs with flowers on them, lamps with fringed shades and bases that looked like vases or Greek columns. It would be cleansed of all doilies, knickknacks, mantelpieces, headboards, and radiator covers. Radiator coils would be left bare as honest, abstract sculptural objects.

But somehow the workers, incurable slobs that they were, avoided Worker Housing, better known as "the projects," as if it had a smell. They were heading out instead to the suburbs—the *suburbs*!—to places like Islip, Long Island, and the San Fernando Valley of Los Angeles—and buying houses with clapboard siding and pitched roofs and shingles and gaslight-style front-porch lamps and mailboxes set up on top of lengths of stiffened chain that seemed to defy gravity, and all sorts of other unbelievably cute or antiquey touches, and they loaded these houses with "drapes" such as baffled all description and wall-to-wall carpet you could lose a shoe in, and they put barbecue pits and fish ponds with concrete cherubs urinating into them on the lawn out back, and they parked twenty-five-foot-long cars out front and Evinrude cruisers up on tow trailers in the carport just beyond the breezeway.*

By the 1960's the common man was also getting quite interested in this business of "realizing his potential as a human being." But once again he crossed everybody up! Once more he took his money and ran—determined to do-it-himself!

4. *Plugging in*

In 1971 I made a lecture tour of Italy, talking (at the request of my Italian hosts) about "contemporary American life." Everywhere I went, from Turin to Palermo, Italian students were interested in just one question: Was it really true that young people in America, no older than themselves, actually left home and lived communally according to their own rules and created their own dress styles and vocabulary and had free sex and took dope? They were talking, of course, about the hippie or psychedelic movement that had begun flowering about 1965. What fascinated them the most, however, was the first item on the list: that the hippies *actually left home and lived communally according to their own rules.*

To Italian students this seemed positively amazing. Several of the students I met lived wild enough lives during daylight hours. They were in radical organizations and had fought pitched battles with police, *on the barricades*, as it were. But by 8:30 p.m. they were back home, obediently washing their hands before dinner with Mom and Dad and Buddy and Sis and the Maiden Aunt. When they left home for good, it was likely to be via the only admissible ticket: marriage. Unmarried sons of thirty-eight and thirty-nine would still be sitting around the same old table, morosely munching the gnocchi.

Meanwhile, ordinary people in America were breaking off from conventional society, from family, neighborhood, and community, and creating worlds of their own. This had no parallel in history, certainly considering the scale of it. The hippies were merely the most flam-

* Ignored or else held in contempt by working people, Bauhaus design eventually triumphed as a symbol of wealth and privilege, attuned chiefly to the tastes of businessmen's wives. For example, Mies's most famous piece of furniture design, the Barcelona chair, now sells for $1,680 and is available only through one's decorator. The high price is due in no small part to the chair's Worker Housing Honest Materials: stainless steel and leather. No chromed iron is allowed, and customers are refused if they want to have the chair upholstered in material of their own choice. Only leather is allowed, and only six shades of that: Seagram's Building Lobby Palomino, Monsanto Chemical Company Lobby Antelope, Arco Towers Pecan, Trans-America Building Ebony, Bank of America Building Walnut, and Architectural Digest Mink.

boyant example. The New Left students of the late 1960's were another. The New Lefters lived in communes much like the hippies' but with a slightly different emphasis. Dope, sex, nudity, costumes, and vocabulary became symbols of defiance of bourgeois life. The costumery tended to be semi-military: non-com officers' shirts, combat boots, commando berets—worn in combination with blue jeans or a turtleneck jersey, however, to show that one wasn't a uniform freak.

That people so young could go off on their own, without taking jobs, and live a life completely of their own design—to Europeans it was astounding. That ordinary factory workers could go off to the suburbs and buy homes and create their own dream houses—this, too, was astounding. And yet the new life of old people in America in the 1960's was still more astounding. Throughout European history and in the United States up to the Second World War, old age was a time when you had to cling to your children or other kinfolk, and to their sufferance and mercy, if any. The Old Folks at Home happily mingling in the old manse with the generations that followed? The little ones learning at Grandpa's and Grandma's bony knees? These are largely the myths of nostalgia. The beloved old folks were often exiled to the attic or the outbuildings, and the servants brought them their meals. They were not considered decorative in the dining room or the parlor.

In the 1960's, old people in America began doing something that was more extraordinary than it ever seemed at the time. They cut through the whole dreary humiliation of old age by heading off to "retirement villages" and "leisure developments"—which quickly became Old Folks communes. Some of the old parties managed to take this to a somewhat psychedelic extreme. For example, the trailer caravaners. The caravaners were (and are) mainly retired couples who started off their Golden Years by doing the usual thing. They went to their children, Buddy and Sis, and gingerly suggested that now that Dad had retired, he and Mom might move in with one of them. They get the old "Uhh . . . sure"—plus a death-ray look. So the two old crocks depart and go out and buy what is the only form of prefabricated housing that has ever caught on in America: the house trailer, or mobile home. Usually the old pair would try to make the trailer look like a real house. They'd park it on a plot in a trailer park and put it up on blocks and put some latticework around the bottom to hide the axles and the wheel housings and put little awnings above the windows and a big one out over the door to create the impression of a breezeway. By and by, however, they would discover that there were people their age who actually moved off dead center with these things and went out into the world and *rolled*. At this point they would join a trailer caravan. And when the trailer caravans got rolling, you had a chance to see some of the most amazing sights of the modern American landscape . . . such as thirty, forty, fifty Airstream trailers, the ones that are silver and have rounded corners and ends and look like silver bullets . . . thirty, forty, fifty of these silver bullets in a line, in a caravan, hauling down the highway in the late afternoon with the sun at a low angle and exploding off the silver surfaces of the Airstreams until the whole convoy looks like some gigantic and improbable string of jewelry, each jewel ablaze with a highlight, rolling over the face of the earth—the million-volt, billion-horsepower bijoux of America!

The caravaners might start off taking the ordinary tourist routes of the West, but they would soon get a taste for adventure and head for the badlands, through the glacier forests of the Northwest and down through western Mexico, not fat green chile relleno red jacaranda blossom mariachi band caballero sombrero Tourist Mexico but *western* Mexico, where the terrain is all skulls and bones and junk frito and hardcheese mestizos hunkered down at the crossroads, glowering, and cows and armadillos by the side of the road on their backs with their bellies bloated and all four feet up in the air. The caravaners would get deeper and deeper into a life of sheer *trailering*. They would become experts at this twentieth-century nomad life. They would begin to look back on Buddy & Sis as sad conventional sorts whom they had left behind, poor turkeys who knew nothing of the initiations and rites of passage of trailering.

The mighty million-volt rites! Every now and then the caravan would have to seek out a trailer camp for a rest in the rush across the face of Western America, and in these camps you'd have to plug a power line from your trailer into the utility poles the camps provide, so as to be able to use the appliances in the trailer when your car engine wasn't generating electricity. In some of the older camps these poles were tricky to use. If you didn't plug your line in in just the right manner, with the right prong up and the right one down, you stood to get a hell of a shock, a feedback of what felt like about two thousand volts. So about dusk you might see the veterans sitting outside their trailers in aluminum-and-vinyl folding chairs, pretending to be just chewing the fat at sunset but in fact nudging one another and keeping everyone on the alert for what is about to happen when the rookie—the rheumy-eyed, gray-haired old Dad who, with Mom, has just joined the caravan—plugs into the malicious Troll Pole for the first time.

Old Dad tries to plug in, and of course he gets it wrong, tries to put the wrong prong in on top and the wrong one on the bottom, and—*bowwwwwwww!*—he gets a thunderbolt jolt like Armageddon itself and does an inverted one-and-a-half gainer and lands on his back—

and the veterans, men and women, just absolutely crack up, bawl, cry, laugh until they're turning inside out. And only after the last whoops and snorts have died down does it dawn on you that this poor wet rookie who plugged in wrong and has just done this involuntary Olympic diving maneuver and landed on his spine with his fingers smoking . . . is a gray-haired party seventy-two years old. But that's also the beauty of it! They always survive! They're initiates! hierophants of the caravan who have moved off dead center! Various deadly rheumatoid symptoms disappear, as if by magic! The Gerontoid Cowboys ride! deep into a new land and a new life they've created for themselves!

5. *Lemon sessions*

It was remarkable enough that ordinary folks now had enough money to take it and run off and alter the circumstances of their lives and create new roles for themselves, such as Trailer Sailor. But simultaneously still others decided to go . . . *all the way.* They plunged straight toward what has become the alchemical dream of the Me Decade.

The old alchemical dream was changing base metals into gold. The new alchemical dream is: changing one's personality—remaking, remodeling, elevating, and polishing one's very *self* . . . and observing, studying, and doting on it. (Me!) This had always been an aristocratic luxury, confined throughout most of history to the life of the courts, since only the wealthiest classes had the free time and the surplus income to dwell upon this sweetest and vainest of pastimes. It smacked so much of vanity, in fact, that the noble folk involved in it always took care to call it quite something else.

Much of the satisfaction well-born people got from what is known historically as the "chivalric tradition" was precisely that: dwelling upon *Me* and every delicious nuance of my conduct and personality. At Versailles, Louis XIV founded a school for girls called Saint-Cyr. At the time most schools for girls were in convents. Louis had quite something else in mind, a secular school that would develop womenfolk for the superior *race guerrière* that he believed himself to be creating in France. Saint-Cyr was the forerunner for what was known up until a few years ago as *the finishing school.* And what was *the finishing school*? Why, a school in which the personality was to be shaped and buffed like a piece of high-class psychological cabinetry. For centuries most of upper-class college education in France and England has been fashioned in the same manner: with an eye toward sculpting the personality as carefully as the intellectual faculties.

At Yale the students on the outside have wondered for eighty years what went on inside the fabled secret senior societies, such as Skull & Bones. On Thursday nights one would see the secret-society members walking silently and single-file, in black flannel suits, white shirts, and black knit ties with gold pins on them, toward their great Greek Revival temples, buildings whose mystery was doubled by the fact that they had no windows. What in the name of God or Mammon went on in those thirty-odd Thursday nights during the senior years of these happy few? What went on was . . . *lemon sessions!*—a regularly scheduled series of the lemon sessions, just like the ones that occurred informally in girls' finishing schools.

In the girls' schools these lemon sessions tended to take place at random on nights when a dozen or so girls might end up in someone's dormitory room. One girl would become "it," and the others would rip into her personality, pulling it to pieces to analyze every defect . . . her spitefulness, her awkwardness, her bad breath, embarrassing clothes, ridiculous laugh, her suck-up fawning, latent lesbianism, or whatever. The poor creature might be reduced to tears. She might blurt out the most terrible confessions, hatreds, and primordial fears. But, it was presumed, she would be the stronger for it afterward. She would be on her way toward a new personality. Likewise, in the secret societies, they held lemon sessions for boys. Is masturbation your problem? Out with the truth, you ridiculous weenie! And Thursday night after Thursday night the awful truths would out, as he who was It stood up before them and answered the most horrible questions. Yes! I do it! I whack whack whack it! I'm *afraid* of women! I'm afraid of *you*! And I get my shirts at Rosenberg's instead of Press! (Oh, you dreary turkey, you wet smack, you little shit!) . . . But out of the fire and the heap of ashes would come a better man, a brother, of good blood and good bone, for the American *race guerrière*. And what was more . . . they loved it. No matter how dreary the soap opera, the star was *Me*.

By the mid-1960's this service, this luxury, had become available for one and all, i.e., the middle classes. Lemon Session Central was the Esalen Institute, a lodge perched on a cliff overlooking the Pacific in Big Sur, California. Esalen's specialty was lube jobs for the personality. Businessmen, businesswomen, housewives—anyone who could afford it, and by now many could—paid $220 a week to come to Esalen to learn about themselves and loosen themselves up and wiggle their fannies a bit, in keeping with methods developed by William C. Schutz and Frederick Perls. Fritz Perls, as he was known, was a remarkable figure, a psychologist who had a gray beard and went about in a blue terry-cloth jumpsuit and looked like a great blue grizzled father bear. His lemon sessions sprang not out of the Manly Virtues & Cold Showers Protestant Prep-School tradition of Yale but out of psychoanalysis. His sessions were a variety of the "marathon encounter."* He put the various candidates for personality change in groups, and they stayed together in close quarters day after day. They were encouraged to bare their own souls and to strip away one another's defensive façade. Everyone was to face his own emotions squarely for the first time.

Encounter sessions, particularly of the Schutz variety, were often wild events. Such aggression! such sobs! tears! moans, hysteria, vile recriminations, shocking revelations, such explosions of hostility between husbands and wives, such mudballs of profanity from previously mousy mommies and workadaddies, such red-mad attacks! Only physical assault was prohibited. The encounter session became a standard approach in many other movements, such as Scientology, Arica, the Mel Lyman movement, Synanon, Daytop Village, and Primal Scream. Synanon had started out as a drug-rehabilitation program, but by the late 1960's the organization was recruiting "lay members," a lay member being someone who had never been addicted to heroin . . . but was ready for the lemon-session life.

Outsiders, hearing of these sessions, wondered what on earth their appeal was. Yet the appeal was simple enough. It is summed up in the notion: "Let's talk about *Me*." No matter whether you managed to renovate your personality through encounter sessions or not, you had finally focused your attention and your energies on the most fascinating subject on earth: *Me*. Not only that, you also put *Me* onstage before a live audience. The popular est movement has managed to do that with great refinement. Just imagine . . . *Me and My Hemorrhoids* . . . moving an entire hall to the most profound outpouring of emotion! Just imagine . . . *my life* becoming a drama with universal significance . . . analyzed, like Hamlet's, for what it signifies for the rest of mankind . . .

The encounter session—although it was not called that—was also a staple practice in psychedelic communes and, for that matter, in New Left communes. In fact, the analysis of the self, and of one another, was unceasing. But in these groups and at Esalen and in movements such as Arica there were two common assumptions that distinguished them from the aristocratic lemon sessions and personality *finishings* of yore. The first was: I, with the help of my brothers and sisters, must strip away all the shams and excess baggage of society and my upbringing in order to find the Real Me. Scientology uses the word "clear" to identify the state that one must strive for. But just what

---

* The real "marathons," in which the group stayed in the same room for twenty-four hours or longer, were developed by George R. Bach and Frederick Stoller of Los Angeles.

is that state? And what will the Real Me be like? It is at this point that the new movements tend to take on a religious or spiritual atmosphere. In one form or another they arrive at an axiom first propounded by the Gnostic Christians some eighteen hundred years ago: namely, that at the apex of every human soul there exists a spark of the light of God. In most mortals that spark is "asleep" (the Gnostics' word), all but smothered by the façades and general falseness of society. But those souls who are clear can find that spark within themselves and unite their souls with God's. And with that conviction comes the second assumption: there is an *other order* that actually reigns supreme in the world. Like the light of God itself, this *other order* is invisible to most mortals. But he who has dug himself out from under the junk heap of civilization can discover it.

And with that . . . the Me movements were about to turn *righteous.*

6. Young faith, aging groupies

By the early 1970's so many of the Me movements had reached this Gnostic religious stage, they now amounted to a new religious wave. Synanon, Arica, and the Scientology movement had become religions. The much-publicized psychedelic or hippie communes of the 1960's, although no longer big items in the press, were spreading widely and becoming more and more frankly religious. The huge Steve Gaskin commune in the Tennessee scrublands was a prime example. A *New York Times* survey concluded that there were at least two thousand communes in the United States by 1970, barely five years after the idea first caught on in California. Both the Esalen-style and Primal Therapy or Primal Scream encounter movements were becoming progressively less psychoanalytical and more mystical in their approach. The Oriental "meditation" religions—which had existed in the United States mainly in the form of rather intellectual and bohemian zen and yoga circles—experienced a spectacular boom. Groups such as the Hare Krishna, the Sufi, and the Maharaj Ji communes began to discover that they could enroll thousands of new members and (in some cases) make small fortunes in real estate to finance the expansion. Many members of the New Left communes of the 1960's began to turn up in Me movements in the 1970's, including two of the celebrated "Chicago Eight." Rennie Davis became a follower of the Maharaj Ji, Jerry Rubin enrolled in both est and Arica. Barbara Garson—who with the help of her husband, Marvin, wrote the agitprop epic of the New Left, *MacBird*—would later observe, with considerable bitterness: "My husband, Marvin, forsook everything (me included) to find peace. For three years he wandered without shoes or money or glasses. Now he is in Israel with some glasses and possibly with some peace." And not just him, she said, but so many other New Lefters as well: "Some follow a guru, some are into primal scream, some seek a rest from the diaspora—a home in Zion." It is entirely possible that in the long run historians will regard the entire New Left experience as not so much a political as a religious episode wrapped in semi-military gear and guerrilla talk.

Meanwhile, the ESP or "psychic phenomena" movement began to grow very rapidly in the new religious atmosphere. ESP devotees had always believed that there was an *other order* that ran the universe, one that revealed itself occasionally through telepathy, *déjà vu* experiences, psychokinesis, and the like. It was but a small step from there to the assumption that all men possess a *conscious energy* paralleling the world of physical energy and that this mysterious energy can unite the universe (after the fashion of the light of God). A former astronaut, Edgar Mitchell, who has a Doctor of Science degree from M.I.T., founded the Institute of Noetic Sciences in an attempt to channel the work of all the ESP groups. "Noetic" is an adjective derived from the same root as that of "the Noösphere"—the name that Teilhard de Chardin gave his dream of a cosmic union of all souls. Even the Flying Saucer cults began to reveal their essentially religious nature at about this time. The Flying Saucer folk quite literally believed in an *other order:* it was under the command of superior beings from other planets or solar systems who had spaceships. A physician named Andrija Puharich wrote a book (*Uri*) in which he published the name of the God of the UFO's: Hoova. He said Hoova had a herald messenger named Spectra, and Hoova's and Spectra's agent on earth, the human connection, as it were, was Uri Geller, the famous Israeli psychic and showman. Geller's powers were also of great interest to people in the ESP movement, and there were many who wished that Puharich and the UFO people would keep their hands off him.

By the early 1970's a quite surprising movement, tagged as the Jesus People, had spread throughout the country. At the outset practically all the Jesus People were young acid heads, i.e., LSD users, who had sworn off drugs (except, occasionally, in "organic form," meaning marijuana and peyote) but still wanted the ecstatic spiritualism of the psychedelic or hippie life. This they found in Fundamentalist evangelical holy-rolling Christianity of a sort that ten years before would have seemed utterly impossible to revive in America. The Jesus People, such as the Children of God, the Fresno God Squad, the Tony and Susan Alamo Christian Foundation, the Sun Myung Moon sect, lived communally and took an ecstatic or "charismatic" (literally: "God-imbued") approach to Christianity, after the manner of the Oneida, Shaker, and Mormon communes of the nineteenth century—

and, for that matter, after the manner of the early Christians themselves, including the Gnostics.

There was considerable irony here. Ever since the late 1950's both the Catholic Church and the leading Protestant denominations had been aware that young people, particularly in the cities, were drifting away from the faith. At every church conference and convocation and finance committee meeting the cry went up: *We must reach the urban young people.* It became an obsession, this business of the "urban young people." The key—one and all decided—was to "modernize" and "update" Christianity. So the Catholics gave the nuns outfits that made them look like World War II Wacs. The Protestants set up "beatnik coffee houses" in the church basement for poetry reading and bongo playing. They had the preacher put on a turtleneck sweater and sing "Joe Hill" and "Frankie and Johnny" during the hootenanny at the Sunday vespers. Both the priests and the preachers carried placards in civil rights marches, gay rights marches, women's rights marches, prisoners' rights marches, bondage lovers' rights marches, or any other marches, so long as they might appear hip to the urban young people.

In fact, all these strenuous gestures merely made the churches look like rather awkward and senile groupies of secular movements. The much-sought-after Urban Young People found the Hip Churchman to be an embarrassment, if they noticed him at all. What finally started attracting young people to Christianity was something the churches had absolutely nothing to do with: namely, the psychedelic or hippie movement. The hippies had suddenly made religion look hip. Very few people went into the hippie life with religious intentions, but many came out of it absolutely *righteous.* The sheer power of the drug LSD is not to be underestimated. It was quite easy for an LSD experience to take the form of a religious vision, particularly if one was among people already so inclined. You would come across someone you had known for years, a pal, only now he was jacked up on LSD and sitting in the middle of the street saying, "I'm in the Pudding at last! I've met the Manager!" Without knowing it, many heads were reliving the religious fervor of their grandparents or great-grandparents—the Bible-Belting lectern-pounding Amen ten-finger C-major-chord Sister-Martha-at-the-keyboard tent-meeting loblolly piney-woods share-it-brother believers of the nineteenth century. The hippies were religious and yet incontrovertibly hip at the same time.

Today it is precisely the most rational, intellectual, secularized, modernized, updated, relevant religions—all the brave, forward-looking Ethical Culture, Unitarian, and Swedenborgian movements of only yesterday—that are finished, gasping, breathing their last. What the Urban Young People want from religion is a little . . . *Hallelujah!*

. . . and *talking in tongues!* . . . *Praise God!* Precisely that! In the most prestigious divinity schools today, Catholic, Presbyterian, and Episcopal, the avant-garde movement—the leading edge—is "charismatic Christianity" . . . featuring talking in tongues, ululalia, visions, holy-rolling, and other non-rational, even anti-rational, practices. Some of the most respectable old-line Protestant congregations, in the most placid suburban settings, have begun to split into the Charismatics and the Easter Christians ("All they care about is being seen in church on Easter"). The Easter Christians still usually control the main Sunday-morning service—but the Charismatics take over on Sunday evening and do the holy roll.

This curious development has breathed new life into the existing fundamentalists, theosophists, and older salvation seekers of all sorts. Ten years ago, if anyone of wealth, power, or renown had publicly "announced for Christ," people would have looked at him as if his nose had been eaten away by weevils. Today it happens regularly . . . Harold Hughes resigns from the U.S. Senate to become an evangelist . . . Jim Irwin, the astronaut, teams up with a Baptist evangelist in an organization called High Flight . . . singers like Pat Boone and Anita Bryant announce for Jesus . . . Charles Colson, the former hard-baller of the Nixon Administration, announces for Jesus . . . The leading candidate for President of the United States, Jimmy Carter, announces for Jesus. O Jesus People.

7. Only one life

In 1961 a copy writer named Shirley Polykoff was working for the Foote, Cone & Belding advertising agency on the Clairol hair-dye account when she came up with the line: "If I've only one life, let me live it as a blonde!" In a single slogan she had summed up what might be described as the secular side of the Me Decade. "If I've only one life, let me live it as a ———!" (You have only to fill in the blank.)

This formula accounts for much of the popularity of the women's liberation or feminist movement. "What does a woman want?" said Freud. Perhaps there are women who want to humble men or reduce their power or achieve equality or even superiority for themselves and their sisters. But for every one such woman, there are nine who simply want to *fill in the blank* as they see fit. If I've only one life, let me live it as . . . a free spirit!" (Instead of . . . a house slave: a cleaning woman, a cook, a nursemaid, a stationwagon hacker, and an occasional household sex aid.) But even that may be overstating it, because often the unconscious desire is nothing more than: *Let's talk about Me.* The great unexpected dividend of the feminist movement has been to elevate an ordinary status—woman, housewife—to the level of drama. One's very existence as *a woman* . . . as *Me* . . . becomes something all the world analyzes, agonizes over, draws cosmic conclusions from, or, in any event, takes seriously. Every woman becomes Emma Bovary, Cousin Bette, or Nora . . . or Erica Jong or Consuelo Saah Baehr.

Among men the formula becomes: "If I've only one life, let me live it as a . . . Casanova or a Henry VIII!" (instead of a humdrum workadaddy, eternally faithful, except perhaps for a mean little skulking episode here and there, to a woman who now looks old enough to be your aunt and needs a shave or else has electrolysis lines above her upper lip, as well as atrophied calves, and is an embarrassment to be seen with when you take her on trips). The right to shuck overripe wives and take on fresh ones was once seen as the prerogative of kings only, and even then it was scandalous. In the 1950's and 1960's it began to be seen as the prerogative of the rich, the powerful, and the celebrated (Nelson Rockefeller, Henry Ford, and Show Business figures), although it retained the odor of scandal. Wife-shucking damaged Adlai Stevenson's chances of becoming President in 1952 and 1956 and Rockefeller's chances of becoming the Republican nominee in 1964 and 1968. Until the 1970's wife-shucking made it impossible for an astronaut to be chosen to go into space. Today, in the Me Decade, it becomes *normal behavior*, one of the factors that has pushed the divorce rate above 50 percent.

When Eugene McCarthy filled in the blank in 1972 and shucked his wife, it was hardly noticed. Likewise in the case of several astronauts. When Wayne Hays filled in the blank in 1976 and shucked his wife of thirty-eight years, it did not hurt his career in the slightest. Copulating with the girl in the office, however, was still regarded as scandalous. (Elizabeth Ray filled in the blank in another popular fashion: "If I've only one life, let me live it as a . . . Celebrity!" As did Arthur Bremer, who kept a diary during his stalking of Nixon and, later, George Wallace . . . with an eye toward a book contract. Which he got.) Some wiseacre has remarked, supposedly with levity, that the federal government may in time have to create reservations for women over thirty-five, to take care of the swarms of shucked wives and widows. In fact, women in precisely those categories have begun setting up communes or "extended families" to provide one another support and companionship in a world without workadaddies. ("If I've only one life, why live it as an anachronism?")

Much of what is now known as the "sexual revolution" has consisted of both women and men filling in the blank this way: "If I've only one life, let me live it as . . . a Swinger!" (Instead of a frustrated, bored monogamist.) In "swinging," a husband and wife give each other license to copulate with other people. There are no statistics on the subject that mean anything, but I do know that it pops up in conversation today in the most unexpected corners of the country. It is an odd experience to be in De Kalb, Illinois, in the very corncrib of America, and have some conventional-looking housewife (not *housewife*, damn it!) come up to you and ask: "Is there much tripling going on in New York?"

"*Tripling?*"

Tripling turns out to be a practice, in De Kalb, anyway, in which a husband and wife invite a third party—male or female, but more often female—over for an evening of whatever, including polymorphous perversity, even the practices written of in the one-hand magazines, such as *Hustler*, all the things involving tubes and hoses and tourniquets and cups and double-jointed sailors.

One of the satisfactions of this sort of life, quite in addition to the groin spasms, is talk: *Let's talk about Me.* Sexual adventurers are given to the most relentless and deadly serious talk . . . about Me. They quickly succeed in placing themselves onstage in the sexual drama whose outlines were sketched by Freud and then elaborated by Wilhelm Reich. Men and women of all sorts, not merely swingers, are given just now to the most earnest sort of talk about the Sexual Me. A key drama of our day is Ingmar Bergman's movie *Scenes from a Marriage*. In it we see a husband and wife who have good jobs and a well-furnished home but who are unable to "communicate"—to cite one of the signature words of the Me Decade. Then they begin to communicate, and thereupon their marriage breaks up and they start divorce proceedings. For the rest of the picture they communicate endlessly, with great candor, but the "relationship"—another signature word—remains doomed. Ironically, the lesson that people seem to draw from this movie has to do with . . . "the need to communicate."

Scenes from a Marriage is one of those rare works of art, like *The Sun Also Rises*, that not only succeed in capturing a certain mental atmosphere in fictional form . . . but also turn around and help radiate it throughout real life. I personally know of two instances in which couples, after years of marriage, went to see *Scenes from a Marriage* and came home convinced of the "need to communicate." The discussions began with one of the two saying, Let's try to be completely candid for once. You tell me exactly what you don't like about me, and I'll do the same for you. At this, the starting point, the whole notion is exciting. We're going to talk about *Me!* (And I can take it.) I'm going to find out what he (or she) really thinks about me! (Of course, I have my faults, but they're minor . . . or else exciting.)

She says, "Go ahead. What don't you like about me?"

They're both under the Bergman spell. Nevertheless, a certain sixth sense tells him that they're on dangerous ground. So he decides to pick something that doesn't seem too terrible.

"Well," he says, "one thing that bothers me is that when we meet people for the first time, you never know what to say. Or else you get nervous and start chattering away, and it's all so banal, it makes me look bad."

Consciously she's still telling herself, "I can take it." But what he has just said begins to seep through her brain like scalding water. What's he talking about?—makes *him* look bad? *He's saying I'm unsophisticated, a social liability and an embarrassment. All those times we've gone out, he's been ashamed of me!* (And what makes it worse—it's the sort of disease for which there's no cure!) She always knew she was awkward. His crime is: he *noticed*! He's known it, too, all along. He's had *contempt* for me.

Out loud she says, "Well, I'm afraid there's nothing I can do about that."

He detects the petulant note. "Look," he says, "you're the one who said to be candid."

She says, "I know. I *want* you to be."

He says, "Well, it's your turn."

"Well," she says, "I'll tell *you* something about when we meet people and when we go places. You never clean yourself properly—you don't know how to wipe yourself. Sometimes we're standing there talking to people, and there's . . . a smell. And I'll tell you something else: People can tell it's you."

And he's still telling *him*self, "I can take it"—but what inna namea Christ is *this?*

He says, "But you've never said anything—about anything like that."

She says, "But I *tried* to. How many times have I told you about your dirty drawers when you were taking them off at night?"

Somehow this really makes him angry . . . All those times . . . and his mind immediately fastens on Harley Thatcher and his wife, whom he has always wanted to impress . . . From underneath my $350 suits I smelled of *shit*! What infuriates him is that this is a humiliation from which there's no recovery. *How often have they sniggered about it later?—or not invited me places? Is it something people say every time my name comes up?* And all at once he is intensely annoyed with his wife, not because she never told him all these years, but simply because she *knows* about his disgrace—and she was the one who *brought him the bad news*!

From that moment on they're ready to get the skewers in. It's only a few minutes before they've begun trying to sting each other with confessions about their little affairs, their little slipping around, their little coitus on the sly—"Remember that time I told you my flight from

Buffalo was canceled?"—and at that juncture the ranks of those *who can take it* become very thin indeed. So they communicate with great candor! and break up! and keep on communicating! and they find the relationship hopelessly doomed.

One couple went into group therapy. The other went to a marriage counselor. Both types of therapy are very popular forms, currently, of *Let's talk about Me.* This phase of the breakup always provides a rush of exhilaration—for what more exhilarating topic is there than . . . *Me*? Through group therapy, marriage counseling, and other forms of "psychological consultation" they can enjoy that same *Me* euphoria that the very rich have enjoyed for years in psychoanalysis. The cost of the new Me sessions is only $10 to $30 an hour, whereas psychoanalysis runs from $50 to $125. The woman's exhilaration, however, is soon complicated by the fact that she is (in the typical case) near or beyond the cutoff age of thirty-five and will have to retire to the reservation.

Well, my dear Mature Moderns . . . Ingmar never promised you a rose garden!

8. *How you do it, my boys!*

In September of 1969, in London, on the King's Road, in a restaurant called Alexander's, I happened to have dinner with a group of people that included a young American named Jim Haynes and an Australian named Germaine Greer. Neither name meant anything to me at the time, although I never forgot Germaine Greer. She was a thin, hard-looking woman with a tremendous curly electric hairdo and the most outrageous Naugahyde mouth I had ever heard on a woman. (I was shocked.) After a while she got bored and set fire to her hair with a match. Two waiters ran over and began beating the flames out with napkins. This made a noise like pigeons taking off in the park. Germaine Greer sat there with a sublime smile on her face, as if to say: "How you do it, my boys!"

Jim Haynes and Germaine Greer had just published the first issue of a newspaper that All London was talking about. It was called *Suck*. It was founded shortly after *Screw* in New York and was one of the progenitors of a line of sex newspapers that today are so numerous that in Los Angeles it is not uncommon to see fifteen coin-operated newspaper racks in a row on the sidewalk. One will be for the Los Angeles *Times*, a second for the *Herald Examiner*, and the other thirteen for the sex papers. *Suck* was full of pictures of gaping thighs, moist lips, stiffened giblets, glistening nodules, dirty stories, dirty poems, essays on sexual freedom, and a gossip column detailing the sexual habits of people whose names I assumed were fictitious. Then

I came to an item that said, "Anyone who wants group sex in New York and likes fat girls, contact L—— R——," except that it gave her full name. She was a friend of mine.

Even while Germaine Greer's hair blazed away, the young American, Jim Haynes, went on with a discourse about the aims of *Suck.* To put it in a few words, the aim was sexual liberation and, through sexual liberation, the liberation of the spirit of man. If you were listening to this speech and had read *Suck*, or even if you hadn't, you were likely to be watching Jim Haynes's face for the beginnings of a campy grin, a smirk, a wink, a roll of the eyeball—something to indicate that he was just having his little joke. But it soon became clear that he was one of those people who exist on a plane quite . . . Beyond Irony. Whatever it had been for him once, sex had now become a religion, and he had developed a theology in which the orgasm had become a form of spiritual ecstasy.

The same curious journey—from sexology to theology—has become a feature of *swinging* in the United States. At the Sandstone sex farm in the Santa Monica Mountains in Los Angeles people of all class levels gather for weekends in the nude. They copulate in the living room, on the lawn, out by the pool, on the tennis courts, with the same open, free, liberated spirit as dogs in the park or baboons in a tree. In conversation, however, the atmosphere is quite different. The air becomes humid with solemnity. Close your eyes, and you think you're at a nineteenth-century Wesleyan summer encampment and tent-meeting lecture series. It's the soul that gets a workout here, brethren. And yet this is not a hypocritical coverup. It is merely an example of how people in even the most secular manifestation of the Me decade —free-lance spread-'em ziggy-zig rutting—are likely to go through the usual stages . . . Let's talk about Me . . . Let's find the Real Me . . . Let's get rid of all the hypocrisies and impediments and false modesties that obscure the Real Me . . . Ah! at the apex of my soul is a spark of the Divine . . . which I perceive in the pure moment of ecstasy (which your textbooks call "the orgasm," but which I know to be heaven) . . .

This notion even has a pedigree. Many sects, such as the Left-handed Shakti and the Gnostic onanists, have construed the orgasm to be the *kairos*, the magic moment, the divine ecstasy. There is evidence that the early Mormons and the Oneida movement did likewise. In fact, the notion of some sort of divine ecstasy runs throughout the religious history of the past twenty-five hundred years. As Max Weber and Joachim Wach have illustrated in detail, every major modern religion, as well as countless long-gone minor ones, has originated not with a theology or a set of values or a social goal or even a vague hope of a life hereafter. They have all originated, instead, with a small circle of people who have shared some overwhelming ecstasy or seizure, a "vision," a "trance," an hallucination; in short, an actual neurological event, a dramatic change in metabolism, something that has seemed to light up the entire central nervous system. The Mohammedan movement (Islam) originated in hallucinations, apparently the result of fasting, meditation, and isolation in the darkness of caves, which can induce sensory deprivation. Some of the same practices were common with many types of Buddhists. The early Hindus and Zoroastrians seem to have been animated by an hallucinogenic drug known as *soma* in India and *haoma* in Persia. The origins of Christianity are replete with "visions." The early Christians used wine for ecstatic purposes, to the point where the Apostle Paul (whose conversion on the road to Damascus began with a "vision") complained that it was degenerating into sheer drunkenness at the services. These great draughts of wine survive in minute quantities in the ritual of Communion. The Bacchic orders, the Sufi, Voodooists, Shakers, and many others used feasts (the bacchanals), ecstatic dancing ("the whirling dervishes"), and other forms of frenzy to achieve the *kairos* . . . the *moment* . . . here and now! . . . the *feeling!* . . . In every case, the believers took the feeling of ecstasy to be the sensation of the light of God flooding into their souls. They felt like vessels of the Divine, of the All-in-One. Only *afterward* did they try to interpret the experience in the form of theologies, earthly reforms, moral codes, liturgies.

Nor have these been merely the strange practices of the Orient and the Middle East. Every major religious wave that has developed in America has started out the same way: with a flood of *ecstatic experiences*. The First Great Awakening, as it is known to historians, came in the 1740's and was led by preachers of the "New Light," such as Jonathan Edwards, Gilbert Tennent, and George Whitefield. They and their followers were known as "enthusiasts" and "come-outers," terms of derision that referred to the frenzied, holy-rolling, pentecostal shout tempo of their services and to their visions, trances, shrieks, and agonies, which are preserved in great Rabelaisian detail in the writings of their detractors.

The Second Great Awakening came in the period from 1825 to 1850 and took the form of a still-wilder hoedown camp-meeting revivalism, of ceremonies in which people barked, bayed, fell down in fits and swoons, rolled on the ground, talked in tongues, and even added a touch of orgy. The Second Awakening originated in western New York State, where so many evangelical movements caught fire it became known as "the Burned-over District." Many new sects, such as Oneida and the Shakers, were involved. But so were older ones, such as the evangelical Baptists. The fervor spread throughout the American frontier (and elsewhere) before the Civil War. The most famous sect of the Second Great Awakening was the Mormon movement, founded by a twenty-five-year-old, Joseph Smith, and a small group of youthful comrades. This bunch was regarded as wilder, crazier, more obscene, more of a threat, than the entire lot of hippie communes of the 1960's put together. Smith was shot to death by a lynch mob in Carthage, Illinois, in 1844, which was why the Mormons, now with Brigham Young at the helm, emigrated to Utah. A sect, incidentally, is a religion with no political power. Once the Mormons settled, built, and ruled Utah, Mormonism became a *religion* soon enough . . . and eventually wound down to the slow, firm beat of respectability . . .

We are now—in the Me Decade—seeing the upward roll (and not yet the crest, by any means) of the third great religious wave in American history, one that historians will very likely term the Third Great Awakening. Like the others it has begun in a flood of *ecstasy*, achieved through LSD and other psychedelics, orgy, dancing (the New Sufi and the Hare Krishna), meditation, and psychic frenzy (the marathon encounter). This third wave has built up from more diverse and exotic sources than the first two, from therapeutic movements as well as overtly religious movements, from hippies and students of "psi phenomena" and Flying Saucerites as well as from charismatic Christians. But other than that, what will historians say about it?

The historian Perry Miller credited the First Great Awakening with helping to pave the way for the American Revolution through its assault on the colonies' religious establishment and, thereby, on British colonial authority generally. The sociologist Thomas F. O'Dea credited the Second Great Awakening with creating the atmosphere of Christian asceticism (known as "bleak" on the East Coast) that swept through the Midwest and the West during the nineteenth century and helped make it possible to build communities in the face of great hardship. And the Third Great Awakening? Journalists—historians have not yet tackled the subject—have shown a morbid tendency to regard the various movements in this wave as "fascist." The hippie movement was often attacked as "fascist" in the late 1960's. Over the past year a barrage of articles has attacked the est movement and the "Moonies" (followers of the Rev. Sun Myung Moon) along the same lines.

Frankly, this tells us nothing except that journalists bring the same conventional Grim Slide concepts to every subject. The word "fascism" derives from the old Roman symbol of power and authority, the *fasces*, a bundle of sticks bound together by thongs (with an ax head protruding from one end). One by one the sticks would be easy to break. Bound together they are indestructible. Fascist ideology called for binding all classes, all levels, all elements of an entire nation together into a single organization with a single will.

The various movements of the current religious wave attempt very nearly the opposite. They begin with . . . "Let's talk about Me." They begin with the most delicious look inward; with considerable narcissism, in short. When the believers bind together into religions, it is always with a sense of splitting off from the rest of society. We, the enlightened (lit by the sparks at the apexes of our souls), hereby separate ourselves from the lost souls around us. Like all religions before them, they proselytize—but always promising the opposite of nationalism: a City of Light that is above it all. There is no ecumenical spirit within this Third Great Awakening. If anything, there is a spirit of schism. The contempt the various gurus and seers have for one another is breathtaking. One has only to ask, say, Oscar Ichazo of Arica about Carlos Castaneda or Werner Erhard of est to learn that Castaneda is a fake and Erhard is a shallow sloganeer. It's exhilarating!—to watch the faithful split off from one another to seek ever more perfect and refined crucibles in which to fan the Divine spark . . . and to *talk about Me.*

Whatever the Third Great Awakening amounts to, for better or for worse, will have to do with this unprecedented post-World War II American luxury: the luxury enjoyed by so many millions of middling folk, of dwelling upon the self. At first glance, Shirley Polykoff's slogan—"If I've only one life, let me live it as a blonde!"—seems like merely another example of a superficial and irritating rhetorical trope (*antanaclasis**) that now happens to be fashionable among advertising copy writers. But in fact the notion of "If I've only one life to live" challenges one of those assumptions of society that are so deep-rooted and ancient they have no name—they are simply lived by. In this case: man's age-old belief in serial immortality.

The husband and wife who sacrifice their own ambitions and their material assets in order to provide a "better future" for their children . . . the soldier who risks his life, or perhaps consciously sacrifices it, in battle . . . the man who devotes his life to some struggle for "his people" that cannot possibly be won in his lifetime . . . people (or most of them) who buy life insurance or leave wills . . . are people who conceive of themselves, however unconsciously, as part of a great

---

* This figure of speech consists of repeating a word (or words with the same root) in such a way that the second usage has a different meaning from the first. "This is WINS, 1010 on your dial—New York wants to *know*, and we *know* it" (1. know = "find out"; 2. know = "realize" or "have the knowledge") . . . "We're American Airlines, *doing* what we *do* best" (1. doing = "performing"; 2. What we do = "our job") . . . "If you think refrigerators cost *too much*, maybe you're looking at *too much* refrigerator" (1. cost; 2. size or complexity). "The smart money *is* on Admiral" (Admiral's italics) . . . There is also an example of the *pun* in the WINS slogan and of *epanadiplosis* in the Admiral slogan (the ABBA pattern of *refrigerator . . . too much/too much refrigerator*).

biological stream. Just as something of their ancestors lives on in them, so will something of them live on in their children . . . or in their people, their race, their community—for childless people, too, conduct their lives and try to arrange their postmortem affairs with concern for how the great stream is going to flow on. Most people, historically, have *not* lived their lives as if thinking, "I have only one life to live." Instead, they have lived as if they are living their ancestors' lives and their offspring's lives and perhaps their neighbors' lives as well. They have seen themselves as inseparable from the great tide of chromosomes of which they are created and which they pass on. The mere fact that you were only going to be here a short time and would be dead soon enough did not give you the license to try to climb out of the stream and change the natural order of things. The Chinese, in ancestor worship, have literally worshipped the great tide itself, and not any god or gods. For anyone to renounce the notion of serial immortality, in the West or the East, has been to defy what seems like a law of nature. Hence the wicked feeling—the excitement!—of "If I've only one life, let me live it as a ———!" Fill in the blank, if you dare.

And now many dare it! In *Democracy in America* de Tocqueville (the inevitable and ubiquitous de Tocqueville) saw the American sense of equality itself as disrupting the stream, which he called "time's pattern": "Not only does democracy make each man forget his ancestors, it hides his descendants from him, and divides him from his contemporaries; it continually turns him back into himself, and threatens, at last, to enclose him entirely in the solitude of his own heart." A grim prospect to the good Alexis de T.— but what did he know about . . . *Let's talk about Me!*

De Tocqueville's idea of modern man lost "in the solitude of his own heart" has been brought forward into our time in such terminology as *alienation* (Marx), *anomie* (Durkheim), the *mass man* (Ortega y Gasset), and *the lonely crowd* (Riesman). The picture is always of a creature uprooted by industrialism, packed together in cities with people he doesn't know, helpless against massive economic and political shifts—in short, a creature like Charlie Chaplin in *Modern Times*, a helpless, bewildered, and dispirited slave of the machinery. This victim of modern times has always been a most appealing figure to intellectuals, artists, and architects. The poor devil so obviously needs *us* to be his Engineers of the Soul, to use a term popular in the Soviet Union in the 1920's. We will pygmalionize this sad lump of clay into a *homo novus*, a New Man, with a new philosophy, a new aesthetics, not to mention new Bauhaus housing and furniture.

But once the dreary little bastards started getting money in the 1940's, they did an astonishing thing—they took their money and ran!

They did something only aristocrats (and intellectuals and artists) were supposed to do—they discovered and started doting on *Me*! They've created the greatest age of individualism in American history! All rules are broken! The prophets are out of business! Where the Third Great Awakening will lead—who can presume to say? One only knows that the great religious waves have a momentum all their own. Neither arguments nor policies nor acts of the legislature have been any match for them in the past. And this one has the mightiest, holiest roll of all, the beat that goes . . . *Me* . . . *Me* . . . *Me* . . . *Me* . . .

The Famous Writer on the College Lecture Circuit

". . . so we are confronted once again with the duality, the bifurcation, the existential dilemma of the writer's task in America, and . . ."

("The little blonde bud from the creative-writing class is a sure thing, but she'll insist on a lot of literary talk first . . . The big redhead on the lecture committee will spare me that, but she talks to me as if I'm seventy years old . . . Little Bud? . . . or Big Red? . . .)

THE INTELLIGENT COED'S GUIDE TO AMERICA

1. O'Hare!

O Mother O'Hare, big bosom for our hungry poets, pelvic saddle for our sexologists and Open Classroom theorists—O houri O'Hare, who keeps her Perm-O-Pour Stoneglow thighs ajar to receive a generation of frustrated and unreadable novelists—

But wait a minute. It may be too early for the odes. Has it even been duly noted that O'Hare, which is an airport outside Chicago, is now the intellectual center of the United States?

Curious, but true. There at O'Hare, on any day, Monday through Friday, from September to June, they sit . . . in row after Mies van der row of black vinyl and stainless steel sling chairs . . . amid soaring walls of plate glass . . . from one tenth to one third of the literary notables of the United States. In October and April, the peak months, the figure goes up to one half.

Masters and Johnson and Erica Jong, Kozol and Rifkin and Hacker and Kael, Steinem and Nader, Marks, Hayden and Mailer, Galbraith and Heilbroner, and your bear-market brothers in the PopEco business, Lekachman & Others—which of you has not hunkered down lately in the prodigious lap of Mother O'Hare!

And why? Because they're heading out into the land to give lectures. They are giving lectures at the colleges and universities of America's heartland, which runs from Fort Lee, New Jersey, on the east to the Hollywood Freeway on the west. Giving lectures in the heartland is one of the lucrative dividends of being a noted writer in America. It

From *Mauve Gloves & Madmen, Clutter & Vine.* First published in *Harper's*, July 1976.

is the writer's faint approximation of, say, Joe Cocker's $25,000 one-night stand at the West Springfield Fair. All the skyways to Lectureland lead through O'Hare Airport. In short, up to one half of our intellectual establishment sits outside of Chicago between planes.

At a literary conference at Notre Dame, I (no stranger to bountiful O'Hare myself) ran into a poet who is noted for his verse celebrating the ecology, née Nature. He lives in a dramatic house nailed together completely from uncut pieces of hickory driftwood, perched on a bluff overlooking the crashing ocean, a spot so remote that you can drive no closer than five miles to it by conventional automobile and barely within a mile and a half by Jeep. The last 7,500 feet it's hand over hand up rocks, vines, and lengths of hemp. I remarked that this must be the ideal setting in which to write about the ecological wonders.

"I wouldn't know," he said. "I do all my writing in O'Hare."

And what is the message that the bards and sages of O'Hare bring to millions of college students in the vast fodderlands of the nation? I'm afraid I must report that it is a gloomy message; morose, even, heading for gangrene.

2. The Frisbee ion

If you happen to attend a conference at which whole contingents of the O'Hare philosophers assemble, you can get the message in all its varieties in a short time. Picture, if you will, a university on the Great Plains . . . a new Student Activities Center the color of butter-almond ice cream . . . a huge interior space with tracks in the floor, along which janitors in green twill pull Expando-Flex accordion walls to create meeting rooms of any size. The conference is about to begin. The students come surging in like hormones. You've heard of rosy cheeks? They *have* them! Here they come, rosy-cheeked, laughing, with Shasta and 7-Up pumping through their veins, talking chipsy, flashing weatherproof smiles, bursting out of their down-filled Squaw Valley jackets and their blue jeans—O immortal denim mons veneris! —looking, all of them, boys and girls, Jocks & Buds & Freaks, as if they spent the day hang-gliding and then made a Miller commercial at dusk and are now going to taper off with a little Culture before returning to the coed dorm. They grow quiet. The conference begins. The keynote speaker, a historian wearing a calfskin jacket and hair like Felix Mendelssohn's, informs them that the United States is "a leaden, life-denying society."

Over the next thirty-six hours, other O'Hare regulars fill in the rest:

Sixty families control one half the private wealth of America, and two hundred corporations own two thirds of the means of production.

"A small group of nameless, faceless men" who avoid publicity the way a werewolf avoids the dawn now dominates American life. In America a man's home is not his castle but merely "a gigantic listening device with a mortgage"—a reference to eavesdropping by the FBI and the CIA. America's foreign policy has been and continues to be based upon war, assassination, bribery, genocide, and the sabotage of democratic governments. "The new McCarthyism" (Joe's, not Gene's) is already upon us. Following a brief charade of free speech, the "gagging of the press" has resumed. Racism in America has not diminished; it is merely more subtle now. The gulf between rich and poor widens daily, creating "permanent ghetto-colonial populations." The decline in economic growth is causing a crisis in capitalism, which will lead shortly to authoritarian rule and to a new America in which everyone waits, in horror, for the knock on the door in the dead of the night, the descent of the knout on the nape of the neck—

How other people attending this conference felt by now, I didn't dare ask. As for myself, I was beginning to feel like Job or Miss Cunégonde. What further devastations or humiliations could possibly be in store, short of the sacking of Kansas City? It was in that frame of mind that I attended the final panel discussion, which was entitled "The United States in the Year 2000."

The prognosis was not good, as you can imagine. But I was totally unprepared for the astounding news brought by an ecologist.

"I'm not sure I want to be alive in the year 2000," he said, although he certainly looked lively enough at the moment. He was about thirty-eight, and he wore a Madras plaid cotton jacket and a Disco Magenta turtleneck jersey.

It seemed that recent studies showed that, due to the rape of the atmosphere by aerosol spray users, by 2000 a certain ion would no longer be coming our way from the sun. I can't remember which one . . . the aluminum ion, the magnesium ion, the neon ion, the gadolinium ion, the calcium ion . . . the calcium ion perhaps; in any event, it was crucial for the formation of bones, and by 2000 it would be no more. Could such a thing be? Somehow this went beyond any of the horrors I was already imagining. I began free-associating . . . Suddenly I could see Lexington Avenue, near where I live in Manhattan. The presence of the storm troopers was the least of it. It was the look of ordinary citizens that was so horrible. Their bones were going. They were dissolving. Women who had once been clicking and clogging down the avenue up on five-inch platform soles, with their pants seams smartly cleaving their declivities, were now mere denim & patent-leather blobs . . . oozing and inching and suppurating along the sidewalk like amoebas or ticks . . . A cab driver puts his arm out the window . . . and it just dribbles down the yellow door like hot Mazola . . . A blind news dealer tries to give change to a notions buyer for Bloomingdale's, and their fingers run together like fettucine over a stack of *New York Posts* . . . It's horrible . . . it's obscene . . . it's the end—

I was so dazed, I was no longer wondering what the assembled students thought of all this. But just at that moment one of them raised his hand. He was a tall boy with a lot of curly hair and a Fu Manchu mustache.

"Yes?" said the ecologist.

"There's one thing I can't understand," said the boy.

"What's that?" said the ecologist.

"Well," said the boy. "I'm a senior, and for four years we've been told by people like yourself and the other gentlemen that everything's in terrible shape, and it's all going to hell, and I'm willing to take your word for it, because you're all experts in your fields. But around here, at this school, for the past four years, the biggest problem, as far as I can see, has been finding a parking place near the campus."

Dead silence. The panelists looked at this poor turkey to try to size him up. Was he trying to be funny? Or was this the native bray of the heartland? The ecologist struck a note of forbearance as he said:

"I'm sure that's true, and that illustrates one of the biggest difficulties we have in making realistic assessments. A university like this, after all, is a middle-class institution, and middle-class life is calculated precisely to create a screen—"

"I understand all that," said the boy. "What I want to know is—how old are you, usually, when it all hits you?"

And suddenly the situation became clear. The kid was no wiseacre! He was genuinely perplexed! . . . For four years he had been squinting at the horizon . . . looking for the grim horrors which he knew—on faith—to be all around him . . . and had been utterly unable to find them . . . and now he was afraid they might descend on him all at once when he least expected it. He might be walking down the street in Omaha one day, minding his own business, when—whop! whop! whop! whop!—War! Fascism! Repression! Corruption!—they'd squash him like bowling balls rolling off a roof!

Who was that lost lad? What was his name? Without knowing it, he was playing the xylophone in a boneyard. He was the unique new creature of the 1970's. He was Candide in reverse. Candide and Miss Cunégonde, one will recall, are taught by an all-knowing savant, Dr. Pangloss. He keeps assuring them that this is "the best of all possible worlds," and they believe him implicitly—even though their lives are one catastrophe after another. Now something much weirder was happening. The Jocks & Buds & Freaks of the heartland have their all-knowing savants of O'Hare, who keep warning them that this is "the worst of all possible worlds," and they know it must be true—and yet life keeps getting easier, sunnier, happier . . . *Frisbee!*

How can such things be?

3. *S-s-s-s-s-s-s-ssssssss*

One Saturday night in 1965 I found myself on a stage at Princeton University with Günter Grass, Allen Ginsberg, Paul Krassner, and an avant-garde filmmaker named Gregory Markopoulos. We were supposed to talk about "the style of the sixties." The auditorium had a big balcony and a lot of moldings. It reminded me of the National Opera House in San José, Costa Rica. The place was packed with about twelve hundred Princeton students and their dates. Before things got started, it was hard to figure out just what they expected. Somebody up in the balcony kept making a sound like a baby crying. Somebody on the main floor always responded with a strange sound he was able to make with his mouth and his cupped hands. It sounded like a raccoon trapped in a garbage can. The baby . . . the raccoon in a can . . . Every time they did it the whole place cracked up, twelve hundred Princeton students and their dates. "Dates" . . . yes . . . this was back before the era of "Our eyes met, our lips met, our bodies met, and then we were introduced."

Anyway, the format was that each man on the stage would make an opening statement about the 1960's, and then the panel discussion would begin. Günter Grass, as Germany's new giant of the novel, the new Thomas Mann, went first. He understood English but didn't feel confident speaking in English, and so he made his statement in German. I doubt that there were ten people in the place who knew what he was saying, but he seemed to speak with gravity and passion. When he finished, there was tremendous applause. Then an interpreter named Albert Harrison (as I recall) delivered Mr. Grass's remarks in English. Sure enough, they were grave and passionate. They were about the responsibility of the artist in a time of struggle and crisis. The applause was even greater than before. Some of the students rose to their feet. Some of the dates rose, too.

The moderator was Paul Krassner, editor of *The Realist* magazine. I remember looking over at Krassner. He looked like one of the trolls that live under the bridge in Norse tales and sit there stroking their molting noses and waiting for hotshots to swagger over the span.

Krassner had to wait for about two minutes for the applause to die down enough to make himself heard. Then he leaned into his microphone and said quite solemnly:

"Thank you, Günter Grass. And thank you, Albert Harrison, for translating . . . Mr. Grass's bar mitzvah speech."

Stunned—like twelve hundred veal calves entering the abattoir. Then came the hissing. Twelve hundred Princeton students & dates started hissing. I had never heard such a sound before . . . an entire hall consumed in hisses . . .

"S-s-s-s-s-s-s-s-s-s-sssssss!"

You couldn't hear yourself talk. You could only hear that sibilant storm. Krassner just sat there with his manic-troll look on, waiting for it to die down. It seemed to take forever. When the storm began to subside a bit, he leaned into the microphone again and said:

"For two years I've been hearing that God is dead. I'm very much relieved to see he only sprung a leak."

For some reason, that stopped the hissing. The kid up in the balcony made a sound like a baby crying. The kid on the main floor made a sound like a raccoon in a garbage can. The crowd laughed and booed, and people tried out new noises. The gyroscope was now gone from the control panel . . . Our trajectory was end over end . . .

The next thing I knew, the discussion was onto the subject of fascism in America. Everybody was talking about police repression and the anxiety and paranoia as good folks waited for the knock on the door and the descent of the knout on the nape of the neck. I couldn't make any sense out of it. I had just made a tour of the country to write a series called "The New Life Out There" for *New York* magazine. This was the mid-1960's. The post-World War II boom had by now pumped money into every level of the population on a scale unparalleled in any nation in history. Not only that, the folks were running wilder and freer than any people in history. For that matter, Krassner himself, in one of the strokes of exuberance for which he was well known, was soon to publish a slight hoax: an account of how Lyndon Johnson was so overjoyed about becoming President that he had buggered a wound in the neck of John F. Kennedy on Air Force One as Kennedy's body was being flown back from Dallas. Krassner presented this as a suppressed chapter from William Manchester's book *Death of a President*. Johnson, of course, was still President when it came out. Yet the merciless gestapo dragnet missed Krassner, who cleverly hid out onstage at Princeton on Saturday nights.

Suddenly I heard myself blurting out over my microphone: "My God, what are you talking about? We're in the middle of a . . . Happiness Explosion!"

That merely sounded idiotic. The kid up in the balcony did the crying baby. The kid down below did the raccoon . . . *Krakatoa, East of Java* . . . I disappeared in a tidal wave of rude sounds . . . Back to the goon squads, search-and-seize and roust-a-daddy . . .

Support came from a quarter I hadn't counted on. It was Grass, speaking in English.

"For the past hour I have my eyes fixed on the doors here," he said. "You talk about fascism and police repression. In Germany when I was a student, they come through those doors long ago. Here they must be very slow."

Grass was enjoying himself for the first time all evening. He was not simply saying, "You really don't have so much to worry about." He was indulging his sense of the absurd. He was saying: "You American intellectuals—you want so desperately to feel besieged and persecuted!"

He sounded like Jean-François Revel, a French socialist writer who talks about one of the great unexplained phenomena of modern astronomy: namely, that the dark night of fascism is always descending in the United States and yet lands only in Europe.

Not very nice, Günter! Not very nice, Jean-François! A bit supercilious, wouldn't you say!

In fact, during the 1960's American intellectuals seldom seemed to realize just how patronizing their European brethren were being. To the Europeans, American intellectuals were struggling so hard (yet once again) to be correct in ideology and in attitude . . . and they were *being* correct . . . impeccable, even—which was precisely what prompted the sniggers and the knowing looks. European intellectuals looked upon American intellectuals much the way English colonial officials used to look upon the swarthy locals who came forward with their Calcutta Toff Oxford accents or their Lagos Mayfair tailored clothes. It was so touching (*then why are you laughing?*) to see the natives try to *do it right*.

I happened to have been in a room in Washington in 1961 when a member of Nigeria's first Cabinet (after independence) went into a long lament about the insidious and seductive techniques the British had used over the years to domesticate his people.

"Just look at *me*!" he said, looking down at his own torso and flipping his hands toward his chest. "Look at this *suit*! A worsted suit on an African—and a *double-breasted waistcoat*!"

He said "double-breasted waistcoat" with the most shriveling self-contempt you can imagine.

"This is what they've done to me," he said softly. "I can't even do the High Life any more."

The High Life was a Low Rent Nigerian dance. He continued to stare down at the offending waistcoat, wondering where he'd left his soul, or his Soul, in any event.

Perhaps someday, if Mr. Bob Silvers's *Confessions* are published, we will read something similar. Silvers is co-editor of *The New York Review of Books.* His accent arrived mysteriously one day in a box from London. Intrigued, he slapped it into his mouth like a set of teeth. It seemed . . . *right.* He began signing up so many English dons to write for *The New York Review of Books* that wags began calling it *The London Review of Bores* and *Don & Grub Street.* He seemed to take this good-naturedly. But perhaps someday we will learn that Mr. Bob Silvers, too, suffered blue moods of the soul and stood in front of a mirror wiggling his knees, trying to jiggle his roots, wondering if his feet could ever renegotiate the Lindy or the Fish or the Hokey-Pokey.

4. Hell's Angels

O how faithfully our native intelligentsia has tried to . . . *do it right!* The model has not always been England. Not at all. Just as frequently it has been Germany or France or Italy or even (on the religious fringe) the Orient. In the old days—seventy-five-or-so years ago—the well-brought-up young intellectual was likely to be treated to a tour of Europe . . . we find Jane Addams recuperating from her malaise in London and Dresden . . . Lincoln Steffens going to college in Heidelberg and Munich . . . Mabel Dodge setting up house in Florence . . . Randolph Bourne discovering Germany's "charming villages" and returning to Bloomfield, New Jersey—*Bloomfield, New Jersey?*—which now "seemed almost too grotesquely squalid and frowsy to be true." The business of being an intellectual and the urge to set oneself apart from provincial life began to be indistinguishable. In July 1921 Harold Stearns completed his anthology called *Civilization in the United States*—a contradiction in terms, he hastened to note—and set sail for Europe. The "Lost Generation" adventure began. But what was the Lost Generation really? It was a post-Great War discount tour in which middle-class Americans, too, not just Bournes and Steffenses, could learn how to become European intellectuals; preferably French.

The European intellectual! What a marvelous figure! A brilliant cynic, dazzling, in fact, set like one of those Gustave Miklos Art Deco sculptures of polished bronze and gold against the smoking rubble of Europe after the Great War. The American intellectual did the best he could. He could position himself against a backdrop of . . . well, not exactly rubble . . . but of the booboisie, the Herd State, the United States of Puritanism, Philistinism, Boosterism, Greed, and the great

Hog Wallow. It was certainly a *psychological* wasteland. For the next fifty years, from that time to this, with ever-increasing skill, the American intellectual would perform this difficult feat, which might be described as the Adjectival Catch Up. The European intellectuals have a real wasteland? Well, we have a psychological wasteland. They have real fascism? Well, we have social fascism (a favorite phrase of the 1930's, amended to "liberal fascism" in the 1960's). They have real poverty? Well, we have relative poverty (Michael Harrington's great Adjectival Catch Up of 1963). They have real genocide? Well, we have cultural genocide (i.e., what universities were guilty of in the late 1960's if they didn't have open-admissions policies for minority groups).

Well—all right! They were difficult, these one-and-a-half gainers in logic. But they were worth it. What had become important above all was to be that polished figure amid the rubble, a vision of sweetness and light in the smoking tar pit of hell. The intellectual had become not so much an occupational type as a status type. He was like the medieval cleric, most of whose energies were devoted to separating himself from the mob—which in modern times, in Revel's phrase, goes under the name of the middle class.

Did he want to analyze the world systematically? Did he want to add to the store of human knowledge? He not only didn't want to, he belittled the notion, quoting Rosa Luxemburg's statement that the "pot-bellied academics" and their interminable monographs and lectures, their intellectual nerve gas, were sophisticated extensions of police repression. Did he even want to change the world? Not particularly; it was much more elegant to back exotic, impossible causes such as the Black Panthers'. Moral indignation was the main thing; that, and a certain pattern of consumption. In fact, by the 1960's it was no longer necessary to produce literature, scholarship, or art—or even to be involved in such matters, except as a consumer—in order to qualify as an intellectual. It was only necessary to live *la vie intellectuelle.* A little brown bread in the bread box, a lapsed pledge card to CORE, a stereo and a record rack full of Coltrane and all the Beatles albums from *Revolver* on, white walls, a huge *Dracaena marginata* plant, which is there because all the furniture is so clean-lined and spare that without this piece of frondose tropical Victoriana the room looks empty, a stack of unread *New York Review of Books* rising up in a surly mound of subscription guilt, the conviction that America is materialistic, repressive, bloated, and deadened by its Silent Majority, which resides in the heartland, three grocery boxes full of pop bottles wedged in behind the refrigerator and destined (one of these days) for the Recycling Center, a small, uncomfortable European car—that pretty well got the job done. By the late 1960's it seemed as if American intellectuals had at last . . . Caught Up. There were riots on the campuses and in the slums. The war in Vietnam had developed into a full-sized hell. War! Revolution! Imperialism! Poverty! I can still remember the ghastly delight with which literary people in New York embraced the Four Horsemen. The dark night was about to descend. All agreed on that; but there were certain ugly, troublesome facts that the native intellectuals, unlike their European mentors, had a hard time ignoring.

By 1967 Lyndon Johnson may have been the very generalissimo of American imperialism in Southeast Asia—but back here in the U.S. the citizens were enjoying freedom of expression and freedom of dissent to a rather astonishing degree. For example, the only major Western country that allowed public showings of *MacBird*—a play that had Lyndon Johnson murdering John F. Kennedy in order to become President—was the United States (Lyndon Johnson, President). The citizens of this fascist bastion, the United States, unaccountably had, and exercised, the most extraordinary political freedom and civil rights in all history. In fact, the government, under the same Johnson, had begun the novel experiment of sending organizers into the slums—in the Community Action phase of the poverty program—to mobilize minority groups to rise up against the government and demand a bigger slice of the pie. (They obliged.) Colored peoples were much farther along the road to equality—whether in the area of rights, jobs, income, or social acceptance—in the United States than were the North Africans, Portuguese, Senegalese, Pakistanis, and Jamaicans of Europe. In 1966 England congratulated herself over the appointment of her first colored policeman (a Pakistani in Coventry). Meanwhile, young people in the U.S.—in the form of the Psychedelic or Flower Generation—were helping themselves to wild times that were the envy of children all over the world.

In short, freedom was in the air like a flock of birds. Just how fascist could it be? This problem led to perhaps the greatest Adjectival Catch Up of all times: Herbert Marcuse's doctrine of "repressive tolerance." Other countries had real repression? Well, we had the obverse, repressive tolerance. This was an insidious system through which the government granted meaningless personal freedoms in order to narcotize the pain of class repression, which only socialism could cure. Beautiful! Well-nigh flawless!

Yet even at the moment of such exquisite refinements—things have a way of going wrong. Another troublesome fact has cropped up, gravely complicating the longtime dream of socialism. That troublesome fact may be best summed up in a name: Solzhenitsyn.

5. *Blaming the messenger*

With the Hungarian uprising of 1956 and the invasion of Czechoslovakia in 1968 it had become clear to Mannerist Marxists such as Sartre that the Soviet Union was now an embarrassment. The fault, however, as *tout le monde* knew, was not with socialism but with Stalinism. Stalin was a madman and had taken socialism on a wrong turn. (Mistakes happen.) Solzhenitsyn began speaking out as a dissident inside the Soviet Union in 1967. His complaints, his revelations, his struggles with Soviet authorities—they merely underscored just how wrong the Stalinist turn had been.

The publication of *The Gulag Archipelago* in 1973, however, was a wholly unexpected blow. No one was ready for the obscene horror and grotesque scale of what Solzhenitsyn called "Our Sewage Disposal System"—in which *tens of millions* were shipped in boxcars to concentration camps all over the country, in which tens of millions died, in which entire races and national groups were liquidated, insofar as they had existed in the Soviet Union. Moreover, said Solzhenitsyn, the system had not begun with Stalin but with Lenin, who had immediately exterminated non-Bolshevik opponents of the old regime and especially the student factions. It was impossible any longer to distinguish the Communist liquidation apparatus from the Nazi.

Yet Solzhenitsyn went still further. He said that not only Stalinism, not only Leninism, not only Communism—but socialism itself led to the concentration camps; and not only socialism, but Marxism; and not only Marxism but any ideology that sought to reorganize morality on an *a priori* basis. Sadder still, it was impossible to say that Soviet socialism was not "real socialism." On the contrary—it was socialism done by experts!

Intellectuals in Europe and America were willing to forgive Solzhenitsyn a great deal. After all, he had been born and raised in the Soviet Union as a Marxist, he had fought in combat for his country, he was a great novelist, he had been in the camps for eight years, he had suffered. But for his insistence that the *isms* themselves led to the death camps—for this he was not likely to be forgiven soon. And in fact the campaign of antisepsis began soon after he was expelled from the Soviet Union in 1974. ("He suffered *too* much—he's crazy." "He's a Christian zealot with a Christ complex." "He's an agrarian reactionary." "He's an egotist and a publicity junkie.")

Solzhenitsyn's tour of the United States in 1975 was like an enormous funeral procession that no one wanted to see. The White House wanted no part of him. *The New York Times* sought to bury his two major speeches, and only the moral pressure of a lone *Times* writer, Hilton Kramer, brought them any appreciable coverage at all. The major television networks declined to run the Solzhenitsyn interview that created such a stir in England earlier this year (it ran on some of the educational channels).

And the literary world in general ignored him completely. In the huge unseen coffin that Solzhenitsyn towed behind him were not only the souls of the *zeks* who died in the Archipelago. No, the heartless bastard had also chucked in one of the last great visions: the intellectual as the Stainless Steel Socialist glistening against the bone heap of capitalism in its final, brutal, fascist phase. There was a bone heap, all right, and it was grisly beyond belief, but socialism had created it.

In 1974, in one of his last speeches, the late Lionel Trilling, who was probably the most prestigious literary critic in the country and had been a professor of English at Columbia for thirty-five years, made what falls under the heading of "a modest proposal." He suggested that the liberal-arts curriculum in the universities be abandoned for one generation.

His argument ran as follows: Children come to the university today, and they register, and they get the student-activity card and the map of the campus and the university health booklet, and just about as automatically they get a packet of cultural and political attitudes. That these attitudes are negative or cynical didn't seem to be what worried Trilling. It was more that they are dispensed and accepted with such an air of conformity and inevitability. The student emerges from the university with a set of ready-mades, intact, untouched by direct experience. What was the solution? Well—why not turn off the packaging apparatus for a while? In time there might develop a generation of intelligent people who had experienced American life directly and "earned" their opinions.

Whether his proposal was serious or not, I couldn't say. But somehow he made me think once more of the Lost Lad of the Great Plains, the Candide in Reverse,

Who asked how old you had to be
Before the O'Hare curse
Coldcocked you like the freight train
Of history—
Tell me, are you willing,
Lost Lad, to pick yourself some
Intelligent lost coed Cunégonde

And head out shank-to-flank in Trilling's
Curriculum?
Will you hector *tout le monde*?
Will you sermonize
On how perceiving
Is believing
The heresy of your own eyes?

Boyhood Dreams

"A sniper? The media coverage is good—but when it's over, they throw you in the nuthouse, and that's that. Me, I want to go to Europe and kidnap industrialists for the Revolution and write a book about it and make a lot of money."

MAUVE GLOVES & MADMEN, CLUTTER & VINE

The well-known American writer . . . but perhaps it's best not to say exactly which well-known American writer . . . they're a sensitive breed! The most ordinary comments they take personally! And why would the gentleman we're about to surprise be any exception? He's in his apartment, a seven-room apartment on Riverside Drive, on the West Side of Manhattan, in his study, seated at his desk. As we approach from the rear, we notice a bald spot on the crown of his head. It's about the size of a Sunshine Chip-a-Roo cookie, this bald spot, freckled and toasty brown. Gloriously suntanned, in fact. Around this bald spot swirls a corona of dark-brown hair that becomes quite thick by the time it completes its mad Byronic rush down the back over his turtleneck and out to the side in great bushes over his ears. He knows the days of covered ears are numbered, because this particular look has become somewhat *Low Rent*. When he was coming back from his father's funeral, half the salesmen lined up at O'Hare for the commuter flights, in their pajama-striped shirts and diamond-print double-knit suits, had groovy hair much like his. And to think that just six years ago such a hairdo seemed . . . so defiant!

Meeting his sideburns at mid-jowl is the neck of his turtleneck sweater, an authentic Navy turtleneck, and the sweater tucks into his Levi's, which are the authentic Original XX Levi's, the original straight stovepipes made for wearing over boots. He got them in a bona fide cowhand's store in La Porte, Texas, during his trip to Houston to be the keynote speaker in a lecture series on "The American Dream: Myth and Reality." No small part of the latter was a fee of two thousand dollars plus expenses. This outfit, the Navy turtleneck

From *Mauve Gloves & Madmen, Clutter & Vine.* First published in *Esquire*, December 1975.

and the double-X Levi's, means work & discipline. *Discipline!* as he says to himself every day. When he puts on these clothes, it means that he intends to write, and do nothing else, for at least four hours. *Discipline*, Mr. Wonderful!

But on the desk in front of him—that's not a manuscript or even the beginnings of one . . . that's *last month's bank statement*, which just arrived in the mail. And those are his canceled checks in a pile on top of it. In that big ledger-style checkbook there (the old-fashioned kind, serious-looking, with no crazy Peter Max designs on the checks) are his check stubs. And those slips of paper in the promiscuous heap are all unpaid bills, and he's taking the nylon cover off his Texas Instruments desk calculator, and he is about to measure the flow, the tide, the mad sluice, the crazy current of the money that pours through his fingers every month and which is now running against him in the most catastrophic manner, like an undertow, a riptide, pulling him under—

—him and this apartment, which cost him $75,000 in 1972; $20,000 cash, which came out of the $25,000 he got as a paperback advance for his fourth book, *Under Uncle's Thumb*, and $536.36 a month in bank-loan payments (on the $55,000 he borrowed) ever since, plus another $390 a month in so-called maintenance, which has steadily increased until it is now $460 a month . . . and although he already knows the answer, the round number, he begins punching the figures into the calculator . . . 536.36 plus . . . 460 . . . times 12 . . . and the calculator keys go *chuck chuck chuck chuck* and the curious little orange numbers, broken up like stencil figures, go trucking across the black path of the display panel at the top of the machine, giving a little orange shudder every time he hits the *plus* button, until there it is, stretching out seven digits long—11956.32—$12,000 a year! One thousand dollars a month—this is what he spends on his apartment alone!—and by May he will have to come up with another $6,000 so he can rent the house on Martha's Vineyard again *chuck chuck chuck chuck* and by September another $6,750—$3,750 to send his daughter, Amy, to Dalton and $3,000 to send his son, Jonathan, to Collegiate (on those marvelous frog-and-cricket evenings up on the Vineyard he and Bill and Julie and Scott and Henry and Herman and Leon and Shelly and the rest, all Media & Lit. people from New York, have discussed why they send their children to private schools, and they have pretty well decided that it is the educational turmoil in the New York public schools that is the problem—the kids just wouldn't be educated!—plus some considerations of their children's personal safety—but—needless to say!—it has nothing to do with the matter of . . . well, *race*) and he punches that in . . . 6750 . . . *chuck chuck chuck chuck* . . . and hits the *plus* button . . . an orange shimmer . . . and beautiful! there's the figure—the three items, the apartment in town, the summer place, and the children's schooling—$24,706.32!—almost $25,000 a year in fixed costs, just for a starter! for lodging and schooling! nothing else included! A grim nut!

It's appalling, and he's drowning, and this is only the beginning of it, just the basic grim nut—and yet in his secret heart he loves these little sessions with the calculator and the checks and the stubs and the bills and the marching orange numbers that stretch on and on . . . into such magnificently huge figures. It's like an electric diagram of his infinitely expanding life, a scoreboard showing the big league he's now in. Far from throwing him into a panic, as they well might, these tote sessions are one of the most satisfying habits he has. A regular vice! Like barbiturates! Calming the heart and slowing the respiration! Because it seems *practical*, going over expenses, his conscience sanctions it as a permissible way to avoid the only thing that can possibly keep him afloat: namely, more writing . . . He's deep into his calculator trance now . . . The orange has him enthralled. Think of it! He has now reached a stage in his life when not only a $1,000-a-month apartment but also a summer house on an island in the Atlantic is an absolute necessity—precisely that, absolute necessity . . . It's appalling! —and yet it's the most inexplicable bliss!—nothing less.

As for the apartment, even at $1,000 a month it is not elegant. Elegance would cost at least twice that. No, his is an apartment of a sort known as West Side Married Intellectual. The rooms are big, the layout is good, but the moldings, cornices, covings, and chair rails seem to be corroding. Actually, they are merely lumpy from too many coats of paint over the decades, and the parquet sections in the floor have dried out and are sprung loose from one another. It has been a long time since this apartment has had an owner who could both meet the down-payment nut *and* have the woodwork stripped and the flooring replaced. The building has a doorman but no elevator man, and on Sundays the door is manned by a janitor in gray khaki work clothes. But what's he supposed to do? He needs seven rooms. His son and daughter now require separate bedrooms. He and his wife require a third one (a third and fourth if the truth be known, but he has had to settle for three). He now needs, not just likes, this study he's in, a workroom that is his exclusively. He now *needs* the dining room, which is a real dining room, not a dogleg off the living room. Even if he is giving only a cocktail party, it is . . . *necessary* that they (one & all) note—however unconsciously—that he *does* have a dining room!

Right here on his desk are the canceled checks that have come in hung over from the cocktail party he gave six weeks ago. They're right in front of him now . . . $209.60 to the florists, Clutter & Vine, for flowers for the hallway, the living room, the dining room, and the study, although part of that, $100, was for a bowl of tightly clustered silk poppies that will become a permanent part of the living-room decor . . . $138.18 to the liquor store (quite a bit was left over however, meaning that the bar will be stocked for a while) . . . $257.50 to Mauve Gloves & Madmen, the caterers, even though he had chosen some of the cheaper hors d'oeuvres. He also tipped the two butlers $10 each, which made him feel a little foolish later when he learned that one of them was co-owner of Mauve Gloves & Madmen . . . $23.91 to the grocery store for he couldn't remember what . . . $173.95 to the Russian Tea Room for dinner afterward with Henry and Mavis (the guests of honor) and six other stragglers . . . $12.84 for a serving bowl from Bloomingdale's . . . $20 extra to the maid for staying on late . . . and he's chucking all these figures into the calculator *chuck chuck chuck chuck* blink blink blink blink *truck truck truck truck* the slanted orange numbers go trucking and winking across the panel . . . 855.98 . . . $855.98 for a cocktail party!—not even a dinner party!—appalling! —and how slyly sweet . . .

Should he throw in the library stairs as a party expense, too? Perhaps, he thought, if he were honest, he would. The checks were right here: $420 to Lum B. Lee Ltd. for the stairs themselves, and another $95 to the customs broker to get the thing through customs and $45 to the trucker to deliver it, making a total of $560! In any event, they're terrific . . . Mayfair heaven . . . the classic English type, stairs to nowhere, going up in a spiral around a central column, carved in the ancient bamboo style, rising up almost seven feet, so he can reach books on his highest shelf . . . He had had it made extra high by a cabinetmaking firm in Hong Kong, the aforementioned Lum B. Lee . . . Now, if the truth be known, the stairs are the result of a habit he has: he goes around the apartment after giving a party and stands where he saw particular guests standing, people who stuck in his mind, and tries to see what they saw from that position; in other words, how the apartment looked in their eyes. About a year ago he had seen Lenny Johns of the *Times* standing in the doorway of his study and looking in, so afterward, after Lenny and everyone else had gone, he took up the same position and looked in . . . and what he saw did not please him. In fact, it looked sad. Through Lenny Johns's eyes it must have looked like the basic writer's workroom out of *Writer's Digest*: a plain Danish-style desk (The Door Store) with dowel legs (dowel legs!), a modernistic (modernistic!) metal-and-upholstery office swivel chair, a low-slung (more Modernismus!) couch, a bank of undistinguished-looking file cabinets, a bookcase covering one entire wall but made of plain white-painted boards and using the wall itself as its back. The solution, as he saw it—without going into huge costs—was the library stairs—the stairs to nowhere!—an object indisputably useful and yet with an air of elegant folly!

It was after that same party that his wife had said to him: "Who was that weepy-looking little man you were talking to so much?"

"I don't know who you're talking about."

"The one with the three strands of hair pulled up from the side and draped over his scalp."

He knew she was talking about Johns. And he knew *she* knew Johns's name. She had met him before, on the Vineyard.

Meeting Lenny Johns socially was one of the many dividends of Martha's Vineyard. They have been going there for three summers now, renting a house on a hill in Chilmark . . . until it has become, well, a *necessity!* It's no longer possible to stay in New York over the summer. It's not fair to the children. They shouldn't have to grow up that way. As for himself, he's gotten to know Lenny and Bill and Scott and Julie and Bob and Dick and Jody and Gillian and Frank and Shelly and the rest in a way that wouldn't be possible in New York. But quite aside from all that . . . just that clear sparkling late-August solitude, when you can smell the pine and the sea . . . heading down the piney path from the house on the hill . . . walking two hundred yards across the marshes on the pedestrian dock, just one plank wide, so that you have to keep staring down at it . . . it's hypnotic . . . the board, the marsh grass, your own tread, the sound of the frogs and the crickets . . . and then getting into the rowboat and rowing across the inlet to . . . the *dune* . . . the great swelling dune, with the dune grass waving against the sky on top . . . and then over the lip of it—to the beach! the most pristine white beach in the world! and the open sea . . . all spread out before you—yours! Just that! the sand, the sea, the sky—and solitude! No gates, no lifeguard stands, no concessions, no sprawling multitudes of transistor radios and plaid plastic beach chairs . . .

It is chiefly for these summers on the Vineyard that he has bought a car, a BMW sedan—$7,200—but very lively! It costs him $76 a month to keep it in a garage in the city for nine months of the year, another $684 in all, so that the hard nut for Martha's Vineyard is really $6,684—but it's a necessity, and one sacrifices for necessities. After three years on the Vineyard he feels very possessive about the place, even though he's a renter, and he immediately joined in with the move to publish a protest against "that little Albanian with a pickup truck," as he was (wrongly) called, some character named Zarno or something who had assembled a block of fifty acres on the Vineyard and was going to develop it into 150 building lots—one third of an acre each! (Only dimly did he recall that the house he grew up in, in Chicago, had been on about one fifth of an acre and hadn't seemed terribly hemmed in.) Bill T—— wrote a terrific manifesto in which he talked about "these Snopes-like little men with their pickup trucks"—Snopes-like!—and all sorts of people signed it.

This campaign against the developers also brought the New York Media & Lit. people into contact for the first time with the Boston people. Until the Media & Lit. people began going there about ten years before, Martha's Vineyard had always been a Boston resort, "Boston" in the most proper social sense of the word. There wasn't much the Boston people could do about the New York people except not associate with them. When they said "New York people," they no doubt meant "Jews & Others," he figured. So when he was first invited to a Boston party, thanks to his interest in the anti-developers campaign, he went with some trepidation and with his resentment tucked into his waistband like a .38. His mood darkened still more when he arrived in white ducks and an embroidered white cotton shirt, yoke-shouldered and open to the sternum—a little eccentric (actually a harmless sort of shirt known in Arizona as Fruit Western) but perfectly in the mood of standard New York People Seaside Funk—and found that the Boston men, to a man, had on jackets and ties. Not only that, they had on their own tribal colors. The jackets were mostly navy blazers, and the ties were mostly striped ties or ties with little jacquard emblems on them, but the pants had a go-to-hell air: checks and plaids of the loudest possible sort, madras plaids, yellow-on-orange window-pane checks, crazy-quilt plaids, giant houndstooth checks, or else they were a solid airmail red or taxi yellow or some other implausible go-to-hell color. They finished that off with loafers and white crew socks or no socks at all. The pants were their note of Haitian abandon . . . weekends by the sea. At the same time the jackets and ties showed they had not forgotten for a moment where the power came from. He felt desolate. He slipped the loaded resentment out of his waistband and cocked it. And then the most amazing thing happened—

His hostess came up and made a fuss over him! Exactly! She had read *Under Uncle's Thumb!* So had quite a few of the men, infernal pants and all! Lawyers and investment counselors! They were all interested in him! Quite a stream—he hardly had to move from the one spot all evening! And as the sun went down over the ocean, and the alcohol rose, and all of their basted teeth glistened—he could almost see something . . . *presque vu!* . . . a glimmer of the future . . . something he could barely make out . . . a vision in which America's best minds, her intellectuals, found a common ground, a natural unity, with the enlightened segments of her old aristocracy, her old money . . . the two groups bound together by . . . but by what? . . . he could *almost* see it, but not quite . . . it was *presque vu* . . . it was somehow a matter of taste . . . of sensibility . . . of grace, natural grace . . . just as he himself had a natural feel for the best British styles, which were after all the source of the Boston manners . . . What were the library stairs, if they weren't that? What were the Lobb shoes?

For here, now, surfacing to the top of the pile, is the check for $248 to John Lobb & Sons Ltd. Boot Makers—that was the way he wrote it out, Boot Makers, two words, the way it was on their bosky florid London letterhead—$248!—for one pair of shoes!—from England!—handmade! And now, all at once, even as *chuck chuck chuck* he punches it into the calculator, he is swept by a wave of sentiment, of sadness, sweet misery—guilt! Two hundred and forty-eight dollars for a pair of handmade shoes from England . . . He thinks of his father. He wore his first pair of Lobb shoes to his father's funeral. Black cap toes they were, the most formal daytime shoes made, and it was pouring that day in Chicago and his incomparable new shoes from England were caked with mud when he got back to his father's house. He took the shoes off, but then he froze—he couldn't bring himself to remove the mud. His father had come to the United States from Russia as a young man in 1922. He had to go to work at once, and in no time, it seemed, came the Depression, and he struggled through it as a tailor, although in the forties he acquired a dry-cleaning establishment and, later, a second one, plus a diaper-service business and a hotel-linen service. But this brilliant man—oh, how many times had his mother assured him of that!—had had to spend all those years as a tailor. This cultivated man!—more assurances—oh, how many yards of Goethe and Dante had he heard him quote in an accent that gripped the English language like a full nelson! And now his son, the son of this brilliant, cultivated but uneducated and thwarted man—now his son, his son with his education and his literary career, his son who had never had to work with his hands more than half an hour at a stretch in his life—his son had turned up at his funeral in a pair of handmade shoes from England! . . . Well, he let the mud dry on them. He didn't touch them for six months. He didn't even put the shoe trees (another $47) in. Perhaps the goddamned boots would curl up and die.

The number . . . 248 . . . is sitting right up there in slanted orange digits on the face of the calculator. That seems to end the reverie. He doesn't want to continue it just now. He doesn't want to see the 6684 for Martha's Vineyard up there again for a while. He doesn't want to see the seven digits of his debts (counting the ones after the decimal point) glowing in their full, magnificent, intoxicating length. It's time to get serious! *Discipline!* Only one thing will pull him out of all this: work . . . writing . . . and there's no way to put it off any longer. *Discipline*, Mr. Wonderful! This is the most difficult day of all, the day when it falls to his lot to put a piece of paper in the typewriter and start on page 1 of a new book, with that horrible arthritic siege—

writing a book!—stretching out ahead of him (a tubercular blue glow, as his mind comprehends it) . . . although it lifts his spirits a bit to know that both *The Atlantic* and *Playboy* have expressed an interest in running chapters as he goes along, and *Penthouse* would pay even more, although he doesn't want it to appear in a one-hand magazine, a household aid, as literary penicillin to help quell the spirochetes oozing from all the virulent vulvas . . . Nevertheless! help is on the way! Hell!—there's not a magazine in America that wouldn't publish something from this book!

So he feeds a sheet of paper into his typewriter, and in the center, one third of the way down from the top, he takes care of the easy part first—the working title, in capital letters:

RECESSION AND REPRESSION
POLICE STATE AMERICA
AND THE SPIRIT OF '76

VIGNETTES*

* From *In Our Time* (New York: Farrar, Straus and Giroux, 1980). First published in *Harper's*.

THE LOWER CLASSES

No. 1. The Down-filled People

They wear down-filled coats in public. Out on the ski slopes they look like hand grenades. They have "audio systems" in their homes and know the names of hit albums. They drive two-door cars with instrument panels like an F-16's. They like High-Tech furniture, track lighting, glass, and brass. They actually go to plays in New York and follow professional sports. The down-filled men wear turtleneck sweaters and Gucci belts and loafers and cover parts of their ears with their hair. The down-filled women still wear cowl-necked sweaters and carry Louis Vuitton handbags. The down-filled people strip wood and have interior walls removed. They put on old clothes before the workmen come over. In the summer they like cabins on fresh water and they go hiking. They regard *Saturday Night Live* and Steve Martin as funny. They say "I hear you," meaning "I understand what you're saying." They say "Really," meaning "That's right." When down-filled strangers are at a loss for words, they talk about real-estate prices.

No. 2. Bliss SoHo Boho

Oh, to be young and come to New York and move into your first loft and look at the world with eyes that light up even the rotting fire-escape railings, even the buckling pressed-tin squares on the ceiling, even the sheet-metal shower stall with its belly dents and rusting seams, the soot granules embedded like blackheads in the dry rot of the window frames, the basin with the copper-green dripping-spigot stains in the cracks at the bottom, the door with its crowbar-notch history of twenty-five years of break-ins, the canvas-bottom chairs that cut off the circulation in the sural arteries of the leg, the indomitable roach that appears every morning in silhouette on the cord of the hot plate, the doomed yucca straining for light on the windowsill, the two cats nobody ever housebroke, the garbage trucks with the grinder whine, the leather freaks and health-shoe geeks, the punkers with chopped hair and Korean warm-up jackets, the herds of Uptown Boutique bohemians who arrive every weekend by radio-call cab, the bag ladies who sit on the standpipes swabbing the lesions on their ankles—oh, to be young and in New York and to have eyes that light up all things with the sweetest and most golden glow!

No. 3. Victims of Inflation

So I go to the place and I tell the guy I want four of those captain's swivel seats for my van, in leather, to go with the lounge banquette underneath the thermo bay in back, and you know what he tells me? One-half down, 20 percent interest on the balance for two years on a five-year payout basis with a $750 balloon payment at the end!"

"I hear you. This dude who's giving my wife flying lessons, he says he's gonna start charging $35 an hour. I told him he can fly that one right up the freaking pipe!"

The Modern Churchman

He was a socially acceptable but obscure minister to the Tassel Loafer & Tennis Lesson Set until the day in 1975 when he announced that he was a pederast. He not only announced it, he enunciated his theory that the sexual life of the child was an essential part of, not an obstacle to, the spiritual life of the child, and that anyone who doubted that God had created a link of sexual attraction between generations was an upland Tennessee aborigine. Half of his congregation walked out, but the other half was stimulated by the television coverage. The diocesan governors had long been troubled by declining church membership and felt that here, at last, was a Modern Churchman who could Reach the Urban Young People. Emboldened by a measure of fame and official support, he enunciated the theory that terrorists were God's Holy Beasts, arguing that Jesus had entered the temple with a flog or cat-o'-nine-tails, according to which Renaissance painting one looked at, to drive the moneychangers out and that the Mexican artist David Alfaro Siqueiros had once led a machine-gun raid on the home of Leon Trotsky. He was a great supporter of the arts, and in his home, an old carriage house redone in nail patterns by Ronaldo Clutter, the interior designer, the painting frame had replaced the cross as a religious symbol. When he held a Holy Roller Disco Night in the sanctuary and urged the recitation of the prayer book "in tongues," he was featured in the Religion sections of both *Time* and *Newsweek*, and his elevation to bishop was said to be imminent.

Primitive Cultures

Professor Nkhrani Emu
Chairman, Department of Anthropology
University of Chembuezi
Babuelu, Chembuezi

Most Esteemed Professor:

As you know, dear Sir, our research team is approaching the end of its field study of "The Sexual Mores of the Americans." I hereby request, most respectfully, that we be granted an extension of the term of our project and a renewal of funding for this work. It is impossible for anyone in a society such as ours to envision from afar the bizarre sexual customs, practices, and rituals to be observed among the American people.

In the republic's largest city, New York, the most prestigious form of entertainment takes place in theaters that have been converted to dance halls. Hundreds of young males may be seen dancing with one another to flashing lights and recorded music in a homoerotic frenzy, while prominent citizens, including politicians, lawyers, financiers, and upper-class matrons, as well as every sort of well-known figure in the arts, most of them heterosexual, look on, apparently greatly stimulated by the atmosphere. This is described in the native press as "disco fever."

In fact, the mores that have grown up among the Americans concerning homosexuality are apt to be most baffling to the investigator first arriving from a society such as ours. In the United States it is the homosexual male who takes on the appearance that in our society is associated with heterosexual masculinity. Which is to say, he wears his hair short in a style known as the *crew cut* or *butch cut*; he wears the simple leather jacket, sleeveless shirt, crew sweater, or steel-toed boot of the day laborer, truck driver, soldier, or sailor; and, if he exercises, he builds up the musculature of his upper arms and chest. The heterosexual male, by contrast, wears long hair, soft open-throated shirts that resemble a woman's blouse, necklaces, gold wristwatches, shapeless casual jackets of a sort worn also by women; and if he exercises, he goes in for a feminine form of running called *jogging*.

The most popular periodicals in America consist of photographs of young women with gaping pudenda and text of a purportedly serious nature, such as interviews with presidents of the republic (!). These are known as "one-hand magazines."

It is the custom throughout the native schools of America to give *sex education* in the classroom to children by the age of thirteen. The children are taught that sexual intercourse is natural, beautiful, and the highest expression of human love. They are also taught that sexual energy is one of a person's most powerful and creative forces, that it will find expression in some form, that it should not be denied. Yet the Americans are at the same time baffled by the fact that the number of pregnancies out of wedlock among schoolgirls rises continually. In this the Americans are somewhat like the Kombanda tribesmen of our country, who, ignorant of the causal relation of activities separated by time, believe that pregnancy is caused by the sun shining on the bare midsections of females of a certain age. The administrators of the American schools remain bewildered, saying that in the sex-education classes females are given pamphlets clearly outlining birth-control procedures. At the same time, their own records show that only a fraction of American secondary-school graduates can read.

So, most revered Sir, we beseech your support in obtaining for us the resources to complete our work. You will recall, Sir, pointing out to us the importance of Diedrich's discovery of the Luloras, the tribe that made its women climb trees and remain there throughout their menstrual periods. Well, Sir—in all humility!—we are convinced that through our work here we have uncovered a yet more primitive layer in the anthropology of human sexual evolution.

Your worshipful student and friend,
Pottho Mboti

New York City
United States of America

The Invisible Wife

The Invisible Wife arrived at the party with Her Husband, but Her Husband was soon vectored off into another room by one of his great manswarm of chums, who began pouring an apparently delicious story down his ear.

The Invisible Wife had gone to the trouble of getting a sideswept multi-chignon hairdo and a Rue St. Honoré Chloe dress with enormous padded shoulders surmounted by piles of beading sewn on as thick as the topping on a peach melba precisely in order to cease being invisible. But from the moment the social current swept her into the path of Her Husband's business friend Earl, her intracranial alarm system warned her that *it* would happen, nonetheless.

After all, she had only been introduced to Earl four times in the past, at four different parties, and this time Her Husband was in another room.

"Hello, Earl," she said clearly and brightly, looking him straight in the eyes.

Earl's lips spread across his face in a great polyurethaned smile. But his eyes were pure panic. They contracted into two little round balls, like a pair of Gift Shop Lucite knickknacks. "Mayday!" they said. "Code Blue! I've met this woman somewhere, but who inna namea Christ is she?"

"Ohh!" he said. "Ahh! Howya doin'! Yes!—"

The little Lucite balls were bouncing all over her, over her hairdo, chignon by chignon, over her blazing shoulders, her dress, her Charles Jourdan shoes, searching for a clue.

"How're the children!" he exclaimed finally, taking a desperate chance.

This was the deepest wound of all for the Invisible Wife. The man had just passed his eyes over $1,650 worth of Franco-American chic and decided that the main thing about her was . . . she looked *matronly*.

How're the children . . . "They've got Legionnaire's disease," she wanted to say, because she knew these people didn't listen to the Invisible Wife. But she went ahead and did the usual.

"Oh, they're fine," she said.

"That's great!" Earl said. "That's great!" He kept saying "That's great" and looking straight through her, frantically trying to devise some way to remove himself from her presence before somebody he knew approached and he was faced with the impossible task of *introducing* her.

At dinner the Invisible Wife sat next to a man who was an investment counselor with an evident interest in convertible debentures. *Convertible debentures!* An adrenal surge of hope rose in the Invisible Wife. Somewhere down Memory Lane she had actually picked up a conversational nugget concerning convertible debentures. This nugget had to do with an extraordinary mathematician from MIT named Edward O. Thorp who, using computers, had devised an *extrinsic formula* for beating the stock market by playing convertible debentures. So she introduced her conversational nugget—Edward O. Thorp and the Convertible Debentures—into the conversation. She dropped it in, just so, ever so lightly; for, being a veteran of dinners like this, she knew that a woman can ask questions, introduce topics, interject the occasional *bon mot*, even deliver a punch line now and again, but she is not to launch into disquisitions or actually *tell long stories* herself.

"Edward O. Thorp!" the Investment Counselor said. "Oh my God!" —and the Invisible Wife was pleased to see that this topic absolutely delighted the Investment Counselor. He launched into an anecdote that lit up his irises like a pair of bed-lamp high-intensity bulbs. There is nothing that a man hungers for more at dinner than to dominate the conversation in his sector of the table.

The Invisible Wife soon noticed, however, that when the man sitting on the other side of her turned their way to listen in, the Investment Counselor looked right past her and directed the entire story into *the man's* face. Not only that, when this man was distracted for a moment by the woman on his other side, the Investment Counselor stopped talking, as if his switch had been turned off. He stopped in mid-sentence, and his eyes clouded up, and he just waited, with his mouth open.

After all, why waste a terrific yarn on an Invisible Wife?

Artistic Vision

Artists from Cincinnati and Cleveland, hot off the Carey airport bus, line up in Soho looking for the obligatory loft.

THE APACHE DANCE

People don't read the morning newspaper, Marshall McLuhan once said, they slip into it like a warm bath. Too true, Marshall! Imagine being in New York City on the morning of Sunday, April 28, 1974, like I was, slipping into that great public bath, that vat, that spa, that regional physiotherapy tank, that White Sulphur Springs, that Marienbad, that Ganges, that River Jordan for a million souls which is the Sunday *New York Times*. Soon I was submerged, weightless, suspended in the tepid depths of the thing, in Arts & Leisure, Section 2, page 19, in a state of perfect sensory deprivation, when all at once an extraordinary thing happened:

I *noticed something!*

Yet another clam-broth-colored current had begun to roll over me, as warm and predictable as the Gulf Stream . . . a review, it was, by the *Times*'s dean of the arts, Hilton Kramer, of an exhibition at Yale University of "Seven Realists," seven realistic painters . . . when I was *jerked alert* by the following:

"Realism does not lack its partisans, but it does rather conspicuously lack a persuasive theory. And given the nature of our intellectual commerce with works of art, to lack a persuasive theory is to lack something crucial—the means by which our experience of individual works is joined to our understanding of the values they signify."

Now, you may say, My God, man! You woke up over *that*? You forsook your blissful coma over a mere swell in the sea of words?

But I knew what I was looking at. I realized that without making the slightest effort I had come upon one of those utterances in search of which psychoanalysts and State Department monitors of the Moscow or Belgrade press are willing to endure a lifetime of tedium: namely,

---

From *The Painted Word*, pp. 3–23 (New York: Farrar, Straus and Giroux, 1975). First published in *Harper's*, April 1975.

the seemingly innocuous *obiter dicta,* the words in passing, that give the game away.

What I saw before me was the critic-in-chief of *The New York Times* saying: In looking at a painting today, "to lack a persuasive theory is to lack something crucial." I read it again. It didn't say "something helpful" or "enriching" or even "extremely valuable." No, the word was *crucial.*

In short: frankly, these days, without a theory to go with it, I can't *see* a painting.

Then and there I experienced a flash known as the *Aha!* phenomenon, and the buried life of contemporary art was revealed to me for the first time. The fogs lifted! The clouds passed! The motes, scales, conjunctival bloodshots, and Murine agonies fell away!

All these years, along with countless kindred souls, I am certain, I had made my way into the galleries of Upper Madison and Lower SoHo and the Art Gildo Midway of Fifty-seventh Street, and into the museums, into the Modern, the Whitney, and the Guggenheim, the Bastard Bauhaus, the New Brutalist, and the Fountainhead Baroque, into the lowliest storefront churches and grandest Robber Baronial temples of Modernism. All these years I, like so many others, had stood in front of a thousand, two thousand, God-knows-how-many thousand Pollocks, de Koonings, Newmans, Nolands, Rothkos, Rauschenbergs, Judds, Johnses, Olitskis, Louises, Stills, Franz Klines, Frankenthalers, Kellys, and Frank Stellas, now squinting, now popping the eye sockets open, now drawing back, now moving closer—waiting, waiting, forever waiting for . . . *it* . . . for *it* to come into focus, namely, the visual reward (for so much effort) which must be there, which everyone (*tout le monde*) knew to be there—waiting for something to radiate directly from the paintings on these invariably pure white walls, in this room, in this moment, into my own optic chiasma. All these years, in short, I had assumed that in art, if nowhere else, seeing is believing. Well—how very shortsighted! Now, at last, on April 28, 1974, I could *see.* I had gotten it backward all along. Not "seeing is believing," you ninny, but "believing is seeing," for *Modern Art has become completely literary: the paintings and other works exist only to illustrate the text.*

Like most sudden revelations, this one left me dizzy. How could such a thing be? How could Modern Art be *literary*? As every art-history student is told, the Modern movement began about 1900 with a complete rejection of the literary nature of academic art, meaning the sort of realistic art which originated in the Renaissance and which the various national academies still held up as the last word.

Literary became a code word for all that seemed hopelessly retrograde about realistic art. It probably referred originally to the way nineteenth-century painters liked to paint scenes straight from literature, such as Sir John Everett Millais's rendition of Hamlet's intended, *Ophelia*, floating dead (on her back) with a bouquet of wildflowers in her death grip. In time, *literary* came to refer to realistic painting in general. The idea was that half the power of a realistic painting comes not from the artist but from the sentiments the viewer hauls along to it, like so much mental baggage. According to this theory, the museum-going public's love of, say, Jean François Millet's *The Sower* has little to do with Millet's talent and everything to do with people's sentimental notions about The Sturdy Yeoman. They make up a little story about him.

What was the opposite of literary painting? Why, *l'art pour l'art*, form for the sake of form, color for the sake of color. In Europe before 1914, artists invented Modern styles with fanatic energy—Fauvism, Futurism, Cubism, Expressionism, Orphism, Suprematism, Vorticism—but everybody shared the same premise: henceforth, one doesn't paint "*about* anything, my dear aunt," to borrow a line from a famous *Punch* cartoon. One just *paints*. Art should no longer be a mirror held up to man or nature. A painting should compel the viewer to see it for what it is: a certain arrangement of colors and forms on a canvas.

Artists pitched in to help make theory. They loved it, in fact. Georges Braque, the painter for whose work the word *Cubism* was coined, was a great formulator of precepts:

"The painter thinks in forms and colors. The aim is not to *reconstitute* an anecdotal fact but to *constitute* a pictorial fact."

Today this notion, this protest—which it was when Braque said it—has become a piece of orthodoxy. Artists repeat it endlessly, with conviction. As the Minimal Art movement came into its own in 1966, Frank Stella was saying it again:

"My painting is based on the fact that only what can be seen there *is* there. It really is an object . . . What you see is what you see."

Such emphasis, such certainty! What a head of steam—what patriotism an idea can build up in three-quarters of a century! In any event, so began Modern Art and so began the modern art of Art Theory. Braque, like Frank Stella, loved theory; but for Braque, who was a Montmartre boho* of the primitive sort, art came first. You can be sure the poor fellow never dreamed that during his own lifetime that order would be reversed.

. . .

* Twentieth-century American slang for *bohemian*, obverse of *hobo*.

All the major Modern movements except for De Stijl, Dada, Constructivism, and Surrealism began before the First World War, and yet they all *seem* to come out of the 1920s. Why? Because it was in the 1920s that Modern Art achieved social chic in Paris, London, Berlin, and New York. Smart people talked about it, wrote about it, enthused over it, and borrowed from it, as I say; Modern Art achieved the ultimate social acceptance: interior decorators did knock-offs of it in Belgravia and the sixteenth arrondissement.

Things like knock-off specialists, money, publicity, the smart set, and Le Chic shouldn't count in the history of art, as we all know—but, thanks to the artists themselves, they do. Art and fashion are a two-backed beast today; the artists can yell at fashion, but they can't move out ahead. That has come about as follows:

By 1900 the artist's arena—the place where he seeks honor, glory, ease, Success—had shifted twice. In seventeenth-century Europe the artist was literally, and also psychologically, the house guest of the nobility and the royal court (except in Holland); fine art and court art were one and the same. In the eighteenth century the scene shifted to the *salons*, in the homes of the wealthy bourgeoisie as well as those of aristocrats, where Culture-minded members of the upper classes held regular meetings with selected artists and writers. The artist was still the Gentleman, not yet the Genius. After the French Revolution, artists began to leave the *salons* and join *cénacles*, which were fraternities of like-minded souls huddled at some place like the Café Guerbois rather than a town house; around some romantic figure, an artist rather than a socialite, someone like Victor Hugo, Charles Nodier, Théophile Gautier, or, later, Edouard Manet. What held the *cénacles* together was that merry battle spirit we have all come to know and love: *épatez la bourgeoisie*, shock the middle class. With Gautier's *cénacle* especially . . . with Gautier's own red vests, black scarves, crazy hats, outrageous pronouncements, huge thirsts, and ravenous groin . . . the modern picture of The Artist began to form: the poor but free spirit, plebeian but aspiring only to be classless, to cut himself forever free from the bonds of the greedy and hypocritical bourgeoisie, to be whatever the fat burghers feared most, to cross the line wherever they drew it, to look at the world in a way they couldn't *see*, to be high, live low, stay young forever—in short, to be the bohemian.

By 1900 and the era of Picasso, Braque & Co., the modern game of Success in Art was pretty well set. As a painter or sculptor the artist would do work that baffled or subverted the cozy bourgeois vision of reality. As an individual—well, that was a bit more complex. As a bohemian, the artist had now left the *salons* of the upper classes—but he had not left their world. For getting away from the bourgeoisie there's nothing like packing up your paints and easel and heading for

Tahiti, or even Brittany, which was Gauguin's first stop. But who else even got as far as Brittany? Nobody. The rest got no farther than the heights of Montmartre and Montparnasse, which are what?—perhaps two miles from the Champs Elysées. Likewise in the United States: believe me, you can get all the tubes of Winsor & Newton paint you want in Cincinnati, but the artists keep migrating to New York all the same . . . You can see them six days a week . . . hot off the Carey airport bus, lined up in front of the real-estate office on Broome Street in their identical blue jeans, gum boots, and quilted Long March jackets . . . looking, of course, for the inevitable Loft . . .

No, somehow the artist wanted to remain within walking distance . . . He took up quarters just around the corner from . . . *le monde*, the social sphere described so well by Balzac, the milieu of those who find it important to be *in fashion*, the orbit of those aristocrats, wealthy bourgeois, publishers, writers, journalists, impresarios, performers, who wish to be "where things happen," the glamorous but small world of that creation of the nineteenth-century metropolis, *tout le monde*, Everybody, as in "Everybody says" . . . the smart set, in a phrase . . . "smart," with its overtones of cultivation as well as cynicism.

The ambitious artist, the artist who wanted Success, now had to do a bit of psychological double-tracking. Consciously he had to dedicate himself to the anti-bourgeois values of the *cénacles* of whatever sort, to bohemia, to the Bloomsbury life, the Left Bank life, the Lower Broadway Loft life, to the sacred squalor of it all, to the grim silhouette of the black Reo rig Lower Manhattan truck-route internal-combustion granules that were already standing an eighth of an inch thick on the poisoned roach carcasses atop the electric hot-plate burner by the time you got up for breakfast . . . Not only that, he had to dedicate himself to the quirky god Avant-Garde. He had to keep one devout eye peeled for the new edge on the blade of the wedge of the head on the latest pick thrust of the newest exploratory probe of this fall's avant-garde Breakthrough of the Century . . . all this in order to make it, to be noticed, to be counted, within the community of artists themselves. What is more, he had to be *sincere* about it. At the same time he had to keep his other eye cocked to see if anyone in *le monde* was watching. *Have they noticed me yet?* Have they even noticed *the new style* (that me and my friends are working in)? Don't they even *know* about Tensionism (or Slice Art or Niho or Innerism or Dimensional Creamo or whatever)? (Hello, out there!) . . . because as every artist knew in his heart of hearts, no matter how many times he tried to close his eyes and pretend otherwise (*History! History!—where is thy salve!*), Success was *real* only when it was success within *le monde*.

He could close his eyes and try to believe that all that mattered was that *he* knew his work was great . . . and that other artists respected it . . . and that History would surely record his achievements . . . but deep down he knew he was lying to himself. *I want to be a Name, goddamn it!*—at least that, a name, a name on the lips of the museum curators, gallery owners, collectors, patrons, board members, committee members, Culture hostesses, and their attendant intellectuals and journalists and their *Time* and *Newsweek*—all right!—even that!—*Time* and *Newsweek*—Oh yes! (ask the shades of Jackson Pollock and Mark Rothko!)—even the goddamned journalists!

During the 1960s this entire process by which *le monde,* the culturati, scout bohemia and tap the young artist for Success was acted out in the most graphic way. Early each spring, two emissaries from the Museum of Modern Art, Alfred Barr and Dorothy Miller, would head downtown from the Museum on West Fifty-third Street, down to Saint Marks Place, Little Italy, Broome Street and environs, and tour the loft studios of known artists and unknowns alike, looking at everything, talking to one and all, trying to get a line on what was new and significant in order to put together a show in the fall . . . and, well, I mean, my God—from the moment the two of them stepped out on Fifty-third Street to grab a cab, some sort of boho radar began to record their sortie . . . *They're coming!* . . . And rolling across Lower Manhattan, like the Cosmic Pulse of the theosophists, would be a unitary heartbeat:

Pick me pick me pick me pick me pick me pick me pick me . . . O damnable Uptown!

By all means, deny it if asked!—what one knows, in one's cheating heart, and what one says are two different things!

So it was that the art mating ritual developed early in the century—in Paris, in Rome, in London, Berlin, Munich, Vienna, and, not too long afterward, in New York. As we've just seen, the ritual has two phases:

(1) The Boho Dance, in which the artist shows his stuff within the circles, coteries, movements, *isms,* of the home neighborhood, bohemia itself, as if he doesn't care about anything else; as if, in fact, he has a knife in his teeth against the fashionable world uptown.

(2) The Consummation, in which culturati from that very same world, *le monde,* scout the various new movements and new artists of bohemia, select those who seem the most exciting, original, important, by whatever standards—and shower them with all the rewards of celebrity.

By the First World War the process was already like what in the Paris clip joints of the day was known as an apache dance. The artist was like the female in the act, stamping her feet, yelling defiance one moment, feigning indifference the next, resisting the advances of her pursuer with absolute contempt . . . more thrashing about . . . more rake-a-cheek fury . . . more yelling and carrying on . . . until finally with one last mighty and marvelous ambiguous shriek—*pain! ecstasy!* —she submits . . . Paff paff paff paff paff . . . How you do it, my boy! . . . and the house lights rise and Everyone, *tout le monde*, applauds . . .

The artist's payoff in this ritual is obvious enough. He stands to gain precisely what Freud says are the goals of the artist: fame, money, and beautiful lovers. But what about *le monde*, the culturati, the social members of the act? What's in it for them? Part of their reward is the ancient and semi-sacred status of Benefactor of the Arts. The arts have always been a doorway into Society, and in the largest cities today the arts—the museum boards, arts councils, fund drives, openings, parties, committee meetings—have completely replaced the churches in this respect. But there is more!

Today there is a peculiarly modern reward that the avant-garde artist can give his benefactor: namely, the feeling that he, like his mate the artist, is separate from and aloof from the bourgeoisie, the middle classes . . . the feeling that he may be *from* the middle class but he is no longer *in* it . . . the feeling that he is a fellow soldier, or at least an aide-de-camp or an honorary cong guerrilla in the vanguard march through the land of the philistines. This is a peculiarly modern need and a peculiarly modern kind of salvation (from the sin of Too Much Money) and something quite common among the well-to-do all over the West, in Rome and Milan as well as New York. That is why collecting contemporary art, the leading edge, the latest thing, warm and wet from the Loft, appeals specifically to those who feel most uneasy about their own commercial wealth . . . See? I'm not like *them*—those Jaycees, those United Fund chairmen, those Young Presidents, those mindless New York A.C. *goyisheh* hog-jowled stripe-tied goddamn-good-to-see-you-you-old-bastard-you oyster-bar trenchermen . . . Avant-garde art, more than any other, takes the Mammon and the Moloch out of money, puts Levi's, turtlenecks, muttonchops, and other mantles and laurels of bohemian grace upon it.

That is why collectors today not only seek out the company of, but also want to hang out amidst, lollygag around with, and enter into the milieu of . . . the artists they patronize. They *want* to climb those vertiginous loft building stairs on Howard Street that go up five flights without a single turn or bend—*straight up!* like something out of a casebook dream—to wind up with their hearts ricocheting around in their rib cages with tachycardia from the exertion mainly but also from the anticipation that just beyond this door at the top . . . in this loft . . . lie *the real goods* . . . paintings, sculptures that are indisputably part of the new movement, the new *école*, the new wave . . . something unshrinkable, chipsy, pure cong, bourgeois-proof.

Great Moments in Contemporary Architecture

The Clients' First Night in the House

"Well, maybe we'll make *Architectural Digest* anyway."
"We damn well better."

THE WHITE GODS

All at once, in 1937, the Silver Prince himself was here, in America. Walter Gropius; in person; in the flesh; and here to stay. In the wake of the Nazis' rise to power, Gropius had fled Germany, going first to England and coming now to the United States. Other stars of the fabled Bauhaus arrived at about the same time: Breuer, Albers, Moholy-Nagy, Bayer, and Mies van der Rohe, who had become head of the Bauhaus in 1930, two years after Gropius, already under pressure because of the left-wing aura of the compound, had resigned. Here they came, uprooted, exhausted, penniless, men without a country, battered by fate.

Gropius had the healthy self-esteem of any ambitious man, but he was a gentleman above all else, a gentleman of the old school, a man who was always concerned about a sense of proportion, in life as well as in design. As a refugee from a blighted land, he would have been content with a friendly welcome, a place to lay his head, two or three meals a day until he could get on his own feet, a smile every once in a while, and a chance to work, if anybody needed him. And instead—

The reception of Gropius and his confreres was like a certain stock scene from the jungle movies of that period. Bruce Cabot and Myrna Loy make a crash landing in the jungle and crawl out of the wreckage in their Abercrombie & Fitch white safari blouses and tan gabardine jodhpurs and stagger into a clearing. They are surrounded by savages with bones through their noses—who immediately bow down and prostrate themselves and commence a strange moaning chant.

The White Gods!
Come from the skies at last!

From *From Bauhaus to Our House*, chapter 3 (New York: Farrar, Straus and Giroux, 1981). First published in *Harper's*, June 1981.

Gropius was made head of the school of architecture at Harvard, and Breuer joined him there. Moholy-Nagy opened the New Bauhaus, which evolved into the Chicago Institute of Design. Albers opened a rural Bauhaus in the hills of North Carolina, at Black Mountain College. Mies was installed as dean of architecture at the Armour Institute in Chicago. And not just dean; master builder also. He was given a campus to create, twenty-one buildings in all, as the Armour Institute merged with the Lewis Institute to form the Illinois Institute of Technology. Twenty-one large buildings, in the middle of the Depression, at a time when building had come almost to a halt in the United States —for an architect who had completed only seventeen buildings in his career—

O white gods.

Such prostrations! Such acts of homage! The Museum of Modern Art honored Gropius with a show called "Bauhaus: 1919–1928," those being the years when Gropius headed it. Philip Johnson, now thirty-four years old, could resist the physical presence of the gods no longer. He decamped to Harvard to study to become an architect at Gropius' feet. Starting from zero! (If the truth be known, he would have preferred to be at Mies' feet, but to a supremely urbane young man like Johnson, we may be sure, the thought of moving to Chicago, Illinois, for three years was a bit more zero than he had in mind.)

It was embarrassing, perhaps . . . but it was the kind of thing one could learn to live with. . . . Within three years the course of American architecture had changed, utterly. It was not so much the buildings the Germans designed in the United States, although Mies' were to become highly influential a decade later. It was more the system of instruction they introduced. Still more, it was *their very presence.* The most fabled creatures in all the mythology of twentieth-century American art—namely, those dazzling European artists poised so exquisitely against the rubble—they were . . . *here!* . . . *now!* . . . in the land of the colonial complex . . . to govern, in person, their big little Nigeria of the Arts.

This curious phase of late colonial history was by no means confined to architecture, for the colonial complex was all-pervasive. Stars of the two great rival movements of European painting, the Cubists and Surrealists, began arriving as refugees in the late 1930s and early 1940s. Léger, Mondrian, Modigliani, Chagall, Max Ernst, André Breton, Yves Tanguy—*O white gods!* The American Scene and Social Realist painting of the 1930s vanished, never to reappear. From the Europeans, artists in New York learned how to create their own clerisy. The first American art compound, the so-called New York School of abstract expressionists, was formed in the 1940s, with regular meetings, manifestos, new theories, new visual codes, the lot. Arnold Schoenberg, the white god of all the white gods in European music, arrived as a refugee in 1936. For the next forty years, serious music in America became a footnote to Schoenberg's theory of serial composition. There was considerable irony here. Many European composers looked to American jazz and to American composers such as George Gershwin, Aaron Copland, and Ferde Grofé as liberating forces, a way out of the hyperrationalization of European avant-garde music as typified by Schoenberg. But serious American composers, by and large, were having none of that. They acted like Saudis being told their tents were marvelous because they were so natural and indigenous and earthy. They wanted the real thing—the European thing—and they fastened onto it with a vengeance. Thereafter, Gershwin, Copland, and Grofé were spoken of with condescension or else plain derision.*

In architecture, naturally, the Silver Prince became the chief executive, the governor of the colony, as it were. The teaching of architecture at Harvard was transformed overnight. Everyone started from zero. Everyone was now taught in the fundamentals of the International—which is to say, the compound—Style. All architecture became nonbourgeois architecture, although the concept itself was left discreetly *unexpressed*, as it were. The old Beaux-Arts traditions became heresy, and so did the legacy of Frank Lloyd Wright, which had only barely made its way into the architecture schools in the first place. Within three years, every so-called major American contribution to contemporary architecture—whether by Wright, H. H. Richardson, creator of the heavily rusticated American Romanesque, or Louis Sullivan, leader of the "Chicago School" of skyscraper architects—had dropped down into the footnotes, into the *ibid.* thickets.

Wright himself was furious and, for one of the few times in his life, bewildered. It was hard to say what got under his skin more: the fact that his work had been upstaged by the Europeans or the fact that he was now treated as a species of walking dead man. He was not deprived of honor and respect, but when he got it, it often sounded like a memorial service. For example, the Museum of Modern Art put on an exhibition of Wright's work in 1940—but it was in tandem with a show of the work of the movie director D. W. Griffith, who had retired in 1931. Mies made a very gracious statement about what a genius Wright was and how he had opened up the eyes of European

* Likewise, in the field of psychology. So many leading Freudian psychoanalysts came to the United States (e.g., Heinz Hartmann and Ernst Kris), the United States became the only important center of Freudian psychology in the world. American contributions to psychology, even those well regarded in Europe, such as William James's, were for the next forty years regarded as backward.

architects . . . back before the First World War . . . As to just what debt he might have felt to the eighty-odd buildings Wright had designed since then, he didn't say.

The late 1920s and early 1930s had been disastrous for Wright. He was already fifty-eight when a fire destroyed his studio at Taliesin, Wisconsin, in 1925. Troubles with his mistress, Miriam Noel, seemed to paralyze his practice. His business had fallen off badly even before the Depression. Wright had finally holed up, like a White Russian on his uppers, in his rebuilt redoubt at Taliesin, with a dozen or so apprentices, known as the Taliesin Fellows his porkpie hats, berets, high collars and flowing neckties, and his capes from Stevenson, the Chicago tailor. Wright himself had been an apprentice of Louis Sullivan and had broken with or been fired by him—each had his own version—but Wright had taken with him Sullivan's vision of a totally new and totally American architecture, arising from the American terrain and the spirit of the Middle West. Well, now, finally, in the late 1930s, there was a totally new architecture in America, and it had come straight from Germany, Holland, and France, the French component being Le Corbusier.

Every time Wright read that Le Corbusier had finished a building, he told the Fellows: "Well, now that he's finished one building, he'll go write four books about it." Le Corbusier made one visit to the United States—and developed a phobia toward America—and Wright developed a phobia toward Le Corbusier. He turned down his one chance to meet him. He didn't want to have to shake his hand. As for Gropius, Wright always referred to him as "Herr Gropius." He didn't want to shake his hand, either. One day Wright made a surprise visit to a site in Racine, Wisconsin, where the first of his "Usonian" houses, medium-priced versions of his Prairie School manor houses, was going up. Wright's red Lincoln Zephyr pulled up to the front. One of his apprentices, Edgar Tafel, was at the wheel, serving as chauffeur. Just then, a group of men emerged from the building. Among them was none other than Gropius himself, who had come to the University of Wisconsin to lecture and was anxious to see some of Wright's work. Gropius came over and put his face at the window and said, "Mr. Wright, it's a pleasure to meet you. I have always admired your work." Wright did not so much as smile or raise his hand. He merely turned his head ever so slightly toward the face at the window and said out of the side of his mouth, "Herr Gropius, you're a guest of the university here. I just want to tell you that they're as snobbish here as they are at Harvard, only they don't have a New England accent." Whereupon he turned to Tafel and said, "Well, we have to get on, Edgar!" And he settled back, and the red Zephyr sped off, leaving

Gropius and entourage teetering on the edge of the curb with sunbeams shining through their ears.*

One up for Daddy Frank!—as the Fellows called Wright, when he was out of earshot. But it was oneupmanship of a hollow sort. Daddy Frank had just seen the face of the German who had replaced him as the Future of American Architecture.

Tafel and the other Fellows were Wright's only followers by now. Among the architecture students in the universities the International Style was all you heard about. Enthusiasm had been building up ever since the pilgrims had returned from Europe and the Museum of Modern Art began touting the compound architects. When the white gods suddenly arrived, enthusiasm became conversion, in the religious sense. There was a zeal about it that went quite beyond the ordinary passions of aesthetic taste. It was the esoteric, hierophantic fervor of the compound that seized them all. "Henceforth, the divinity of art and the authority of taste reside *here with us . . .*" The university architecture departments themselves became the American version of the compounds. Here was an approach to architecture that turned the American architect from a purveyor to bond salesman to an engineer of the soul. With the Depression on, the bond salesmen weren't doing much for the architecture business anyway. New building had come to almost a dead halt. This made it even easier for the architectural community to take to the white gods' theories of starting from zero.

Studying architecture was no longer a matter of acquiring a set of technical skills and a knowledge of aesthetic alternatives. Before he knew it, the student found himself drawn into a movement and entrusted with a set of inviolable aesthetic and moral principles. The campus itself became the physical compound, as at the Bauhaus. When students talked about architecture, it was with a sense of mission. The American campus compounds differed one from the other—to an ever so slight degree, just as de Stijl differed from Bauhaus. Harvard was pure Bauhaus. At Yale they would experiment with variations. At one point the principle of "the integrally jointed wooden frame" seemed exhilaratingly rebellious—but it would have taken the superfine mind of Doctor Subtilis himself to have explained why. This, too, was after the manner of the European compounds.

Faculty members resisted the compound passion at their peril. Students were becoming unruly. They were drawing up petitions—manifestos in embryo. No more laying down laborious washes in china ink in the old Beaux-Arts manner! No more tedious Renaissance

* Edgar Tafel, *Apprentice to Genius: Years with Frank Lloyd Wright* (New York: McGraw-Hill Book Company, 1979).

renderings! After all, look at Mies' drawings. He used no shading at all, just quick crisp straight lines, clean and to the point. And look at Corbu's! His draftsmanship—a veritable scribble! A pellmell rush of ideas! His renderings were watercolors in mauve and brown tones, as fast and terribly beautiful as a storm! Genius!—you had to let it *gush out!* We declare: No more stone-grinding classical Renaissance details! —and the faculties caved in. By 1940, the sketchiness of Corbu's quivering umber bird had become the modern standard for draftsmanship. With the somewhat grisly euphoria of Savonarola burning the wigs and fancy dresses of the Florentine fleshpots, deans of architecture went about instructing the janitors to throw out all plaster casts of classical details, pedagogical props that had been accumulated over a half century or more. I mean, my God, all those Esquiline vase-fountains and Temple of Vesta capitals . . . How very bourgeois.

At Yale, in the annual design competition, a jury always picked out one student as, in effect, best in show. But now the students rebelled. And why? Because it was written, in the scriptures, by Gropius himself: "The fundamental pedagogical mistake of the academy arose from its preoccupation with the idea of individual genius." Gropius' and Mies' byword was "team" effort. Gropius' own firm in Cambridge was not called Gropius & Associates, Inc., or anything close to it. It was called "The Architects Collaborative." At Yale the students insisted on a group project, a collaborative design, to replace the obscene scramble for individual glory.

Now, in the late 1940s and early 1950s, Buckminster Fuller came into his own. Fuller was an American designer with an endless stock of ingenious notions, one of which was his geodesic dome, a dome created of thousands of short, thin metal struts arranged in tetrahedra. Fuller's dome fit in nicely with the modern principle of creating large structures with light surfaces out of machine-made materials and using tensions and stresses to do the work that massive supports had done for the old (bourgeois) order. But Gropius and the others never felt very comfortable with Fuller. It was hard to tell whether he was an architect, an engineer, a guru, or simply that species of nut known all around the world: *the inventor.* But to American university students he was a guru at the very least. He would give amazing twelve-hour lectures, great seamless geodesic domes of words that youths with supple spines and good kidneys found uplifting, even intoxicating. At Yale, after one of Fuller's amazing performances, the architecture students were swept up into an ecstasy of rebellious and collaborative action. They constructed an enormous geodesic dome of cardboard struts and put it up on top of Yale's stony gray Gothic Revival architecture school building, Weir Hall, and as much as dared the dean of architecture to try to do anything about it. He didn't, and the dome slowly rotted in its eminence.

In 1950, Yale got its own Bauhäusler when Josef Albers arrived from North Carolina to become the head of fine-arts instruction. Albers immediately instituted the fabled Bauhaus Vorkurs, except that now he wasn't interested in depositing sheets of newspaper on the table. Now he deposited squares of Color-aid paper on the table and told the students to create works of art. As a painter, Albers himself had spent the preceding fourteen years seeking to solve the problem (if any) of superimposing squares of color, one upon the other. Now he had the Yale students doing it . . . and month after month went by. Yale, simply because it was Yale, attracted outstanding artists from high schools all over America. Some young lad who could take a piece of marble and carve you a pillow that looked so full of voluptuous downy billows you would have willingly tried to bury your head in it —this reincarnation of Bernini himself would sit there with Albers' implacable Color-aid paper in his hands . . . *starting from zero* . . . and watch Albers point to some gristle-brained photographer's little playpretty layers of colored squares and hear him say: "But *this!*—is form sculpted by light!" And the walls of the compound box closed in yet a few more inches.

As for the compound taboos concerning what was bourgeois and nonbourgeois, these soon became the very central nervous system of architecture students in the universities, as if they had been encoded in their genes. There was a bizarre story in the press at the time about a drunk who had put a gun to the head of an upland Tennessee foot-washing Baptist and ordered him to utter a vile imprecation regarding Jesus Christ. The victim was in no mood to be a martyr; in fact, he desperately wished to save his own hide. But he was a true believer, and *he could not make the words pass his lips*, try as he might, and his brains were blown out. So it was with the new generation of architects by the late 1940s. There was *no circumstance* under which a client could have prevailed upon them to incorporate hipped roofs or Italianate cornices or broken pediments or fluted columns or eyebrow lintels or any of the rest of the bourgeois baggage into their designs. Try as they might, they could not make the drafting pencil describe such forms.

O white gods.

An intellectual weakness—and saving grace—of American students has always been that they are unable to sit still for ideology and its tight flemish-bonded logics and dialectics. They don't want it and don't get it. Any possible connection that worker housing or antibourgeois ideals might have had with a political program, in Germany, Holland, or anywhere else, eluded them. They picked up the sentimental side of it only. I can remember what brave plans young architects at Yale and Harvard had for the common man in the early 1950s. That was the term they used, *the common man.* They had a vague notion that the common man was a workingman, and not an advertising account executive, but beyond that it was all Trilby and Dickens. They were designing things for the common man down to truly minute details, such as lamp switches. The new liberated common man would live as the Cultivated Ascetic. He would be modeled on the B.A.-degree Greenwich Village bohemian of the late 1940s—dark wool Hudson Bay shirts, tweed jackets, flannel pants, briarwood pipes, sandals & simplicity—except that he would live in an enormous hive of glass and steel, i.e., an International Style housing project with elevators, instead of a fourth-floor walkup in a brownstone. So much for ideology. But the design side of the compounds they comprehended in all its reductionist, stereotaxic-needle-implant fineness. At Yale the students gradually began to notice that everything they designed, everything the faculty members designed, everything that the visiting critics (who gave critiques of student designs) designed . . . looked the same. Everyone designed the same . . . box . . . of glass and steel and concrete, with tiny beige bricks substituted occasionally. This became known as The Yale Box. Ironic drawings of The Yale Box began appearing on bulletin boards. "The Yale Box in the Mojave Desert"—and there would be a picture of The Yale Box out amid the sagebrush and the joshua trees northeast of Palmdale, California. "The Yale Box Visits Winnie the Pooh"—and there would be a picture of the glass-and-steel cube up in a tree, the child's treehouse of the future. "The Yale Box Searches for Captain Nemo"—and there would be a picture of The Yale Box twenty thousand leagues under the sea with a periscope on top and a propeller in back. There was something gloriously nutty about this business of The Yale Box!—but nothing changed. Even in serious moments, nobody could design anything *but* Yale Boxes. The truth was that by now architectural students all over America were inside that very box, the same box the compound architects had closed in upon themselves in Europe twenty years before.

Every young architect's apartment, and every architecture student's room, was that box and that shrine. And in that shrine was always the same icon. I can still see it. The living room would be a mean little space on the backside of a walkup tenement. The couch would be a mattress on top of a flush door supported by bricks and covered with a piece of monk's cloth. There would be more monk's cloth used as curtains and on the floor would be a sisal rug that left corduroy ribs on the bottoms of your feet in the morning. The place would be lit by clamp-on heat lamps with half-globe aluminum reflectors and ordinary bulbs replacing the heat bulbs. At one end of the rug, there it would be . . . *the Barcelona chair.* Mies had designed it for his German Pavilion at the Barcelona Exposition of 1929. The Platonic ideal of *chair* it was, pure Worker Housing leather and stainless steel, the most perfect piece of furniture design in the twentieth century. The Barcelona chair commanded the staggering price of $550, however, and that was wholesale. When you saw that holy object on the sisal rug, you knew you were in a household where a fledgling architect and his young wife had sacrificed everything to bring the symbol of the godly mission into their home. Five hundred and fifty dollars! She had even given up the diaper service and was doing the diapers by hand. It got to the point where, if I saw a Barcelona chair, no matter where, I immediately—in the classic stimulus-response bond—smelled diapers gone high.

But if they already had the chair, why was she still doing the diapers by hand? Because one chair was only halfway to Mecca. Mies always used them in pairs. The state of grace, the Radiant City, was two Barcelona chairs, one on either end of the sisal rug, before the flush-door couch, under the light of the heat-lamp reflectors.

If a young man had suffered and sacrificed in this way and stripped the fat from his mental life and revealed the Mazda gleam at the apex of his soul—who, in the mundane world outside, could stop him now?

It was about this time, the late 1940s and early 1950s, that The Client in America began to realize that something very strange had taken place among the architects. At Yale the first of the rude jolts—many more would follow—came in 1953 with an addition to the Yale Art Gallery. Barely ten years before, on the eve of the Second World War, Yale had completed a building program of vast proportions that had turned the campus into as close an approximation of Oxford and Cambridge as the mind of man could devise on short notice in southern Connecticut. Edward Harkness, a partner of John D. Rockefeller, and John Sterling, who had a railroad fortune, donated most of the money. Eighteen medieval fortresses rose up, tower upon tower, in High Collegiate Gothic, to house ten residential colleges (Yale Mid-Atlantic for dormitories), four graduate schools, a library, a power plant, whose buttressed smokestack reminded people of the Cathedral at Rheims, a ten-story gymnasium known as the Cathedral of Sweat, and the twenty-one-story Harkness Tower, which had a carillon on top. All these soaring structures had rusticated stone façades. Gothic Revivalism was carried to the point not only of putting leaded panes in the casement windows but also of having craftsmen blow, etch, and stain panes with medieval designs, many of them detailed representations of religious figures and mythical animals, and installing them at seemingly random intervals. The result was a campus almost as unified, architecturally, as Jefferson's University of Virginia. For better or worse, Yale became the business baron's vision of a luxurious collegium for the sons of the upper classes who would run the new American empire.

The art-gallery addition, at York and Chapel Streets in New Haven, was Yale's first major building project following the Second World War. A gray little man named Louis Kahn was appointed as architect. His main recommendation seemed to be that he was a friend of the chairman of the architecture department, George Howe. The existing gallery, built just twenty-five years earlier, was an Italian Romanesque palazzo designed by Egerton Swartwout, a Yale architect, and paid for by Harkness. It had massive cornices and a heavy pitched slate roof. On the Chapel Street side, it featured large windows framed in compound arches of stone.

Kahn's addition was . . . a box . . . of glass, steel, concrete, and tiny beige bricks. As his models and drawings made clear, on the Chapel Street side there would be no arches, no cornice, no rustication, no pitched roof—only a sheer blank wall of small glazed beige brick. The only details discernible on this slick and empty surface would be four narrow bands (string courses) of concrete at about ten-foot intervals. In the eyes of a man from Mars or your standard Yale man, the building could scarcely have been distinguished from a Woolco discount store in a shopping center. In the gallery's main public space the ceiling was made of gray concrete tetrahedra, fully exposed. This gave the interior the look of an underground parking garage.

Yale's administrators were shocked. Kahn had been an architect for twenty years but had done little more than work as assistant architect, under Howe, among others, on some housing projects. He was not much to look at, either. He was short. He had wispy reddish-white hair that stuck out this way and that. His face was badly scarred as the result of a childhood accident. He wore wrinkled shirts and black suits. The backs of his sleeves were shiny. He always had a little cigar of unfortunate hue in his mouth. His tie was always loose. He was nearsighted, and in the classrooms where he served as visiting critic, you would see Kahn holding some student's yard-long blueprint three inches from his face and moving his head over it like a scanner.

But that was merely the exterior. Somewhere deep within this shambles there seemed to be a molten core of confidence . . . and *architectural destiny* . . . Kahn would walk into a classroom, stare blearily at the students, open his mouth . . . and from the depths would come a remarkable voice:

"Every building must have . . . its own *soul.*"

One day he walked into a classroom and began a lecture with the words: "Light . . . *is.*" There followed a pause that seemed seven days long, just long enough to re-create the world.

His unlikely physical appearance only made these moments more striking. The visionary passion of the man was irresistible. Everybody was wiped out.

Kahn stared at the administrators in the same fashion, and the voice said: What do you mean, "It has nothing to do with the existing building"? You don't understand? You don't *see* it? You don't see the string courses? They express the floor lines of the existing building. They *reveal* the *structure*. For a quarter of a century, those floors have been hidden behind masonry, completely concealed. Now they will be *unconcealed*. Now the entire structure will be *unconcealed*. Honest form—*beauty*, as you choose to call it—can only result from *unconcealed structure!*

Unconcealed structure? Did he say *unconcealed structure*? Baffled but somehow intimidated, as if by Cagliostro or a Jacmel hoongan, the Yale administration yielded to the destiny of architecture and took it like a man.

Administrators, directors, boards of trustees, municipal committees, and executive officers have been taking it like men ever since.

The Maternal Instinct

"How's your little boy?"

"Oh, I don't know what to do with him. He's sick, but he won't stay in bed. He had an angina attack sprinting on the beach, trying to impress the boys at his big conference. He had another one in his room trying to impress the little researcher I'm not supposed to know about. He had another one hanging some shutters in the kitchen trying to deal with his guilt."

THE ANGELS

Within five minutes, or ten minutes, no more than that, three of the others had called her on the telephone to ask her if she had heard that something had happened out there.

"Jane, this is Alice. Listen, I just got a call from Betty, and she said she heard something's happened out there. Have you heard anything?" That was the way they phrased it, call after call. She picked up the telephone and began relaying this same message to some of the others.

"Connie, this is Jane Conrad. Alice just called me, and she says something's happened . . ."

Something was part of the official Wife Lingo for tiptoeing blindfolded around the subject. Being barely twenty-one years old and new around here, Jane Conrad knew very little about this particular subject, since nobody ever talked about it. But the day was young! And what a setting she had for her imminent enlightenment! And what a picture she herself presented! Jane was tall and slender and had rich brown hair and high cheekbones and wide brown eyes. She looked a little like the actress Jean Simmons. Her father was a rancher in southwestern Texas. She had gone East to college, to Bryn Mawr, and had met her husband, Pete, at a debutante's party at the Gulph Mills Club in Philadelphia, when he was a senior at Princeton. Pete was a short, wiry, blond boy who joked around a lot. At any moment his face was likely to break into a wild grin revealing the gap between his front teeth. The Hickory Kid sort, he was; a Hickory Kid on the deb circuit, however. He had an air of energy, self-confidence, ambition, *joie de vivre*. Jane and Pete were married two days after he graduated from Princeton. Last year Jane gave birth to their first child, Peter. And today, here in Florida, in Jacksonville, in the peaceful year 1955, the sun shines through the pines outside, and the very air takes

From *The Right Stuff*, chapter 1 (New York: Farrar, Straus and Giroux, 1979).

on the sparkle of the ocean. The ocean and a great mica-white beach are less than a mile away. Anyone driving by will see Jane's little house gleaming like a dream house in the pines. It is a brick house, but Jane and Pete painted the bricks white, so that it gleams in the sun against a great green screen of pine trees with a thousand little places where the sun peeks through. They painted the shutters black, which makes the white walls look even more brilliant. The house has only eleven hundred square feet of floor space, but Jane and Pete designed it themselves and that more than makes up for the size. A friend of theirs was the builder and gave them every possible break, so that it cost only eleven thousand dollars. Outside, the sun shines, and inside, the fever rises by the minute as five, ten, fifteen, and, finally, nearly all twenty of the wives join the circuit, trying to find out what has happened, which, in fact, means: to whose husband.

After thirty minutes on such a circuit—this is not an unusual morning around here—a wife begins to feel that the telephone is no longer located on a table or on the kitchen wall. It is exploding in her solar plexus. Yet it would be far worse right now to hear the front doorbell. The protocol is strict on that point, although written down nowhere. No woman is supposed to deliver the final news, and certainly not on the telephone. The matter mustn't be bungled!—that's the idea. No, a man should bring the news when the time comes, a man with some official or moral authority, a clergyman or a comrade of the newly deceased. Furthermore, he should bring the bad news in person. He should turn up at the front door and ring the bell and be standing there like a pillar of coolness and competence, bearing the bad news on ice, like a fish. Therefore, all the telephone calls from the wives were the frantic and portentous beating of the wings of the death angels, as it were. When the final news came, there would be a ring at the front door—a wife in this situation finds herself staring at the front door as if she no longer owns it or controls it—and outside the door would be a man . . . come to inform her that unfortunately something has happened out there, and her husband's body now lies incinerated in the swamps or the pines or the palmetto grass, "burned beyond recognition," which anyone who had been around an air base for very long (fortunately Jane had not) realized was quite an artful euphemism to describe a human body that now looked like an enormous fowl that has burned up in a stove, burned a blackish brown all over, greasy and blistered, fried, in a word, with not only the entire face and all the hair and the ears burned off, not to mention all the clothing, but also the *hands* and *feet*, with what remains of the arms and legs bent at the knees and elbows and burned into absolutely rigid angles, burned a greasy blackish brown like the bursting body itself, so that this husband, father, officer, gentleman, this *ornamentum* of some mother's eye, His Majesty the Baby of just twenty-odd years back, has been reduced to a charred hulk with wings and shanks sticking out of it.

My own husband—how could this be what they were talking about? Jane had heard the young men, Pete among them, talk about other young men who had "bought it" or "augered in" or "crunched," but it had never been anyone they knew, no one in the squadron. And in any event, the way they talked about it, with such breezy, slangy terminology, was the same way they talked about sports. It was as if they were saying, "He was thrown out stealing second base." And that was all! Not one word, not in print, not in conversation—not in this amputated language!—about an incinerated corpse from which a young man's spirit has vanished in an instant, from which all smiles, gestures, moods, worries, laughter, wiles, shrugs, tenderness, and loving looks—*you, my love!*—have disappeared like a sigh, while the terror consumes a cottage in the woods, and a young woman, sizzling with the fever, awaits her confirmation as the new widow of the day.

The next series of calls greatly increased the possibility that it was Pete to whom something had happened. There were only twenty men in the squadron, and soon nine or ten had been accounted for . . . by the fluttering reports of the death angels. Knowing that the word was out that an accident had occurred, husbands who could get to a telephone were calling home to say *it didn't happen to me*. This news, of course, was immediately fed to the fever. Jane's telephone would ring once more, and one of the wives would be saying:

"Nancy just got a call from Jack. He's at the squadron and he says something's happened, but he doesn't know what. He said he saw Frank D—— take off about ten minutes ago with Greg in back, so they're all right. What have you heard?"

But Jane has heard nothing except that other husbands, and not hers, are safe and accounted for. And thus, on a sunny day in Florida, outside of the Jacksonville Naval Air Station, in a little white cottage, a veritable dream house, another beautiful young woman was about to be apprised of the *quid pro quo* of her husband's line of work, of the tradeoff, as one might say, the subparagraphs of a contract written in no visible form. Just as surely as if she had the entire roster in front of her, Jane now realized that only two men in the squadron were unaccounted for. One was a pilot named Bud Jennings; the other was Pete. She picked up the telephone and did something that was much frowned on in a time of emergency. She called the squadron office. The duty officer answered.

"I want to speak to Lieutenant Conrad," said Jane. "This is Mrs. Conrad."

"I'm sorry," the duty officer said—and then his voice cracked. "I'm sorry . . . I . . ." He couldn't find the words! He was about to cry! "I'm—that's—I mean . . . he can't come to the phone!"

He can't come to the phone!

"It's very important!" said Jane.

"I'm sorry—it's impossible—" The duty officer could hardly get the words out because he was so busy gulping back sobs. *Sobs!* "He can't come to the phone."

"Why not? Where is he?"

"I'm sorry—" More sighs, wheezes, snuffling gasps. "I can't tell you that. I—I have to hang up now!"

And the duty officer's voice disappeared in a great surf of emotion and he hung up.

The duty officer! *The very sound of her voice was more than he could take!*

The world froze, congealed, in that moment. Jane could no longer calculate the interval before the front doorbell would ring and some competent long-faced figure would appear, some Friend of Widows and Orphans, who would inform her, officially, that Pete was dead.

Even out in the middle of the swamp, in this rot-bog of pine trunks, scum slicks, dead dodder vines, and mosquito eggs, even out in this great overripe sump, the smell of "burned beyond recognition" obliterated everything else. When airplane fuel exploded, it created a heat so intense that everything but the hardest metals not only *burned* —everything of rubber, plastic, celluloid, wood, leather, cloth, flesh, gristle, calcium, horn, hair, blood, and protoplasm—it not only burned, it gave up the ghost in the form of every stricken putrid gas known to chemistry. One could smell the horror. It came in through the nostrils and burned the rhinal cavities raw and penetrated the liver and permeated the bowels like a black gas until there was nothing in the universe, inside or out, except the stench of the char. As the helicopter came down between the pine trees and settled onto the bogs, the smell hit Pete Conrad even before the hatch was completely open, and they were not even close enough to see the wreckage yet. The rest of the way Conrad and the crewmen had to travel on foot. After a few steps the water was up to their knees, and then it was up to their armpits, and they kept wading through the water and the scum and the vines and the pine trunks, but it was nothing compared to the smell. Conrad, a twenty-five-year-old lieutenant junior grade, happened to be on duty as squadron safety officer that day and was supposed to make the on-site investigation of the crash. The fact was, however, that this squadron was the first duty assignment of his career, and he had never been at a crash site before and had never smelled any such revolting stench or seen anything like what awaited him.

When Conrad finally reached the plane, which was an SNJ, he found the fuselage burned and blistered and dug into the swamp with one wing sheared off and the cockpit canopy smashed. In the front seat was all that was left of his friend Bud Jennings. Bud Jennings, an amiable fellow, a promising young fighter pilot, was now a horrible roasted hulk—with no head. His head was completely gone, apparently torn off the spinal column like a pineapple off a stalk, except that it was nowhere to be found.

Conrad stood there soaking wet in the swamp bog, wondering what the hell to do. It was a struggle to move twenty feet in this freaking muck. Every time he looked up, he was looking into a delirium of limbs, vines, dappled shadows, and a chopped-up white light that came through the treetops—the ubiquitous screen of trees with a thousand little places where the sun peeked through. Nevertheless, he started wading back out into the muck and the scum, and the others followed. He kept looking up. Gradually he could make it out. Up in the treetops there was a pattern of broken limbs where the SNJ had come crashing through. It was like a tunnel through the treetops. Conrad and the others began splashing through the swamp, following the strange path ninety or a hundred feet above them. It took a sharp turn. That must have been where the wing broke off. The trail veered to one side and started downward. They kept looking up and wading through the muck. Then they stopped. There was a great green sap wound up there in the middle of a tree trunk. It was odd. Near the huge gash was . . . tree disease . . . some sort of brownish lumpy sac up in the branches, such as you see in trees infested by bagworms, and there were yellowish curds on the branches around it, as if the disease had caused the sap to ooze out and fester and congeal—except that it couldn't be sap because it was streaked with blood. In the next instant—Conrad didn't have to say a word. Each man could see it all. The lumpy sac was the cloth liner of a flight helmet, with the earphones attached to it. The curds were Bud Jennings's brains. The tree trunk had smashed through the cockpit canopy of the SNJ and knocked Bud Jennings's head to pieces like a melon.

In keeping with the protocol, the squadron commander was not going to release Bud Jennings's name until his widow, Loretta, had been located and a competent male death messenger had been dispatched to tell her. But Loretta Jennings was not at home and could not be found. Hence, a delay—and more than enough time for the other wives, the death angels, to burn with panic over the telephone lines. All the pilots were accounted for except the two who were in the woods, Bud Jennings and Pete Conrad. One chance in two, acey-deucey, one finger-two finger, and this was not an unusual day around here.

Loretta Jennings had been out at a shopping center. When she returned home, a certain figure was waiting outside, a man, a solemn Friend of Widows and Orphans, and it was Loretta Jennings who lost the game of odd and even, acey-deucey, and it was Loretta whose child (she was pregnant with a second) would have no father. It was this young woman who went through all the final horrors that Jane Conrad had imagined—*assumed!*—would be hers to endure forever. Yet this grim stroke of fortune brought Jane little relief.

On the day of Bud Jennings's funeral, Pete went into the back of the closet and brought out his bridge coat, per regulations. This was the most stylish item in the Navy officer's wardrobe. Pete had never had occasion to wear his before. It was a double-breasted coat made of navy-blue melton cloth and came down almost to the ankles. It must have weighed ten pounds. It had a double row of gold buttons down the front and loops for shoulder boards, big beautiful belly-cut collar and lapels, deep turnbacks on the sleeves, a tailored waist, and a center vent in back that ran from the waistline to the bottom of the coat. Never would Pete, or for that matter many other American males in the mid-twentieth century, have an article of clothing quite so impressive and aristocratic as that bridge coat. At the funeral the nineteen little Indians who were left—Navy boys!—lined up manfully in their bridge coats. They looked so young. Their pink, lineless faces with their absolutely clear, lean jawlines popped up bravely, correctly, out of the enormous belly-cut collars of the bridge coats. They sang an old Navy hymn, which slipped into a strange and lugubrious minor key here and there, and included a stanza added especially for aviators. It ended with: "O hear us when we lift our prayer for those in peril in the air."

Three months later another member of the squadron crashed and was burned beyond recognition and Pete hauled out the bridge coat again and Jane saw eighteen little Indians bravely going through the motions at the funeral. Not long after that, Pete was transferred from Jacksonville to the Patuxent River Naval Air Station in Maryland. Pete and Jane had barely settled in there when they got word that another member of the Jacksonville squadron, a close friend of theirs, someone they had had over to dinner many times, had died trying to take off from the deck of a carrier in a routine practice session a few miles out in the Atlantic. The catapult that propelled aircraft off the deck lost pressure, and his ship just dribbled off the end of the deck, with its engine roaring vainly, and fell sixty feet into the ocean and sank like a brick, and he vanished, *just like that.*

Pete had been transferred to Patuxent River, which was known in

Navy vernacular as Pax River, to enter the Navy's new test-pilot school. This was considered a major step up in the career of a young Navy aviator. Now that the Korean War was over and there was no combat flying, all the hot young pilots aimed for flight test. In the military they always said "flight test" and not "test flying." Jet aircraft had been in use for barely ten years at the time, and the Navy was testing new jet fighters continually. Pax River was the Navy's prime test center.

Jane liked the house they bought at Pax River. She didn't like it as much as the little house in Jacksonville, but then she and Pete hadn't designed this one. They lived in a community called North Town Creek, six miles from the base. North Town Creek, like the base, was on a scrub-pine peninsula that stuck out into Chesapeake Bay. They were tucked in amid the pine trees. (Once more!) All around were rhododendron bushes. Pete's classwork and his flying duties were very demanding. Everyone in his flight test class, Group 20, talked about how difficult it was—and obviously loved it, because in Navy flying this was the big league. The young men in Group 20 and their wives were Pete's and Jane's entire social world. They associated with no one else. They constantly invited each other to dinner during the week; there was a Group party at someone's house practically every weekend; and they would go off on outings to fish or waterski in Chesapeake Bay. In a way they could not have associated with anyone else, at least not easily, because the boys could talk only about one thing: their flying. One of the phrases that kept running through the conversation was "pushing the outside of the envelope." The "envelope" was a flight-test term referring to the limits of a particular aircraft's performance, how tight a turn it could make at such-and-such a speed, and so on. "Pushing the outside," probing the outer limits, of the envelope seemed to be the great challenge and satisfaction of flight test. At first "pushing the outside of the envelope" was not a particularly terrifying phrase to hear. It sounded once more as if the boys were just talking about sports.

Then one sunny day a member of the Group, one of the happy lads they always had dinner with and drank with and went waterskiing with, was coming in for a landing at the base in an A3J fighter plane. He came in too low before lowering his flaps, and the ship stalled out, and he crashed and was burned beyond recognition. And they brought out the bridge coats and sang about those in peril in the air and put the bridge coats away, and the Indians who were left talked about the accident after dinner one night. They shook their heads and said it was a damned shame, but he should have known better than to wait so long before lowering the flaps.

Barely a week had gone by before another member of the Group was coming in for a landing in the same type of aircraft, the A3J, trying to make a 90-degree landing, which involves a sharp turn, and something went wrong with the controls, and he ended up with one rear stabilizer wing up and the other one down, and his ship rolled in like a corkscrew from 800 feet up and crashed, and he was burned beyond recognition. And the bridge coats came out and they sang about those in peril in the air and then they put the bridge coats away and after dinner one night they mentioned that the departed had been a good man but was inexperienced, and when the malfunction in the controls put him in that bad corner, he didn't know how to get out of it.

Every wife wanted to cry out: "Well, my God! The *machine* broke! What makes *any* of you think you would have come out of it any better!" Yet intuitively Jane and the rest of them knew it wasn't right even to suggest that. Pete never indicated for a moment that he thought any such thing could possibly happen to him. It seemed not only wrong but dangerous to challenge a young pilot's confidence by posing the question. And that, too, was part of the unofficial protocol for the Officer's Wife. From now on every time Pete was late coming in from the flight line, she would worry. She began to wonder if—no! *assume!*—he had found his way into one of those corners they all talked about so spiritedly, one of those little dead ends that so enlivened conversation around here.

Not long after that, another good friend of theirs went up in an F-4, the Navy's newest and hottest fighter plane, known as the Phantom. He reached twenty thousand feet and then nosed over and dove straight into Chesapeake Bay. It turned out that a hose connection was missing in his oxygen system and he had suffered hypoxia and passed out at the high altitude. And the bridge coats came out and they lifted a prayer about those in peril in the air and the bridge coats were put away and the Indians were incredulous. How could anybody fail to check his hose connections? And how could anybody be in such poor condition as to pass out *that quickly* from hypoxia?

A couple of days later Jane was standing at the window of her house in North Town Creek. She saw some smoke rise above the pines from over in the direction of the flight line. Just that, a column of smoke; no explosion or sirens or any other sound. She went to another room, so as not to have to think about it but there was no explanation for the smoke. She went back to the window. In the yard of a house across the street she saw a group of people . . . standing there and looking at her house, as if trying to decide what to do. Jane looked away—but she couldn't keep from looking out again. She caught a glimpse of *a certain figure* coming up the walkway toward her front door. She knew exactly who it was. She had had nightmares like this. And yet this was no dream. She was wide awake and alert. Never more alert in her entire life! Frozen, completely defeated by the sight, she simply waited for the bell to ring. She waited, but there was not a sound. Finally she could stand it no more. In real life, Jane was both too self-possessed and too polite to scream through the door: "Go away!" So she opened it. There was no one there, no one at all. There was no group of people on the lawn across the way and no one to be seen for a hundred yards in any direction along the lawns and leafy rhododendron roads of North Town Creek.

Then began a cycle in which she had both the nightmares and the hallucinations, continually. Anything could touch off an hallucination: a ball of smoke, a telephone ring that stopped before she could answer it, the sound of a siren, even the sound of trucks starting up (crash trucks!). Then she would glance out the window, and a certain figure would be coming up the walk, and she would wait for the bell. The only difference between the dreams and the hallucinations was that the scene of the dreams was always the little house in Jacksonville. In both cases, the feeling that *this time it has happened* was quite real.

The star pilot in the class behind Pete's, a young man who was the main rival of their good friend Al Bean, went up in a fighter to do some power-dive tests. One of the most demanding disciplines in flight test was to accustom yourself to making precise readings from the control panel in the same moment that you were pushing the outside of the envelope. This young man put his ship into the test dive and was still reading out the figures, with diligence and precision and great discipline, when he augered straight into the oyster flats and was burned beyond recognition. And the bridge coats came out and they sang about those in peril in the air and the bridge coats were put away, and the little Indians remarked that the departed was a swell guy and a brilliant student of flying; a little too *much* of a student, in fact; he hadn't bothered to look out the window at the real world soon enough. Beano—Al Bean—wasn't quite so brilliant; on the other hand, he was still here.

Like many other wives in Group 20 Jane wanted to talk about the whole situation, the incredible series of fatal accidents, with her husband and the other members of the Group, to find out how they were taking it. But somehow the unwritten protocol forbade discussions of this subject, which was the fear of death. Nor could Jane or any of the rest of them talk, really *have a talk*, with anyone around the base. You could talk to another wife about being worried. But what good did it do? Who *wasn't* worried? You were likely to get a look that said: "*Why dwell on it?*" Jane might have gotten away with divulging the matter of the nightmares. But *hallucinations*? There was no room in Navy life for any such anomalous tendency as that.

By now the bad string had reached ten in all, and almost all of the dead had been close friends of Pete and Jane, young men who had been in their house many times, young men who had sat across from Jane and chattered like the rest of them about the grand adventure of military flying. And the survivors still sat around *as before*—with the same inexplicable exhilaration! Jane kept watching Pete for some sign that his spirit was cracking, but she saw none. He talked a mile a minute, kidded and joked, laughed with his Hickory Kid cackle. He always had. He still enjoyed the company of members of the group like Wally Schirra and Jim Lovell. Many young pilots were taciturn and cut loose with the strange fervor of this business only in the air. But Pete and Wally and Jim were not reticent; not in any situation. They loved to kid around. Pete called Jim Lovell "Shaky," because it was the last thing a pilot would want to be called. Wally Schirra was outgoing to the point of hearty; he loved practical jokes and dreadful puns, and so on. The three of them—*even in the midst of this bad string!*—would love to get on a subject such as accident-prone Mitch Johnson. Accident-prone Mitch Johnson, it seemed, was a Navy pilot whose life was in the hands of two angels, one of them bad and the other one good. The bad angel would put him into accidents that would have annihilated any ordinary pilot, and the good angel would bring him out of them without a scratch. Just the other day—this was the sort of story Jane would hear them tell—Mitch Johnson was coming in to land on a carrier. But he came in short, missed the flight deck, and crashed into the fantail, below the deck. There was a tremendous explosion, and the rear half of the plane fell into the water in flames. Everyone on the flight deck said, "Poor Johnson. The good angel was off duty." They were still debating how to remove the debris and his mortal remains when a phone rang on the bridge. A somewhat dopey voice said, "This is Johnson. Say, listen, I'm down here in the supply hold and the hatch is locked and I can't find the lights and I can't see a goddamned thing and I tripped over a cable and I think I hurt my leg." The officer on the bridge slammed the phone down, then vowed to find out what morbid sonofabitch could pull a phone prank at a time like this. Then the phone rang again, and the man with the dopey voice managed to establish the fact that he was, indeed, Mitch Johnson. The good angel had not left his side. When he smashed into the fantail, he hit some empty ammunition drums, and they cushioned the impact, leaving him groggy but not seriously hurt. The fuselage had blown to pieces; so he just stepped out onto the fantail and opened a hatch that led into the supply hold. It was pitch black in there, and there were cables all across the floor, holding down spare aircraft engines. Accident-prone Mitch Johnson kept tripping over these cables until he found a telephone. Sure enough, the one injury he had was a bruised shin from tripping over a cable. The man was accident-prone! Pete and Wally and Jim absolutely cracked up over stories like this. It was amazing. Great sports yarns! Nothing more than that.

A few days later Jane was out shopping at the Pax River commissary on Saunders Road, near the main gate to the base. She heard the sirens go off at the field, and then she heard the engines of the crash trucks start up. This time Jane was determined to keep calm. Every instinct made her want to rush home, but she forced herself to stay in the commissary and continue shopping. For thirty minutes she went through the motions of completing her shopping list. Then she drove home to North Town Creek. As she reached the house, she saw a figure going up the sidewalk. It was a man. Even from the back there was no question as to who he was. He had on a black suit, and there was a white band around his neck. It was her minister, from the Episcopal Church. She stared, and this vision did not come and go. The figure kept on walking up the front walk. She was not asleep now, and she was not inside her house glancing out the front window. She was outside in her car in front of her house. She was not dreaming, and she was not hallucinating, and the figure kept walking toward her front door.

The commotion at the field was over one of the most extraordinary things that even veteran pilots had ever seen at Pax River. And they had all seen it, because practically the entire flight line had gathered out on the field for it, as if it had been an air show.

Conrad's friend Ted Whelan had taken a fighter up, and on takeoff there had been a structural failure that caused a hydraulic leak. A red warning light showed up on Whelan's panel, and he had a talk with the ground. It was obvious that the leak would cripple the controls before he could get the ship back down to the field for a landing. He would have to bail out; the only question was where and when, and so they had a talk about that. They decided that he should jump at 8,100 feet at such-and-such a speed, directly over the field. The plane would crash into the Chesapeake Bay, and he would float down to the field. Just as coolly as anyone could have asked for it, Ted Whelan lined the ship up to come across the field at 8,100 feet precisely and he punched out, ejected.

Down on the field they all had their faces turned up to the sky. They saw Whelan pop out of the cockpit. With his Martin-Baker seat-parachute rig strapped on, he looked like a little black geometric lump a mile and a half up in the blue. They watched him as he started dropping. Everyone waited for the parachute to open. They waited a few more seconds, and then they waited some more. The little shape was getting bigger and bigger and picking up tremendous speed. Then there came an unspeakable instant at which everyone on the field who knew anything about parachute jumps knew what was going to happen. Yet even for them it was an unearthly feeling, for no one had ever seen any such thing happen so close up, from start to finish, from what amounted to a grandstand seat. Now the shape was going so fast and coming so close it began to play tricks on the eyes. It seemed to stretch out. It became much bigger and hurtled toward them at a terrific speed, until they couldn't make out its actual outlines at all. Finally there was just a streaking black blur before their eyes, followed by what seemed like an explosion. Except that it was not an explosion; it was the tremendous *crack* of Ted Whelan, his helmet, his pressure suit, and his seat-parachute rig smashing into the center of the runway, precisely on target, right in front of the crowd; an absolute bull's-eye. Ted Whelan had no doubt been alive until the instant of impact. He had had about thirty seconds to watch the Pax River base and the peninsula and Baltimore County and continental America and the entire comprehensible world rise up to smash him. When they lifted his body up off the concrete, it was like a sack of fertilizer.

Pete took out the bridge coat again and he and Jane and all the little Indians went to the funeral for Ted Whelan. That it hadn't been Pete was not solace enough for Jane. That the preacher had not, in fact, come to her front door as the Solemn Friend of Widows and Orphans, but merely for a church call . . . had not brought peace and relief. That Pete still didn't show the slightest indication of thinking that any unkind fate awaited him no longer lent her even a moment's courage. The next dream and the next hallucination, and the next and the next, merely seemed more real. For she now *knew*. She now knew the subject and the essence of this enterprise, even though not a word of it had passed anybody's lips. She even knew why Pete—the Princeton boy she met at a deb party at the Gulph Mills Club!—would never quit, never withdraw from this grim business, unless in a coffin. And God knew, and she knew, there was a coffin waiting for each little Indian.

Seven years later, when a reporter and a photographer from *Life* magazine actually stood near her in her living room and watched her face, while outside, on the lawn, a crowd of television crewmen and newspaper reporters waited for a word, an indication, anything—perhaps a glimpse through a part in a curtain!—waited for some sign of what she felt—when one and all asked with their ravenous eyes and, occasionally, in so many words: "How do you feel?" and "Are you scared?"—America wants to know!—it made Jane want to laugh, but in fact she couldn't even manage a smile.

"Why ask *now*?" she wanted to say. But they wouldn't have had the faintest notion of what she was talking about.

The Joggers' Prayer

Almighty God, as we sail with pure aerobic grace and striped orthotic feet past the blind portals of our fellow citizens, past their chuck-roast lives and their necrotic cardiovascular systems and rusting hips and slipped discs and desiccated lungs, past their implacable inertia and inability to persevere and rise above the fully pensioned world they live in and to push themselves to the limits of their capacity and achieve the White Moment of slipping through the Wall, borne aloft on one's Third Wind, past their Cruisomatic cars and upholstered lawn mowers and their gummy-sweet children already at work like little fat factories producing arterial plaque, the more quickly to join their parents in their joyless bucket-seat landau ride toward the grave—help us, dear Lord, we beseech Thee, as we sail past this cold-lard desolation, to be big about it.

YEAGER

Anyone who travels very much on airlines in the United States soon gets to know the voice of *the airline pilot* . . . coming over the intercom . . . with a particular drawl, a particular folksiness, a particular down-home calmness that is so exaggerated it begins to parody itself (nevertheless!—it's reassuring) . . . the voice that tells you, as the airliner is caught in thunderheads and goes bolting up and down a thousand feet at a single gulp, to check your seat belts because "it might get a little choppy" . . . the voice that tells you (on a flight from Phoenix preparing for its final approach into Kennedy Airport, New York, just after dawn): "Now, folks, uh . . . this is the captain . . . ummmm . . . We've got a little ol' red light up here on the control panel that's tryin' to tell us that the *land*in' gears're not . . . uh . . . *lock*in' into position when we lower 'em . . . Now *I* don't believe that little ol' red light knows what it's *talk*in' about—I believe it's that little ol' red *light* that iddn' workin' right" . . . faint chuckle, long pause, as if to say, *I'm not even sure all this is really worth going into—still, it may amuse you* . . . "*But* . . . I guess to play it by the rules, we oughta *humor* that little ol' light . . . so we're gonna take her down to about, oh, two or three hundred feet over the runway at Kennedy, and the folks down there on the ground are gonna see if they caint give us a *vis*ual inspection of those ol' landin' gears"—with which he is obviously on intimate ol'-buddy terms, as with every other working part of this mighty ship—"and if I'm right . . . they're gonna tell us everything is copa*cet*ic all the way aroun' an' we'll jes take her on in" . . . and, after a couple of low passes over the field, the voice returns: "Well, folks, those folks down there on the ground—it must be too early for 'em or somethin'—I 'spect they still got the *sleep*ers in their eyes . . . 'cause they say they

From *The Right Stuff*, chapter 3.

caint tell if those ol' landin' gears are all the way down or not . . . But, you know, up here in the cockpit we're convinced they're all the way down, so we're jes gonna take her on in . . . And oh" . . . (*I almost forgot*) . . . "while we take a little swing out over the ocean an' empty some of that surplus fuel we're not gonna be needin' anymore—that's what you might be seein' comin' out of the wings—our lovely little ladies . . . if they'll be so kind . . . they're gonna go up and down the aisles and show you how we do what we call 'assumin' the position' " . . . another faint chuckle (*We do this so often, and it's so much fun, we even have a funny little name for it*) . . . and the stewardesses, a bit grimmer, by the looks of them, than *that voice*, start telling the passengers to take their glasses off and take the ballpoint pens and other sharp objects out of their pockets, and they show them *the position*, with head lowered . . . while down on the field at Kennedy the little yellow emergency trucks start roaring across the field—and even though in your pounding heart and your sweating palms and your broiling brainpan you *know* this is a critical moment in your life, you still can't quite bring yourself to be*lieve* it, because if it were . . . how could *the captain*, the man who knows the actual situation most intimately . . . how could he keep on drawlin' and chucklin' and driftin' and lollygaggin' in that particular voice of his—

Well!—who doesn't know that voice! And who can forget it!—even after he is proved right and the emergency is over.

That particular voice may sound vaguely Southern or Southwestern, but it is specifically Appalachian in origin. It originated in the mountains of West Virginia, in the coal country, in Lincoln County, so far up in the hollows that, as the saying went, "they had to pipe in daylight." In the late 1940's and early 1950's this up-hollow voice drifted down from on high, from over the high desert of California, down, down, down, from the upper reaches of the Brotherhood into all phases of American aviation. It was amazing. It was *Pygmalion* in reverse. Military pilots and then, soon, airline pilots, pilots from Maine and Massachusetts and the Dakotas and Oregon and everywhere else, began to talk in that poker-hollow West Virginia drawl, or as close to it as they could bend their native accents. It was the drawl of the most righteous of all the possessors of the right stuff: Chuck Yeager.

Yeager had started out as the equivalent, in the Second World War, of the legendary Frank Luke of the 27th Aero Squadron in the First. Which is to say, he was the boondocker, the boy from the back country, with only a high-school education, no credentials, no cachet or polish of any sort, who took off the feed-store overalls and put on a uniform and climbed into an airplane and lit up the skies over Europe.

Yeager grew up in Hamlin, West Virginia, a town on the Mud River not far from Nitro, Hurricane, Whirlwind, Salt Rock, Mud, Sod, Crum, Leet, Dollie, Ruth, and Alum Creek. His father was a gas driller (drilling for natural gas in the coalfields), his older brother was a gas driller, and he would have been a gas driller had he not enlisted in the Army Air Force in 1941 at the age of eighteen. In 1943, at twenty, he became a flight officer, i.e., a non-com who was allowed to fly, and went to England to fly fighter planes over France and Germany. Even in the tumult of the war Yeager was somewhat puzzling to a lot of other pilots. He was a short, wiry, but muscular little guy with dark curly hair and a tough-looking face that seemed (to strangers) to be saying: "You best not be lookin' me in the eye, you peckerwood, or I'll put four more holes in your nose." But that wasn't what was puzzling. What was puzzling was the way Yeager talked. He seemed to talk with some older forms of English elocution, syntax, and conjugation that had been preserved up-hollow in the Appalachians. There were people up there who never said they disapproved of anything, they said: "I don't hold with it." In the present tense they were willing to *help* out, like anyone else; but in the past tense they only *holped.* "H'it weren't nothin' I hold with, but I holped him out with it, anyways."

In his first eight missions, at the age of twenty, Yeager shot down two German fighters. On his ninth he was shot down over German-occupied French territory, suffering flak wounds; he bailed out, was picked up by the French underground, which smuggled him across the Pyrenees into Spain disguised as a peasant. In Spain he was jailed briefly, then released, whereupon he made it back to England and returned to combat during the Allied invasion of France. On October 12, 1944, Yeager took on and shot down five German fighter planes in succession. On November 6, flying a propeller-driven P–51 Mustang, he shot down one of the new jet fighters the Germans had developed, the Messerschmitt-262, and damaged two more, and on November 20 he shot down four FW-190s. It was a true Frank Luke-style display of warrior fury and personal prowess. By the end of the war he had thirteen and a half kills. He was twenty-two years old.

In 1946 and 1947 Yeager was trained as a test pilot at Wright Field in Dayton. He amazed his instructors with his ability at stunt-team flying, not to mention the unofficial business of hassling. That plus his up-hollow drawl had everybody saying, "He's a natural-born stick 'n' rudder man." Nevertheless, there was something extraordinary about it when a man so young, with so little experience in flight test, was selected to go to Muroc Field in California for the X–1 project.

Muroc was up in the high elevations of the Mojave Desert. It looked like some fossil landscape that had long since been left behind by the rest of terrestrial evolution. It was full of huge dry lake beds, the biggest being Rogers Lake. Other than sagebrush the only vegetation was Joshua trees, twisted freaks of the plant world that looked like a cross between cactus and Japanese bonsai. They had a dark petrified green color and horribly crippled branches. At dusk the Joshua trees stood out in silhouette on the fossil wasteland like some arthritic nightmare. In the summer the temperature went up to 110 degrees as a matter of course, and the dry lake beds were covered in sand, and there would be windstorms and sandstorms right out of a Foreign Legion movie. At night it would drop to near freezing, and in December it would start raining, and the dry lakes would fill up with a few inches of water, and some sort of putrid prehistoric shrimps would work their way up from out of the ooze, and sea gulls would come flying in a hundred miles or more from the ocean, over the mountains, to gobble up these squirming little throwbacks. A person had to see it to believe it: flocks of sea gulls wheeling around in the air out in the middle of the high desert in the dead of winter and grazing on antediluvian crustaceans in the primordial ooze.

When the wind blew the few inches of water back and forth across the lake beds, they became absolutely smooth and level. And when the water evaporated in the spring, and the sun baked the ground hard, the lake beds became the greatest natural landing fields ever discovered, and also the biggest, with miles of room for error. That was highly desirable, given the nature of the enterprise at Muroc.

Besides the wind, sand, tumbleweed, and Joshua trees, there was nothing at Muroc except for two quonset-style hangars, side by side, a couple of gasoline pumps, a single concrete runway, a few tarpaper shacks, and some tents. The officers stayed in the shacks marked "barracks," and lesser souls stayed in the tents and froze all night and fried all day. Every road into the property had a guardhouse on it manned by soldiers. The enterprise the Army had undertaken in this godforsaken place was the development of supersonic jet and rocket planes.

At the end of the war the Army had discovered that the Germans not only had the world's first jet fighter but also a rocket plane that had gone 596 miles an hour in tests. Just after the war a British jet, the Gloster Meteor, jumped the official world speed record from 469 to 606 in a single day. The next great plateau would be Mach 1, the speed of sound, and the Army Air Force considered it crucial to achieve it first.

The speed of sound, Mach 1, was known (thanks to the work of the physicist Ernst Mach) to vary at different altitudes, temperatures, and wind speeds. On a calm 60-degree day at sea level it was about 760 miles an hour, while at 40,000 feet, where the temperature would be at least 60 below, it was about 660 miles an hour. Evil and baffling things happened in the transonic zone, which began at about .7 Mach. Wind tunnels choked out at such velocities. Pilots who approached the speed of sound in dives reported that the controls would lock or "freeze" or even alter their normal functions. Pilots had crashed and died because they couldn't budge the stick. Just last year Geoffrey de Havilland, son of the famous British aircraft designer and builder, had tried to take one of his father's DH 108s to Mach 1. The ship started buffeting and then disintegrated, and he was killed. This led engineers to speculate that the g-forces became infinite at Mach 1, causing the aircraft to implode They started talking about "the sonic wall" and "the sound barrier."

So this was the task that a handful of pilots, engineers, and mechanics had at Muroc. The place was utterly primitive, nothing but bare bones, bleached tarpaulins, and corrugated tin rippling in the heat with caloric waves; and for an ambitious young pilot it was perfect. Muroc seemed like an outpost on the dome of the world, open only to a righteous few, closed off to the rest of humanity, including even the Army Air Force brass of command control, which was at Wright Field. The commanding officer at Muroc was only a colonel, and his superiors at Wright did not relish junkets to the Muroc rat shacks in the first place. But to pilots this prehistoric throwback of an airfield became . . . shrimp heaven! the rat-shack plains of Olympus!

Low Rent Septic Tank Perfection . . . yes; and not excluding those traditional essentials for the blissful hot young pilot: Flying & Drinking and Drinking & Driving.

Just beyond the base, to the southwest, there was a rickety windblown 1930's-style establishment called Pancho's Fly Inn, owned, run, and bartended by a woman named Pancho Barnes. Pancho Barnes wore tight white sweaters and tight pants, after the mode of Barbara Stanwyck in *Double Indemnity*. She was only forty-one when Yeager arrived at Muroc, but her face was so weatherbeaten, had so many hard miles on it, that she looked older, especially to the young pilots at the base. She also shocked the pants off them with her vulcanized tongue. Everybody she didn't like was an old bastard or a sonofabitch. People she liked were old bastards and sonofabitches, too. "I tol' 'at ol' bastard to get 'is ass on over here and I'd g'im a drink." But Pancho Barnes was anything but Low Rent. She was the granddaughter of the man who designed the old Mount Lowe cable-car system, Thaddeus S. C. Lowe. Her maiden name was Florence Leontine Lowe. She was brought up in San Marino, which adjoined Pasadena and was one of Los Angeles' wealthiest suburbs, and her first husband—she was married four times—was the pastor of the Pasadena Episcopal Church, the Rev. C. Rankin Barnes. Mrs. Barnes seemed to have few of the conventional community interests of a Pasadena matron. In the late 1920's, by boat and plane, she ran guns for Mexican revolutionaries and picked up the nickname Pancho. In 1930 she broke Amelia Earhart's air-speed record for women. Then she barnstormed around the country as the featured performer of "Pancho Barnes's Mystery Circus of the Air." She always greeted her public in jodhpurs and riding boots, a flight packet, a white scarf, and a white sweater that showed off her terrific Barbara Stanwyck chest. Pancho's desert Fly Inn had an airstrip, a swimming pool, a dude ranch corral, plenty of acreage for horseback riding, a big old guest house for the lodgers, and a connecting building that was the bar and restaurant. In the barroom the floors, the tables, the chairs, the walls, the beams, the bar were of the sort known as extremely weatherbeaten, and the screen doors kept banging. Nobody putting together such a place for a movie about flying in the old days would ever dare make it as dilapidated and generally go-to-hell as it actually was. Behind the bar were many pictures of airplanes and pilots, lavishly autographed and inscribed, badly framed and crookedly hung. There was an old piano that had been dried out and cracked to the point of hopeless desiccation. On a good night a huddle of drunken aviators could be heard trying to bang, slosh, and navigate their way through old Cole Porter tunes. On average nights the tunes were not that good to start with. When the screen door banged and a man walked through the door into the saloon, every eye in the place checked him out. If he wasn't known as somebody who had something to do with flying at Muroc, he would be eyed like some lame goddamned mouseshit sheepherder from *Shane*.

The plane the Air Force wanted to break the sound barrier with was called the X–1. The Bell Aircraft Corporation had built it under an Army contract. The core of the ship was a rocket of the type first developed by a young Navy inventor, Robert Truax, during the war. The fuselage was shaped like a 50-caliber bullet—an object that was known to go supersonic smoothly. Military pilots seldom drew major test assignments; they went to highly paid civilians working for the aircraft corporations. The prime pilot for the X–1 was a man whom Bell regarded as the best of the breed. This man looked like a movie star. He looked like a pilot from out of *Hell's Angels*. And on top of everything else there was his name: Slick Goodlin.

The idea in testing the X–1 was to nurse it carefully into the transonic zone, up to seven-tenths, eight-tenths, nine-tenths the speed of sound (.7 Mach, .8 Mach, .9 Mach) before attempting the speed of sound itself, Mach 1, even though Bell and the Army already knew the X–1 had the rocket power to go to Mach 1 and beyond, if there *was* any *beyond*. The consensus of aviators and engineers, after Geoffrey de Havilland's death, was that the speed of sound was an absolute, like the firmness of the earth. The sound barrier was a farm you could buy in the sky. So Slick Goodlin began to probe the transonic zone in the X–1, going up to .8 Mach. Every time he came down he'd have a riveting tale to tell. The buffeting, it was so fierce—and the listeners, their imaginations aflame, could practically see poor Geoffrey de Havilland disintegrating in midair. And the goddamned aerodynamics—and the listeners got a picture of a man in ballroom pumps skidding across a sheet of ice, pursued by bears. A controversy arose over just how much bonus Slick Goodlin should receive for assaulting the dread Mach 1 itself. Bonuses for contract test pilots were not unusual; but the figure of $150,000 was now bruited about. The Army balked, and Yeager got the job. He took it for $283 a month, or $3,396 a year; which is to say, his regular Army captain's pay.

The only trouble they had with Yeager was in holding him back. On his first powered flight in the X–1 he immediately executed an unauthorized zero-g roll with a full load of rocket fuel, then stood the ship on its tail and went up to .85 Mach in a vertical climb, also unauthorized. On subsequent flights, at speeds between .85 Mach and .9 Mach, Yeager ran into most known airfoil problems—loss of elevator, aileron, and rudder control, heavy trim pressures, Dutch rolls, pitching and buffeting, the lot—yet was convinced, after edging over .9 Mach, that this would all get better, not worse, as you reached Mach 1. The attempt to push beyond Mach 1—"breaking the sound barrier"—was set for October 14, 1947. Not being an engineer, Yeager didn't believe the "barrier" existed.

October 14 was a Tuesday. On Sunday evening, October 12, Chuck Yeager dropped in at Pancho's, along with his wife. She was a brunette named Glennis, whom he had met in California while he was in training, and she was such a number, so striking, he had the inscription "Glamorous Glennis" written on the nose of his P–51 in Europe and, just a few weeks back, on the X–1 itself. Yeager didn't go to Pancho's and knock back a few because two days later the big test was coming up. Nor did he knock back a few because it was the weekend. No, he knocked back a few because night had come and he was a pilot at Muroc. In keeping with the military tradition of Flying & Drinking, that was what you did, for no other reason than that the sun had gone down. You went to Pancho's and knocked back a few and listened to the screen doors banging and to other aviators torturing the piano and the nation's repertoire of Familiar Favorites and to lonesome mouse-turd strangers wandering in through the banging doors and to Pancho classifying the whole bunch of them as old bastards and miserable peckerwoods. That was what you did if you were a pilot at Muroc and the sun went down.

So about eleven Yeager got the idea that it would be a hell of a kick if he and Glennis saddled up a couple of Pancho's dude-ranch horses and went for a romp, a little rat race, in the moonlight. This was in keeping with the military tradition of Flying & Drinking and Drinking & Driving, except that this was prehistoric Muroc and you rode horses. So Yeager and his wife set off on a little proficiency run at full gallop through the desert in the moonlight amid the arthritic silhouettes of the Joshua trees. Then they start racing back to the corral, with Yeager in the lead and heading for the gateway. Given the prevailing conditions, it being nighttime, at Pancho's, and his head being filled with a black sandstorm of many badly bawled songs and vulcanized oaths, he sees too late that the gate has been closed. Like many a hard-driving midnight pilot before him, he does not realize that he is not equally gifted in the control of all forms of locomotion. He and the horse hit the gate, and he goes flying off and lands on his right side. His side hurts like hell.

The next day, Monday, his side still hurts like hell. It hurts every time he moves. It hurts every time he breathes deep. It hurts every time he moves his right arm. He knows that if he goes to a doctor at Muroc or says anything to anybody even remotely connected with his superiors, he will be scrubbed from the flight on Tuesday. They might even go so far as to put some other miserable peckerwood in his place. So he gets on his motorcycle, an old junker that Pancho had given him, and rides over to see a doctor in the town of Rosamond, near where he lives. Every time the goddamned motorcycle hits a pebble in the road, his side hurts like a sonofabitch. The doctor in Rosamond informs him he has two broken ribs and he tapes them up and tells him that if he'll just keep his right arm immobilized for a couple of weeks and avoid any physical exertion or sudden movements, he should be all right.

Yeager gets up before daybreak on Tuesday morning—which is supposed to be the day he tries to break the sound barrier—and his ribs still hurt like a sonofabitch. He gets his wife to drive him over to the field, and he has to keep his right arm pinned down to his side to keep his ribs from hurting so much. At dawn, on the day of a flight, you could hear the X–1 screaming long before you got there. The fuel for the X–1 was alcohol and liquid oxygen, oxygen converted from a gas to a liquid by lowering its temperature to 297 degrees below zero.

And when the lox, as it was called, rolled out of the hoses and into the belly of the X–1, it started boiling off and the X–1 started steaming and screaming like a teakettle. There's quite a crowd on hand, by Muroc standards . . . perhaps nine or ten souls. They're still fueling the X–1 with the lox, and the beast is wailing.

The X–1 looked like a fat orange swallow with white markings. But it was really just a length of pipe with four rocket chambers in it. It had a tiny cockpit and a needle nose, two little straight blades (only three and a half inches thick at the thickest part) for wings, and a tail assembly set up high to avoid the "sonic wash" from the wings. Even though his side was throbbing and his right arm felt practically useless, Yeager figured he could grit his teeth and get through the flight—except for one specific move he had to make. In the rocket launches, the X–1, which held only two and a half minutes' worth of fuel, was carried up to twenty-six thousand feet underneath the wings of a B–29. At seven thousand feet, Yeager was to climb down a ladder from the bomb bay of the B–29 to the open doorway of the X–1, hook up to the oxygen system and the radio microphone and earphones, and put his crash helmet on and prepare for the launch, which would come at twenty-five thousand feet. This helmet was a homemade number. There had never been any such thing as a crash helmet before. Throughout the war pilots had used the old skin-tight leather helmet-and-goggles. But the X–1 had a way of throwing the pilot around so violently that there was danger of getting knocked out against the walls of the cockpit. So Yeager had bought a big leather football helmet—there were no plastic ones at the time—and he butchered it with a hunting knife until he carved the right kind of holes in it, so that it would fit down over his regular flying helmet and the earphones and the oxygen rig. Anyway, then his flight engineer, Jack Ridley, would climb down the ladder, out in the breeze, and shove into place the cockpit door, which had to be lowered out of the belly of the B–29 on a chain. Then Yeager had to push a handle to lock the door airtight. Since the X–1's cockpit was minute, you had to push the handle with your right hand. It took quite a shove. There was no way you could move into position to get enough leverage with your left hand.

Out in the hangar Yeager makes a few test shoves on the sly, and the pain is so incredible he realizes that there is no way a man with two broken ribs is going to get the door closed. It is time to confide in somebody, and the logical man is Jack Ridley. Ridley is not only the flight engineer but a pilot himself and a good old boy from Oklahoma to boot. He will understand about Flying & Drinking and Drinking & Driving through the goddamned Joshua trees. So Yeager takes

Ridley off to the side in the tin hangar and says: Jack, I got me a little ol' problem here. Over at Pancho's the other night I sorta . . . dinged my goddamned ribs. Ridley says, Whattya mean . . . *dinged*? Yeager says, Well, I guess you might say I damned near like to . . . *broke* a coupla the sonsabitches. Whereupon Yeager sketches out the problem he foresees.

Not for nothing is Ridley the engineer on this project. He has an inspiration. He tells a janitor named Sam to cut him about nine inches off a broom handle. When nobody's looking, he slips the broomstick into the cockpit of the X–1 and gives Yeager a little advice and counsel.

So with that added bit of supersonic flight gear Yeager went aloft.

At seven thousand feet he climbed down the ladder into the X–1's cockpit, clipped on his hoses and lines, and managed to pull the pumpkin football helmet over his head. Then Ridley came down the ladder and lowered the door into place. As Ridley had instructed, Yeager now took the nine inches of broomstick and slipped it between the handle and the door. This gave him just enough mechanical advantage to reach over with his left hand and whang the thing shut. So he whanged the door shut with Ridley's broomstick and was ready to fly.

At 26,000 feet the B–29 went into a shallow dive, then pulled up and released Yeager and the X–1 as if it were a bomb. Like a bomb it dropped and shot forward (at the speed of the mother ship) at the same time. Yeager had been launched straight into the sun. It seemed to be no more than six feet in front of him, filling up the sky and blinding him. But he managed to get his bearings and set off the four rocket chambers one after the other. He then experienced something that became known as the ultimate sensation in flying: "booming and zooming." The surge of the rockets was so tremendous, forced him back into his seat so violently, he could hardly move his hands forward the few inches necessary to reach the controls. The X–1 seemed to shoot straight up in an absolutely perpendicular trajectory, as if determined to snap the hold of gravity via the most direct route possible. In fact, he was only climbing at the 45-degree angle called for in the flight plan. At about .87 Mach the buffeting started.

On the ground the engineers could no longer see Yeager. They could only hear . . . that poker-hollow West Virginia drawl.

"Had a mild buffet there . . . jes the usual instability . . ."

Jes the usual instability?

Then the X–1 reached the speed of .96 Mach, and that incredible caint-hardlyin' aw-shuckin' drawl said:

"Say, Ridley . . . make a note here, will ya?" (*if you ain't got nothin' better to do*) ". . . elevator effectiveness *re*gained."

Just as Yeager had predicted, as the X–1 approached Mach 1, the stability improved. Yeager had his eyes pinned on the machometer. The needle reached .96, fluctuated, and went off the scale.

And on the ground they heard . . . that voice:

"Say, Ridley . . . make another note, will ya?" (*if you ain't too bored yet*) ". . . there's somethin' wrong with this ol' machometer . . ." (faint chuckle) ". . . it's gone kinda screwy on me . . ."

And in that moment, on the ground, they heard a boom rock over the desert floor—just as the physicist Theodore von Kármán had predicted many years before.

Then they heard Ridley back in the B–29: "If it is, Chuck, we'll fix it. Personally I think you're seeing things."

Then they heard Yeager's poker-hollow drawl again:

"Well, I guess I am, Jack . . . And I'm still goin' upstairs like a bat."

The X–1 had gone through "the sonic wall" without so much as a bump. As the speed topped out at Mach 1.05, Yeager had the sensation of shooting straight through the top of the sky. The sky turned a deep purple and all at once the stars and the moon came out—and the sun shone at the same time. He had reached a layer of the upper atmosphere where the air was too thin to contain reflecting dust particles. He was simply looking out into space. As the X–1 nosed over at the top of the climb, Yeager now had seven minutes of . . . Pilot Heaven . . . ahead of him. He was going faster than any man in history, and it was almost silent up here, since he had exhausted his rocket fuel, and he was so high in such a vast space that there was no sensation of motion. He was master of the sky. His was a king's solitude, unique and inviolate, above the dome of the world. It would take him seven minutes to glide back down and land at Muroc. He spent the time doing victory rolls and wing-over-wing aerobatics while Rogers Lake and the High Sierras spun around below.

On the ground they had understood the code as soon as they heard Yeager's little exchange with Ridley. The project was secret, but the radio exchanges could be picked up by anyone within range. The business of the "screwy machometer" was Yeager's deadpan way of announcing that the X–1's instruments indicated Mach 1. As soon as he landed, they checked out the X–1's automatic recording instruments. Without any doubt the ship had gone supersonic. They immediately called the brass at Wright Field to break the tremendous news. Within two hours Wright Field called back and gave some firm orders. A top security lid was being put on the morning's events. That the press was not to be informed went without saying. But neither was anyone else, anyone at all, to be told. Word of the flight was not to go beyond the flight line. And even among the people directly involved—who were there and knew about it, anyway—there was to be no celebrating. Just what was on the minds of the brass at Wright is hard to say. Much of it, no doubt, was a simple holdover from wartime, when every breakthrough of possible strategic importance was kept under wraps. That was what you did—you shut up about them. Another possibility was that the chiefs at Wright had never quite known what to make of Muroc. There was some sort of weird ribald aerial tarpaper mad-monk squadron up on the roof of the desert out there . . .

In any case, by mid-afternoon Yeager's tremendous feat had become a piece of thunder with no reverberation. A strange and implausible stillness settled over the event. Well . . . there was not supposed to be any celebration, but come nightfall . . . Yeager and Ridley and some of the others ambled over to Pancho's. After all, it was the end of the day, and they were pilots. So they knocked back a few. And they had to let Pancho in on the secret, because Pancho had said she'd serve a free steak dinner to any pilot who could fly supersonic and walk in here to tell about it, and they had to see the look on *her* face. So Pancho served Yeager a big steak dinner and said they were a buncha miserable peckerwoods all the same, and the desert cooled off and the wind came up and the screen doors banged and they drank some more and bawled some songs over the cackling dry piano and the stars and the moon came out and Pancho screamed oaths no one had ever heard before and Yeager and Ridley roared and the old weatherbeaten bar boomed and the autographed pictures of a hundred dead pilots shook and clattered on the frame wires and the faces of the living fell apart in the reflections, and by and by they all left and stumbled and staggered and yelped and bayed for glory before the arthritic silhouettes of the Joshua trees. Shit!—there was no one to tell except Pancho and the goddamned Joshua trees!

Over the next five months Yeager flew supersonic in the X-1 more than a dozen times, but still the Air Force insisted on keeping the story secret. *Aviation Week* published a report of the flights late in December (without mentioning Yeager's name) provoking a minor debate in the press over whether or not *Aviation Week* had violated national security—and *still* the Air Force refused to publicize the achievement until June of 1948. Only then was Yeager's name released. He received only a fraction of the publicity that would have been his had he been presented to the world immediately, on October 14, 1947, as the man who "broke the sound barrier." This dragged-out process had curious effects.

In 1952 a British movie called *Breaking the Sound Barrier*, starring

Ralph Richardson, was released in the United States, and its promoters got the bright idea of inviting the man who had actually done it, Major Charles E. Yeager of the U.S. Air Force, to the American premiere. So the Air Force goes along with it and Yeager turns up for the festivities. When he watches the movie, he's stunned. He can't believe what he's seeing. Far from being based on the exploits of Charles E. Yeager, *Breaking the Sound Barrier* was inspired by the death of Geoffrey de Havilland in his father's DH 108. At the end of the movie a British pilot solves the mystery of "the barrier" by *reversing the controls* at the critical moment during a power dive. The buffeting is tearing his ship to pieces, and every rational process in his head is telling him to *pull back* on the stick to keep from crashing—and he *pushes it down* instead . . . and zips right through Mach 1 as smooth as a bird, regaining full control!

Breaking the Sound Barrier happened to be one of the most engrossing movies about flying ever made. It seemed superbly realistic, and people came away from it sure of two things: it was an Englishman who had broken the sound barrier, and he had done it by reversing the controls in the transonic zone.

Well, after the showing they bring out Yeager to meet the press, and he doesn't know where in the hell to start. To him the whole goddamned picture is outrageous. He doesn't want to get mad, because this thing has been set up by Air Force P.R. But he is not happy. In as calm a way as he can word it on the spur of the moment, he informs one and all that the picture is an utter shuck from start to finish. The promoters respond, a bit huffily, that this picture is not, after all, a documentary. Yeager figures, well, anyway, that settles that. But as the weeks go by, he discovers an incredible thing happening. He keeps running into people who think he's the first *American* to break the sound barrier . . . and that he learned how to *reverse the controls* and zip through from the Englishman who did it first. The last straw comes when he gets a call from the Secretary of the Air Force.

"Chuck," he says, "do you mind if I ask you something? Is it true that you broke the sound barrier by reversing the controls?"

Yeager is stunned by this. The Secretary—*the Secretary!*—of the U.S. Air Force!

"No, sir," he says, "that is . . . not correct. Anyone who reversed the controls going transonic would be dead."

Yeager and the rocket pilots who soon joined him at Muroc had a hard time dealing with publicity. On the one hand, they hated the process. It meant talking to reporters and other fruit flies who always hovered, eager for the juice . . . and invariably got the facts screwed up . . . *But that wasn't really the problem, was it!* The real problem was that reporters violated the invisible walls of the fraternity. They blurted out questions and spoke boorish words about . . . all the unspoken things!—about fear and bravery (they would say the words!) and how you *felt* at such-and-such a moment! It was obscene! They presumed a knowledge and an intimacy they did not have and had no right to. Some aviation writer would sidle up and say, "I hear Jenkins augered in. That's too bad." *Augered in!*—a phrase that belonged exclusively to the fraternity!—coming from the lips of this *ant* who was *left behind* the moment Jenkins made his first step up the pyramid long, long ago. It was repulsive! But on the other hand . . . one's healthy pilot ego loved the glory—wallowed in it!—lapped it up!—no doubt about it! The Pilot Ego—ego didn't come any bigger! The boys wouldn't have minded the following. They wouldn't have minded appearing once a year on a balcony over a huge square in which half the world is assembled. They wave. The world roars its approval, its applause, and breaks into a sustained thirty-minute storm of cheers and tears (moved by my righteous stuff!). And then it's over. All that remains is for the wife to paste the clippings in the scrapbook.

A little adulation on the order of the Pope's; that's all the True Brothers at the top of the pyramid really wanted.

Yeager received just about every major decoration and trophy that was available to test pilots, but the Yeager legend grew not in the press, not in public, but within the fraternity. As of 1948, after Yeager's flight was made public, every hot pilot in the country knew that Muroc was what you aimed for if you wanted to reach the top. In 1947 the National Security Act, Title 10, turned the Army Air Force into the U.S. Air Force, and three years later Muroc Army Air Base became Edwards Air Force Base, named for a test pilot, Glenn Edwards, who had died testing a ship with no tail called the Flying Wing. So now the magic word became *Edwards*. You couldn't keep a really hot, competitive pilot away from Edwards. Civilian pilots (almost all of whom had been trained in the military) could fly for the National Advisory Committee for Aeronautics (NACA) High Speed Center at Edwards, and some of the rocket pilots did that: Scott Crossfield, Joe Walker, Howard Lilly, Herb Hoover, and Bill Bridgeman, among them. Pete Everest, Kit Murray, Iven Kincheloe, and Mel Apt joined Yeager as Air Force rocket pilots. There was a constant rivalry between NACA and the Air Force to push the rocket planes to their outer limits. On November 20, 1953, Crossfield, in the D–558–2, raised the speed to Mach 2. Three weeks later Yeager flew the X–1A to Mach 2.4. The rocket program was quickly running out of frontiers within the atmosphere; so NACA and the Air Force began planning a new project, with a new rocket plane, the X–15, to probe altitudes as high as fifty miles, which was well beyond anything that could still be called "air."

My God!—to be a part of Edwards in the late forties and early fifties!—even to be on the ground and hear one of those incredible explosions from 35,000 feet somewhere up there in the blue over the desert and know that some True Brother had commenced his rocket launch . . . in the X–1, the X–1A, the X–2, the D–558–1, the horrible XF–92A, the beautiful D–558–2 . . . and to know that he would soon be at an altitude, in the thin air at the edge of space, where the stars and the moon came out at noon, in an atmosphere so thin that the ordinary laws of aerodynamics no longer applied and a plane could skid into a flat spin like a cereal bowl on a waxed Formica counter and then start tumbling, not spinning and not diving, but tumbling, end over end like a brick . . . In those planes, which were like chimneys with little razor-blade wings on them, you had to be "afraid to panic," and that phrase was no joke. In the skids, the tumbles, the spins, there was, truly, as Saint-Exupéry had said, only one thing you could let yourself think about: *What do I do next?* Sometimes at Edwards they used to play the tapes of pilots going into the final dive, the one that killed them, and the man would be tumbling, going end over end in a fifteen-ton length of pipe, with all aerodynamics long gone, and not one prayer left, and he knew it, and he would be screaming into the microphone, but not for Mother or for God or the nameless spirit of Ahor, but for one last hopeless crumb of information about the loop: "I've tried A! I've tried B! I've tried C! I've tried D! Tell me what else I can try!" And then that truly spooky click on the machine. *What do I do next?* (In this moment when the Halusian Gulp is opening?) And everybody around the table would look at one another and nod ever so slightly, and the unspoken message was: Too bad! There was a man with the right stuff. There was no national mourning in such cases, of course. Nobody outside of Edwards knew the man's name. If he were well liked, he might get one of those dusty stretches of road named for him on the base. He was probably a junior officer doing all this for four or five thousand a year. He owned perhaps two suits, only one of which he dared wear around people he didn't know. But none of that mattered!—not at Edwards—not in the Brotherhood.

What made it truly beautiful (for a True Brother!) was that for a good five years Edwards remained primitive and Low Rent, with nothing out there but the bleached prehistoric shrimp terrain and the rat shacks and the blazing sun and the thin blue sky and the rockets sitting there moaning and squealing before dawn. Not even Pancho's changed—except to become more gloriously Low Rent. By 1949 *the girls* had begun turning up at Pancho's in amazing numbers. They were young, lovely, juicy, frisky—and there were so many of them, at all hours, every day of the week! And they were not prostitutes, despite the accusations made later. They were just . . . well, just young juicy girls in their twenties with terrific young conformations and sweet cupcakes and loamy loins. They were sometimes described with a broad sweep as "stewardesses," but only a fraction of them really were. No, they were lovely young things who arrived as mysteriously as the sea gulls who sought the squirming shrimp. They were moist labial piping little birds who had somehow learned that at this strange place in the high Mojave lived the hottest young pilots in the world and that this was *where things were happening.* They came skipping and screaming in through the banging screen doors at Pancho's—and it completed the picture of Pilot Heaven. There was no other way to say it. Flying & Drinking and Drinking & Driving and Driving & Balling. The pilots began calling the old Fly Inn dude ranch "Pancho's Happy Bottom Riding Club," and there you had it.

All of this was fraternal bliss. No pilot was shut off from it because he was "in the public eye." Not even the rocket aces were isolated like stars. Most of them also performed the routine flight-test chores. Some of Yeager's legendary exploits came when he was merely a supporting player, flying "chase" in a fighter plane while another pilot flew the test aircraft. One day Yeager was flying chase for another test pilot at 20,000 feet when he noticed the man veering off in erratic maneuvers. As soon as he reached him on the radio, he realized the man was suffering from hypoxia, probably because an oxygen hose connection had come loose. Some pilots in that state became like belligerent drunks—prior to losing consciousness. Yeager would tell the man to check his oxygen system, he'd tell him to go to a lower altitude, and the man kept suggesting quaint anatomical impossibilities for Yeager to perform on himself. So Yeager hit upon a ruse that only he could have pulled off. "Hey," he said, "I got me a problem here, boy. I caint keep this thing running even on the emergency system. She just flamed out. Follow me down." He started descending, but his man stayed above him, still meandering. So Yeager did a very un-Yeager-like thing. He *yelled* into the microphone! He yelled: "Look, my dedicated young scientist—*follow me down!*" The change in tone —*Yeager yelling!*—penetrated the man's impacted hypoxic skull. *My God! The fabled Yeager! He's yelling—Yeager's yelling!—to me for help! Jesus H. Christ!* And he started following him down. Yeager knew that if he could get the man down to 12,000 feet, the oxygen content of the air would bring him around, which it did. *Hey! What happened?* After he landed, he realized he had been no more than a minute or two from passing out and punching a hole in the desert. As he got out of the cockpit, an F–86 flew overhead and did a slow roll sixty feet off the deck and then disappeared across Rogers Lake. That was Yeager's signature.

Yeager was flying chase one day for Bill Bridgeman, the prime pilot for one of the greatest rocket planes, the Douglas Skyrocket, when the ship went into a flat spin followed by a violent tumble. Bridgeman fought his way out of it and regained stability, only to have his windows ice up. This was another common danger in rocket flights. He was out of fuel, so that he was now faced with the task of landing the ship both deadstick and blind. At this point Yeager drew alongside in his F–86 and became his eyes. He told Bridgeman every move to make every foot of the way down . . . as if he knew that ol' Skyrocket like the back of his hand . . . and this was jes a little ol' fishin' trip on the Mud River . . . and there was jes the two of 'em havin' a little poker-hollow fun in the sun . . . and that lazy lollygaggin' chucklin' driftin' voice was still purrin' away . . . the very moment Bridgeman touched down safely. You could almost hear Yeager saying to Bridgeman, as he liked to do:

"How d'ye hold with rockets now, son?"

That was what you thought of when you saw the F–86 do a slow roll sixty feet off the deck and disappear across Rogers Lake.

Yeager had just turned thirty. Bridgeman was thirty-seven. It didn't dawn on him until later that Yeager always called him *son.* At the time it had seemed perfectly natural. Somehow Yeager was like the big daddy of the skies over the dome of the world. In keeping with the eternal code, of course, for anyone to have suggested any such thing would have been to invite hideous ridicule. There were even other pilots with enough Pilot Ego to believe that *they* were actually better than this drawlin' hot dog. But no one would contest the fact that as of that time, the 1950's, Chuck Yeager was at the top of the pyramid, number one among all the True Brothers.

And *that voice* . . . started drifting down from on high. At first the tower at Edwards began to notice that all of a sudden there were an awful lot of test pilots up there with West Virginia drawls. And pretty soon there were an awful lot of fighter pilots up there with West Virginia drawls. The air space over Edwards was getting so caint-hardly super-cool day by day, it was terrible. And then that lollygaggin' poker-hollow air space began to spread, because the test pilots and fighter pilots from Edwards were considered the pick of the litter and had a cachet all their own, wherever they went, and other towers and other controllers began to notice that it was getting awfully drawly and down-home up there, although they didn't know exactly why. And then, because the military is the training ground for practically all airline pilots, it spread further, until airline passengers all over America began to hear that awshuckin' driftin' gone-fishin' Mud River voice coming from the cockpit . . . "Now, folks, uh . . . this is the captain . . . ummmm . . . We've got a little ol' red light up here on the control panel that's tryin' to tell us that the *lan*din' gears're not . . . uh . . . *lock*in' into position . . ."

But so what! What could possibly go wrong! We've obviously got a man up there in the cockpit who doesn't have a nerve in his body! He's a block of ice! He's made of 100 percent righteous victory-rolling True Brotherly stuff.